Historicizing Colonial
Nostalgia

Historicizing Colonial Nostalgia

European Women's Narratives of Algeria and Kenya 1900–Present

Patricia M. E. Lorcin

First published in 2012 by
PALGRAVE MACMILLAN® in the United States – a division of
St. Martin's Press LLC, 175 Fifth Avenue, New York, NY 10010.

Where this book is distributed in the UK, Europe and the rest of the world,
this is by Palgrave Macmillan, a division of Macmillan Publishers Limited,
registered in England, company number 785998, of Houndmills, Basingstoke,
Hampshire RG21 6XS.

Palgrave Macmillan is the global academic imprint of the above companies
and has companies and representatives throughout the world.

Palgrave® and Macmillan® are registered trademarks in the United States, the
United Kingdom, Europe and other countries.

ISBN 978-0-230-33865-4

Library of Congress Cataloging-in-Publication Data is available from the
Library of Congress.

A catalogue record of the book is available from the British Library.

Design by MPS Limited, A Macmillan Company

First edition: January 2012

10 9 8 7 6 5 4 3 2 1

Printed in the United States of America.

For Oliver and Melissa with Love

I feel kind of homesick for those old times, although I never knew them.

Greg Francis a 30-year-old Anglo-Indian from Calcutta quoted in
The New York Times, International Sunday, August 15, 2010

Contents

List of Figures   viii

Acknowledgements   ix

Introduction   1

**Part I   1900–1930. Colonial Women and Their
Imagined Selves**

1   Paradoxical Lives: Women and their Colonial Worlds   21

2   Nostalgia Personified: Isabelle Eberhardt and
    Karen Blixen   45

**Part II   1920–1940. Political Realities and Fictional
Representations**

3   Reality Expressed; Reality Imagined: Algeria
    and Kenya in the Twenties   67

4   Writing and Living the Exotic   85

5   Women's Fictions of Colonial Realism   107

**Part III   Imperial Decline and the Reformulation
of Nostalgia**

6   Nationalist Anger; Colonial Illusions: Women's
    Responses to Decolonization   143

7   Happy Families, *Pieds-Noirs*, Red Strangers, and "a Vanishing
    Africa": Nostalgia Comes Full Circle   171

Conclusion   195

Notes   205

Bibliography   273

Index   307

LIST OF FIGURES

1.1 Frontispiece to the first French edition of *Une Femme Chez les Sahariennes* by Mme. Jean Pommerol Reproduced with permission from the Bibliothèque Nationale de France   33

2.1 Isabelle Eberhardt c. 1898   51

2.2 Karen Blixen. Photograph taken by the late Sophus Juncker Jensen in 1913 Reproduced with permission from the Royal Library, Copenhagen   55

3.1 Magali Boisnard. Image from Marie Cardinal's *Les Pieds-Noirs* reproduced with permission from the deceased's husband   74

4.1 Elissa Rhaïs, c. 1920. Reproduced with permission from the Bibliothèque Marguerite Durand, Paris   87

4.2 Nora Strange. Reproduced with permission from the National Portrait Gallery, London   102

5.1 Elspeth Huxley. Reproduced with permission from the National Portrait Gallery, London   115

ACKNOWLEDGEMENTS

It is impossible to do justice to all the people who contributed in one way or another to the genesis of this book. Unlike my first book, which was written in somewhat of an academic vacuum when I was part of a diplomatic milieu, this work has benefited enormously from the contacts and connections I have made as a Jeannie-come-lately to the profession. These acknowledgements, therefore, not only signal the institutions, colleagues, and friends whose support I appreciated, but they also trace my trajectory from the diplomatic to the academic world.

In my first academic post, at Florida International University, I participated in a forum on women and gender, which started my formal research into this project, although, as the opening pages of the book suggest, the original inspiration came earlier. My colleagues during the year I spent at Rice, in particular Dan Sherman, Lynne Huffer, Richard Wolin, Paula Saunders, Peter Caldwell, and Michael Mass greatly encouraged me in many ways. Discussions with and support from colleagues at Texas Tech, Catherine Miller, Ed Steinhart, Jim Brink, and José Santos, propelled the project along as did the conference I helped to organize with Hafid Gafaiti and David Troyansky in 2002 on *Transnational Cultures, Diasporas and Immigrant Identities in France and the Francophone World*. My move to the University of Minnesota in 2004 proved to be propitious as I was able to participate in and present work at the workshops that are organized by the Department of History. In particular listening to the presentations and comments from colleagues and students attending the GWSS collaborative, the Mediterranean Collaborative and the monthly Monday presentations stimulated me to think about issues not necessarily related to my research, but which informed the way in which I thought about what I was doing. Anna Clark commented on a chapter of my work and M. J. Maynes on the whole manuscript. Kay Reyerson and John Watkins, co-conveners in the Mediterranean collaborative provided encouragement when I presented there. My thanks to all of them. The discussions in my graduate classes on Western imperialism, Post-colonialism, and French Imperialism were always lively and I benefited greatly from having interested and engaging students. Numerous grants from Texas Tech and the University of Minnesota have helped me complete my research.

From beyond the confines of these institutions, my thanks also go to Lou Roberts then at Stanford, Leonard Smith at Oberlin, Bertrand Taithe at the University of Manchester, Judy Surkis and Mary Lewis at Harvard, Gabi Piterberg and Susan Slimovics at U.C.L.A., and Jim Le Sueur at the University of Nebraska for inviting me to present papers at their workshops and seminars on my work-in-progress. The comments and observations I received at these and many other institutions where I was invited to speak were invariably helpful and made me rethink and improve different aspects of my work. My very special thanks also goes to Julia Clancy-Smith and Martin Thomas for their close reading of the manuscript and their helpful suggestions and comments.

Then too there were the colleagues with whom I have discussed issues related to my interests or whose work helped me think things through: Robert Aldrich, Jennifer Boittin, Raphaëlle Branche, Alice Conklin, Eric Jennings, Dane Kennedy, Joby Margadant (who also kindly let me use her painting as the cover image), Ted Margadant, Kim Munholland, Mireille Rosello, Todd Shepard, Emmanuelle Sibeud, Bonnie Smith, Tyler Stovall, Owen White, and Angela Woollacott.

If colleagues were vital to the genesis of this project, so too were my friends and family who have encouraged and supported me. In particular I would like to thank Liz Smitten, Jon Miller, and Sally Brotherton who encouraged me in ways of which they were certainly unaware. My thanks, too, to my erstwhile partner and close friend, Roger Horrell, for our discussions on colonial Kenya in particular and colonialism in general. But above all, a very special thanks to my spouse Claude, who patiently accompanied me to the various sites of my research, read parts of my manuscript and encouraged and supported me from the project's beginning to end.

Like all researchers I am greatly indebted to the archivists and librarians where I worked: the Centre des archives d'outre mer, the Archives du Feminisme in Angers, the Bibliothèque Marguerite Durand in Paris, to Françoise Gicquel, Cultural Director at the Archives de la Prefecture de Paris, and Lucy McCann at Rhodes House, who helped me locate seemingly elusive documents. The executors of the Huxley estate granted permission to reproduce the citations from the letters of Nellie Grant and Elspeth Huxley, for which I am most grateful.

Finally, my thanks to Chris Chappell and Sarah Whalen at Palgrave whose support and help was invaluable in getting the manuscript ready for publication in record time.

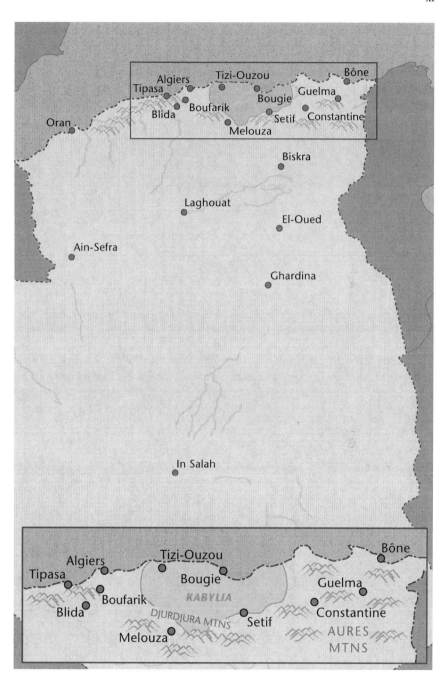

Colonial Algeria. Created by the University of Minnesota Cartography Lab

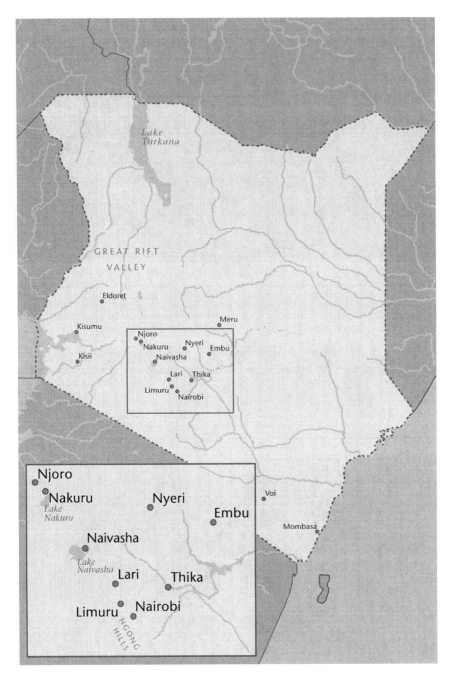

Colonial Kenya. Created by the University of Minnesota Cartography Lab

Introduction

Although I did not realize it at the time, the seed for what follows was inadvertently sown as a result of a holiday I took in August 1994, while living in the Ivory Coast. On the recommendation of friends, I had journeyed to Sinématiali, in the North of the country, to stay with a French couple who had a farm nearby, where they received guests. Near Sinématiali, we turned off the main road and drove for several miles along a dusty track which appeared to be leading nowhere. The instructions we had been given seemed decidedly vague to our urban sensibilities referencing, as they did, baobab trees and clusters of huts as the relevant signposts that would head us in the right direction. Any doubts we had about finding the place were dispelled when we found ourselves on a eucalyptus lined dirt "avenue," which led us to the farm. *Vidalkaha, La ferme africaine,* as it was called, was in fact a mango plantation or at that time the early stages of one (it is now an export business) to which the owners had added accommodation for guests in the form of a collection of small wattle huts. We were shown to our accommodation and told that drinks were served at sundown on the veranda of the reception hut, which was set on a sharp incline overlooking the plantation below. We arrived before our hosts and after admiring the magnificent view over the valley below we wandered into the sitting room.

A few years earlier I had read Karen Blixen's *Letters from Africa* and was familiar with most of her fiction. Thanks to Judith Thurman, I was also familiar with her life story.[1] As I walked around the sitting room, looking at the pictures on the wall, the zebra skins on the floor and heard the roar of the lion (they had a pet lion), I had a feeling of déjà vu. At dinner, when our hostess appeared in an elegant long dress and we sat down to a table dressed with fine silver and multibranched candelabras, with dinner served by an impeccably liveried African "boy" in white gloves, the parallels with Blixen's Africa came into focus. The next day when our hostess, dressed in jodhpurs and a straw hat shaped like a pith helmet, showed us around her farm and her "people" (Ivorians who lived on their land), I couldn't resist asking if she had ever read the works of Karen Blixen. She looked pleased. She told me that before moving to the North from Abidjan, where she had been living, she had spent some time in Paris recovering from a personal setback. An acquaintance had recommended the works of Blixen as a way of reconnecting to her temporarily shattered African life. She knew nothing of Blixen's works but by the time she had finished reading them, she had emerged from her doldrums and had decided what she wanted to do. She persuaded her husband to take an early retirement from his lucrative business in the Ivorian capital and invest in a plantation in the North. He would run the plantation and take guests trekking, hunting (game and photographic) in "the bush" and fishing on the nearby river, while she would provide an elegant end to the guests' day, a beguiling combination of the "primitive" and the "civilized." As I listened, what intrigued me the most was the starting point for our hostess' recreation as it was from a British colonial setting rather than a French one. Much later, when I started to think in a more structured way about the significance of nostalgia and the choices our hostess had made, I realized that the concept of nostalgia was not solely framed, as some scholars would have it, by the home or nation. The usual analysis of nostalgia as a longing to return home could be complicated by rethinking the concept in relation to notions of space and time and their use in women's personal strategies.

****

This is a study of the writing and strategies of European women in two colonies, French Algeria and British Kenya, the aim of which is to historicize nostalgia. I make a distinction between imperial and colonial nostalgia, concentrating on the latter and arguing that women's writing made a singular contribution to its development. I differentiate colonial nostalgia and colonial myths: namely that the former was the embellishment of lived experience, whereas the latter was either the misinterpretation or incomprehension of the colonized territory and its people or the fabrication of a nonexistent dimension of colonial life.

My interest in the social history of ideas, in fiction as a historical source, and in the nature of women's roles in the colonies drew me to the subject. I became interested in the ideological aspects of colonial literature when I was writing my first book, a social history of French ideas on ethnicities in nineteenth-century Algeria. After writing a few articles on colonial literature from Algeria, I decided that I wanted to extend my field of vision beyond French North Africa and write a comparative study.[2] My first question was whether or not to make it gender specific. I opted for concentrating on women because, in the case of Algeria, a colony I wanted to use as one of my case studies, works on colonial literature were weighted toward male writers.[3] The next question was which colonies? I considered comparing the writing of colonial women in different parts of the French empire, but the promise of a more intellectually rewarding enterprise stimulated me to consider women writers from different geographical areas of empire as well as from different empires. I knew that socio-economic and political dissimilarities in different parts of the French empire produced a literature shaped by the desires and mythologies of the people who settled there, people whose socio-economic background often determined the colonies they, or their forebears, chose to inhabit. Such differences might be even greater in considering the literatures of two competing empires, France and Britain. All the monographs on literature and empire focused on one empire (usually the British) or on one colony (India, Kenya, Algeria, Indochina).[4] Hardly any compared colonies from two different empires unless the focus was thematic, and even then there is not a great deal to chose from.[5] George Steinmetz has recently examined three German colonies in very different parts of the globe to provide "a corrective to hasty generalizations about colonialism per se"; my aim is to add to this corrective by focusing on two colonies from two different empires.[6]

WHY ALGERIA? WHY KENYA? WHY THIS PARTICULAR COMPARISON?

The choice of Algeria and Kenya was not random. There were socio-political, cultural, and thematic reasons why these two colonies would make a good comparison. Both were important settler colonies in their respective empires, the decolonization of which in each case was violent. This suggested that the stakes in their loss were similar, that is to say a land that settlers considered their own. The similarity is deceptive, however. Historians now categorize French Algeria as a colony, but at the time the mainland French, the colonists and even a minority of Algerian *évolués* considered the territory to be part of France. In contrast, although British settlers laid claim to the Kenya highlands as "white man's country," it never became an administrative part of Britain in the manner of Algeria, nor indeed was Kenya ever considered an extension of the British mainland, even if some settlers imagined that it was. Furthermore, territorial expropriation was an essential feature of both and was contested, leading to conflict and uprisings, but the fact that land in Algeria was imagined as French and in Kenya as African but "empty," hence available, shaped colonial writing.

Socio-political differences were also connected to my chosen time frame. By 1900, the approximate starting point of my analysis, Algeria had been occupied by the French for 70 years. Kenya was part of what was then known as the British East African Protectorate. It was established in 1895, one year before work began on the Uganda railway, which eventually transformed the region.[7] Only in 1920 did Kenya acquire its name and officially became a colony. In Algeria the military administration was replaced by a civilian one in 1871, and it was during the last three decades of the nineteenth century that the colony was transformed into a bona fide settler "state." The differences in the length of colonization meant that by 1900 Algeria had an urban culture, whereas, Kenya did not. Even before the French occupation there were important urban centers in the territory: Algiers, Oran, Constantine, Bone, Bougie. As settlement increased these centers were transformed, to a greater or lesser degree, into French towns.[8] In Kenya the only real town, Nairobi (or Nyrobe, from the Maasai *Engore Nyorobe)*, was a twentieth-century creation. Its emergence was connected to the construction of the Kenya-Uganda railway and its development into a true urban space was slow. In essence, therefore, Kenya was a rural settler culture, whereas Algeria was an urban one. The preoccupations of each, land in Kenya and cultural hegemony in Algeria, shaped the narratives and predominant literary themes and figures of speech of each.

Colonial theory and practice were also different. French colonial policies varied. The two theories were Assimilation and Association. Assimilation emerged from the revolutionary doctrine of the equality of man and the Utopian Socialist assumption of the superiority of European, and in particular French civilization with the concurrent desire to civilize and educate "lesser" civilizations. Assimilationists sought to absorb the colony into the French administrative and cultural framework, and socialize its inhabitants into becoming French men and women. By the early twentieth century, however, in many French territories colonial policy shifted to Association as assimilation of the "natives" was not longer considered to be feasible. Instead they were to be allowed to maintain their culture and develop at their own rate in tandem with the French. In either case direct rule was the structural framework. In Algeria there was never a watershed date separating Assimilation and Association, nor was there any coherence in the implementation of one policy or the other.[9] Colonial policy in Algeria had a haphazard, changeable quality to it, largely because it was considered to be a part of France and settler lobbies were strong. In Kenya, on the other hand, from the outset the policy was one of indirect rule, expressed definitively by Lord Lugard in his *The Dual Mandate in British Tropical Africa*. In it he stated that Britain was responsible for promoting the social, political, and economic development of its African dependencies.[10] These differences in approach shaped the attitudes of the settlers to the inhabitants of their colony. This study seeks to address how these differences in colonial ideology and policy were written into women's fiction and nonfiction.

Literary differences were also noticeable. In contrast to Kenya, by the interwar period Algeria had developed a lively literary scene. The urban culture and greater size of the settler population in Algeria produced more women novelists than the rural culture of Kenya. A comparison of their respective novelists suggested a study predominantly about Algeria. A possible solution was to compare the novelists in both territories, using the limited output of colonial women in Kenya as a foil for those from Algeria. A more promising approach, however, was to enlarge the scope of women's writing to include memoirs, letters, and various types of nonfictional writing. This redresses the imbalance and enables an assessment of how fiction and nonfiction converge to reinforce colonial themes within their respective territories or whether each genre responds differently to colonialism. Furthermore, memoir and letter writing are as much a cultural practice as is writing novels. If the former is, at the outset, a more private pursuit than the latter it is no less defining of a society. Examining why this was so can tell us as much about women's attitudes as it can about the society in which they functioned.

A final point of difference has to do with settler demographics. In both colonies the white settler population was a minority, but the similarity ends there. Not only was the settler population much larger in Algeria, but the majority was also of non-French origin, coming from the countries of the northern shores of the Mediterranean: principally Spain, Italy, and Malta. By 1900 most had been granted French citizenship, as had the Jews indigenous to Algeria. In Kenya, on the other hand, the majority of non-British settlers were Indian. Initially brought in to construct the railroad, their numbers had multiplied and they had established commercial roots. Indians were not granted full citizenship nor were they given the same rights as European settlers. These differences in demographics were mirrored in the ideological imaginings of the settlers and in the social hierarchies that emerged in each colony. Settler ideologues in Algeria looked to what they considered to be the Latin roots of Algeria and developed the concept of a melting pot of "Latins," which was producing a "virile, hardworking, hedonistic race" with the potential to "regenerate" France.[11] Kenyan settler mythologies were more closely connected to class and the pastimes of the settler "aristocracy," most famously the "Happy Valley Set," which in spite of the numerical (and actual) insignificance of its members became stereotypically associated with a certain white Kenyan lifestyle, overshadowing the reality of settler existence.

WOMEN, GENDER, AND SPACE/PLACE

In considering colonial women's activities in the colonies and their influence on the development of colonial society, feminist scholars have tended to focus on issues of gender, race, and sexuality.[12] Partially a response to the idea, prevalent until the 1970s but still evident as late as 1995, that women were the real source of racism in the colonies, these thematic categories were a convenient way of writing women back into the colonial power structures from which they had been excluded.[13] There has also been a tendency among scholars to divide women into types: travelers, missionaries, educators, medical personnel, etc.; typological categories that proved useful in recuperating women from the imperial limbo.[14] Whereas the categories of race, gender, and sexuality are valuable in analyzing the social structures of the colonies, the typological ones are useful in pinpointing the chronology and development of women's involvement in the Empire. How then does one tie these themes and categories together to recreate the theoretical and practical complexities of women's association with the colonies?

Listening to women's voices is one way of gauging what women feel and think or, more to the point, what they think listeners should know about what they do or do not feel and think. The writing of women travelers and missionaries (mostly British) has received considerable attention from historians, whereas colonial women novelists have been examined mainly by literary scholars. The approach is thematic and very often deconstructive, in the Derridaian sense; an approach that is excellent from a literary point of view but often falls short from a historical one. Subaltern and Francophone studies have concentrated on the writings of the "colonized" (men and women), in both the colonial and post-independence settings; colonial women have received less attention.[15] Yet an examination of all types of women's writing—fiction and nonfiction—offers the possibility of crossing categorical boundaries and typologies, whereas a historical rather than a literary analysis can demonstrate the impact of national and international politics and events.

In their recent theoretical analysis of the relevance of personal narratives to the social sciences, Maynes, Pierce, and Laslett take issue with the way in which dominant theories and methods of the social sciences view individuals and their actions primarily through categories, arguing that by doing so individuals are reduced "to clusters of social variables that serve as proxies for persons" and human agency becomes defined in terms of social positions. An analysis of personal narratives, on the other hand, can provide "important insights into the history of the self and its variations," while potentially "enrich[ing] theories of social action and human agency."[16] The written narratives that are discussed and analyzed in the ensuing chapters are as important for understanding the personal and professional strategies of their writers as they are to situating their authors within the social, cultural, and political structures of the two colonies. Women had an ideological role to play in the colonies, whether it was consciously assumed or not. Personal narratives help us to understand just how important this role was.

The scholarship on European women in the colonies has expanded greatly in the past decade, enhancing our understanding of the dynamics of colonialism and their involvement in it. From its original recuperative stance this literature has become more nuanced as scholars have sought out and analyzed women's texts in an endeavor to understand exactly what that role was, the extent to which they were complicit with or resistant to the imperialism enterprise, and the way in which gender, race, and sexuality had an impact on the lives and interactions of colonial society.[17] Although much of the early scholarship in this vein focused on the British Empire, other European empires have now engaged scholars in much the same way.[18] Scholarship on colonial women's writing has, for the most part, either focused on travel writing, on the works of individual writers, or on the way in which literary tropes were used to colonial ends, whereas comparisons of women's writings in the colonies have tended to remain anchored to one empire.[19] Edited volumes on gender and empire, or women and empire, include articles from different European empires, and hence have a comparative dimension, but there has been no history monograph that specifically and extensively compares colonial women's writing from the colonies of two different European empires.

An examination of women's writing raises the question of how the relationship between discourse and experience should be prioritized. To be sure, women's narratives must be contextualized by their colonial experience. It is not only women's colonial experiences that are relevant to what follows, however. As a historian rather than a literary scholar I am as interested in women's personal strategies and responses to given political and social situations as I am in their literary ends. Although discursive narratives are at the center of this study, arranging them thematically separates them from the chronological trajectory of women's experiences. Doing so can thus diminish the impact of women's colonial agency and overlook their personal and cultural ambitions. It can also obscure political, cultural, and social developments that framed their writings. The structure of this work is not therefore thematic, as a discourse-oriented literary study would necessarily be. My intention is to elucidate the way women mapped the patterns of colonial nostalgia by demonstrating how women writers used the colonial space to further their personal, intellectual, and political (in the broadest sense of the term) agendas, and how these changed over time; changes due not only to developments within the colony but also to political pressures from outside. My subsequent aim is to provide a better understanding of how their writing is situated within the colonial narratives and literary discourses of their day. It is not enough to highlight socio-political divergences from one colony to another for, within individual colonies, there were divergences over time. As discursive narratives were not neatly contained within chronological, or indeed geographical borders, but crossed over them, my comparisons are organized into three discrete yet overlapping sections: colonial women and their imagined selves (1900–1930); political realities and fictional representations (c.1920–1940); the end of empire and the reformulation of nostalgia (1940–present). By exploring women's (self) representations in this way, my aim is to throw light on what it was about the colonial context that made women write, and write the way they did, when they did.

SPACE, NOSTALGIA, AND MODERNITY

When I embarked on this study, themes of gender and race were prevalent themes while examining colonial women. I was certainly interested in exploring the different ways in which gender and race shaped, or were shaped by, women's attitudes toward colonialism and I published a number of articles in this vein on Algeria.[20] As I progressed I became more absorbed by the concepts of space, nostalgia, and modernity and the way they impinged on, or were shaped by, the lives of colonial women. Colonies provided an important space for the personal and professional development of European women. Shirley Ardener has argued that space is an ordering principle of society. Like gender and race, to which it is often linked, it structures the lives of the men and women who are associated with it. The social and political mapping of space in the patriarchal societies of the colonies depended on "ground rules" that created gender- or race-specific locations, where gender or race-related activities were carried out. Space can thus be associated with political and social power. Although these spaces were largely the domain of men, they were not impenetrable.[21] Women in the colonies transgressed boundaries of space in the colonies that, at the time, would have been difficult to do in the metropole. Colonial power structures, furthermore, were not binary, colonizer or colonized, even if some scholars have preferred to see it that way.[22] European women may not have been part of the ruling political elite until near the end of empire, and then in very small numbers, but they were part of the dominating culture from its inception. They were, therefore, in a paradoxical situation. A framework of separate spheres, problematic at best, is totally inappropriate in the colonial context, as the domestic or private space was also a political space when it came to the issue of race. Women who wrote could and did transgress spatial boundaries of gender, power, and patriarchy.

In thinking about colonial women and space, one should be mindful of the fact that expatriation for settler women was comparable to self-imposed exile. Unlike true expatriates, who left their homelands for a limited period of time, for most settler women expatriation, like exile, was permanent. The perception of permanence was more pronounced in colonies that were furthest from the homeland (Kenya as opposed to Algeria) particularly in the early stages of colonization when travel was complicated and the voyage home was long. The voyage from Mombasa to Tilbury, for example, took six weeks. Socioeconomic factors were also relevant as travel was expensive and trips back "home" could be infrequent. More importantly, when settlers did return home they did so in a time warp as the metropole had evolved socially, politically, and culturally at a different pace from the colony. Whatever settlers may have thought of their homeland, it was the colony that became their new home—socially, politically, and culturally. A culturally hybrid home, to be sure but home nonetheless. As Peter Fritzsche has said in another context: "exiles at once mapped the center at which they had once stood and the margins to which they had been displaced."[23] In such circumstances, space and its gendering become linked in various ways to nostalgia. There was, nonetheless, an important difference between the colonial situation and that of exiled or diasporic communities. Whereas the latter adapted their minority culture to the majority culture of their new home, in the colonial situation the culture of the minority was imposed on the majority. Thus, space and its gendering become allied to nostalgia in altogether different ways. By reinventing and remapping the spaces of the colonies in their texts, colonial women sowed the seeds of post-independence colonial nostalgia.

COLONIAL NOSTALGIA BUT NOT IMPERIAL NOSTALGIA

When associated with European imperialism, nostalgia brings to mind a rose-colored reminiscence of lost empire, understood as a response to a diminished global position. It is a regressive sentiment that circumvents the real issues of colonialism and obscures the extent of its violence. Like the gendered tropes associated with the discourse of imperialism, this type of nostalgia is often gendered in that an imagined or regretted past is associated with female or male representations or protagonists. Films such as *Indochine* or *Chocolat*, have central characters personifying France as benevolent and magnanimous, as in the case of Eliane in *Indochine*, or even as innocent as in the case of France in *Chocolat*.[24] Symbolism of this sort is a recurring theme in postcolonial representation, whether through film, in novels or other depictions of the colonial or postcolonial situation.[25] But, such nostalgia is not restricted to the retrospective daydreams of the colonizing powers, as scholars such as William Bissell have shown.[26] Bissell, who examines nostalgia for the colonial past among Africans of Zanzibar, suggests that it is part of a social imaginary triggered by economic, political, and social instability. As he rightly points out, nostalgia is "an irreducibly plural phenomenon, [which] takes on very different forms and dimensions, engaging an array of social agents, interest, forces and locations."[27]

As the above paragraph suggests the concepts of imperial and colonial nostalgia are often elided. I distinguish between the two. Imperial nostalgia, I argue, is associated with loss of empire; colonial nostalgia with the loss of socio-cultural standing. The former is connected to power politics exemplified by events such as the 1982 Falklands and the 1986 Operation Epervier to shield Chad from Libyan invasion, which echoed notions of former British and French imperial grandeur; the latter to colonial lifestyle, illustrated by films, such as those mentioned above. Women's role in constructing colonial nostalgia is an important one for, as numerous scholars have pointed out, colonial women were vital to the development of the social and domestic structures of colonial society and were, therefore intimately involved in creating the colonial lifestyle. Colonial nostalgia, furthermore, is not a monolithic concept, but one whose parameters are defined by the particular lifestyles of specific colonies. This study focuses on these differences and their development over time.

The term nostalgia, a combination of the Greek *nostos* (return home) and *algos* (pain), was coined by Johannes Hofer in the seventeenth century (c. 1688) to describe an affliction of Swiss mercenaries serving outside their native land. Those suffering from the ailment grew despondent, sickened, wasted away and in some cases died or committed suicide. From the outset, therefore, nostalgia has been associated with dislocation. In the culture of capitalism the concept of nostalgia splintered into multiple forms associated with class, power, and the displacements engendered by a capitalist economy. Or as Kathleen Stewart has put it, capitalism created "nostalgias of hegemony or resistance."[28] Nostalgia in this light is the resistance of tradition to modernity. In the context of the colonies, however, the oppositional poles of nostalgia and modernity, past and present, were often transgressed or elided. Linked to collective or personal identity, nostalgia as a symptom of social, political, or economic angst can therefore mean different things to different people(s).

Janelle Wilson has rightly pointed out that nostalgia is both a cultural phenomenon and a personally subjective experience.[29] Wilson argues that the shift from personal to cultural is largely due to commercialization. In other words, nostalgia sells. Writing a quarter of a century before Wilson, Fred Davis also made the distinction between private and collective nostalgia stating that the former is shaped by the images and illusions relevant to a person's biography, whereas the latter is associated to symbols and objects of a "highly public, widely shared, and familiar character."[30] For Davis nostalgia is a deeply social emotion. Using this analysis in the colonial context one can, therefore argue that a letter or an unpublished memoir forms part of the private archive of nostalgia but a novel or memoir, once published, enters the public domain and, therefore becomes part of the collective archive of nostalgia. But what if the two "archives" have the same themes, figures of speech, and patterns? What if those themes, figures of speech, and patterns are not only an essential part of the creation of settler women's identity, but also form part of the post-independence nostalgia for a lifestyle that has disappeared? I argue that colonial women played an important part in the creations of the themes, tropes, and patterns of a colonial lifestyle that became a part of colonial (as opposed to imperial) nostalgia. What follows is an attempt to historicize colonial nostalgia.

In her sensitive analysis of the significance and dynamics of longing, Svetlana Boym argues that nostalgia has two manifestations: restorative and reflective. The former is associated with *nostos*, the home, and a desire to reconstruct it; the latter with *algia*, the pain of loss and the wistfulness of memory. Nostalgia, therefore, is not just about the past; it is also about the future. It is both prospective and retrospective.[31] Nor is nostalgia only about loss and displacement, it is also about "a romance with one's own fantasy"[32] It appears in times of upheaval and rapid changes of lifestyle and is not a flight from modernity but is coeval with it. Fantasies of the past are defined by the necessities of the present.[33] To this I would add that in settler colonies such fantasies were also a way of preparing for the future, by creating a community where the reinvention of metropole tradition, to paraphrase Hobsbawm and Ranger, became rooted to the colonial land in space-specific ways.[34] As Roxanne Panchasi has pointed out in another context, "[n]ostalgia is generated in advance of loss as well as in its wake."[35] In the colonial context, the possibility of loss—of power, of territory, of the upper hand—was an ever-present, if subliminal, anxiety. Nostalgia, therefore, was inherent to the settler psyche and colonial nostalgia was built into the settler system from its outset.

The questions of exile and nostalgia, a yearning for a lost past or a past that never was, have interested a number of scholars concerned with diaspora and migration, in particular when related to a postcolonial situation.[36] In the latter context, Shaden Tageldin elaborates on Boym's argument by demonstrating that the specificity of the postcolonial migrant's nostalgia "is not that it yearns for a futurized past (or an anteriorized future), but why and how it does so."[37] In the chapters that follow it is the why and the how that I shall develop.

In *Yesterday's Self,* Andreea Decíu Rítívoí's study of nostalgia and immigrant identity, Rítívoí states that "[n]ostalgia prompts questions regarding the . . . distinctions between escapist fantasy and the imagination as repository of ideals, considerations of identity as a self-sufficient entity or as a culture- and context bound entity." In short, it functions "as a potent interpretive stance, a comparison and analysis."[38] For Rítívoí, then, nostalgia in the context of the immigrant is about adjustment to new surroundings, the success of which depends on building bridges between the past and the present. It is a narrative of identity that is part of self-preservation in an alien culture or environment. I shall build on her thesis by arguing that the bridges settler women built between their metropole past (nostalgia) and their colonial present (imposing "modernity") formed the repertoire, to borrow Charles Tilly's concept, of post-independence nostalgia. Colonial women's writing became a significant repository for this repertoire.

Nostalgia inherently occludes the less desirable and highlights what is desired. The language and narratives of nostalgia therefore include, to quote, Michael Dorland in another context, "figures of speech or acts of figuration [that] give shape to, form, or stylize what is being said or written so that it will say, or attempt to say, *this* as opposed to *that*. Figuration is precisely the point of contact between a writer and the world outside the writer's mind . . ."[39] In other words the occlusions of narrative of the colonial period, the *this* as opposed to the *that,* formed the basis of colonial nostalgia. If my basic argument is that women's writing developed the themes and figures of speech that made up colonial nostalgia, what endowed their writing with such power? In the processes of colonization it is colonial men rather than colonial women, who are associated with the active role in the brutality of colonization (warfare, land-grabbing, repression), an erroneous perception perhaps but a significant one all the same. The nature of women's role in colonization was of course no less active nor less powerful, as scholars such as Ann Stoler, Antoinette Burton and many others have shown. It was just different. Furthermore, the social construction of European women during much of the colonial period was formulated around a gendered ideal of helpmate and do-gooder, who instructed her children in the niceties of civilized behavior, knew how to keep her house in order—in both the metaphorical and literal senses—and when appropriate involved herself in philanthropic activities. Women's power lay in the very fact they were perceived as the more benign partners in the colonial process. As Glenda Riley, paraphrasing Ngugi Wa Thiong'o, put it in the context of her comparison between pioneer women in Kenya and the American West, "Whereas most men excelled in colonizing the body, most women [were] especially adept at colonizing the mind."[40] Women as educators, as role models, as guardians of national cultural and social traditions—this provided the colonial project with a familial and more compassionate dimension, the dimension in which colonial nostalgia is anchored.

Linking modernity to the concept of nostalgia helps to complicate the picture. In her book *Modernity and Nostalgia, art and politics in France between the wars*, Romy Golan demonstrates that in spite of the fact France was considered to be in the forefront of the avant-garde a retrenchment took place after World War I. This led to reactionary responses such as the return to the soil, anti-urbanism and the questioning of technology with ideological corollaries of agrarianism, regionalism, and corporatism, which exercised a profound influence on French modernism.[41] The intersection of modernity and nostalgia was an equally important feature in the colonies of Kenya and Algeria, as will be demonstrated below.

The connection of modernity to empire has received considerable attention from scholars. Antoinette Burton, for example, argues that modernity developed through colonialism. Dipesh Chakrabarty, on the other hand, suggests that imperialism shaped both modern European national cultures and the way in which Western history was written. The essays in Howard J. Booth's and Nigel Rigby's volume on modernism and empire deal with their connection and their relevance to the theory and literature of British territories, whereas Phyllis Lassner looks at the way British women writing about the colonies were central to the postcolonial debates rooted in the "racial modernities" that emerged as a result of World War II. These works have greatly helped me to develop my own ideas, but unlike them my focus is on the different ways in which the concept of modernity was used and performed in the two colonies, while intersecting with nostalgia and women's role in creating the colonial link between the two.[42] The construction of nostalgia, I argue, was not an ex post-facto development but was embedded in the colonial period and, especially in the lives and experiences of colonial women, who, as numerous scholars have shown, were essential to creating and maintaining the identity and lifestyle of a given settler colony.

Equally important to this study, is the way in which modernity was linked to women. The "new woman" of the Edwardian period and the "modern woman" of the interwar period were defined by their independence and enterprising spirit. As Whitney Chadwick and Tirza Latimer have pointed out in the context of interwar France, popular representations of the "modern woman" in the media in France often focused on the expatriate phenomenon.[43] Women who chose to go to the colonies were also seen in this light. Furthermore, as will be demonstrated in the chapters that follow, whether colonial women were actually "modern" or not did not much matter. They were held up as exemplars of modernity to the local population of the colonies in which they lived.

Modernity can mean many things: liberalism, secularism, democracy, progress—economic, political, or social. It is associated with rationality, efficiency and change and contrasted with a traditionalism that connotes fatalism, superstition, and lack of scientific or technological sophistication. Modernity can be a theory or a practice. Its meaning can be precise or imprecise and, as such, the concept can be manipulated and, of course, it can also be associated with violence.[44] At the end of the nineteenth century European concepts of modernity were teleological and linear. In the colonial context the concept of modernity became a tool of control in so far as

the British and the French colonizers saw themselves as harbingers of progress and improvement, whether that improvement was moral, economic, or
political. The "white man's burden" was the "onerous duty" to enlighten the
"black man"; the *mission civilisatrice* was the didactic desire to bring French
enlightenment to the "benighted." The purported aim may have been the
same, but the means were different. Modernity was performed differently in
the two colonies, both in discourse and in practice. Gertrude Himmelfarb,
in her study of the French, British, and American Enlightenments, has suggested that the paths to modernity were nuanced according to a nation's
ideological and political concerns.[45] In the colonies, where the colonizing
power was deemed not only to symbolize modernity but also to introduce
and advance it, economic, cultural, racial, and political concerns in the two
colonies created dissimilar patterns by which modernity was performed.
Women's colonial experiences and their narratives were inevitably shaped by
these patterns, which were then picked up, consciously or sub-consciously,
in women's writing.

Jo Burr Margadant has rightly pointed out that, "No one 'invents' a self
apart from cultural notions available to them in a particular historical setting."[46] In the case of women in the colonies, however, the cultural and
social markers were those of the metropole they had left behind **and** of
the colony in which they had chosen to settle. In this paradoxical situation
nostalgia and modernity were conflated. Nostalgia was inherently written
into their daily lives in the sense that women reproduced metropole patterns
of behavior in an altogether different environment, whether they actually
longed for the absent metropole or not. This type of nostalgia was masked
by the activities of modernity. Whether it was the "civilizing mission" or the
mise en value of the French or the "white man's burden" and the introduction to capitalism of the British, the underlying message was one of bringing
progress to backward civilizations or primitive peoples; of showing them
how to live the civilized (hence modern) way. In the colonies, therefore,
nostalgia and modernity were not just about the antithesis between the past
and the present, between the traditional and the modern, they were closely
linked. It is the ambiguity of this situation that is explored below.

NOVELS, MEMOIRS, AND LETTERS

Novels, memoirs and letters—three distinctive genres that can each be used
as historical sources in their own right—highlight the role of the authors
in society, and lead to an understanding of the society's social and cultural
framework. As Diana Holmes has pointed out, the novel is "one of the cultural forms through which a society shapes its sense of reality."[47] Seen from
this perspective, an examination of colonial women's novels in Algeria and
Kenya will illustrate the differences in the shared meaning of each colony.
Among the scholarly preoccupations with regard to women's writing has
been its relationship to, or its subversion of, the patriarchal order.[48] In the
period covered by this study, with very few exceptions, women writers were

considered to be subordinate to their male counterparts. As a response to the patriarchal situation in which they found themselves, at different times and in different places, women have used a variety of strategies to reconcile "the female self as 'other' with the female self as author."[49] In the colonies these strategies were complicated by the presence of the colonized peoples who served (metaphorically and literally) as foils for women writers in their quest to achieve their ends. In the pages that follow, I shall identify the different ways in which this relationship was played out.

During the colonial period covered in this study, virtually no published works by colonized women existed. In Algeria there were one or two exceptions; in Kenya there was none.[50] This was due to the fact that for most of the colonial period colonized women in these colonies did not have a Western education, if they had an education at all. In Algeria there certainly were literate women among the elite, but Arabic was the foundation of their literacy, not French. It was only by the late 1930s that a limited number of colonized women had acquired the sort of French education that would have permitted them to write for a metropole audience and even then publishing was a major hurdle and could only be achieved through sponsorship.[51] In Kenya the process to acquire publishing literacy was even slower.[52] In both colonies, however, a strong oral tradition of songs, poems, and epics existed among the colonized peoples and women were essential to their propagation. Their respective oral traditions helped to reinforce their identities at a time of social and political disruption and if on occasion it was threaded through with nostalgia for a precolonial time, it did not contribute to the type of nostalgia discussed in this study. Their voices are, therefore, silent in this study but in spite of this silence their contribution is not negligible. The significance of colonized women to colonial nostalgia was not through their voices, oral or written, but rather in the way in which settler women interacted with Algerian or Kenyan women in what the settlers considered to be their philanthropic activities, or in the way in which settler women envisaged their every day exchanges with the women they colonized, or in the manner in which they wrote them into (or out of) their novels. Colonized women could therefore be emblematic of the "feel good" dimension of colonial nostalgia, or in the case of their occlusion from colonial novels, suggestive of the power structures of the colony. In what follows, therefore, wherever appropriate I analyze the implications of the representations of colonized women if and when they appear in novels.[53]

If novels are a form of self-construction and performance that elucidate the workings of a society and its culture, so too are memoirs and letters. Like novels they are sites of reconstructed memory; an immediate past (letters), an intermediate or distant past (memoirs), all selectively recreated. Each of the three genres conflates the facts and fictions of a particular time and place in a singular way, but taken together they contribute to the makeup of the colony's collective identity. Scholars have focused extensively on the inextricable nature of individual and collective memory and the way in which each constructs a reality.[54] Although the connection between these two types of memory and their respective realities is a component of the writings of colonial women, the three genres are all odysseys of sorts in which imagination is the vehicle of self-creation. It is the way in which the imagination is used in each that I would like to stress. Whereas the fiction of the novel can mask the "reality" of society, the "reality" of the memoir can mask society's fictions. As for the letters, they take the reader on an odyssey through the daily life of the writer, a writer who makes deliberate choices of what to include and not include. Analyzing these choices sheds light on both the way the reader views the writer and the way the writer sees herself. Unfortunately, with rare exceptions, few complete collections of the letters of individual women from the colonies have survived.[55] Most have been lost or destroyed during the peregrinations of the writers or at decolonization when families left, often in haste. The letters that are examined in this volume were all written by articulate women who prided themselves on their style, both literary and cultural. They are, therefore, cultural artifacts representative of a certain class. The writing under consideration was nearly all penned by women whose origins were middle or upper class. It was this class that set the cultural and social tone of colonial society and it was the women who stabilized the colonial structure of society. A few women writers came from less privileged backgrounds but profited socially and culturally from their colonial experience. Although there was a pecking order among settlers, whatever their original background and whatever their position in settler society, in relation to the metropole a settler's social standing was always enhanced due to the dominant position that the racial framework of the colony ensured. The distinction achieved by colonial women, whose work was published, consolidated (or improved) their social position in the colony. The way in which this distinction was experienced in the colony and the metropole differed. I shall analyze these differences whenever relevant.

But Where Are the Men?

Colonial nostalgia was not, of course, the prerogative of women. Men were as engaged in its production as women. A study combining both men and women's contribution to colonial nostalgia in two colonies structured along the lines of what follows would have required two volumes. Besides, a considerable literature already exists on men's direct or indirect contribution to colonial nostalgia, although most is limited either to one colony or to one empire.[56] Nostalgia was not, of course, just reproduced in European writing as the work of scholars such as Gwendolyn Wright, Zeynep Çelik, Felix Driver, and David Gilbert have demonstrated.[57] Architectural design and the way in which cities were designed or redesigned in the colonies, formed part of the restorative element of nostalgia that accompanies the creation of an identity away from "home." If the architects and urban designers sought to recreate Paris or London in Africa or Asia it was not only to impose modernity on "backward" nations, even if that was the rationale. It was also to alleviate the culture shock and the desire to recreate familiar architectural surroundings and public space in which they could function more comfortably, the *nostos* of nostalgia that so often accompanies permanent expatriation, exile and in the colonial case, conquest. Women's involvement was, perhaps, less flamboyant but it was nonetheless equally important. If women in the colonies were able to contribute more readily to the public space than they were in the metropole, they still were the essential element in the reconstruction of the private space. They also played an important role in socializing their children, and defining the way in which colonial society developed, as scholars like Stoler, Gouda, Strobel and others have shown. By helping to structure the colonial lifestyle they laid the groundwork for the development of colonial nostalgia. It is in their letters, memoirs, and novels that this groundwork can best be read.

The Structure of the Study

Themes and chronology are equally important in analyzing narratives from a historical point of view. Whereas themes make up the substance of the work, chronology situates the narratives in relation to national and international events, and the way in which they were played out in the colony. Had what follows been a literary analysis, my organizational choice would have been thematic. But I am more interested in the way in which women's lives were shaped by the colonial space and how they responded to events and circumstances over time. A thematic approach would privilege discourse and obscure the importance of event and circumstance in shaping their writing. Without knowledge of the experience one cannot truly understand the discourse; nor can one separate what is subjective from what is objective in a particular narrative. My preference for an essentially chronological framework is geared to move away from the standard analyses of women's writing, which is so often thematic, in order to highlight the paradoxical experiences of colonial women's lives over time and space, and to demonstrate how they transformed these experiences through writing.[58]

The first chapter is an overview of the development of settler society and its female presence in Algeria and Kenya. The second chapter focuses on the lives and African writing of two women, Isabelle Eberhardt in Algeria and Karen Blixen in Kenya. I demonstrate the importance of the colonial space as a source of their creativity and what it was about their personal strategies that shaped their images for posterity. I argue that Eberhardt and Blixen became personifications of colonial nostalgia and I show that it was the way they lived their lives—or *performed* their colonial experience—that established their iconic status. Just how their strategies set them apart from other colonial women writers will become clearer in ensuing chapters. It is also in this chapter that I introduce the idea of nostalgia as a continuum, that is to say the formulation of romanticized fantasies, which persist beyond the colonial period as post-independence signifiers of expatriation and adventure. It introduces some of the patterns and themes of nostalgia-in-the-making that appear and are elaborated in the ensuing chapters. Part I, therefore, sets the stage for what follows. The three chapters of Part II cover women's writing in the interwar period. Whereas, overall the chapters demonstrate the way in which women's narratives responded to the politics and events both in the colonies and in the respective metropoles, each focuses on a different component of women's writing. Chapter 3 looks at letters, memoirs, fiction and nonfiction and is concerned with the way women performed and thought modernity and nostalgia. Chapter 4 concentrates on the fictional works of four authors: Elissa Rhaïs and Magali Boisnard, writing about Algeria, and Florence Riddell and Nora K. Strange writing about Kenya. In this chapter, I examine and analyze the development of narratives of nostalgia and modernity in the fiction of the two colonies. Chapter 5 is concerned with women's responses to the national and international political developments of the thirties. Issues of governance and inter-racial relations were the main colonial preoccupations, but the Depression and the rise of fascism also featured in women's writing, particularly in Kenya. The political turbulence of the period created a "realist" response to the colonial situation and an enforcement of the nostalgic patterns of settler identity. Part III comprises two chapters that cover the period of decolonization. Chapter 6 explores the differences in the way the two colonies were decolonized, women's responses to decolonization, and the fracturing of their identity. Chapter 7 highlights the way the nostalgia narratives of the colonial period were picked up and reshaped as an identity mechanism for women whose family roots were in the colony of Algeria or Kenya.

Finally, a word about terminology: in Algeria the settlers viewed themselves as *Algériens* and referred to the local population (comprised largely of ethnic Arabs and Berbers) as *indigènes* or *musulmans*. This, of course, suggested that the settlers were the "real" Algerians, whereas the population native was "other." I prefer to use settler, *pied-noir* or *colon* and Algerian for the Arabs and Berbers unless I want to refer specifically to one of these two ethnicities. In quotes from settler literature the word *Algérien* is a self-reference. In Kenya, the situation was slightly different due to the presence of an imported Indian population. I therefore use African or Kenyan for the inhabitants native to Kenya and only refer to specific ethnicities such as the Kikuyu, Maasi, or Somali if they appear as such in women's texts or if the ethnicity is relevant to my discussion. Although the Indian population was a settler population, I refer to them as Indian and use the term settler to refer to the British and Europeans, who were the politically dominant group. As this study is not a literary analysis, in the interest of uniformity and unless otherwise stated, all translations from the French are mine.

PART I

1900–1930. COLONIAL WOMEN AND THEIR IMAGINED SELVES

CHAPTER 1

PARADOXICAL LIVES: WOMEN AND THEIR COLONIAL WORLDS

L'Afrique est le pays de mon imagination, la France la patrie de mon coeur.

Pauline Noirfontaine (1856)

We felt at times as if we might be living in the Garden of Eden . . .

Marion Dobbs (c. 1920)

SETTING THE SCENE

Space and Place

The territories of Algeria and Kenya lie on either side of the Sahara desert; the former to the north, the latter to the south. Geographically Algeria can be divided into two regions, the temperate coastal plains bordering the Mediterranean and the arid southern desert. The two regions are separated by a series of mountainous sections that form part of the Atlas range. With the exception of a short border with Libya to the east, during the colonial period covered by this study, the remaining land borders were with territories occupied by the French, providing a sense of French continuity along the southern Mediterranean shore. As the bulk of the colony's territory lay in the arid south, existence for Europeans was difficult and settlers gravitated to the temperate Mediterranean region settling first in towns along the coast before moving more slowly inland. Arabs and the Berbers were the predominant ethnic groups, both being followers of Islam. Although a small number of other ethnicities existed, the indigenous Jews formed the only other group relevant to this study.[1] When the French first moved into Algeria the territory was not a complete unknown. Economic and migratory relations had existed with North Africa and in particular the Regency of Algiers for centuries.[2] If the image of the area, largely shaped by Western perceptions of Islam, that had developed over time was a distorted one, there was nonetheless a sense of a shared Mediterranean history, and hence of some familiarity with the region.[3]

In contrast to Algeria, the territory of Kenya was situated on the equator in the sub-Saharan tropics. It is bordered to the east by the Indian Ocean, where the climate is hot and humid, but running through the country is the Rift Valley with its mountainous spine rising in places as high as 12,000 feet and its savannah flat lands harboring great herds of game. With the exception of Somalia and Ethiopia in the north and northeast, British occupied territories formed its inland borders.[4] Ethnically more diverse than Algeria, the territory was (and is) home to about 40 different peoples, of which the most relevant to this study are the Kikuyu, the Luo, the Masai, and the Somalis.[5] It was also religiously more diverse. Arabs and Somalis had settled along the coast, as the port of Mombasa was an important link between East Africa and South Asia, leaving their cultural and religious mark on the area. Religious practices inland were predominantly animist, although Islam was present along the borderlands of the north as well as on the coast. A Christian presence had existed since the arrival of Protestant and Catholic missionaries in the early nineteenth century, but Christian and animist practices were often mixed. In spite of the fact that East Africa had been the object of interest during the nineteenth century as explorers set out to find the origins of the Nile, the Mountains of the Moon, or some imagined El Dorado, the region was still largely unknown territory. The image of "darkest Africa" that so tantalized the Victorians was also a distorted one, but the distortion came through complete ignorance of the terrain and its peoples rather than the perceived familiarity arising from a shared space and history, as was the case in Algeria.

These differences in the spaces colonial women occupied were to influence the way in which their colonial life was experienced and, above all, imagined. But, if geographic and ethnic spaces were contributing factors to women's imaginings, so too were the politics and economics of occupation in particular in relation to the deployment of land.

Algeria

Under the military administration (1830–1870) European settlement in Algeria progressed in fits and starts mainly due to high mortality and inconsistent colonial policies.[6] Land expropriation on the other hand started immediately, thanks in part to officers like General Clauzel, who were early advocates of settlement. The expropriation of land continued throughout the military regime occurring on a truly large scale after the Kabyle insurrection of 1871, and the ensuing transfer of the administration from the military to the civilians.[7] A 1873 law, known as the *Loi Warnier*, started a process which was to make all land transactions subject to French law, thus transforming Algerian collective and individual landholdings either into

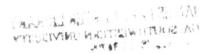

individual French holdings or into property of the Colonial State. In 1887 a second law *(La loi du 23 avril)* was passed that effectively completed the process. The issuing of land deeds in accordance with French law, which this process entailed, created a situation whereby property transactions nearly always benefited the French. On the one hand they understood the law and could therefore manipulate it to their advantage and, on the other hand, land collectively owned under the precolonial system now became subject to individual land ownership procedures, whereby deeds were required to prove ownership. From 1872 to 1901 European landholding more than doubled, reaching 1,912,000 hectares (4,724,655 acres) in 1901.[8] In addition, large swathes of forest were declared to be property of the state and placed under the French forestry commission. In spite of this, however, at the turn of the century only 39% of the settler population was rurally based.[9] The remaining 61% of the European population was situated in the urban centers of Algiers, Oran, Bône, and Constantine, or in smaller towns where its members were involved in commercial activities of different sorts.

The centrality of land apart, the two main concerns during the initial period of the civilian administration were the numerical imbalance between the French and the Algerian populations and the question of labor. Colonial anxieties about the former led to the promulgation in 1889 of a law, which granted French citizenship to the children born in Algeria of non-French Europeans, who had settled in the colony. Nineteen years earlier, in 1870, the *Crémieux Law* had granted French citizenship to the indigenous Jews of Algeria. It was a contested move, giving rise to anti-Semitic outbursts, most notably in 1898 and in the 1930s. The ethnic distinctions in the colony led to a complex racial and class stratification of indigenous ethnicities (Arab and Berber), naturalized French indigenous ethnicities (Jews and *évolué* Arabs and Berbers), naturalized French European ethnicities (predominantly Spanish, Italian, and Maltese), and the French. [10]

During the first two decades of occupation the local population was put under severe economic pressure. Not only was their land seized but they were also obliged to pay special taxes, the *impôts arabes*. These measures impoverished them further and forced them into the labor market. By 1900, 70 years of occupation had led to considerable pauperization of the native population, thus creating the prerequisites for the emergence of a cheap labor force. The need for labor increased as the agriculture sector developed following the draining of the swampy plains of the Mitidja and the establishment of the wine industry in Algeria in the wake of the 1880s phylloxera disaster in France. By 1900, furthermore, prophylactics and improved hygiene had stabilized the demographics of the settler population. Colonial society, therefore, was finally "coming into its own".

Kenya

In Kenya the situation was very different. European missionaries had been present in East Africa since the 1840s, but the British economic presence only started in 1888, when the chartered Imperial British East Africa Company moved from Zanzibar into the territories of Kenya and Tanganyika (Tanzania). The aim was to manage the area on a no-cost basis. In less than a decade, however, it became clear that the company was not succeeding in its aims. As a result, in 1895 the British government stepped in creating the protectorate of British East Africa under the aegis of the Foreign Office and the guiding hand of Sir Arthur Hardinge, then Consul-General in Zanzibar and later Commissioner for the protectorate. It was to become "one of the most controversial dependencies in the British Empire."[11] The first settlers straggled into Kenya in the 1890s, but their endeavors were mostly unsuccessful.[12] In 1900, Sir Charles Eliot was appointed Commissioner for the protectorate and a year later the Uganda railway was completed. The convergence of these two events gave settlement a significant boost. The completion of the 582-mile railway, linking Mombasa to the Uganda hinterland, opened the way to the economic development of the area along European lines. Although Eliot only remained in his East African post for four years, he promoted white settlement, encouraging "men of position and means" to come to Kenya by offering them large concessions.[13] Initially, alienated land was designated Crown Land and leased to would-be settlers. The leasehold stipulated by the 1902 Crown Land Ordinance was 99 years, but in 1915 it was increased to 999 years. Land was divided into three categories: farms (5,000 acres/2023 hectares or more), homesteads (640 acres/259 hectares), and residential and small business plots (1–2 acres/0.4–0.8 hectares).[14] Eliot's belief in white supremacy and the leadership attributes of the British upper classes, led him to favor the more aristocratically inclined settlers and to encourage their settlement in the highlands, considered at the time to be the most salubrious spot for Europeans. For example, Lord [Hugh] Delamere, who was the greatest publicist for the colony and would eventually become the leading settler spokesman, was granted 100,000 acres (40,500 hectares) at an annual rent of £200 pounds.[15] The proceeds of the property leased by the Crown were not geared to bring revenue into the colonial administration's coffers, rather by encouraging the acquisition of large tracts of land at relatively low leasehold prices the intention was to establish an export economy that would keep the colony solvent.[16] The need for labor led to the imposition of taxes on the Kenyans, the first of which was the 1902 hut tax.[17] As Africans were required to pay the tax in cash, which they did not have, or in kind, it created the conditions which would push them into the labor market in much the same way as settler measures had in Algeria. Kenyans residing on land that was "alienated" were moved into native reserves by tribe. Those who were not shifted into the reserves became squatters on the farms, thus providing a ready source of labor. There was also a growing population of Indians, originally brought in to work on the railway. Once it was completed, many of the Indians, who had survived the harsh conditions under which they worked, remained in Kenya moving into trade and commerce.[18] In 1903 Eliot issued an order prohibiting the alienation of highland territory to the Indians. A scheme was drawn up to assist the immigration of British Indians to the regions near the coast and Victoria Nyanza, both considered areas "not suitable for settlement by Europeans."[19] These measures effectively created a three-tiered racial hierarchy, which was further complicated by notions of class or rank within each group.

The Foreign Office did not approve of the aggressive methods by which Eliot was privileging the settlers, and the ensuing tension led to his resignation in 1904.[20] His departure did little to redress the situation as far as land alienation was concerned: land applications had increased from 117 to 300 and with it the European presence.[21] From a few hundred residents at the turn of the century the European population increased to 1,813 in 1905 and to 5,438 in 1914.[22] Compared to other British territories in Africa, such as Southern Rhodesia, the settler population was low, so measures were taken at different times to attract new settlers.[23] The most notable of these occurred in the immediate aftermath of World War I, when 2.54 million acres (1.03 million hectares) were made available for white settlement. Much of this land came from the African reserves. A Soldier Settlement Scheme was implemented for demobilized military personnel, whereby two categories of farms (160 acres/65 hectares and 3,000–5,000 acres/1,200–2,000 hectares) were distributed by raffle, and restrictions imposed on colonial officials owning land were relaxed.[24] Land that was not alienated to Europeans was transformed into forestry or "native" reserves, each of which was restricted to a particular tribe.

THE MYTHOLOGIES AND DISCOURSES OF SETTLEMENT

The concept of "pioneer" used by settlers of expanding nations, whether in Africa, the Americas or elsewhere, to describe what they consider to be their heroic or epic period, was incorporated into the discourses of nostalgia of Algeria and Kenya. The positive imagery associated with the pioneer—hardworking, tough, no-nonsense types whose backbreaking work had created something out of nothing—was a staple of post-pioneer era literature. So, too was the narrative that the occupied territory was demographically empty and economically unexploited, ripe for the civilizing influences of the occupying power. Positive imagery and narratives of this sort masked the land grabbing and the marginalization, or elimination, of the native population that accompanied the process. The justificatory myths and discourses inherent in the process of colonial settlement were of course geared to anchor the settlers to the land.[25]

In the final years of the nineteenth century, Algeria was a settler society in the process of definition, whereas Kenya was hardly a settler society at all. Colonial Algeria had emerged from it's "frontier pioneering" phase, Kenya was just entering it. Yet, by the early twentieth century each had an established territorial discourse: Algeria as a Latin land, Kenya as a "white man's country." In Algeria colonial officials, ideologues, and novelists promoted the idea that France was recovering North Africa's sacred Latin past, thus diminishing the importance of Islam and marginalizing its indigenous inhabitants.[26] In Kenya it was the period of early settlement, from the end of the 1890s to 1920 when Kenya became a colony, that the idea took hold of a land where the white man would reign supreme and live by the noble occupations of the hunt and the fruits of the estate.[27] Both these narratives had strong elements of reflective nostalgia; both were strongly masculine. If, as Raymond Williams has suggested, literature is the form "through which the meanings . . . valued by the community are shared and made active," then an examination of women's literature in Algeria and Kenya will deepen our understanding of the gender relationships and sexual identities within those societies, as well as how the racial and social constraints helped to shape them.[28]

WOMEN IN THE COLONIES

The change in women's circumstances over the course of the nineteenth century contributed to their mobility, whether it was from rural to urban centers in the metropole or from the metropole to the colonies. Education for women improved in both France and Britain over the century providing women with better formal educational opportunities. Additionally the reform movements that took shape in both countries during the century raised women's political awareness and encouraged the emergence of feminist and women's labor movements. Although the feminist movement in France was a shadow of its British counterpart, the end of the nineteenth century marked the emergence of a strain of feminist writing in both countries.[29] This was due to the fact that, as the century progressed, there had been a noticeable increase in the number of women writers. In France this development accelerated during the last decade of the century.[30] European women writers, who had always had to use a variety of strategies or subterfuges to get into print and, when they did, to be accepted on a par with male writers, found the hurdles less daunting even if unqualified acceptance was not usually forthcoming. The European colonies as "exotic" settings or their inhabitants as counterpoints in the elaboration of the metropole nation and its values were part of the development of the novel in the nineteenth century. The colonies, therefore, were a stimulus to literary output in the nineteenth century as much as they have been to the literary movements of postcolonial France and Britain.[31]

Women's mobility also increased as a result of the security afforded by European expansion into hitherto "hostile" areas. For French women, Algeria was the privileged choice due to its proximity and to the fact that after 1848 it was administratively absorbed into France as three departments. For British women, it was originally India and South Africa but by the end of the nineteenth century the charms of British East Africa were exercising their influence. Women went to the colonies for a number of reasons; some voluntarily, others because they had no choice. Missionaries, travellers, wives, feminists, and professionals found their way to the colonies at different times. In the case of Algeria, there was also the category of political exiles or escapees who had been deported as a result of, or fled from, social or political upheavals in France such as the closing of the National Workshops, the Paris Commune or the 1870 annexation of Alsace-Lorraine by the Germans. Other women arrived in the colonies for economic reasons because there were better opportunities than the areas from which they came. In many ways the development of colonial society during the fin-de-siècle and early decades of the twentieth century in Algeria and Kenya created a privileged space for women. In spite of the fact both were patriarchal societies with their own specific gender traditions, as will be seen in the chapters that follow, there was also an element of the frontier—initially actual and eventually imagined—in each, which meant that women were required to pull their weight both from an economic and a natalist point of view. But the presence of "cheap and abundant" local labor, both in the home and in the work place, allowed for a leeway that many women could not have in the metropole. They could fulfill the roles expected of them from society and yet have the leisure to shape their lives in more substantial ways. Another advantage was that social mobility was easier and could be more spectacular. In Algeria, for example, Aurelie Picard (1849–1933), was plucked out of domestic service in France to marry a wealthy Algerian dignitary and rose to an exalted position in the Tidjanniya, an important Sufi brotherhood.[32] In Kenya, although British class sensibilities were a feature of the social scene, and hence more traditional class divisions existed among Europeans than in Algeria, women could and did make the most of colonial opportunities to cross class boundaries. Mary Roseveare came to Kenya to act as governess to the four daughters of the McDonell family, settlers in Limuru. In 1912 she established a small school that became the Limuru Girls High School of which she was the first headmistress.[33] Alice Hammond, a cook-house-keeper in England came to the colony as a housekeeper and found that there was a solidarity that transcended class. "There is" she said "something different about pioneer work. One has a sense of achievement, a feeling of being first".[34] Before examining these issues in detail and moving on to the women, who are the main focus of this work, it is necessary to set out the way in which a female presence was established in each colony.

THE GROWTH OF A EUROPEAN FEMALE PRESENCE IN ALGERIA

The first women to arrive in Algeria of their own accord were travellers and missionaries.[35] Among these was the missionary, Emilie de Vialar (1797–1856), who came to Algeria in 1835 to run a hospital with the Sisters of St. Joseph, a charitable religious order she had founded and whose charter she had drawn up in 1832. Sarah Curtis has shown that she was a woman of means who left Gaillac in France, where she had gained a bad press for her headstrong ways, remaining in Algeria with her order until 1843. At the outset, de Vialar was welcomed by the authorities of the Catholic Church as, being a woman, her service was valuable for its proselytizing potential. She would have easier access than her male counterparts to the homes, and thus to the women, of the local population where she would be able to spread French values, both religious and secular. The prevailing beliefs that (a) local women were the "guardians" of traditional social values and perpetrated "archaic" customs together and (b) women generally were more easily influenced than men meant that an ability to enter the home was a prized asset. (The medical profession was similarly esteemed for the ability to spread the civilizing mission.) In the course of her sojourn in Algeria, de Vialar and her coworkers gained widespread popularity among the Muslims for their charitable work. Instead of seeing this as an important initial step in the implementation of the civilizing mission that the Church adhered to, the Bishop of Algiers, Mgr. Dupuch, saw her independence and growing popularity as a threat.[36] Curtis uses the Vialar/Dupuch clash to foreground the ambiguities of the Church's involvement in the colonial enterprise, but it is also worth noting that for as long as Vialar remained in Algeria the colonial setting served her well, allowing her to set up and run her own establishment in a way she would have had more difficulty to achieve in France.[37] Furthermore, her experience there served as the dress rehearsal for her role in spreading the order throughout the Middle East.[38] Vialar, then, is an early example of the way in which the colonial space could be beneficial to women.

Within a few years of Vialar's departure in 1843 the colony became a privileged site for travellers and artists in search of inspiration and light. Théophile Gautier, Eugène Fromentin, and Eugène Delacroix, are among the better known, but women such as Pauline de Noirfontaine, Barbara Leigh Smith Bodichon, Louise Vallory, and Matilda Betham-Edwards also left records in writing or on canvas of their activities in Algeria.[39] In a letter written in 1849, Noirfontaine, an aspiring poet and celebrated hostess whose Parisian salon was "noted for its soirées," encapsulated the effect Algeria had on travellers and visitors:

> . . . there are two distinct parts to a traveller's account: the reality and the dream. It is usually the dream that predominates: the truth is the exception. Some dream with their minds; others with their souls; the former make a science of style; the latter of imagination and sentiment. Somewhere in between are those who simply tell it as it is . . . "[40]

Noirfontaine classed herself in the latter category and her account, written in epistolary form and dedicated to Count Adolphe d'Houdelot, is a detailed description of her impressions and observations. Travel writing has always been, and probably always will be, inherently romantic in that the writer, in travelling, is seeking new sensations and experiences.[41] Noirfontaine was no different, but unlike so many other travellers, one thing she did not romanticize was the resentment and recalcitrant resistant of the Arabs to French occupation:

> Neither our rich intelligence, nor our petulant spirit, nor the elegance of our manners, nothing has been able to rid these opinionated men of their savage

harshness or their cold courage . . . It's in vain that we pretend that they are seeing the light . . . No matter how much the Arab people rub shoulders with our civilisation, eternal Lazarus that they represent, they will never sign a social pact with us.[42]

Unlike Noirfontaine, Barbara Bodichon (1827–1891) was a foreigner and a feminist. She is of particular interest as a comparison and feminist precursor to Hubertine Auclert (1848–1914), the French activist who came to the colony at the end of the century and to Isabelle Eberhardt (1877–1904), another foreign observer of Algeria, discussed in the next chapter. Barbara Bodichon was the daughter of Anne Longden and Benjamin Leigh Smith, a Unitarian radical Member of Parliament for Norwich and fervent supporter of the French revolution. The couple never married. Bodichon is best known for her feminist activities, in particular her work with Emily Davis in founding Girton College at the University of Cambridge, her role in establishing *The Englishwoman's Journal,* her founding of the *Women's Suffrage Committee,* and her outspoken views against marriage.[43] In spite of the latter, however, she married Eugène Bodichon, a French physician and former army officer with a practice in Algeria. After her marriage in 1857 she divided her time between Europe and Algeria, where she painted. She soon acquired a reputation as a landscape artist, exhibiting at the Royal Academy in London and the National Academy of Design in New York.[44] The only full-length publication on Algeria she put her name to was entitled *Algeria; considered as a winter residence for the English* (1858). As its name suggests, it was a guidebook.[45] Although Bodichon wrote the passages pertaining to the artistic possibilities offered by Algeria and the chapter on "life in Algeria" describing her surroundings and excursions into the hinterland, her real contribution was to translate extracts from the works of her husband, Eugène and introduce them, together with "other parts . . . written in English by him."[46] Why did Bodichon put her name to his work (rather than using joint names) and what was the relevance of doing so? To be sure, she was a better-known figure in Britain than he was and as such the book would have a ready-made public, thus ensuring steady initial sales. However, her husband was a respected physician in Algeria at the time, whose ideas were well known. Could it be that it was not quite right for a person of his standing to author such a lightweight genre as a guidebook when he had written on much weightier subjects? The book was never translated into French, which might add some credence to this speculation. More concretely though, it suggests the beginning of the need, that was then just emerging, of attracting foreign tourists to what was considered to be a part of France. Barbara Bodichon was therefore using her activist prestige to further the French colonial cause in British circles.

If Bodichon was an activist for women's causes in Britain, she was uninterested in those of the Algerians.[47] They were, for her, indistinguishable but picturesque figures in an alien setting.[48] Eugène Bodichon's writing on the various groups making up the local population was shot through with the pseudo-scientific ideas on race that were starting to be the vogue at the time, and Barbara Bodichon's support of his work suggests that she was in line with his opinions.[49] In one of the passages she wrote herself, she records a conversation between her husband and her friend, Lady A., who remarks on the dreariness of the life of a "Moorish lady of distinction," she had recently visited. Bodichon's husband replies: " . . . like all people in a barbarous state, they are simple, and all very much alike . . . The wife of a French workman is a thousand times more civilized than the richest Moorish lady."[50] It would have been a difficult task to agitate on their behalf, and one she was ill-equipped culturally to undertake as the following passage, describing a visit to her friend's, suggests:

> We found at Lady A.'s, Madame Luce, the originator and energetic teacher and conductor of the Moorish school for girls, the first Christian woman who has made a break into the prison life of the Eastern women. All honour to her name and success to her endeavour, the difficulty of which no one who has not examined her schools, can be aware.[51]

Bodichon's interest in the Arabs and Berbers, who made up most of the indigenous population of Algeria, was purely artistic. Algeria was a source of inspiration for her painting. That she reiterated her husband's ideas on the inhabitants of Algeria reflected less on her relationship with him than on the ideological trends and beliefs of the time. Ideas on the races of man, which had emerged during the Enlightenment, were crystallizing into an ideology of difference. Utopian socialists had promoted the idea that one of the measures of a civilization's "worth" was its treatment of women. Although Arabs were deemed to be sadly wanting in this regard and their civilization was considered to be in decline, such settlers as there were had not yet developed the desire to use Arab women as a "stick" with which to beat Arab men.[52] In the 1840s, when Bodichon was in Algeria, settler society was relatively small and many of its members were not yet French. Notwithstanding its administrative inclusion into France as three departments, Algeria was still very much an outpost whose main noneconomic attraction was its "local colour."

Bodichon's attitude toward Algerian women is in contrast to that of the French feminist, Hubertine Auclert (1848–1914). Auclert accompanied Antonin Lévrier to Algeria in 1888 when ill health prompted him to take up a position of magistrate in the colony. She returned to France four years later as a widow. Auclert had no first-hand knowledge of colonialism when she arrived and unlike Bodichon's husband, who had come to Algeria as an officer and decided to settle as a civilian physician, Lévrier's choice of Algeria was dictated by its proximity and its felicitous climate. Auclert did not, therefore, have the "advantage" of a settler husband to "inform" her about the colonial situation; she had to find out for herself. In spite of the fact both women had been active in feminist circles in their homelands before coming to Algeria, only Auclert sought out Algerian women with a view to examining their lives and the conditions under which they lived. Although she never returned to Algeria, she did write up her experiences and they appeared in 1900 as *Les*

Femmes arabes en Algérie. The title of the work and Auclert's reputation as an outspoken feminist in France creates the impression that this is a feminist tract highlighting the ills of Algerian women.[53] But the fact she treats Algerian women in a monolithic manner rather than analyzing their problems in the light of their ethnic diversity, suggests that it is more than an exposé of Algerian women's inferior status, with calls for changes and improvements in their lives. The real focus of her opprobrium is colonial society with European men coming in for as much criticism, if not more, than the Arab man. In a section entitled "Quel est le barbare?" [Who is the barbarian?] Auclert declares, "Far from the motherland, men living among men, deprived of the female element, return to the savage state; only this can explain the cruelty of the [French] civil servants toward the natives."[54] On occasion she also uses the text as a forum for presenting her ideas on women's suffrage: "If French women voted and passed laws, their African sisters would long since have been delivered from outrageous polygamy and the intolerable promiscuity of [living with] their co-wives."[55] For all her outrage, Auclert was not without her cultural prejudices, which led her occasionally to echo the arguments prevalent among the colonialists regarding some Arab practices. "Polygamy," she wrote, "not only hastens physical decrepitude, it leads to intellectual degeneration. By concentrating all cerebral activity on the bestial instinct, the Arabs annihilate their intelligence and atrophy their brains."[56] The question of polygamy was the subject of debate among anthropologists and scholars in the nineteenth century, when women's position in society was considered an indicator of its moral progress. Monogamy was seen to have evolved from a prior promiscuous state and the monogamous family was deemed by many scholars to be the culmination of the social evolutionary process.[57] With regard to her evaluation of Algerian women, about which I have written elsewhere, Auclert shared the settler view that they were beasts of burden.[58] But, like many officials and pro-colonialists from France, she believed that in women lay one of the keys successfully to convince the Arabs of the benefits of French rule:

> For us, French, our interests in Algeria must take precedence over all else. But, *we have a real interest, a political interest, in educating Muslim women* for, through them, we will be able to influence and create the well-being of Muslim men.[59]

In spite of her critical stance of colonial society and her desire to see the Algerians treated with respect, she did not envisage relinquishing the colony. "What is most important now," she wrote, "is to criss-cross *our* North Africa with roads and railways, so that both the settler and indigenous population can benefit from their produce."[60] She believed that if the Arabs were provided with the rights they deserved they would be valuable auxiliaries and serve France well.[61] To buttress her argument she pointed to the restraint the Arabs had shown during the anti-Semitic riots that took place at the end of the century.[62] As these few examples suggest, there was considerable ambiguity in Auclert's attitudes to both the colonial enterprise and to the Algerians themselves. Had she stayed in Algeria longer she would, perhaps, have clarified some of her ideas in presenting her case. It is to be noted that *Les Femmes arabes* was published in 1900, eight years after she left Algeria, at a time when there was a great deal of agitation as to the future political shape of the colony.[63] The lapse in time must also have blurred her initial impressions. Furthermore, her Algerian hiatus from her feminist activities in France caused her to lose her former stature once she returned.[64] *Les Femmes arabes,* therefore, was as much an attempt to reassert herself in the metropolitan political scene as it was an attack on the activities in the colony.

In 1900, the same year as *Les Femmes arabes* appeared, the novelist, Mme. Jean Pommerol's *Une femmes chez les Sahariennes: entre Laghouat et In-salah* was published simultaneously in French and English. As its name suggests it was a travelogue, a *"carnet de route"* compiled "betwixt heaven and sand, beneath the magic of the great sun" dedicated to Captain Charles Richard, who had written numerous books on Arab society in Algeria in the nineteenth century, and was considered an authority.[65] The illustration (fig. 1.1) on the title page of the French edition is of a nubile, bare-breasted Arab woman lounging on cushions on a carpet against a background sketch, by the author, of palm trees. (This illustration is absent from the English edition.) The imposition of the photograph on the sketch gives the image an unreal dimension, thus suggesting both the sexual and magical attractions of the orient. The English edition was advertised as a new and exciting book tracing Pommerol's "experiences in a series of very vivid word-pictures . . . [with] photographs taken under great difficulties for the women of the Sahara look upon the camera as an uncanny sentient being with the power of the evil eye."[66] These various introductions to *Une femme chez les Sahariennes,* encapsulate the contradictions inherent in her writing. Pommerol, who was a well-published author, choose to present herself as Mrs. Jean Pommerol, rather than using her own Christian name with her husband's surname or a pen name.[67] By doing so, she benefits from a male name (only Jean Pommerol appears on the outside cover), often a necessary way of gaining literary acceptance, while acknowledging her place as a wife in the existing gender hierarchy. The dedication to Charles Richard suggests the authenticity of her observations, whereas the title page illustration in the French edition and the English-language advertisement draw attention to the attractions of the book as a study of a very different and more primitive society.[68]

In the opening sentence of the book she acknowledges the advantages of being a French woman in Algeria, as it allows her to get to know the women of the Sahara as a man could not and "to penetrate in their imperfect minds, breathing the same air . . . camping on the same sands [and being] honoured by their intense and over demonstrative friendship."[69] During her peregrinations in the Sahara, Pommerol visited a number of different tribes, describing in detail her experiences with the women of each as well as their physical, moral, and social attributes. She was granted permission to enter the female quarters by the male members of the families because they believed doing so would

UNE FEMME

chez les Sahariennes

ENTRE

LAGHOUAT ET IN-SALAH

90 Illustrations d'après les Dessins et Photographies de l'Auteur

PARIS

ERNEST FLAMMARION, ÉDITEUR

RUE RACINE, 26, PRÈS L'ODÉON

Figure 1.1 Frontispiece to the first French edition of *Une Femme chez les Sahariennes*
Reproduced with permission from the Bibliothèque Nationale de France

please the military authorities and would help rectify French misconceptions about indigenous women.[70] The one exception she encountered was among the Mozabites, who adamantly resisted her various attempts to gain access to their women. She even went as far as trying to gate-crash a wedding only to be thrown out by the women "beating, shoving and scratching" her.[71] Her "nightmare" experience in the "pious, hypocritical [territory of the] M'zab" was the only misadventure in an otherwise serene, if at times arduous trip.[72] Mozabites apart, her general impression was that the desert women "were friv-olous (légère), childlike, sly—unscrupulous because, in accordance with their Islamic faith, they believed their souls were half-formed."[73] In Dakhla, one of the villages she visited, Pommerol conversed at length with the Agha, Dejel-loul-ben-el-Hadj-Lakhdar, about the differences in customs between Euro-pean and Arab women. He was astounded at her ideas [about Arab women], she said, and informed her that the Arab women of the Sahara were;

> relatively very happy . . . were not confined . . . were never overburdened with difficult work . . . nor ever badly treated . . . nor ever beaten except when caught in *flagrante delicto* with another man. [Furthermore] they had too much influence over their husbands and their husbands had too little influence over them.

Pommerol concluded the passage with: "Hem! Hem! I cough politely. The good Agha seems to be such a gallant man!"[74] Pommerol's response, naturally enough, was conditioned by existing ideas on the morality of Arab women and the belief that women in indigenous societies were not as enlightened as women from European societies. Making very few direct comparisons, Pommerol uses the condition of women and their mores to suggest the differences between the civilized and the less civilized; the modern and the archaic. Drawing attention to these disparities was a way of signaling the effort required for their eventual assimilation. The use of the condition of women as a signifier of progress—or lack of it—was part of the teleological modernity narrative, which was universal to European colonies but had precedents in the Enlightenment. Indeed, in a slightly different guise it is still prevalent today.[75]

The stylistic tone of the French edition, however, sets it apart from the English edition. Although this is probably an indication that Pommerol was being advised by media-savvy British publishers in order to ensure good sales, the French original is an example of the literary strategies women employed to ensure publication and a good reception. Chapter Four, entitled "Virtue," opens with the statement that it is the most awkward (embarrassant) section and so will surely elicit contempt (me faire honnir) from the husbands of the Saharan women whose virtue is in question. "In my opinion," Pommerol declares:

> . . . there are no honest women in these climes or among these races. There are no chaste fiancées. No virtue. For virtue, honesty, chastity are voluntary means of maintaining a state of moral and physical purity. An instinct, or an effort, that comes from the person herself. Why is it that the Southern Arab wife,

fiancée, young girl, does not feel or desire this? You will remember, I compared them above [p. 4] to gazelles and pussies (*chattes*). Can you imagine a virtuous pussy? A modest pussy, other than as a result of capriciousness or disdain?[76]

I need hardly dwell on the erotic innuendoes of this brief extract, which are totally absent in the English edition, where *chatte* is translated as cat.[77] French Orientalism had an overtly sexual dimension, which in its British counterpart was not as blatant due to the bowdlerization that was a feature of publishing in Victorian Britain. To be sure, this indicates that Pommerol was in tune with the French taste for Oriental exoticism, but it also illustrates the ways in which women could subtly transgress gender borders by adopting the male gaze and using it to eroticize their descriptions of Arab women.

By the end of the nineteenth century, therefore, women were not only active in settler society, but a number of women, whether they were settlers or just passing through, found inspiration in the colony. In the process of promoting their own political, social, or cultural agendas, they laid the foundation of a nostalgic space, linked to the exoticism of its people and the ruggedness of its landscape. Algeria proved to be the perfect haven to discover and experience firsthand, the pull of the Orient and the fascination it exercised on artists and writers, women as much as men, that so permeated the arts in the nineteenth century.[78]

THE GROWTH OF A EUROPEAN FEMALE PRESENCE IN KENYA

Unlike Algeria, the early decades of settlement in Kenya did not occur in the shadow of a military administration, whose purported and actual intentions were not economic. From its inception as part of British East Africa the economic motives for settlement were made clear. Although missionaries preceded settlement, when settlement began in earnest wives and companions were part of the first wave. Indeed the first settler baby was born in 1897.[79] It was an appropriately symbolic event, being the year of Queen Victoria's Diamond Jubilee. Unlike Algeria, the early settlers who came to East Africa were mainly from the British upper classes or were aristocratic or wealthy foreigners. This was due to a number of reasons. To begin with there was a certain amount of publicity in the shape of handbooks that presented the charms of Kenya and emphasized the profits to be made from coffee and sisal plantations, cattle and sheep farming, and retail and manufacturing.[80] Additionally, aristocrats like Lord Delamere, who had wandered around Africa in the late nineteenth century and decided to settle in Kenya, actively promoted expatriation to the colony. He believed that the colony's development would mean the "opening of a new world" and "influence a whole continent."[81] Writing to the manager of his estate in Britain in the opening years of the century, Delamere stated:

Help me advertise this country in any way you can . . . . If any Cheshire or Lancashire man brings me a letter from you I will see he gets a good 640

acres . . . Settlers . . . say it compares with the best of New Zealand . . . A South
African who has had much experience was here the other day and said he
wouldn't take 20 acres in South Africa for one here.[82]

The draw of such publicity, which was no doubt instrumental in attracting
members of the upper classes to the colony, was compounded by economic
and financial factors. An agricultural depression in the United Kingdom dealt
a serious blow to many landed families, whose scions attached more importance to family pedigree and the public school ethos than to the technical
and meritocratic skills necessary to combat the economic downturn in agriculture.[83] Kenya was to provide them with the land and manpower to recreate the patterns of landholding and labor with which they were accustomed.
Secondly, setting up in Kenya required a considerable investment, as will be
seen in the ensuing chapter. This requirement effectively excluded working
class or lower middle class individuals, unless they accompanied, or came to
work for, moneyed settlers in some service capacity. What it meant for the
women, who accompanied their moneyed spouses, was that they were freed
to take a more active role in the economic functioning of the colony. As Eleanor Cole, wife of the Honorable Galbraith Cole, explained: "I was able to get
an English nanny so was free to help Galbraith on the farm".[84] Furthermore,
the importance of women as vectors of the social tone of a society meant that
class codes and values were incorporated into the "civilizing system." Marion
Dobbs, who married the district officer C. M. Dobbs, in Dublin, in 1906,
and followed him out to Kenya three years later stated that on her arrival in
Mombasa, the port of arrival for all incoming settlers, she discovered that:

> All higher officials or their wives called on us, and from 5–6 p.m. each day was
> usually taken up returning these calls. In Mombasa it was the custom to leave
> a wooden box, resembling an alms box, on the verandah, so that people could
> drop their cards in it when calling.[85]

Although up-country such niceties were often eschewed, and even ridiculed,
as Dobbs discovered when returning a call in Kisumu where she "found
a certain chamber utensil placed just inside the verandah, presumably as a
receptacle for visiting cards,"[86] upper class behavioral patterns were maintained by women and shaped much of settler life in the colony. They were,
of course, also equated with being "civilized." In her memoirs Dobbs insists
on detailing the family ancestry, opining that a well endowed genealogy was
a hallmark of the British colonist:

> When reading a biography some people are inclined to omit the details relating
> to ancestry and early life, under the impression that these must necessarily be
> dull. If this is ever true, surely it cannot be the case in the lives of those who
> went out to the distant parts of the British Empire half a century or so ago.
> Something of their make-up, physical and mental, must have been derived
> from their forebears who fought difficulties, and perhaps endured hardship, in
> the distant past.[87]

An early social exception to this rule was a group of about 50 Afrikaner families, who trekked up from South Africa, settling initially in German East Africa but moving on to Kenya when the Germans created difficulties due to their poverty and independence of spirit.[88] Although in Kenya they did not encounter the pressure to leave that they had in German East Africa, they kept to themselves, seldom mixing with the other settlers and, with few exceptions, failing to move up the social scale. The novelist Florence Riddell had one of her characters declare that they were "Awful people! . . . So dirty!"[89] Even in the twilight of the colonial period, the status of the Afrikaners had not changed much. Most remained poor and were disparagingly called "munts" or "kaffirs" [an interesting inversion as both were derogatory terms used by white South Africans for black Africans] by the more-racially inclined non-Afrikaner settlers.[90] Christine Nicholls explained that when she was a child living in Eldoret, where there was a community of Afrikaners, she was aware of their presence, but when she moved away "it was as if they had never existed."[91] The racial slurs and the segregation that the eradication from memory implies was not just one of class, however. The Boer War (1899–1902) anchored conflict in settler memory, often playing itself out in an antagonistic relationship between British and Afrikaner, in those European colonies in Africa where both groups resided, until long after World War II. The social structure that the settlers eventually created, therefore, was a complex combination of class, race, memory and nostalgia.

The first real wave of settlers occurred in 1903, in the wake of the Land Ordinance Act. According to the records of the European Pioneers' Society, in the period leading up to World War I, there were 82 women pioneers, 42 of whom listed a profession.[92] Although these figures are incomplete, given that the European population in 1905 was over 1,000, it is an indication that women assumed a variety of roles even in the earliest days of settlement. A sense of adventure and a sense of duty were the two main motives that led women to Kenya. Margaret Elkington, who arrived with her parents in 1905, sums it up as follows:

> Most of the others [settlers] had come to B. E. A. out of a sense of adventure. Mrs. Jim [her mother] had not. She had merely been an obedient Victorian wife. But this isn't to say that she hadn't a thought in her head. She had most definitely, and she also had a strong character and a great deal of common sense.[93]

Although the majority of women were, like Mrs. Jim Elkington, accompanying their husbands, even they, obedient housewives that they were, soon had to take the sort of initiatives that were not required of them in their homeland social milieu. Elkington's mother was taken aback on her arrival at her new home:

> When Mrs. Jim first entered the house she must have felt horrified. It was a three roomed, unlined tin hut with an earth floor, which gave us the shudders as immediatelly [sic] we entered we were covered with fleas.[94]

Being the "dutiful woman" she was, however, she set about "making the most" of the situation: "Mrs. Jim had never cooked a thing in her life, but now with tremendous optimism she set herself the task of learning."[95] As she put European order into her African existence "to her own surprise she found that this strange country was becoming less strange and more beautiful and desirable as the days went by."[96] The point I want to make is not that she was exceptional in any way; successful pioneer women across time and space have always responded to unfamiliar situations and places in enterprising ways.[97] What is important to retain is that by creating a home away from home women, like Mrs. Jim, were endorsing the colonial discourse of bringing modernity to the primitive society at the same time as they were escaping aspects of modernity they found disagreeable in their homeland. Modernity in the colony was synonymous with "civilization," and the faster it was achieved the more laudable were those who imposed it. Marion Dobbs, who joined her husband in 1909, discovered that "[w]hen [her husband] landed in Mombasa in November 1906 conditions were still very primitive up-country." On her arrival, three years later "wonderful progress had been made, for civilization had to a certain extent replaced ignorance and savagery."[98] If, as Kennedy has suggested, the upper classes gravitated to the colonies due to their inability to adapt their public school ethos to the technological and meritocratic needs of modern estate management, the manifestation of modernity some colonial women, in particular settler wives, were happy to escape was the questioning and fracturing of traditional gender relations that the feminist movements of the late nineteenth century had put into motion. As put by another "very determined woman," Eleanor [Nellie] Cole, daughter of the 2nd Earl of Balfour and wife of the Hon. Galbraith Cole, "When women become a dominating influence in a nation, that nation begins to go downhill morally. It was the undoing of Rome, and it is taking place in America and England today . . ."[99] If by 1912, British East Africa, the "portion of the 'Dark Continent' which only twenty to thirty years ago was considered the typical habitat of savage tribes . . .," was in the process of being "civilized" [modernized], the process entailed a concomitant process of nostalgic recreation, both of estate management and gender structures.[100] Settler wives were bound up in this paradoxical process.

One of the principal attractions of the colony, which convinced many a settler to put down roots, was the presence of big game. Well-to-do men, such as Delamere or the Americans Northrup MacMillan (also spelt McMillan) and Billy Sewell, came to Kenya to hunt big game and stayed.[101] It may have been the men who were initially attracted to Kenya by the hunt, but once women were in the colony big game exercised its fascination on them too. Hilda MacNaghten, who joined her husband in 1906, was quick to see big game's romantic dimension. "Is this unique, being charged by a rhinoceros on your honeymoon, in real wild country?" she wondered.[102] Cara Buxton, who left her native Norfolk to travel in Africa in 1910, walking from the North African coast to Kenya and settling there in 1913 to farm coffee and maize, wrote to her nephew extolling the pleasures of pioneer life and declaring that "when one shoots it is because one is hungry," although there were apparently exceptions to mere necessity as she goes on to say that she "had one thrilling leopard hunt but did not get the leopard."[103] Margit Bursall, whose husband initially went to work on Karen Blixen's farm, but went on to buy his own land, declared that during the time they were establishing their concern "we lived on game, which we shot on Sundays."[104] Hunting was not just about killing to eat, however. Women from well-to-do European families came primed for its pleasures. The photographer, Gretchen Cron, who went to Africa to shoot game and pictures because "a lot of romance is still there," describes her preparation for the trip:

> Herman taught me to shoot and instructed me in the sporting etiquette one must conform to on such preserves, which, with their ideals of chivalry and good sportsmanship, are like fascinating survivals of the Middle Ages.[105]

Big game was an essential feature of the exoticism of Kenya, but so too was the temporal nostalgia inherent in hunting it.[106]

The hunt, as either a blood or a viewer sport, was not the only pleasure women derived from animals, however. Wild animals could also be pets and few families did not have one or two specimens. The Northrup MacMillans had a whole menagerie, including a pet lion. Indeed, lions are the animals most often mentioned in women's memoirs. Margaret Elkington's lion, Paddy, "was perfectly tame" and was allowed to roam around the house until he got too big. He remained with the family for 17 years.[107] For Helen Cleland Scott, like Joy Adamson many years later, life was all about lions. She bred them from an initial pair called Adam and Eve, eventually providing zoos with their offspring.[108] Just how significant animals were to the lives of some of these women is illustrated by K. A. Hill-Williams, known to her friends as Tuppence, who wrote in her memoirs: "Most of my early memories are connected with wild animals."[109]

It is worth reflecting on the two activities of women in regard to animals. On the one hand, by hunting, women were transgressing gender boundaries by participating in an activity that was traditionally considered to be male. On the other hand, caring for animals was an extension of the nurturing-caring activity traditionally considered to be female. The taming of, and caring for, wild animals by women on their farms was of course symbolic; a microcosm of the taming of the "savagery" of Africa. Whether by hunting or through caring, women's involvement with wild animals in Kenya created a space that combined the restorative nostalgia of the aristocratic hunt in Britain with the aspect of the modern woman, who was on par with men in being able to shoot and handle wild animals. The importance of this had less to do with the appearance of gender equality within the settler community than with their place in relation to the Africans. African women, who were "primitive," did not hunt, European women, who were "civilized" (hence modern), did.

If the hunt was an important signifier in colonial society so too was the club.[110] Of all the colonial institutions the club was undoubtedly one of the most indispensable. Clubs were sites of pleasure, politicking and business and few settlers did not belong to at least one. One of the earliest was the Mombasa club, established at the end of the nineteenth century. Families arriving in Kenya inevitably stopped off there on their way up-country. A bell at 7 p.m. was the sign for the premises to be cleared of women, a reminder to new arrivals that traditional gender structures were in place in the colony. As settlement progressed local clubs sprang up catering to the localized settler populations. Among the most important were the East African Turf Club and the Muthaiga Club in Nairobi.[111] Horses were an essential part of settler life, whether as work animals or as accessories to the social life of the settlers. The Turf Club was the breeding and training ground for both race horses and polo ponies, both sports that were practiced and viewed regularly. Women, however, were more than spectators as they were involved in both the breeding and training of horses.

The compartmentalization of space by gender and race that was a feature of some of the clubs prompted women to create their own group activities. Victorian patterns of philanthropy and welfare provision in Britain were emulated in the colony by women settlers and administrators' wives. Women opened small schools on their farms and administered elementary medical care to their laborers and their staff. Activities of this sort were seen as a step in "modernizing" the colony, while enforcing gender perceptions of the nurturing/caring dimension of women's abilities. In 1917 colonial women activists formed the East African Women's League.[112] The dual aims of the League were to secure votes for white women in local council elections and "to study and take action on, where necessary, all matters affecting the welfare and happiness of women and children of all races in East Africa."[113] Like many of its male counterparts, whose gender and racial segregations were maintained until the 1950s, the League was gender- and race-exclusive.

An interest in race relations was symptomatic of developments in both the French and British empires at the turn of the century. The upheaval caused to the local populations by the settlers' quests for land and labor, produced tension and conflict. A desire to dissipate such strains was strong grounds for improving relations. Women's involvement in this process was motivated as much by the desire to assert themselves by some sort of activism as it was to contribute to the overall colonial aim. An interest in race relations was an obvious avenue for women's involvement, particularly as their experiences with Africans often extended beyond the domestic sphere of the home to the management of labor on the farms. The benevolence of women's activities with regard to the local population factors in to the creation of a nostalgic space. It shades the ugliness of domination with a tone of goodwill, which, however genuine its intentions, is never the complete picture but only the picture that nostalgia evokes.

Obviously, race relations in the colony were shaped by the need for labor. As of 1912 increased settlement meant that demand increasingly outstripped supply.[114] Furthermore, Africans were not inclined to work for the settlers. The latter sought to redress the situation by introducing forms of coercion that were legally binding. In 1906 the Master and Servant Ordinance was passed imposing criminal penalties on Africans who broke their contracts.[115] The Native Registration Ordinance followed in 1915, requiring all African males over 16 to carry a *kipandi*, an identification-cum-reference book.[116] As Marion Dobbs remarked in her memoirs "it facilitated the exercise of more effective control over them," but "caused much discontent among the natives, who were fined if found anywhere without their *kipandis.*" Settlers were also somewhat peeved as "it entailed a lot of extra book-work."[117] Labor was obtained by offering Africans wages, food, and the rudimentary medical services provided by settler women. A squatter system was also established, which allowed Africans who were forbidden from owning land in the white farming areas, to "squat" on the land of their employers. In exchange for 180 days of work each year on the farms, they could grow their own crops and keep animals.[118] It was, of course, a throwback to the tenant/farmer system of the large estates.

Disciplining Africans for infractions of various sorts was a dimension of race relations that was deemed to be part of the civilizing process. Although District Officers dealt with meeting out justice in cases between Africans that were brought before the local colonial courts, on the farms, more often than not, settlers resolved matters themselves. Dobbs, whose husband was a Colonial Administrator, tells us that "the usual punishment for male offenders was imprisonment or flogging, or both. The flogging was carried out by a *kiboko*, a whip made of hippo hide."[119] In March 1907, Ewart Stewart Grogan administered a public flogging to three of "his Kikuyu rickshaw boys" because he felt they had insulted his sister and her friend.[120] In addition to the cruelty and disproportion of the punishment, what is noteworthy is the reason for it. By beating Africans for disrespect of white women, Grogan publicly reinforced the barrier between black men and white women as well as the traditional gender structure by implying that women could not look after themselves and needed men to do it for them. Shortly after this incident, restrictions were imposed on flogging. It is useful, nonetheless, to bear in mind that birching was an accepted punishment in Britain, particularly for young males. An edifying parallel between metropole and colony can be drawn from an article that appeared in the Yorkshire paper, *Eastern Morning News,* in 1911. Two boys were convicted for stealing equipment from a stable. In passing sentence "[t]he stipendiary said that it was a boys' offence, and he should award a boys' punishment—six strokes with the birch."[121] The colonials emulated the technique, substituting a *kiboko* for the birch to punish their "children." Women, who oversaw both the domestic service and the labor on the farms, were not averse to administering punishments, although these usually took the form of threats of docking of salary. When

Nellie Grant, scion of the Duke of Westminster and mother of the author Elspeth Huxley discovered that her laborers' wage money had disappeared, she informed her laborers that she

> would set alight every hut on the farm (strictly illegal of course). Before the hour was up a somewhat sheepish gentleman arrived with the bag of rupees, saying he had found it under the sitting turkey, "Oh the naughty bird," I said, but gave him no reward.[122]

Corporal punishment, if and when inflicted by women, was usually in the form of slaps although there were some exceptions. Pioneer Mary [Walsh], better known as *bibi kiboko,* was inseparable from her rhino-hide whip and had no compunction about using it.

Women in Kenya immersed themselves in colonial existence from the very beginning of settlement. Naturally enough, they reacted to the realities of pioneer life in very different ways. Some, like Mrs. Jim, made the best of a difficult situation and eventually managed to create a satisfactory life for themselves. Others were swept away by the romance of Kenya existence. Marion Dobbs declared that to her "there was romance and glamour in this life far above that to be found on sophisticated European dance floors."[123] Hilda MacNaghten found adventure in her contact with African women:

> The local village women all collected to see the white child . . . These women were most friendly and loved seeing a "white" child, and what appealed to them very much were his little boots! Here was adventure, and I loved every minute of it.[124]

Although most of the women's memoirs, collected for the Oxford Colonial Records Project, overlook the problematic or unhappy aspects of their lives in Kenya, some like, Madeleine La Vie Platts, whose husband's position often took him on safari, were more straightforward:

> Alone, I would try and cheer myself with a little culture, my music and books, the gospels in Greek, some French translating, study of Swahili, a dip into some favourite Thackeray, Bröntes, Jane Austen, Shakespeare, as well as frequent light novels. But the nights were both melancholy and terrifying.[125]

Alyse Simpson, whose Kenya memoir was published in 1937 shortly after she and her husband left for good, found the settler experience overwhelming:

> It made me smile when I looked back, when I remembered the things I had imagined about Kenya before we left our house [in Britain] . . . The grim reality was . . .anything but romantic . . . The Kenya of my dreams, the country of my fertile imagination crashed to pieces . . . . We weren't making any money . . . . The park like beauty of Kenya existed only in the highlands . . . life was far from idyllic.[126]

There is no doubt that life was not easy for many women, but whenever their memoirs were written—long after they had left or while they were still there—and whatever their experiences, the image most of them wanted to project was positive.[127] Whether it was the fabric of memory or the stiff-upper-lip of the stalwart woman pioneer, these women created a nostalgic space that was integral to the colonial image of Kenya. As Simpson so rightly noted:

> There was, I thought, a great deal of make-belief in people's lives, and it took more courage than was generally realised to face up and admit the truth. When I studied those who called Kenya beautiful, the opinion seemed mostly to come from the wealthy, the sport-loving and those who had no choice.[128]

CONCLUSION

During the "Belles Epoques" of colonial Algeria and Kenya, women lived and imagined their lives in ways that reflected both the values and customs of their homelands and the opportunities and experiences of their "adopted" land. The hybrid result was a nostalgic space that was unique to the respective colony. In Algeria it was the mingling of French cultural values, republican ideas of modernity, and the ambiguities inherent in French Orientalism as manifested by the eroticism of the exotic and anxieties about Islam. In Kenya it was the British traditions of the landed gentry with their class convictions and their love of the hunt. Wild animals were as essential to the creation of Kenya's nostalgic space, as sexuality was to that of Algeria. Colonial women's writing was grounded in these frameworks.

Before moving on to the interwar period when women's writing in each colony acquired new dimensions, I want to turn my attention to two women, Isabelle Eberhardt and Karen Blixen. If, as Michel de Certeau has argued, writing is the essential process through which individuals produce themselves as subjects, the "African" personas that Eberhardt and Blixen created also made them objects of emulation and desire.[129] Their writing and colonial experiences personify the nostalgic creation of each colony in so far as the paradoxes of their lives made them icons of sorts, whose attraction as unconventional women extended beyond the colonial period to the present.

CHAPTER 2

NOSTALGIA PERSONIFIED: ISABELLE EBERHARDT AND KAREN BLIXEN

"Les lieux où l'on a aimé et où l'on a souffert, où l'on a pensé et rêvé, surtout, les pays quittés sans espoir de jamais les revoir, nous apparaissent plus beaux par le souvenir qu'ils le furent en réalité.

Isabelle Eberhardt (1901)

. . . when one comes to realize the whole nature of life, which is: that nothing lasts and in that very fact lies some of its glory . . .

Karen Blixen (1931)

Iconic personalities, who represent elements of a given time or event, become poles around which nostalgia can form. European colonies had their share of such figures but few women transcended the notoriety of colonialism to have a true post-independence appeal. Two literary personalities, Isabelle Eberhardt in Algeria and Karen Blixen in Kenya, managed to do so as much by the manner in which they conducted themselves in their respective colonies as by the way their admirers and champions reimagined their colonial lives for them. In the introduction to the recent volume, *Constructing Charisma*, Edward Berenson and Eva Giloi point out that "charisma is both a social and an individual trait" for charismatic personalities are as dependent on their followers in defining their charisma as they are in projecting the personal traits that define them as such.[1] Although neither Blixen nor Eberhardt qualify as charismatic, as defined by Berenson and Giloi, their status as icons of nostalgia was dependent, in much the same way, on the manner their lives were imaged and reconstructed by their "followers."[2] The endorsement of their celebrity occurred, not in the colonial space but outside of it, when the colonial moment of both these women had passed. The renown of both was posthumous: Eberhardt's in a literal sense after her death; Blixen's in a metaphoric sense, at the demise of her emotional, entrepreneurial and colonial life, for her departure from Kenya coincided with the death of her lover, Dennis Finch Hatton, and the collapse of her farming venture. Recapturing what their lives were thought to have been, rather than what they actually were, was the essential element in constructing the aura of nostalgia that came to surround both these women in the aftermath of their passage through the colonies. It is the slippage between the life lived and the life imagined with which this chapter is concerned.

In an article from the volume cited above, Mary Louise Roberts argues that eccentricity was a critical attribute in propelling women to fame at the end of the Nineteenth Century. Using the actress, Sarah Bernhardt, and the artist, Rosa Bonheur, as her examples she demonstrates that "by failing to match normative expectations" and performing a marginality that made them seem "odd" rather than conventional, they achieved the sort of celebrity that was usually reserved for men.[3] She goes on to show that their eccentricity was linked to the *androgynous* and *therianthropic* qualities of their public image, which defied the normative expectations of the society and time in which they lived.[4] Eberhardt and Blixen also defied normative expectations. In the first instance, by leaving what was socially familiar and going to the colonies to carve out a life for themselves and, in the second, by the choice of lifestyle once there. Colonial women were ambiguous figures negotiating between the public and the private when it came to gender and race, and Eberhardt and Blixen were not exceptions. Ambiguity of this sort has led to the debate as to colonial women's complicity with or resistance to the colonial oeuvre.[5] To be sure the paradoxes of Eberhardt's and Blixen's experiences rested on the fact complicity and resistance formed an essential part of their colonial identities, but it was not just the fact they *transgressed* the norms of race and gender, but how they did so that endowed them with their emblematic status.[6] They were oddities, one Russian the other Danish, whose ideas and behavior did not always conform to the norms of French or British colonial society. Unlike Bernhardt and Bonheur, however, their oddness or eccentricity did not endear them to the society in which they lived; nor, while they resided there, did it enable them to achieve celebrity of the Bernhardt/Bonheur caliber. Nonetheless, it was a combination of their eccentricity, imagined and performed, that singled them out and eventually enveloped them with nostalgic kudos.

A significant scholarly literature exists on both Eberhardt and Blixen, but either it has focused on them as individuals, or examined their works in relation to other women in Francophone or Anglophone territories, respectively, or else deconstructed their texts by means of literary analysis.[7] Although they are not the only colonial women with a post-independence literary reputation, they are the only two whose lives have resonated so strongly posthumously providing them with the transgressive appeal intrinsic to the image of a woman icon.

SETTLER SOCIETIES IN THE MAKING

The settler population of Algeria rose from 236,000 to 621,000 during the first three decades of civilian rule. The intensification of land sequestration, detailed in the preceding chapter, and the growth of labor-intensive capitalist agriculture, especially in the newly cleared swamp area of the coastlands, contributed to the increase in their numbers. When Eberhardt arrived in Algeria at the turn of the century, therefore, settler society was being redefined along civilian lines. Blixen's arrival in Kenya just before World War I coincided with a similar process as settlers arrived to buy up land and "to establish in East Africa a new, loyal, white dominion securely founded in the principles of British tradition and civilisation."[8] During the period 1905 to 1914 settler landholdings increased from 263 to 312 representing a rise in acreage from 368,165 to 639,640. In 1919 an additional 2.5 million acres were parceled out.[9] Most of this land was in the hands of a few dozen landowners.[10] Conscious of their status, they discouraged the arrival of poor whites, wanting to avoid the emergence of a poor white class such as had been established in South Africa.[11] As a result, in these early years of settlement, in contrast to Algeria, settler society in Kenya was relatively homogenous socially. Nonetheless, like Algeria, it was in a period of self-definition. Eberhardt and Blixen came into their own, therefore, in settler colonies where colonial identities were taking root. The two colonies shared the social and political configurations of settler societies, but were different in geography and cultural heritage (both African and European). The personal choices of Eberhardt and Blixen were determined by the spatial and cultural configurations of colonial Africa; it became a mythical terrain where they reinvented themselves, finding a personal and cultural liberation that stimulated their creativity. But this reinvention was framed in terms of an imagined space and time, where a woman could be free, could run wild.

In March 1931, on the eve of her definitive departure from Africa, in a letter to her mother, Karen Blixen, who would take the pen name Isak Dinesen (1885–1962) wrote:

> She may be more gentle to others, but I hold in the belief that I am one of Africa's <u>favourite children.</u> A great world of poetry has revealed itself to me and taken me to itself here, and I have loved it . . . I have plucked the best rose of life . . .[12]

Thirty years earlier, in January 1901, in another part of Africa, Isabelle Eberhardt (1877–1904) confided to her diary:

> . . . no other place on earth has bewitched me, charmed me as much as the moving solitude of the great dry ocean . . . I love my Sahara with a love that is obscure, mysterious, profound, inexplicable but real and indestructible.[13]

These two quotations, written in the imperial heyday, exemplify the importance of space and place to the personal and professional development of the two women. Eberhardt's literary output was almost exclusively connected to Algeria, either as the site where it was produced or as its subject matter. She was drowned there in 1904. Unlike Eberhardt, Blixen lived to see the African colonies gain independence, but she never returned to Kenya after 1931 and her masterpiece, *Out of Africa*, which catapulted her to fame, was published simultaneously in English and Danish in 1937.[14] The fact they were colonial writers, whose work is impregnated with the attitudes of their era, has not detracted from their appeal. Literary talent alone cannot explain this. Blixen's artistic merit may be undisputed, but Eberhardt had and still has her detractors.[15] Besides, there were other colonial women writers who, in spite of an engaging style and content, did not manage to shake off their colonial mantle.[16] Eberhardt and Blixen, both writing before nationalist movements could shape or color their views, created personal and literary narratives that made them compelling enough to endow them with their iconic status, a status that signified approval.

Approval, in the colonial context, was synonymous with acceptance. Conditioned by an adherence to the cultural and social norms of the colony as well as to economic accomplishment, it was one of the requisites for social integration and success. For both these women, acceptance had a particular relevance, given that Eberhardt was Russian and Blixen was Danish. In Africa, they found themselves in a setting where cultural-specificity, French or British, was intensely reinforced. As "foreigners" they assessed the colony with the gaze of the outsider, but they were in turn categorized as "other" and profiled negatively or positively according to political or social exigencies. Both women were, at one time or another, the butt of colonist criticism. Acceptance, therefore, had a two-fold dimension. On the one hand there was their acceptance of colonial society and its narratives and, on the other, their acceptance by the colonists as *bona fide* members of their society. Degrees of acceptance (of or by colonial society) all too often shape our perceptions of colonial women, relegating them to the role of pawns in the imperial game, and obscuring their strategies of survival, adaptability and personal empowerment in a political, social, and cultural structure that was weighted against them. The multiple paradoxes in the lives of Eberhardt and Blixen imply that by manipulating the "ground rules" of colonial society they were transcending ordinary colonial mentalities. It was the strategies they used to negotiate the spaces of gender and race that established their identities and led to the creation of their literary persona, while also contributing to their post-independence attraction.

WHY AFRICA?

Both Eberhardt and Blixen went to Africa at a time when recruitment for settlement was being actively promoted. In January 1897, Joseph Chailley-Bert spoke at a conference of the *Union coloniale française*, stressing the need "to people [French] colonies with women of an age to serve as work mates and life companions to the settlers."[17] Although, the "demographic crisis" was not as acute in the British colonies as expatriation was more readily undertaken by the British than the French, Kenya was the focus of propaganda campaigns by both official bodies and the likes of Delamere, as mentioned above. Both women were thus caught up, consciously or inadvertently, in the drive to increase settlement.

Eberhardt arrived in Africa in 1897; Blixen in 1914. Although both women certainly had a well-developed sense of adventure, neither chose their destination for this reason and the independence such a choice provided as did, for example, Mary Kingsley or Mary Hall.[18] Nor did they go to Africa for vocational reasons, as did missionary women like Emilie de Vialar (1797–1856), Anna Martin Hinderer (1827–1870), or Mary Slessor (1848–1915). Rather they found themselves propelled toward Africa for the more conventional reasons of family problems or ties. Eberhardt arrived in Bône in eastern Algeria with her mother, having sold up their family house in Geneva. Although the exact reasons for the move are unclear, the decision was not Eberhardt's alone. Her mother, her resident tutor Alexander Trophimowsky, and her brother Augustin all had their say.[19] Eberhardt's desire to learn Arabic fluently, her attraction to Islam, instilled in her by Trophimowsky, and her belief in her Muslim birthright must certainly have made the decision seem like part of the destiny *(mektoub),* she so fervently believed in, but more prosaic reasons underlay the final choice. Family connections in Bône would provide a residence and initial contacts in an alien environment.[20]

Eberhardt did not seek her Islamic destiny at the cultural nerve center of Islam in the Middle East, but in the safety net of what was considered to be a French territory, where the culture of empowerment was not Islamic. The geo-political location, therefore, ensured that the transition from the culture of the empowered to the culture of the subordinate, which, in Algeria, Eberhardt's espousal of Islam implied, blurred her real affinity to Islam and provided her with the possibility of selectively espousing those aspects of each culture, which suited her best. Whatever her personal sentiments with regard to the colonial hierarchy, she was a European and was therefore perceived to be a member of the "ruling class." This provided her with a freedom of movement and behavior that would have been more difficult to come by, or taken much more time to acquire, had she opted to find her Islamic self in an independent Muslim territory.

Blixen's decision to go to Africa involved not only her family but also her future husband, Baron Bror Blixen-Finecke, whom she married on her first day in Kenya. In spite of mutual warm feelings, the union had the trappings of a marriage of convenience. He provided her with an aristocratic title she coveted and her family provided the financial backing for the farm they together planned to establish in British East Africa, recommended to them as the "land of the future."[21] Coffee was the means by which they would make their fortune. The choice of crop was not random. Blight had destroyed the coffee plantations in Ceylon at the turn of the century and the British government started to encourage coffee production in other parts of the Empire to counteract the sole remaining coffee-producing area of Latin America, which was a virtual United States monopoly. Research conducted in Kenya from 1905 to 1907 as to the feasibility of successful coffee production had produced positive results. By the time the Blixens were contemplating marriage, coffee was already a money-spinner in Kenya and its cultivation was a European monopoly.[22]

A limited liability company, Karen Coffee Company Ltd., was created in Denmark for the express purpose of financing the Blixen project. Most of the initial financing was put up by Karen Blixen's mother, Ingeborg, and her uncle, Aage Westenholz, but many members of the family bought shares.[23] It was a capitalist venture involving a sizeable investment, property, and Kenyan labor.[24] On her arrival in 1914 she possessed 4,500 acres to be worked by 1,200 Kenyan farm hands and 6 European managers; a further 1,500 acres would be added at a later date.[25] Blixen, however, was inclined to interpret her family's participation as part of a European cultural mission to civilize Africa.[26] From her earliest days in Kenya she considered herself as an aristocrat, surrounded by her people, or "my Africans" as she would often called them. Her concept of aristocracy was as much of mind as of social hierarchy, but the notion of "position" was important to her. Even after her marriage failed, a tragedy, which she told her brother Thomas, was worse for her than the death of her sister Ea, she declared that she would marry again if it was "to achieve a position" she "was really suited to fill."[27] The life Blixen created for herself in Africa was in line with her sense of position. Furthermore, she found in Africa, echoes of Denmark in 1700: the same "huge flock of utterly superfluous servants . . . clustering around one," the same rough conditions, the same challenge to educate, to tame nature and to build "a realm of beauty."[28] It was the perfect setting to develop her aristocratic sense of self.

For both Eberhardt and Blixen, Africa provided a relatively safe haven for adventure. Their expatriation, which certainly entailed risks unfamiliar today, was nonetheless undertaken within the confines of a certain familiarity. For Eberhardt, the juxtaposition of European and Islamic cultures in Algeria provided the means of gradual or, should it suit her, partial transition to Muslim identity. Algeria was a cultural halfway house which, due perhaps to her premature death, Eberhardt never truly vacated. For Blixen too there was familiarity in an alien land, but unlike Eberhardt it was social. She arrived with an aristocratic husband and the promise of a life that she could fashion to suit her sense of position and style. As societies-in-the-making, the two colonies provided a sense of freedom from the established cultural and social configurations of mainland Europe, without breaking away from them completely. But there was an ambiguity to these two women. They were intermediary figures, halfway between the female loner, whose sense of adventure leads her away from all that is familiar, and the socially confined woman, whose personal development takes place within the parameters of custom. Such ambivalence made them difficult to situate in comfortable analytical categories and endowed them with the ambiguous emblematic status that could (and would) be used selectively by detractors and supporters alike.

GENDER AND IDENTITY: EBERHARDT AND THE FLIGHT INTO MASCULINITY

Neither Eberhardt nor Blixen had difficulty adapting to the gendered structure of colonial society with its predominantly male framework. Albeit in totally different ways, both identified almost at once with the masculine element. Even before her arrival in Algeria, Eberhardt had started to assume the masculine identity of Nicolas Podolinsky when writing to her Tunisian friend, Ali Abdul Wahab. Once in Algeria she took the process a step further by adopting male dress. She had always been partial to wearing a variety of costumes, but in Algeria her sartorial habits became almost exclusively masculine (fig. 2.1). Dressed in "the egalitarian outfit of the Bedouins," as she put it, she was able to wander unnoticed through the Arab quarters.[29] "It was a man's world, she declared, 'which the attire of a staid young European woman would prevent her from entering.'"[30] As an aspiring writer, she sought the freedom of movement to which only a man was privy. On the one hand, therefore, male dress enabled her to explore every avenue of Arab society, a necessity she felt would enrich her writing; on the other hand, it facilitated her desire for a nomadic and reclusive life.

Her admiration of the nomads, whom she considered stalwart in body and soul, stemmed from her own deep-felt identification with the desert.[31] "The desert," she wrote, "was bewitching, unique; a place where silence and a centuries-old peace was to be found. It was a land of dreams and mirages where the sterile agitation of modern Europe could never penetrate."[32] If the desert provided the peace and solitude necessary for creativity, its mirages

Figure 2.1   Isabelle Eberhardt, c. 1898

stimulated the imagination. Access to this privileged site of creativity, which was essentially an Arab space, was achieved more readily through the use of male identity. Accordingly, she recreated herself in a number of different male identities: Mahmoud, Mahmoud-ben-Abdullah, and Mahmoud Saadi or Si Mahmoud, the pseudonym she finally adopted. With male clothes and a male identity she traveled in the company of students, *spahis* (cavalry) and *goumis* (troops from a particular tribe) both in Algeria and Tunisia. A few may have been unsuspecting of her disguise, but most knew her real identity due, according to Eberhardt, to the repeated "indiscretions" of the settlers. Robert Randau, her friend and biographer, put it down to the "innate politeness of the Arabs," who would never expose a person against their wishes.[33] Unlike the Europeans, therefore, the Arabs respected Eberhardt's sartorial unconventionality.[34] Whatever was at the root of Arab willingness to overlook her transvestism, the fact she was a European allowed for more indulgence in any matter of cultural sensitivity. Eberhardt's transgression of identity, whether or not it was problematic for the Arabs, would not have elicited the type of response it did from the Europeans. Whereas the European reaction (in so far as Eberhardt's transvestism was Arab) was prompted by sentiments of "betrayal of one's own" and accompanied by the vociferations designed to bring the errant individual back into line, any negative Arab response would have been less forthright, due to differences in underlying motive, and would have been muted due to colonial power structures.

Her husband, Slimène Ehnni, was one of the very few Algerian *spahis* with French nationality. Eberhardt described him as her "best friend, chosen brother and profound love," and he responded to her need to assert herself in a masculine world and understood the motives behind her transvestism.[35] He would introduce her as "Isabelle Eberhardt, my wife, and Mahmoud Saadi, my companion . . . "[36] As an Algerian, who had opted for French nationality, Ehnni would naturally have been more open to deviations from the cultural norm. His family, furthermore, had long been in the service of the French. His father, a descendent of an important maraboutic (holy) family had been head of indigenous recruiting for the French Army and was appointed Head of the Security Service in Constantine in 1882.[37] Like Eberhardt, therefore, Ehnni was something of a hybrid at a time when hybridity was not much of an asset. His union with Eberhardt and acceptance of her anomalies was as much contingent on colonial circumstance as it was to his ties to the woman he described as "the only person who loves and is devoted to me."[38]

Her switch, on arrival in Algeria, to an Arab male persona was of course an extension of her religious affiliation to Islam, her efforts to acquire fluency in Arabic, and her desire to familiarize herself with Islamic customs and laws. With few exceptions she did not make much attempt to identify with Arab women, whose company she considered boring, "the bleak boredom of life among unintelligent beings, in the midst of the mediocrity and indiscretion of indigenous females."[39] Her chosen companions were male, whether they were Arab *spahis* and fellow travelers, or French officers and legionnaires. According to one German soldier who knew her well and appreciated her literary command of his language, Eberhardt was especially friendly with the foreign legionnaires and, on the whole, preferred men from the ranks to officers. She was interested in their personal lives, their activities, and their motives for enlisting. In exchange she captivated them with her stories and accounts of her adventures in the Algerian *bled*.[40] This ability to captivate a male audience in the capacity of storyteller was one she shared with Blixen.

Among Eberhardt's admirers was General Hubert Lyautey who, after her death, declared that he would always "cherish the memory of the exquisite conversational evenings passed together" with the free spirit whose refractory nature he so admired. "I loved her," he wrote, "for her prodigious artistic talent and for the fact she so disturbed (*faire tressaillir*) the notaries and mandarins of all sorts."[41] It was Lyautey, who ordered his men to search for her papers in the ruins of the house in which she was drowned in Aïn Sefra, which he assembled and helped to preserve.[42] He believed that few people knew "Africa" as well as Eberhardt, and he made use of this knowledge.[43] She assisted Lyautey in reconnaissance work, an activity facilitated by her journalistic ties that provided her with a cover.[44] More important, Eberhardt had been initiated in 1899 into the Sufi brotherhood, the Quadiriya, to which her future husband belonged and which, unlike the equally powerful Tijaniya brotherhood, had strongly resisted French penetration of Algeria.[45] Her insider knowledge, therefore, placed her in an exceptional position. In more ways than one, therefore, the colonial space facilitated Eberhardt's flight into masculinity as a means of empowerment.

Gender and Identity : Blixen and the Masculine Chivalric Ideal

To some degree Blixen's experience replicated the patterns of Eberhardt's identification with the masculine elements of colonial society. Unlike Eberhardt, however, Blixen did not invest in the outward trappings of male identity. To be sure she adopted the male *nom de plume* of Isak Dinesen, but it was for publication purposes after she left the colony and there was no attempt to transform herself physically through male attire. Where she did resemble Eberhardt was in her identification with the male members of colonial society, whether they were African or European. From her earliest days in Kenya, Blixen felt that she was bound to the Africans by a sort of "covenant."[46] They were "her own people" and the semi-mystical bond she believed linked her to them arose out of her chivalric sense of aristocratic obligation, on the one hand, and her initial sense of alienation in a British colony, on the other. "It is unfortunate that Denmark and Sweden have no colonies," she wrote to her mother shortly after her arrival, as "the English are particularly foreign to me, so it is lucky that I feel for the Somalis and natives like brothers . . ."[47] Fifteen years later, when she had reconciled herself to the ways of the British and had even found traits she considered admirable among her aristocratic friends, the bond was even stronger. "It is clear to me now," she wrote, "that my black brother here in Africa has become the great passion of my life and that this cannot be changed. Even Denys (her lover) . . . carries no weight in comparison."[48] In fact, for all the fraternal claims, Blixen's relationship with "her Africans" was one of the munificent overlord. Her concern and affection for them was genuine, but it was strongly paternalistic and she was not averse to inflicting corrections when the occasion arose.[49] Her protective paternalism extended to keeping the police at bay when one of "her people" had brushed with the law. On her farm she was the only one who could "regulate her people."[50] While in Africa, Blixen's creative spirit and strong sense of artistic destiny took the form of feudal benevolence. Her creativity would be her success as a coffee-grower, and her destiny would be to provide a great future for her "dear black people."[51] "The passion of my life," she wrote to Thomas, "has become *my love* for my black brother." [52] In other words, she invested her creative energy, her artistic temperament, in what she considered to be her role as benefactress to the Africans.

Blixen's sense of the aristocratic defined her relationships with all Africans. Nowhere is this more obvious than with her Somali manservant, Farah, whom she came to consider as her "best friend."[53] From her earliest days in Africa she identified with Somali men, whose bearing she compared to Spanish grandees.[54] (Like Eberhardt she did not relate as well to the women whom she considered uncivilized and childlike.[55]) But it was not just a question of an attraction to shared aristocratic values of discretion, honor, and dignity. A Somali manservant was a distinguishing feature in the hierarchy of the colony.[56] Blixen's relationship with Farah enabled her to identify with the blue bloods of British colonial society, all males of aristocratic origin, who were "accustomed to proud servants."[57] In a passage from *Shadows on the Grass*, she describes this privileged bond:

> So it came that our particular clan of early settlers—arrogantly looking upon ourselves as Mayflower people—might be characterized as those Europeans who kept Somali servants and to whom a house without a Somali would be like a house without a lamp. Here were Lord Delamere and Hassan, Berkeley Cole and Jama, Denys Finch—Hatton and Bilea, and I myself and Farah. We were the people who, wherever we went, were followed, at a distance of five feet, by those noble, vigilant and mysterious shadows.[58]

Blixen's ability to associate with Delamere's set placed her at the pinnacle of colonial society. The order of precedence in the social hierarchy of colonial Kenya was defined by the length of time a settler had been in the colony. The "old" settlers clubbed together and looked down on new arrivals. As Blixen put it: "people like Delamere and Cole . . . are quite unbeatable and those who arrived last year or this are of absolutely no consequence."[59] By definition this elite set was masculine and Blixen placed herself in its midst. Her relationship with Denys Finch Hatton, who became her mentor and lover, reinforced her association with the male elite of the society.[60] Denys was "one of the old settlers, like Delamere" and, being the son of Lord Winchilsea "a much better type than the later ones."[61] It was a fortunate country

Figure 2.2 Karen Blixen. Photograph taken by the late Sophus Juncker Jensen in 1913
Reproduced with permission from the Royal Library, Copenhagen

that had a class of such people "who had nothing better to do than follow
their own bent" and who were "brought up to observe the phenomena of
life from above." [62] Blixen never hid the importance she attached to class,
nor her desire to seek out and associate with "the best" in order to be considered the same[63] (fig. 2.2). By her own admission she felt class differences
much more than racial ones, preferring, as she put it, the company of "an
Arabian chief or an Indian priest" to that of "a waiter from home."[64] There
is a certain irony in this last statement and Blixen's admiration for and desire
to be so closely associated with the male aristocratic presence in the colony.
As Kennedy and Duder have shown, aristocrats such as Cole thought nothing of assuming the role of laborer and "mucking" in on their farms. Upper
crust they may have been but they often indulged in decidedly unaristocratic
activities, which reinforced a notion of the leveling of class structures and
was hardly viewing "life from above."[65] In fact it was personal bearing and
social behavior that was their defining feature, not their pioneering activities.
A social behavior that was revealed by class fraternization in clubs and social
gatherings rather than the deprecation of manual labor or "trade," as was the
case of the aristocrats in Europe.[66]

Blixen's identification with the male elite of Kenya society was taken to
its logical conclusion in her enthusiastic espousal of the most aristocratic of
pastimes, the hunt.[67] Within weeks of her arrival in Kenya, Bror Blixen was

teaching her how to shoot and this in spite of his belief that "gentlemen do not like ladies to be at the butts."[68] She had obviously succeeded in changing his views as to a woman's unsuitability for participating in shooting parties for no sooner had she settled into her new home than they were off on safari. In July 1914 she wrote to her mother describing one of their hunting exhibitions. "We had an *absolutely marvelous* (Blixen's emphasis) time, I have never in my life enjoyed myself more. It was a tremendously successful safari, six big lions, four leopards, one cheetah. I shot one lion and one big leopard."[69] She soon acquired a reputation as a "first-rate shot" among her African "boys" earning their respect not only for her ability to protect the farm from marauders but also as their provider of game, a role which she appeared to relish.[70] She shared her exhilaration of the hunt with her brother Thomas, as the one person in Denmark who would appreciate the depth of her feeling:

> I have spent four weeks in the happy hunting grounds and have just emerged from the depths of the great wide open spaces . . . from meeting with the great beasts of prey, which enthrall one, which obsess one so that one feels that lions are all that one lives for . . . There is nothing in the world like it . . . I shot 20 different kinds of game—all the ordinary species of deer, zebra . . . one lion, one leopard.[71]

The lion was of course the ultimate trophy to bag, both for its majesty and for the danger it represented. For Blixen the majesty of the lion represented "thousands of generations of unrestricted supreme authority," which made everything else appear trite.[72] This majesty was both awe-inspiring and awe-endowing. To be able to shoot lion successfully enhanced Blixen's social prestige among both Africans and Europeans. The great cats preyed on Kenyan cattle and on occasion on the Kenyans themselves. Her ability to shoot them thus inspired confidence among her staff, some of whom had lost relatives in this way. It also gave her access to social occasions of considerable significance in the colony. Shooting parties were the order of the day for visiting dignitaries and Blixen's letters attest to the fact she was often involved. The visit of the Prince of Wales was one such occasion, and although the actual shooting party never materialized Blixen, as member of the shooting set, was included. The experience was as enthralling for her as the aborted hunt would have been, leading her to declare that the Prince was "absolutely charming, and I am so much in love with him that it hurts."[73]

Blixen's unabashed attraction to majesty, whether of humans or beasts, was bound up with her elite sense of herself. When her mother questioned her love of lion hunting, she replied "if someone should come and shoot me in the full vigour of youth, so that I died in five minutes. I would be *sincerely* grateful to them and not resent them standing looking at my last moments, with deep admiration for my greatness."[74] Blixen's identification with lions and lion hunting was such that by 1928 she had earned the sobriquet of Lioness von Blixen, which evidently pleased her for she thought it was "rather grand."[75] Blixen did not identify with the feminine desire to nurture and domesticate lions, as did Margaret Elkington or Helen Cleland-Scott, but rather with the masculine urge to hunt.

In the same way as Eberhardt responded to the setting of colonial Algeria, therefore, Blixen responded to that of colonial Kenya. Both women aligned themselves with male power structures in the colony: Eberhardt with the military, Blixen with the male aristocratic elite. Both identified with an essentially male space: Eberhardt with the desert, terrain of the nomadic Tuareg and the military; Blixen with the aristocratic terrain of the hunt. Both used the indigenous population in conjunction with a surrogate male identity to develop a latent affinity. Without the colonial setting, Blixen could not have recreated the aristocratic paternalism of her farm at Ngong; nor would Eberhardt have been able to negotiate the venues of Islam with the ease she was able to do in Algeria.

FICTION AND REALITY

The different mode of gender identification of these two women was mirrored in their literary works. Blixen, whose mode of identification was circumscribed by creating an image of herself as singularly able to negotiate the masculine domain, had little space for women in her works on Africa. *Out of Africa* and *Shadows on the Grass* describe the man's world she felt so comfortable in. Farah's women appear briefly in *Out of Africa* and, on occasion a colonial figure such as Lady Macmillan, the wife of William Northrup MacMillan.[76] Femininity makes an appearance in the form of allegory, as in the description of the antics of Lulu the gazelle, but the cast of characters is essentially male.[77] Similarly, Eberhardt, who identified more aggressively with the masculine gender, mirrors this stance in her short stories. Yasmina, her best-known heroine, was a nubile Bedouin shepherdess whose passionate affair with an aristocratic young French officer led to her ruin in a Madame Butterfly-like denouement. Yasmina exuded a "mystical charm" which, for the Frenchman, was an essential part of the enchanting spell of Africa, a chimerical world into which he entered with abandon.[78] The eroticism of the pliant oriental female is a recurrent theme in her short stories. In her most seemingly autobiographical short story, "the Anarchist," she once again identifies with the masculine and provides a stereotypical version of the attractions of oriental women. Andreï, the hero, shares many circumstantial features of Eberhardt's life and his relationship with Saharan women mirror the extent of Eberhardt's gender identification. Whether or not Eberhardt was attracted to her own sex is moot, but her short stories suggest that her assumption of masculine identity stopped short of a sexual attraction for women. Arab women are stereotyped in the Orientalist manner as voluptuous, mysterious, often superstitious, but nearly always the pathway to the unbridled erotic experience of the Orient, thus indicating a response to imagined male desires rather than a sensual appreciation of other women.[79]

The creation of fiction in the writer's own image is par for the course in literary works and it is not, therefore, surprising that fiction and reality merged both in the life and work of these two women. Blixen, whose literary ambitions were not realized until after she left Africa, was often worried that she would not be able to make "something of her life." In a letter to Thomas expressing her fears of this eventuality she wrote: "Here I am living an idyll, which is only an idyll because I want to make it one."[80] Her desire for exceptional achievement created the fictional idyll that eclipsed the reality of the endless difficulties she encountered on the farm and eventually led to its bankruptcy and her return to Europe.[81] To her family, whose financial support enabled her to remain in Kenya for so long, she was not always able to gloss over the vicissitudes of her life, but once in Europe she had free rein to create the fiction she had wanted the reality to be. The magnificence of *Out of Africa* and *Shadows on the Grass* lies not only in the compelling prose, but also in the "idyll" she created from the combination of an atavistic nostalgia for a distant chivalric past, and the desire to rearrange the immediate past to suit an aristocratic image of herself. The reader is transported to a bewitching world of aristocratic benevolence, where the beauty of life is exalted and its ugliness recedes in the artifice of a tale well told. Blixen's Kenyan experience developed her aristocratic yearnings and honed her capacity for fictionalizing reality. With Blixen's departure from Africa, the actuality of her imagined "idyll" was over but its true fictionalization began.

The fact that Eberhardt wrote extensively while in Africa did not make her less prone to fictionalizing reality than Blixen. Quite apart from the fact her transvestism was itself a fictional rendition of herself, she acknowledged her need to fictionalize her life, describing it to her friend Ali Abdul Wahab, as a "novel," which had started in Algeria and had ended so miserably."[82] For Eberhardt the interlacing of fact and fiction had an urgent quality. Her life in Algeria had not evolved in the way she had anticipated. The death of her mother, "the light of her life" as she called her, so soon after her arrival in Algeria and her intractable financial problems added to her sense of social and familial alienation and developed her triple association of suffering, destiny and creativity, by which she rationalized her problems.[83] "Suffering was ennobling . . . for it alone produced the splendors of true courage and deep devotion . . . in the same way as it created great sentiments and grand ideas."[84] It was her destiny to suffer, as it was her destiny to write. "I write because I love the process of literary creation," she wrote to Ali Abdul Wahab, "I write, in the same manner as I love, because such is my destiny."[85] In her fiction, much of which has a discernible autobiographical content, Eberhardt ennobled suffering, transforming the mental attrition of its relentlessness into imperious disdain or valiant stoicism. The sordid spiral of decline engendered by personal misfortune, which Eberhardt experienced, was glossed with her contempt of complacency and regard for the ameliorating and creative impetus of difficulty.[86] The suffering of her fictional characters increased their stature, rather than diminishing it.

Writing was not just a means of exorcising her suffering and accomplishing her creative destiny, it was also a channel for her "mystical" attraction to the Orient; her flight to the East to escape the strictures of the West. All her fiction is set in North Africa and resonates with her passion for the East. Her work is an exaltation of the nomadic life and her prose a transliteration of her vision of the plaintive song of the nomad. "The reflective, carefree, sensual soul of the nomads," she wrote "can be heard in their poignant, wildly beautiful songs which speak to the heart and senses and envelope (the) soul with an infinitely sad, yet soothing, gentleness."[87] Her positive response to the nomad was in contrast to her reaction against the "self-satisfaction" and "foolish boasting" of the insensitive "bourgeois," who never reconsidered their opinions or deviated from their ideas.[88] Through the fictionalization of her life she escaped the constricting world of middle-class mediocrity. By identifying with the nomads, whom she saw as free-spirits like herself, she was able to repudiate those aspects of her own culture and society she found disagreeable, and embrace the aspects of a culture and society she found congenial. Her fiction allowed her the leeway to create the "novel" she had sought to make of her life when coming to Algeria but which reality had robbed her of.

PARADOX AND AMBIGUITY: AN OPEN DOOR TO POSTERITY?

If the colonial space favored the creative development of these two women, it is the paradoxical way they moved through this space that has intrigued posterity. Although both women were critical of colonial society, neither came out in direct opposition to the colonial state. Eberhardt, whose outsider status was reinforced by her adoption of indigenous dress, was content to be the loner on the margins of a society whose European members she characterized as a "grey banality . . . of vapidly gossiping civil servants and socialites."[89] Her distaste for this milieu stopped short of open criticism. "I have no intention of railing against the French in public," she wrote. "It would only get me into trouble and disrupt my future plans."[90] Blixen's reactions were very similar. She privately protested against the "prigs" in Kenyan society, declaring that they were "the most abominable . . . of all human types."[91] Publicly, however, she held her peace believing that her influence as a woman and foreigner should be confined to setting an example:

> if I start to preach I shall lose my power, which must be won through being a hostess and friend; even my glasses and my big cupboard must work in my mission for my "black brothers," but the example takes effect so slowly and sometimes one feels like firing off a broadside right in their silly faces, when that typical English stupidity starts braying too loudly.[92]

It was the narrow-mindedness of the settlers rather than the imperial framework, which the two women criticized. Indeed Eberhardt acknowledged the ideal of France's *mission civilisatrice*, lamenting its flagrant distortions in the colony.[93] She even defended herself against the accusations of the settlers in an open letter to the *Petite Gironde*, stating that far from stirring up trouble among the indigenous population, she spent her time telling her Muslim friends that French occupation was infinitely better than Ottoman.[94]

Both women identified in some way with the local population and were criticized for it. Both felt much more should be done for the local population but any remonstrance they made was, on the whole, private. Eberhardt believed improving the lot of the Algerians would be in the best French tradition *(la plus française des œuvres)* and, in 1902, found it encouraging that the Socialists were moving in this direction.[95] Blixen believed in the importance of "native production" and in the need for African involvement in the economy to ensure the future success of the colony.[96] She also made every effort to resettle her squatters and find employment for her staff before she left Kenya.[97] Neither Eberhardt nor Blixen, however, became embroiled in colonial politics; their interest was that of educated observers rather than outspoken critics. Whereas Eberhardt found, what she termed, the *kitchen politics* of Algeria repugnant and tried to avoid open involvement, Blixen adopted a backstairs approach.

Their gender identification was also ambiguous. Both women criticized the unequal nature of gender relations and vociferated in their letters or diaries against the social and professional limitations of being a woman, but both emigrated to a society whose cultural configurations were even more emphatically masculine than the one they had left behind. They furthered their personal goals by identifying with these structures. Their relations with contemporaneous feminists were tenuous. By her own admission, Eberhardt's attempts to link up with French feminists were a failure. She sent a manuscript to the French feminist paper, *La Fronde,* but received no response. Eberhardt tried to see Marguerite Durand, the paper's director, but was unsuccessful due, she opined, to her masculine attire.[98] Her friend and colleague, J. Bonneval, director of *L'Athénée* tried to intervene on her behalf with Durand but fared no better: "[She] must have lost [the manuscript] or cannot be bothered to look for it," he wrote.[99] It may well be that Durand believed Eberhardt's close identification with the masculine sex made her too suspect to further their cause, but more likely is the fact that the colonies, for which the paper did not show a great deal of interest, were already covered by someone else.[100] Furthermore, Durand was not an exception: Eberhardt's approaches to Séverine were also ignored.[101] Was she altogether too subversive? Or was it that she was not interested enough in the French feminist cause to be acceptable to the mandarins of the movement? As for Blixen, she believed that feminism was probably the most important movement of the nineteenth century and had a fine grasp of the politics from which it emerged and the direction in which the movement was going, but she did not align herself with its politically minded participants.[102] Both women were too far removed from metropole activities and too entrenched in a masculine framework of the colony to become involved in feminist activism.

NOSTALGIA AND THE CREATION OF FEMALE ICONS

When Eberhardt's Algerian odyssey was cut short by her death in 1904, the journalist Séverine, who had ignored Eberhardt in her lifetime, published an article comparing her to Bakunin. It was the beginning of her transformation from an "undesirable troublemaker" to a radical icon.[103] Although the controversy about her literary merits would continue, her transgender dressing, her perceived sexual excesses, her substance abuse, and her familiarity with the Arabs, all of which had elicited so much criticism during her lifetime, ceased to be the focus of opprobrium. In 1922, Lucienne Crespin, writing for *Akhbar,* wondered what "Eberhardt['s reputation] would be in ten years time, "because since her death twenty years earlier, it has not ceased to grow."[104] In a book published in 1925, the journalist and traveller, Henriette Celarié, visited her house at El-Oued, where she had lived for a while, and described the atmosphere as one where "her thoughts *(pensées)* still formed part of the air one breathed . . . [a] strange, near brilliant *(presque géniale)* woman whose immense curiosity is so appealing, her boldness of spirit, her freedom from social conventions, from petty actions, and her soul shrouded in melancholy. "[105] Three years later, an article in *La Revue de France* declared Eberhardt to be "an exquisite and profound writer who, with Fromentin, had understood North Africa the best and described most perfectly the profound, mysterious and *nostalgic charm of Islam.*"[106] As time progressed, the sobriquets she acquired suggest the form her rehabilitation took: *la bonne nomade, l'amazone des sables, l'aventureuse du Sahara, La Passionaria du désert, Notre Dame d'Afrique, Isabelle d'Afrique* and *la Séverine musulmane;* an irony given her relationship with Séverine.[107] In 1930 a society to her memory, *Le Couvenir d'Isabelle Eberhardt,* was established and a commemorative plaque was placed on the house in which she drowned in Aïn Sefra.[108] Local newspapers vied to claim their support (alleged or real) of her when she was still alive:

> When our contributor (collaboratice) Isabelle Eberhardt was being odiously attacked by some small Algerian newspapers, our colleague Lys du Pac, editor of the *Dépêche Algérienne* was, at our request, pleased to accept her collaboration . . . Isabelle also had a good position in the *Revue Blanche.*"[109]

By the end of the decade the places she had frequented during her lifetime had become sites of pilgrimage and her life had been romanticized for theatrical effect.[110] Thus, glamour was added to a decidedly unglamorous existence. Eberhardt was reinvented as a T. E. Lawrence of sorts, who had not only understood the desert and the Arabs in a unique way but also had the attraction of being a free-spirited woman. Her own nostalgic yearning to achieve fulfillment in the solitary spaces of the desert became associated with a communal wistfulness for a romanticized past. She became a figure of personal and collective nostalgia: a woman whose artistic temperament had been hemmed in by tragedy, but whose spirit represented the adventurous creativity perceived to be the hallmark of the early colonial period. Unlike other women writing in colonial Algeria, or indeed other women closely associated with Arabs, her reputation as a colonial renegade persisted into the post-independence period. As we shall see in the ensuing chapters the authors

Magali Boisnard and Elissa Rhaïs were also sartorially unconventional: they both affected Muslim dress (although neither adopted male attire). Furthermore Rhais, who was a Jewess, assumed Muslim identity. Aurélie Picard, the working class woman who married a sheikh of the Tidjania brotherhood, achieved more respect within it than Eberhardt had in the Quadiriya, yet Ursula Hart's account of the two women, the sole comparative study, portrays Eberhardt in a positive light and Picard in a negative one.[111] What was it about Eberhardt that struck such a sympathetic chord? To be sure the disapproval of the colonial authorities and her rejection by "genteel" colonial society elevated her above the colonial norm, but it was the space she appropriated as her own, the fringes of the Sahara, that gave her the gloss of exceptionality. She contributed to the creation of a nostalgic space in Algeria, whose cultural origins were rooted in French fascination with the eroticism of the Orient. Her fin-de-siècle "Orientalism" was construed as Romanticism, a throwback to a heroic cultural past. Her revolt against conservative morality and personal insincerity, her assertion of individuality, her emphasis on intensity and imagination, and her belief in the transcendental quality of emotions were all hallmarks of the true Romantic. She was an unconventional figure with a hint of eroticism: an emblem of the free-spirited adventuress. The nostalgia that eventually attached to her persona was as much cultural as it was of her subversive lifestyle. Her appeal transcended the period in which she lived by providing a multi-faceted pole of attraction with which to identify.

The nostalgia for a heroic past was also integral to Blixen's appeal. Unlike Eberhardt, Blixen's literary reputation, and her reinvention of herself as part of an ancient tribe of storytellers, did much to enhance her iconic status, although it was her association with Africa that has made her universally known.[112] Stanley Pollack's 1985 film, *Out of Africa,* a highly romanticized and inaccurate version of her life, did much to transform her into a household name, cement her association with Africa, and reinforce the nostalgia for the pioneer spirit that sought out life in the "wilds" of Africa. There is, however, more to the phenomenon than a Hollywood interpretation. Blixen's appropriation of Africa as an "untamed" space on which to carve out a patrician identity became such a powerful image that it has been emulated repeatedly, creating a quasi-stereotypical dimension to the process. Perhaps the most flagrant example of this is illustrated in Kuki Gallmann's African memoir, *I Dreamed of Africa,* first published in 1991. It quickly became a best seller and has also been made into a film. *I Dreamed of Africa* does more than echo Blixen's work; it practically mimics it. While the events of Gallmann's life are, in many ways, an uncanny replica of Blixen's, it is the way the memoir is constructed that is the real indication of Blixen's emblematic status. Like Blixen, Gallmann uses the trials and tribulations of her life to create an African idyll that sucks the reader into a world of heroic dimensions shot through with nostalgia for all that is lost. Even the prose is reminiscent of Blixen's. Of Farah's death Blixen had written: "more than once before now I had sent him ahead, to some unknown place, to pitch camp for me there."[113] In a similar vein, Gallmann tells her young daughter at her son's funeral: "He is gone ahead, you know he always walked faster than us."[114] Like Blixen, Gallmann referred to the Kenyan staff on her Kenyan ranch as "our people" or "my people" and in the way Blixen had identified strongly with a particular "tribe," the Somali; so too did Gallmann, the Turkana. Her attraction to an aristocratic demeanor also parallels Blixen's. Weaving into her narrative tales of Blixen's aristocratic friends, she draws a connection to their way of life and hers. She merges the past and present in this and other ways throughout her memoir, but she echoes Blixen's sentiments, especially, strongly in describing the first lover she had after her husband's death. He had "a patrician quality," Gallmann writes "a presence, an aura of adventure and of times past. Of wild remote places where time still follows the sun and the seasons."[115] Examples of the mimetic quality of Gallmann's life and work are legion and an article could be devoted to analyzing their extent and significance.

The linking in one work of differing nostalgias—for heroic times past, for people and places lost, for lifestyles of days gone by—creates a compelling female narrative in which the author herself becomes the object of longing, of the reader's nostalgic identification with loss. Gallmann's close friend Oria Douglas–Hamilton (another woman of Kenya renown), when speaking at the funeral of Gallmann's son, manages succinctly to evoke the power of the wild and its connection to loss:

> We come from the seed of wild men
> We married wild men
> Wild children we bore
> *Wild men who caught and sang the sun in flight* (my italics)

She ends her oration with the fourth verse of one of Dylan Thomas' best-loved poems, the first line of which connects the freedom of spirit that Thomas sought to express with the independent spirit of their own lives. The melancholy of the occasion is captured in the next line: *And learn, too late, they grieved it on its way* and the final refrain: *Do not go gentle into that good night* is a reminder, in the context of the occasion, not to forget.[116] Thus, adding to Dylan Thomas' lines her own perception of their heritage and the choices that led them to Africa, Douglas-Hamilton encapsulates the strong human identification with the wild and the nostalgia provoked by opportunities lost. It is as much an epitaph for the works of Blixen and Eberhardt as it is for her friend's son.

CONCLUSION

During their colonial lives Eberhardt and Blixen transgressed the boundaries of gender and race, while maintaining and adhering to the structures of imperialism. Although they were not alone in this, they did so by creating colonial identities for themselves that departed from the colonial norm. By inclination Eberhardt was an anarchist; Blixen an aristocrat. In spite of these seemingly opposing political poles, in many ways their strategies were similar. They aligned themselves with the masculine element of the colony and repudiated the mean-spirited treatment of the local population by the settlers. Both were imperialists insofar as they believed in the "civilizing mission" and used the colonial space to further their own personal ends. Although neither woman was able to make an economic success of their African adventure, both used their failure to create an imaginary world that procured them literary renown when their African "adventure" was over. By transgressing the boundaries of gender and race but failing as true colonialists they broke three molds of tradition contemporary to their time, and are thus perceived to have functioned outside accepted paradigms.

Nostalgia, as a response to alienation, to the disruption of exile and expatriation, provides equilibrium by conflating time and space. Both Eberhardt and Blixen responded to the alienation they felt from their own societies by expatriation to a colony where they each created a spatial time warp. Eberhardt chose the desert in which to romanticize the nomad; Blixen chose the Kenyan "wild" in which to develop her sense of a bygone aristocracy. Both were "exotic" women in a society where most colonial women were hidebound. But exoticism, as Chris Bongie has ably demonstrated, is a way of indicating loss.[117] By responding to their personal losses with an exoticism that extended beyond their lifestyles to their literature, they represented a type of personality around which admiration coalesced; a personality closely associated with colonial time and space but reimagined outside of them by a succession of other writers. Their celebrity as writers of the colonial moment was a celebrity of nostalgia.

Colonial society has sometimes been evaluated as one peopled with escapees from modernity, bent on recreating a world that had more to do with eighteenth-century absolutism than it did with the nineteenth or twentieth centuries. But this type of reasoning is a simplification. In many ways, Eberhardt and Blixen were modern for their times. Eberhardt was a writer and journalist who flaunted social conventions to achieve her professional ends. Blixen was a capitalist and a woman entrepreneur, albeit not a very successful one. They were not really escaping Western modernity, however much they believed they were. To do so would have meant integration with the nomads by Eberhardt, and with "her" Africans by Blixen. Neither chose to do so. Instead they used the spaces associated with these to groups to spin an imaginative web of nostalgia for a space and time that never was. They were ambiguous figures whose own nostalgias responded to multiple alienations: from their homeland, from the colonists (as opposed to colonization), from their middle-class roots, from certain types of women, from the gender and racial norms of the colonial society in which they chose to live. Ambiguity can be a hook for many coats. As romanticizers of loss they are emblematic of the disruption in the lives of postcolonial migrants, whether expatriates or exiles. As such the echoes of their nostalgia can still be heard today.

PART II

1920–1940. POLITICAL REALITIES AND FICTIONAL REPRESENTATIONS

CHAPTER 3

REALITY EXPRESSED; REALITY IMAGINED:
ALGERIA AND KENYA IN THE TWENTIES

*A great deal of nonsense has been written about a fellow hearing the irresist-
ible Call of Africa, if he has once lived there. I have yet to meet the man who
honestly yearns for a life such as we were living . . .*

Alyse Simpson

*Je voudrais que la Gauloise (qui a souvent du sang sarrazin dans les
veines), je voudrais que la Franque prennent beaucoup à leur soeur ainée
l'Algérienne musulmane.*

J. Annette Godin

Algeria and Kenya emerged from World War I territorially unscathed but
in turmoil. The impact of the war was economic, social, and psychological.
Colonial troops had been sent from both colonies to the fronts, suffering
heavy casualties and being short-changed in their expectations of what was
their due when they returned. Any anticipation they may have had for an
improvement in their status was not fulfilled. Furthermore, the superiority of
western civilization, which was the lynchpin of colonial ideology, French and
British, was called into question by the horrific and mindless bloodletting of
the war. Whereas the European populations of the two colonies struggled
to consolidate their grip, discontent among the non-European populations
triggered the process that would lead to the formation of nationalist movements. Tensions were not limited to the colonizer and colonized, however.
The settler populations in Kenya and Algeria sought to distance themselves
from the metropole by demanding more autonomy. The resultant friction
between the colonial offices and ministries in the metropole, and the settler
establishment in the colonies played itself out in the colony between administrators and settlers. During the war, women in both colonies covered for

the absence of their men by taking over some of their roles, in much the same way as they had in the metropole. Similarly, after the war they were instrumental in picking up the pieces of their shattered lives. Although colonial realities of power and domination were similar in both colonies, there were also striking differences, due as much to the social and cultural makeup of each colony as to their politics.

KENYA: REALITY EXPRESSED—REALITY IMAGINED

The presence of German territory adjacent to Kenya meant that East Africa was directly involved in the war. The East African campaign led to the death of nearly 50,000 men, African, Indian and British, and huge losses of horses, mules and oxen, vital to farming.[1] Male settlers joined up leaving their farms to be run by their wives or neighbor's wives. One woman was often in charge of several farms.[2] The adventuress and farmer Cara Buxton, for example, supervised a number of farms in different parts of the country. "She wandered from farm to farm with a Boy, two mules, and a sack containing her belongings."[3] Until the outbreak of the war, most settler wives had remained in the traditional role of helpmate, but the necessity of taking over farm management in the absence of their partners meant that by war's end, women had acquired the experience and expertise to run farms on their own. Their experiences during the war convinced some, like Nellie Grant (1885–1977), that it was best "to strike out on her own, running a farm in the way she thought best and not having to consider Jos," her husband.[4] In spite of knowing little about coffee, Grant planted over 30,000 seedlings, which by 1922 had yielded 10 tons of coffee.[5] The Bostonian Lucy Macmillan (later Lady Macmillan), with her African-American companion, Louise Decker, converted her residence, Juja House into a convalescent home for officers. She was a keen fund-raiser and went on to create the Woman's War Work League.[6] Lucy's efforts no doubt contributed to the fact her husband, Northrup, was knighted in 1918 for his contribution to the British war effort. After his death in 1925 she commissioned the Sir Northrup MacMillan Memorial Library, which was inaugurated in his memory in 1931. The impressive library, which became a pivotal landmark in colonial Nairobi for the use of Europeans only, is still standing. Lucy MacMillan may have built it in memory of her larger-than-life husband but its legacy as a memorial has a gendered element, for it is a reminder of the way in which women could and did shape colonial institutional and racial spaces.

The enlistment of settlers and administrators meant that many districts had few remaining male authority figures.[7] In Kisii, in the southwest of the colony, Marion Dobbs recorded in her memoir, that the Africans vandalized the District Commissioner's quarters "stick[ing] spears into the D.C.'s tins of food, destroy[ing] the papers in his office, and [doing] any other mischief that occurred to them." Whereas they were, no doubt, expressing their resentment of British occupation, settlers interpreted it as a breach of trust. "They were to regret the action," she adds, as "a heavy cattle fine

(3,000 [rupees] a head) was imposed on them as punishment."[8] To prevent what was considered to be disorderly conduct, the administration passed a number of ordinances. The Pass and Registration ordinances restricted the movement of Kenyan workers, thus facilitating the apprehension of deserters and monitoring "troublemakers."[9] The Crown Land Ordinance, passed in 1915, deprived Kenyans of virtually all rights to land, thus effectively disinheriting them and placing the colonial administration in full control of their rights.[10] Grievances over land, thus, became a focal point of protest for both Kenyans and Indians. The Europeans did not, of course, see it that way. Writing of the highlands, Elspeth Huxley (1907–1997), Nellie Grant's daughter and one of colonial Kenya's leading women writers, stated that a "point which is often overlooked is that regions most favoured by Europeans may be those least suited to Africans." [11] It was a lame justification for the land grabbing and spatial segregation that went on, but it was one that the settlers chose to believe and, as such, it became incorporated into the narratives of settler identity.[12]

In the two years that followed the armistice, the colony established its true colonial foundations. In 1919 the British acquired Germany's East African colonies, which led to the carving up of the British East African protectorate into individual colonies. In 1919 Sir Edward Northey was appointed governor of what, in 1920, became the protectorate of Kenya. By 1920, therefore, Kenya was no longer a subdivision of a larger territorial protectorate but a colony in its own right. The appointment of Northey started an administrative struggle between metropole and colony that would end, with his departure in 1923, in favor of the metropole, but whose social and economic legacy in the colony would persist for much longer. Northey was strongly pro-settler and therefore, espoused the settler line that Africans were economically only suited for labor on settler farms and had little or no future as independent producers.[13] The ideal of white dominance was, therefore, anchored at the colony's inception, and even if, as Maxon has suggested, the Colonial Office recaptured the imperial initiative in Kenya, preventing settler self-rule and avoiding some of the excesses that were to characterize South Africa and Southern Rhodesia, the belief in white supremacy did not disappear.[14] As Huxley, writing in the 1930s about the early period, put it: "Settlement was, in fact—as it still remains—an economic necessity. But it was more that that; it was part of a world necessity. It was also part of a cultural conviction."[15]

During the war and its immediate aftermath, therefore, a twofold process developed. On the one hand, most Kenyans were relegated to the status of laborers on the land, whether they actually held that position or not.[16] A social structure was thus created, whose hierarchy was a throwback to the type of manorial/tenant relationship that had been disappearing in Britain prior to the war and that petered out entirely afterward. On the other hand, the claiming of the best land as a European space whose proper exploitation, as part of the capitalist world economy, was the prerogative of the settlers, reinforced the claim that modernity, as capitalist enterprise, was a European phenomenon, which the traditional African was in no position to emulate. The structural underpinning of the colonial narrative of modernity, which was so important to its ideology, was therefore a nostalgic recreation of a master/servant relationship, which in Britain had been shattered by the war.[17]

The attitudes of, and the measures taken by, the settlers resulted in protest by both Africans and Indians. The missionaries had encouraged an African engagement with politics— under their tutelage—as part of their message of modernity.[18] They encouraged Christian Africans to represent themselves by forming councils of African elders within the churches. This led, in 1921, to senior Kikuyu landholders and chiefs within the missions forming a single association, the Kikuyu Association.[19] Furthermore, the decade of the 1920s saw the emergence of a Kikuyu politician, Harry Thuku, who started to voice African grievances, eventually creating the more radical East African Association; the first of the Kikuyu political associations, which actually sought redress.[20] For their part, in the years immediately after the war, the Indians started to demand equality with the European settlers. As the Hon. Mrs. K. Armstrong, who arrived in Kenya in 1919, and settled with her parents on a coffee farm just outside Nairobi, put it in her memoirs:

> 1922 was the year of the Indian Question. Indians demanded equal votes with white people and rights to buy lands in the Highlands. This created tremendous feelings among the settlers as there were barely 20,000 whites in the country and something like 120,000 Indians. There was a lot of talk of an armed revolt if this happened and a lot of settlers boycotted the Indians."[21] [According to the 1921 census figures there were 9,651 Europeans, 22,822 Indians and 2,431 Goans]

The uproar in settler society created by these demands occasioned an extensive debate.[22] Educated Africans were offended that Indians might be given privileges that were denied to them. An article appearing in the *Sekanyola,* a Ugandan African paper published in the vernacular, declared:

> It is true that we educated Africans recognise the great superiority of whites over Africans and are willing to learn and obey their laws, but the idea of being subjected to a race whom we do not admit to be our superiors, who would then come to our shores in their thousands and prevent us from learning trades and useful work, and therefore robbing us of our livelihood, and ever keeping us in the dark, would be an unjust, intolerable law and opposed to our sense of justice.[23]

Whether the author of the article had interiorized colonial ideology about white superiority or whether he was pandering to the white administration for political purposes is not relevant here. The extract indicates that feelings were running high among Africans and, more to the point for this study, that the inappropriateness of the blanket category of laborer, beyond which so many settlers seemed incapable of seeing, was challenged early on.

On January 27, 1922 Winston Churchill spoke at the East African Dinner on the question of African and Indian rights, stating:

> No doubt you know that we have laid down the principle that, so far as practicable throughout the whole range of the British Empire, colour is by no means to be a bar, . . . We shall apply broadly and comprehensively, so far as is practical, Mr. Rhodes's principle of equal rights for all civilised men. That means that natives and Indians alike, who reach and conform to well-marked European standards, shall not be denied the fullest exercise and enjoyment of civic and political rights.[24]

Lord Delamere, who was at the dinner, responded that given the fact there were 25,000 Indians to only about 10,000 whites, the settlers had to ensure that "European ideas of Government, Western ideals, were not swamped by the ideals of another civilisation."[25] Settler anxiety regarding Colonial Office intentions was such that in February 1923, leading white farmers had held a secret meeting, where they took an oath to rebel against the British government if it acceded to Indian demands.[26] As Nellie Grant wrote, shortly afterward, to her brother-in-law, Robin:

> The political situation has been the devil, we really thought 'direct action' would be our only way out . . . The white community was absolutely unanimous about rejecting the proposals for Indian rights as set out by the Colonial Office and everything was ready, when, mercifully, the Col. Office suggested the Governor going [sic] home with delegates to discuss everything at home. We are pledged not to take 'direct action' while the Governor is out of the country and the Col. Office is pledged not to introduce further legislation on the matter until the Governor and delegates are back again.[27]

As a result of this move, the East Africa Women's League wrote to Sir Robert Corydon, who had replaced Northey as Governor, declaring that: "We place our interests unreservedly in your hands, knowing that it is your Excellency's desire to bring about a settlement which will be in the best interests of the future destinies of this Colony, and of the resident races, both native and white."[28] The equivocal nature of the response was due to their allegiance to settler society on the one hand, and the purported aim of the League to promote the interests of women of all races, on the other. The outcome was the Devonshire Declaration, which stated the interests of "African natives to be paramount" and was engineered to maneuver between Indian and settler demands. In fact it did little to change the existing state of affairs.[29]

To resolve the tensions existing in the colony and to ensure the settlers' security, measures were taken to attract more settlers to the colony. The Soldier Settlement Scheme was introduced both as a way to provide veterans with a possibility for a new life and to attract new settlers to the colony. A few women qualified for this scheme. Those who did, like Mary Roberts, had served in some auxiliary capacity such as nurse or hospital matron.[30] The various settlement promotions were relatively successful, but the older settlers were not always enamored of the new arrivals. As early as 1919, Cara Buxton wrote to her brother that she was rowing with a neighbor who had beaten one of the Kenyan children from her farm. She put his behavior down to the fact "we have such a mixed crowd and certainly during these years of war all the good settlers are away and the bad ones get worse and worse. I wish we could drown all the bad ones." Not only were they bad; as far as Buxton was concerned, they were also cowardly: "Of course none of them would fight so there was no hope of any getting killed."[31] What is of note in this passage is the way that Buxton, whose parents were part of the Norwich gentry, equates race relations with behavior that is defined by class. Race and class in the colonies are usually analyzed merely as different categorizations of hierarchy. But Buxton's attitude, much like Blixen's, suggests that the relationship between class and race was more nuanced. Settlers whose violence and uncouth behavior created interracial problems were seen as disruptive to the colony's harmony. Benevolent paternalism, a characteristic of an upper class that "knew" how to treat its African retainers and laborers, could only enhance relations. In Kenya, therefore, the usual conflation of class and race in the colonies as white/upper and black/lower is nuanced within the colony by the settlers who had a nostalgic vision of a master/servant relationship whose harmony—or lack of it—was defined by the behavior of class.

If the complaints of the likes of Buxton demonstrate the awareness of class among the settlers, the desire for more European immigration to the colony produced various schemes and promotions to attract settlers. As the community increased and prospered so too did the merchants and service sector employees, but in spite of the steady influx of settlers, many did not stay. The number of Europeans emigrating from the colony nearly matched those immigrating to it. In his introduction to Alyse Simpson's *The Land that Never Was*, Kennedy states that for every ten persons who entered Kenya in the interwar period nine departed.[32] In 1921 Kenya was on the verge of bankruptcy. The worldwide depression in the wake of the war and the collapse of commodity prices fueled the political discontent in the colony and had serious repercussions on its economy. To try and alleviate the situation, the currency was converted from rupees to shillings and wages were reduced. Elspeth Huxley, who was 14 at the time, wrote to her aunt and uncle that: "there is awful excitement going on over the currency . . . but the great excitement is about reducing wages. They are trying to get every man in the country to reduce the wages of all Natives. It is more or less fixed up now."[33] Converting the currency to shillings was a means of revaluing the currency but the switch from the rupee, the Indian monetary denomination, to the shilling, a British denomination, was also a step toward the imposition of a British identity on the colony and a way of keeping Kenyan wage demands in check.

Drought, locusts and other afflictions, with which most settlers had little experience, compounded the economic depressions of the interwar period. As Alyse Simpson noted: "It is difficult, if not impossible for me to convey on paper the extreme monotony of months and months of drought, when the dust rises high about the trees and nothing of interest really happens."[34] In the five and a half years she farmed there with her husband, they only had one decent crop of maize.[35] "Kenya was a cruel country, if truth be told," she wrote.[36] Cruel enough for the novelist Florence Riddell to declare in her memoirs that during her four years in Kenya, "more of the people whom I met there committed suicide than I can count in all the other years of my life put together."[37] Although the relativity of this statement leaves the door open to an interpretative range of casualties, it does drive home the fact that not everybody made a success of their Kenya experience. Indeed in the very early years of settlement the Kikuyu, more experienced with the vicissitudes of the climate and territory, fared better with their farming than the settlers.[38] The fact was, to make a success of farming in Kenya, a settler needed money; enough to ride out lean periods and crop failures. Although, the minimum capital investment was deemed to be £2,000, the more realistic figure was twice that amount; even more if the settler was trying to convert what they considered to be virgin land.[39] However disillusioned new settlers became or, however realistically they viewed the colonial situation, their loyalties nonetheless lay to each other. Alyse Simpson, who throughout her memoir emphasized settler dominance by capitalizing the words White Man expressed it as follows: "Attached as I was to the natives as well as conscious of having intruded into their own province, of having helped to deprive them of some of their freedom, my pity was all for the plodding White Man."[40]

Women experienced the precarious economic situation of the colony according to their wealth, status, and personal circumstances and their voices mirrored these differences. As Juanita Carberry, who came from a privileged background, put it, "Life in Africa in the twenties and thirties was still fairly primitive, even for rich settlers."[41] Those whose economic or social positions enabled them to stay imagined their lives in terms of success, romanticizing, or disregarding its difficulties. For those, like Simpson, who left because of economic failure, the realities of their Kenya lives overshadowed or eradicated altogether the romantic attractions that characterized the accounts of those who chose to stay, whether they were successful or not. Putting a brave face on things is a behavioral pattern of identity, which in the case of the British was associated with the comportment of "good breeding." But putting a brave face on things is also a mechanism of incipient nostalgia; it allows for the effacement of the unpalatable and the accentuation of the desirable, which, of course, is what is remembered. It is, therefore, as much an expression of the real as it is of the imagined.

ALGERIA: NARRATING MODERNITY AS "TEACHING THE NATIVE"

Unlike pre-World War I Kenya where women were only just beginning to arrive in significant numbers, by 1900 women in Algeria, whether Algerian or French, were essential elements in the colonial narrative. "The Muslim woman in North Africa," according to Ferdinand Duchène's writing in 1908, "was placed on the second rung of humanity by the will of God and was reduced to slavery by the will of man." The woman question, he went on, was "the moral malady of Islam, whose remedy would appear to be very difficult to administer."[42] Although this opinion of women in Islam was not new, in resisting the French the Algerians had retrenched, using Islam as a refuge. Breeching the strength of the Islamic bulwark was not an easy task. Women, deemed to be more docile and malleable than men, appeared to be a possible way to this end. The difficulty lay in the fact Algerian women were inaccessible and, hence beyond the reach of French men and their colonial propaganda. French women, on the other hand, could and did have access to their "Muslim sisters." One woman who realized that writing about North African women could be both a literary and a public spirited plus was Magali Boisnard. Boisnard (1882–1945) was born in the Vaucluse in France but raised in the Algerian Atlas, where her parents had a large forestry domain. She spoke fluent Arabic and was deeply interested in Islam and its culture (fig. 3.1). According to the critic(s) Marius-Ary Leblond she gave an unforgettable talk "at the Sorbonne on the relations between French thought and North African Islam."[43] Her memoir-novel, *Les Endormies,* is a description of the exchanges between two cultures: French and Islamic. It is worth noting that the comparison is not between two religions, Catholic and Islam, or between two peoples, French and Arab [Algerian], but between two types of civilization, one secular and the other religious. Boisnard presents Islam as a once great civilization, which was now slumbering.[44] She compares it to a sick man and like a sick man it was curable.[45] In her preface, Boisnard

Figure 3.1 Magali Boisnard. Image from Marie Cardinal's *Les Pieds-Noirs* reproduced with permission from the deceased's husband

declares that she has seen the soul and face of the *Endormies* of the title [slumbering women of Islam] from beneath their Muslim veils.[46] Noura Le Gall, the central character of the work, states that she has come as an educator whose mission is one of kindred spirit, to uplift *(relèvement)* her "Muslim sisters."[47] Like Boisnard, who claimed that she had a Muslim soul but a Gallic heart, Noura Le Gall, an Arab orphan raised by a French family, sees herself as a cultural go-between of two lifestyles. *Les Endormies* is, in effect, an educatory dialogue between the modern woman assimilated to the culture of France and the traditional woman of Islam. Called Noura—light—by her French "aunt," she felt "destined to bring enlightenment to those who were still in obscurity."[48] But, Noura finds herself "up against absurdity, a discreet irony, often an unexpected logic or a certain inertia that seemed to be a gracious form of calculated incomprehension, if not hostility."[49] Toward the end of the book, Noura, sitting on the tomb of a marabout, thinks wistfully of these "enchanted, slumbering women" and the way in which she, who "had no magical powers, was able to penetrate into their kingdom of magical spells." She reflects that she has witnessed their tranquility and peace of mind and "that nonchalance, required by ancient tradition, which enslaved them." They had been enveloped for so long by the odor *(parfum)* of a tradition that their ties to it were either indestructible or else too dangerous to break.[50] Boisnard's work spoke to the attraction of the Orient, while underscoring the fact that the differences between the two cultures were too great to bridge with any real success. Like Eberhardt, Boisnard had an affinity with Islam, which she believed placed her in a unique position to understand the Algerians. On a number of occasion in *Les Endormies*, she refers, with respect, to the rare talent and nomadic temperament of Si Mahmoud Saâdi [Eberhardt], who, dressed in a student's burnouse [Arab cloak], sang the song of the South and the Bedouin soul."[51] If an understanding of Islam and an attraction to the exoticism of the Orient was a bond of sorts between the two writers, unlike Eberhardt, Boisnard came from an established settler background. Unlike Eberhardt, whose relationship to Islam was defined by mysticism and an association to the masculine, Boisnard's affinity to Islam translated into a desire to educate and improve the Algerian, and the means to this end was to be through women. Her association, therefore, was to the feminine.

A year after the publication of *Les Endormies,* on November 20, 1910 Charles René-Garnier, a Parisian lawyer and former secretary of the Geographical Society of North Africa, gave a speech at the Geographical Society of Normandy, in which he dwelt on the importance of Muslim women to the French cause. It was to become a tenet of French colonial practice in Algeria. Addressing the French women in the audience, he stated:

> Do not for a moment believe, dear ladies, that these [Muslim] women have no heart. Like you, they have young girls who are very sentimental with poetic oriental souls; they become perfect wives, spending their entire lives working at home, preparing food and clothes for their husbands, who beat them when

angry, yet they care for their children like good mother hens. And nearly
remain scrupulously faithful to their husbands . . .

It is to the mothers of Muslim families who must be endowed with French souls
for they will in turn model the virgin souls of their children. It is to them that you
must demonstrate what they can expect from such a change *(cette evolution)*.[52]

This extract from a speech that was often ambiguous in its depiction of
Arab women, was as much a call for French women to do good works in
the North African colonies as it was an object lesson in proper feminine
behavior, at a time when agitation for women's rights was perturbing gender
norms.[53] Although the war temporarily suspended such preoccupations, in
its aftermath anxieties of gender and, in the colony, of interracial relations
resurfaced and the call for women's involvement in the colonization process
was reanimated. The interwar period in Algeria was characterized by political (the vote) and social (race relations) struggles that pitted nostalgic ideas
about tradition against "modern" ideas about society.

At war's end there were important differences between Kenya and Algeria,
which shaped political and social relations and women's responses to them.
In the first place, unlike Kenya, in Algeria only about 10% of the settler
population lived off the land.[54] Most of the settler community was therefore
urban, with the largest concentrations being in Algiers, Oran, Constantine,
and Bône.[55] Whereas Nairobi, the largest European center in Kenya, was
still a "collection of huts," Algiers and its surroundings in 1921 had a total
population of 206,595 souls. Of the 195,655 in the city itself 47,669 were
Muslim (Arab and Berber), 117,050 were French, and 30,936 were foreigners, mostly European.[56] Although Constantine retained much of its Algerian
identity, Algiers, Oran, and Bône had acquired a definite aura of Frenchness.[57]
Additionally, the fact that Algeria was considered to be an extension of France
reinforced the idea among the settlers that their dominance was not only
assured but, as personifications of what it meant to be French, domination
was their right. Differences in the urban rural settler ratio in Kenya and Algeria, differences in British and French ideas of dominance, and the differences
in the colonial policies of indirect and direct rule, defined interracial relations
in the two colonies. Unlike Kenya where the relationship of the majority of
settlers with Africans was in terms of labor, as members of an essentially urban
population, settlers in Algeria came into contact with Algerians from across
the social spectrum. The length of French occupation also meant that urban
Algerian men had acquired enough familiarity with French ways, to make
their presence felt both politically and socially. Urban living socializes and
introduces individuals more rapidly to change than rural existence and in the
colonial context this meant socializing to the French language and culture.
However much settlers may have vaunted their superiority and dominance;
in the interwar period anxiety about race was conditioned by the complexity
of the relations between the colonizer and the colonized. In Algeria the more
complex racial relations of urban existence triggered settler anxieties about
the Algerians that were social, political, and economic. In Kenya where, with

the exception of labor concerns, Anglo-African relations were left largely to the officers of the colonial administration, settler anxieties were shaped by economic and political concerns; socially the Africans could be and nearly always were overlooked.

The similarity between the two colonies came from the settler desire for low-cost labor, on the farms, in the home, and at the lowest ranks of the tertiary sector. Settlers consistently took measures to maintain the status quo and keep the upper hand so that the supply of cheap labor remained steady. Unlike Kenya, where the Indians contributed in significant numbers to the merchant and trader class and to the tertiary sector of the economy, in Algeria, Europeans were invested in these sectors. The bulk of the settlers formed a middle class, which was made up of artisans, traders, civil servants, and professionals. As in Kenya there were distinctions between settlers, but unlike Kenya where these distinctions arose out of behavioral patterns based on social class, in Algeria, where class was meritocratically based, in theory if not in practice, distinctions "were founded on an order that scorned the defeated, the weak, and the poor, denying them true humanity. As such the Arab and the Spaniard [or the French citizen of Spanish origin] provoked the same degree of contempt."[58] For whatever reason, the less successful settlers were relegated to the bottom of the European hierarchy in the colonies, their ultimate degradation being "to go native." Unlike Kenya where interracial unions were socially "inconceivable," in Algeria it was not so much miscegenation that was the "sin," but the loss of French cultural identity that such a union implied.

Contempt was not the only factor that soured relations between the settlers and their "subjects." The disparity between French humanist ideas and colonial reality created tensions among Algerians that increased steadily throughout the interwar period. Whereas Algerian resistance to French rule in the nineteenth century had been characterized essentially by revolts and uprisings occurring outside the main urban centers; in the early twentieth century Algerians switched from instigating revolts to organizing strikes and campaigns for reform in urban centers.[59] Additionally, written protest appeared in the form of newspaper articles, poems, and plays penned by Algerian men.[60] Throughout the interwar period, Algerian men agitated for increased rights and inclusion in the franchise.[61] There were two conflicting responses to the recriminations and demands of the Algerians. On the one hand, the settlers blocked Algerian demands for the franchise and, hence inclusion in the French political fold; French women played a role in preventing this. On the other hand, there was the desire to inculcate French [read secular] values into the local population; French women contributed through their communication with Arab women.

In the 1920s colonial women responded to Garnier's call to use their influence among Arab women to spread the French word. Women were deemed to have an advantage over men in their ability to portray the intimacies of Arab society, due to their access to Arab women. "The doors of the gynaecium, which remain closed to European [male] travelers, open before her. Thanks to her [it holds] no more secrets."[62] During the interwar period, therefore, the feminization of the colony gathered speed as women consciously moved into the public sphere using the opportunities the colonial situation provided. Although most such women were wives first and public figures second, their high profile helped to create the much-vaunted image of dynamism attached to the colony. One such woman was Marie Bugéja (1875?–1957).[63] The daughter of administrators who had come to Algeria from Brittany, she married an administrator and started to take an interest in the lives of Algerian women, although she was initially discouraged by her fellow colonists, who felt Muslim women should be left in obscurity.[64] The conflict between Bugéja's convictions and settler disapproval of her activities illustrates the tensions that so often existed between administrators and settlers and more pertinent to what follows, the differences in their narratives. Administrators who toed the metropole imperial line and mainland French, who visited or settled temporarily in the colony, were seen as idealists who lacked the pragmatism of the settlers when it came to dealing with colonial issues and in particular with the "natives." Bugéja's research, in spite of being carried out against the "better judgment" of her peers led to the publication in 1921 of *Nos Soeurs musulmanes.* It was a paean to Algeria and French colonization as well as a defense of Algerian women. Bugéja argued that by educating them French interests would be served, as they would pass on French values to their children and husbands.[65] She stressed that as a daughter and wife of administrators in Algeria, she had gained an in-depth knowledge of Algerians from across the social spectrum, and she knew that French women could "conquer the hearts" of their Algerian counterparts and thus promote integration.[66] Her enthusiasm for integration with the Algerians stopped short at the prospect of inter-marriage. Citing the work of a certain C. Mairin, as advocating inter-marriage for solving integration, she pointed to the poor results of such unions formed during or immediately after World War I, when French women married Algerian servicemen.[67] These women, she declared, had no idea what they were letting themselves in for and once in Algeria they either tried to escape the "hell" *(enfer)* they found themselves in or, if they chose to remain, they immersed themselves in the "native" milieu and avoided all contact with Europeans. These civilized women would become embittered, angry *Mauresques.*[68] It was the loss of French identity that was so deplorable; the secular modernity of French civilization being engulfed by antiquated theocratic Islam. Bugéja felt strongly enough about the question of inter-marriage to write a novel about the impossibility of its success.[69] During the twenties, Bugéja had communicated her ideas by means of a series of lectures, which were published in 1929.[70] Bugéja's switch to fiction in the early thirties extended her audience, allowing her to popularize her views on colonial society.[71] In 1930 Bugéja's colonizing and, as yet rudimentary, literary efforts were crowned when she became a laureate of the *Grand Concours littéraire du centenaire de l'Algérie de la Ville de Paris.* By 1938 she had acquired the added distinction of *"laureate de l'Institut de France."*

Another woman who became interested in the educational relationship between French and Arab women was Annette Godin (1875–1958). Unlike Bugéja, Godin saw it as a two-way learning process:

> I do not know what the Arab woman will gain from us, or indeed whether she will gain anything, but I am certain that, [her] lessons will not be lost on us, and our spouses have much to gain if we Arabize a little. The French woman will become more of a homebody (*plus casanière*) more flexible, more tender and more submissive; coquette in her home but not outside (*pour la rue*); more truly a woman.
>   Isn't this form of feminism equal to the other? Our spouses prefer it and society has nothing to lose—And thus—we would have more children and more happiness.[72]

Godin was born in Saint-Maixint but grew up and trained as a primary school teacher in Algeria.[73] She first taught in Bougie and then in Constantine together with her husband, Henri Paulignan, also a teacher, with whom she had three children. The couple held a number of posts together in Algeria, and Godin turned to poetry and novels to describe different aspects of the country she considered her home. She was associated with the *Algérianiste* school, whose founding member and leading literary light of the colony, Robert Randau, described her as one of those authors who, under the general heading of *Barbaresque*, published tales of local (*indigène*) intrigue in classical style.[74] She was a member of the Association of Algerian writers, formed in the 1920s, whose purported aim was to rectify the misinterpretations of writers who wrote about Algeria without any real knowledge of the land and its people and "to enlighten the French public on the exact psychology of their Algerian compatriots, Muslim and non-Muslim . . . to soothe misunderstandings between the races."[75]

Au pays du Myrte, from which the above extract is taken, was not a novel, but a homage to Algeria. Written during the last years of the war and published in 1921 it was Godin's first book. The underlying message that emerges as one reads is that the beguiling beauty of Algeria, where traditional gender relations are valued, make it an ideal place to escape from the turmoil of the metropole. The natalism expressed in the passage above is echoed in less overt ways at intervals throughout the text. It responds to the demographic fears of the metropole, but it also reflects the importance to colonial society of traditional gender norms. Lisette Martini, an author of *pied-noir* origin, writing with a certain degree of wistfulness 75 years later, described the family unit in Algerian settler society as a place where gender roles were very clear. Men, who alone worked to support the family, were respected and women venerated. It was a society whose unwritten rules, and here she quotes Albert Camus, were "never to let one's mother down, to respect women in the street, and to show consideration to women who were pregnant."[76] In short, it was the fecundity of women that made them objects of veneration. Godin's first work reflects the attraction for the exotic that characterized much fin-de-siècle literature and was picked up after the war as an escapist panacea. If her suggestion that French women had something to learn from their Arab counterparts underlines the colony's aspiration to maintain traditional gender norms, it also points to the feature that characterized so much of colonial women's writing in Algeria, and set it apart from colonial women's writing in Kenya, namely its focus on the relationship between the races.

Godin's first novel, *L'Erreur de Nedjma,* published two years after *Au pays du Myrte,* is the story of Nedjma d'Astier, who, as her name suggests, is the product of a Franco-Arab union, the daughter of a wealthy Arab and a French officer. That her given name is Arabic and her family name is French perpetuates the gendered imagery of colonialism as a masculine power dominating a female colony. Torn between two identities, traditional Arab and modern French, it is the Frenchness of her Father that wins out. Nedjma cannot bring herself to identify with Arab women, who "are so calm, those carefree child-women, whose whole life is cloistered, controlled, spoilt, without temptation or emotion . . . No! I do not want a bridle, I want to run free, to have knowledge, to feel." [77] Two aspects of this passage are noteworthy. The first is that some women writers were countenancing mixed unions, which in Kenya they did not. Whereas sexual relations between Africans and Kenyan settlers were unpardonable; in Algeria the attraction of the "erotic Orient" excused interracial sexual relations (nearly always French men and Arab women). More often than not, however, the fictional outcome was a failure, echoing the *colon* adage that "boiling a French person with an Arab in the same pot always produces two stocks."[78] The second point to retain is the notion of the Arab woman as a woman-child *(femme-enfant).* The woman-child concept, which was a recurring image in colonial writing, implies that like children, Arab women were in need of socializing. It also suggests their subjugation to parental control—in this case the Arab male—a hindrance that separated them from what it meant to be modern; an irony given Godin's apparent preference for traditional gender roles.

The works of Godin, and Bugéja reflect the social debates about gender and race that were taking place in the colony. The difference in their attitudes toward interracial union was conditioned by gender, reflecting both metropole attitudes toward equality and the legal debates in the colonies regarding the acquisition of French citizenship for the offspring of mixed unions. Whereas its acquisition in all cases hinged on the importance of acquired Frenchness, a patrilineal descent was nearly always favored over a matrilineal one in a court of law.[79] In the traditional gender framework the sexuality of French men made it acceptable for them to be attracted to the alluring mystery of colonized women, it was not so for French women, who would lose their Frenchness and their virtue by doing so. Godin's appeal for a return to the traditions of the virtuous, submissive wife, and her acceptance of the French man/Arab woman relationship, and Bugéja's condemnation of the French woman/Arab man relationship were each, in their own way, defining a traditional gender framework as the desirable one for the colony. But there was a paradox in the narratives of well-defined gender roles and the need to introduce the Arab woman to progress along French lines. The former was nostalgic in its desire to recreate a traditional stability that had seemingly been lost, the latter was deemed to be progressive insofar as it advocated endowing traditional Arab women with the values of modern French civilization.

The emphasis, in these works, on the beauties and attractions of Algeria was also a means of promoting the colony's multiple attractions at a time when its economy was under considerable strain. As Bugéja was to put it in 1935, "It is agreeable *(doux)* for me to transcribe the sensations one feels, to exalt its beauties, and to deepen its secrets."[80] The lyric descriptions of Algeria expressed did not only target metropole readers. They reinforced among the settlers, a love of the land, which as "an extension of the motherland [was] ours to the very fiber of its soul."[81] The role of colonial women as educators was as important to the settler community as it was seen to be for Arab women. Women who wrote, read and believed in these colonial narratives of nostalgia-in-the making socialized colonial children.

There was a didactic quality to all these works. For women like Bugéja, who was conscious of her role as a member of the "mother race of the World . . . that had won over territories *(les Terres)* to its language, its science, its spiritualism and its inextinguishable valor; the mother race that would exist until the end of time," preaching its mission was natural.[82] Bugéja made an imperialist virtue of being an administrator's wife, blurring the distinction between private and public by using her position as a dutiful spouse to further her own and her country's agenda. As settler society developed women took opportunities to move into the public sphere where, in the metropole, they might have been less likely to do so. The point to emphasize about settler society is that although it was structured along traditional gender lines and social positions were clearly differentiated, competition for such positions was much more limited than in the metropole. Thus an administrator's wife or a schoolteacher, for example, could attain wider social recognition in the colony than would be possible in the metropole.

By the end of the decade, the attention colonial women focused on Arab women was being echoed by some Algerian men. An article in the news bulletin *Akhbar*, reproduced a letter to the newspaper, the *Dépêche Algérienne*, by a certain Monsieur Mohammed Taouti, who declared that:

> the beneficial work *(oeuvre bienfaisante)* of the French in Algeria will never bear fruit if [Algerian] women do not benefit from this grand education . . . The indigenous woman remains cloistered in her home . . . From France, our adoptive mother, she can expect help . . . Let us educate Muslim women, for the good of the country as well as for the women themselves, let us guide them toward progress and emancipation.[83]

Much like the African letter about the Indian question, Taouti's letter can be interpreted as an opportunistic endorsement of colonial ideologies. The more appropriate interpretation, however, is that whatever the Algerians may have felt about the French occupation, the carrot of modernity, which the colonial powers dangled in front of their "subjects," was not yet seen to be the mirage it actually was. For if the colonial powers preached the benefits of modernity, settler society remained anchored to traditions of social inequality that belied its modern stance.

It was in the political sphere, with the question of the franchise that the manifestation of this inequality was brought out into the open. Interwar Algeria was a period of struggle for the vote involving Algerian men and women and, of course, French women who, unlike their counterparts in many democratic countries, had not yet been granted the vote. With regard to Algerian men and women, the first article of the 1865 Sénatus-Consulte established that the Algerian *(l'indigène algérien)* was French, but governed by Muslim law. French rights would only be bestowed if the individual accepted governance by French civil and political laws, in other words renouncing the personal statute of Islam. There was no mention of the Algerian woman in this document. In 1919, however, a law was promulgated containing a clause pertaining to Algerian women married to men who had been naturalized.[84] Whereas married women could thus become citizens, single women could not. The 1919 law provided certain Algerians with political rights, that is, voting rights. These rights were, of course, reserved for men. The fear appears to have been that granting rights to unmarried Algerian women, who were beyond the reach of French patriarchy, might cause unrest in the colony and, furthermore, disturb French gender norms by provoking demands for the vote by French women. On July 10, 1925 in a debate in the National Assembly, the Deputy, M. Roux-Freissineng, asked, "how can the indigenous woman lay claim to the rights of a French citizen [i.e., the vote], which are not accorded to the French woman?"[85] The question of women and the franchise, which, in relation to Algeria, will be discussed in more detail in chapter five, was being debated in France throughout the twenties.[86] Those in favor believed women's exceptional activities during the war entitled them to the vote. As Raymond Poincaré stated in a speech to the *Ligue française pour le droit des femmes* at the Tro- cadero Palace in December 1921: "They were men's equals during the war; in peace time we do not want to deny them the means of making their voice heard; nor do we want to prevent them from working with us to uplift our nation."[87] In spite of a substantial backing on the part of French deputies, successive attempts to grant women the vote were blocked by the Senate. The denial of the vote to French women in the metropole was to become an additional argument in denying the vote to Algerians.

Conclusion

Colonial women's voices in postwar Kenya and Algeria reflected different realities, insofar as Kenya was in a much earlier stage of settlement than Algeria. But World War I was a pivotal moment in both colonies as wit- nessed by the elevation of settler women from helpmate on family farms and in businesses to proprietor or manager, where they held their own until the return of their partners from the front and often well beyond. In the aftermath of the war, the Soldier Settlement Scheme and other attempts to draw settlers to Kenya led to extensive land expropriations. In Algeria natalist ideologies that emerged in France as a result of the catastrophic losses during the war, were echoed among the settlers in the preoccupation with fertility and the maintenance of traditional gender roles. Furthermore, the political issues in each colony, although grounded in the inequality of the races, were experienced and approached differently. In both colonies, an increased need for cheap labor and demographic anxieties about racial imbalance led to colony-specific ways of differentiation. In Kenya class and a strict adherence to maintaining all round racial distance determined the shape and power structures of settler society, whereas in Algeria where the social hierarchy was more complex and intermixing did occur, it was degrees of Frenchness that became the signifier of colonial clout. Inevitably, modernity and civilization in Kenya and Algeria was imagined as the quintessential essence of what it meant to be British in the former or French in the latter.

Women's voices in both colonies combined strains of restorative nostalgia with narratives of modernity, that is to say what was perceived to be a "civilized" social, cultural, and political framework. If women's letters, memoirs, and nonfiction provide us with an image of colonial women's realities, imagined or otherwise, the fictionalization in colonial women's novels of the situation in twenties Kenya and Algeria complicates this image. Reality is deflected into narratives of exoticism and nostalgia, and modernity is fictionalized in terms of cultural difference. The personal strategies and literary ends of women writers were inevitably shaped as much by the environment of the individual colonies as their responses to it and, as we shall now see, these lived differences defined the way in which they wrote modernity and created patterns of nostalgia.

CHAPTER 4

WRITING AND LIVING THE EXOTIC

I loved those walks in the quiet darkness of Africa . . . All these things wove their spell upon me. They were part of the strange soul of Africa—the land that had taken us as her own, to make or to break . . .

Florence Riddell

Oh! Cette patrie d'Afrique! Maintenant qu'on l'arrachait à elle, combien il l'aimait

Elissa Rhaïs

The twenties saw an increase in the literary output of women in both colonies.[1] In Kenya it was the early beginning of a literature that would expand in the thirties and forties; in Algeria the period marked the consolidation of colonial women's voices into a "female" genre that was seen to have a true understanding of interracial relations, and thus to be its most accurate representation. Colonial women's novels, whether in Kenya or Algeria, reflected metropole anxieties as much as they depicted a particular vision of the colony. In the aftermath of World War I, when the need was to forget the horror and devastation by recreating a semblance of stability, women responded by producing fiction in which the prewar status quo was packaged in an exoticism that belied colonial realities, while formulating a seductive image of the colony. The representational tropes they created and used laid the groundwork for the nostalgia that would become a part of the post-independence collective memory of the colonial past. The exotic in both Algeria and Kenya was perceived in the land and its peoples, and performed by the settlers in their leisure activities. In Algeria it was associated with the Mediterranean beauty of the land and the eroticism of Orientalism; in Kenya it was associated with the wildness of the flora, fauna and landscape and the pleasures their proximity could bring. In Algeria, Elissa Rhaïs (1876–1940) and Magali Boisnard (1882–1945) wrote and performed via the medium of the exotic.[2] In Kenya, Nora K. Strange (1884–1974) and Florence Riddell (c.1885–1960) exemplified colonial women, who wrote about and lived an adventure under "the wonderful spell of Kenya," as the promotional blurb put it.[3]

NOSTALGIA AS UNDERSTANDING "THE NATIVE"

In 1919 Rosine Boumendil, a Jewish woman indigenous to Algeria, made her entry onto the Parisian literary scene as Elissa Rhaïs, author of the novel *Saâda, la Marocaine*. At the time of her literary debut, Rhaïs was presented as an "Arab Muslim" woman, whose authenticity arose out of her personal experience of "indigenous" society.[4] Boumendil, which is an Arab-Jewish name, suggests that she may have been ethnically Arab, but she was not Muslim.[5] The fact she was categorized as an "Arab Muslim" was no mere publicity ploy; it was also indicative of the colonial discourse that elided the ethnic entity of Arab with the religious entity of Muslim. Rhaïs was born in Blida in 1876, where she attended primary school and then continued her education at the *École des Religeuse de la Doctrine* until 1894. Her first marriage to Rabbi Moise Amar produced three children. She divorced Amar in 1914 and re-married another Jew, the wealthy merchant Mardochée (Maurice) Chemouil.[6] The choice of her pen name is noteworthy: Elissa is the less familiar name of Dido of Carthage and Rhaïs is the homophone of Raïs, or leader in Arabic. According to Jean Déjeux, her son Roland claimed it was his classics professor, M. Da Costa, who provided her with the pseud-onym.[7] But it has also been imputed to Plon as her contract with that press states that she was "born in Blida of Muslim origin, [and] learned French at the village school."[8] Whoever it was, it obviously resonated with the colonial author and ideologue, Louis Bertrand, who encouraged her to go to Paris and promoted her work, and with René Doumic, editor of the *Revue des Deux Mondes,* who first serialized her work.[9] Whether the choice was just a marketing gambit or an attempt to create a more authoritative self with the added aura of enchantment, her acceptance of this new identity helped to land her a five year contract with the French publishing house, Plon. Over a period of 20 years, she published 12 volumes of fiction (10 novels and 5 novellas) and had short stories included in two anthologies, appearing in one of these alongside Luigi Pirandello.[10] Although the authenticity of her identity was sometimes questioned she was deemed to have "a great depth of knowledge of the Arab soul and customs."[11] Such was her popularity that some of her works were translated into Norwegian, Finnish, Swedish, and Russian.[12] In Paris, she held court in her apartment in the Left Bank, where she reinforced her image of the "authentic and exotic Muslim" by receiving her guests in the "oriental" finery of turbans and caftans. Rhaïs wrote sen-timental romances, which today would be classed as *romans de bibliothèque de gare* or romantic fiction[13] (fig. 4.1). As one rather patronizing reviewer put it: "if ever there were doubts as to whether mediocre adventures could charm and move merely by accentuating the primitive aspects of humanity,

Figure 4.1 Elissa Rhaïs, c. 1920. Reproduced with permission from the Bibliothèque Marguerite Durand, Paris

Elissa Rhaïs dispels them."[14] Her plots evoked the perceived sexuality and mystery of the Orient, her descriptions were often titillating, and the violence and passion of her Arab characters reflected stereotypes of Islam as violent. Nonetheless, Robert Randau, one of the leading literary figures of the colony, grouped her with Godin and Boisnard as one of the "exquisite women novelists" *(exquises romancières)* of the colony, thus endorsing the authenticity of her portrayals of "indigenous" society.[15]

Boisnard, meanwhile, lived with her physician husband, Pierre Crespin, whom she married in 1910, in the Algerian town of Biskra in an Arab-style house, decorated with local textiles and rugs.[16] There, she would greet her guests, often dressed in Arab or Berber dress, thus emphasizing her love of Islam and all things Islamic and reflecting the fact, as one contemporary opined, "She [had] been brought up to live the Arab life among the Arabs."[17] She created an "oasis" of her own, where she grew date palms and other local fruits and vegetables, which she would serve with camel's milk in olive-wood containers hewn from local trees. She was, as her friend and fellow author Robert Randau put it, "[A]n Orientalist to her very soul *(elle est orientaliste dans l'âme)* . . . more closely allied to schools of Arab poetry than she was to our [French] literature" "whose work was suffused by the sun (*pénétré de soleil*)."[18] Boisnard's immersion in "indigenous" culture was a manifestation of her interest in the history and ethnography of Algeria, an interest that was mirrored in the subject matter of her novels.[19] Her numerous works included an account of the Sultans of Touggourt and historical fictions of the fourteenth-century North African historian, Ibn Khaldoun, and the seventh-century Berber heroine, the Kahena, which she stated were based on Arab texts.[20] She was a more accomplished writer than Rhaïs, receiving literary accolades of a more prestigious nature.[21] Nonetheless, both women, in their own ways, were instrumental in establishing a fictional space in which an "understanding" of the "indigenous" population palliated settler-Algerian antagonisms.

Rhaïs' first novel, *Saâda la Marocaine* (1919) was serialized in the *Revue des Deux Mondes* and was followed in quick succession by a series of novels and novellas.[22] Although there were critics who had reservations about her work, her success was such that her novels were reedited multiple times and her fiction was published in some of the best literary journals of her day.[23] She found favor with established figures such as Colette and Paul Morand, and became popular in literary circles, where her tales of the lives and loves of Muslim men and women were hailed for their exoticism.[24] Muslim women, she told the journalist Hugette Champy, "were terribly spoilt by their husbands, who only sought to please their wives, even though they were insanely jealous of them . . . Arab men are sensual," she explained "and their wives are their most precious earthly jewel."[25] She was, according to one critic, "[A] writer of great imagination, whose rare talent was coupled with the temperament of both a poet and a landscape artist."[26] The aim of her storytelling "was to explain the complex character of the Oriental," for, she knew Arab men well. Describing their relationship to France, she said:

> They come to Paris to educate themselves, they wear dinner jackets with ease, dance perfectly, become Western in appearance, but their soul does not change, it remains poetic, childlike and refined. As soon as they return to their homeland, they reject their dark dress and put on their white burnouses and matching turbans . . . With these vestments they slip back into their true mindset intact, that of the perpetually voluptuous, ablaze *(embrasés)* with endless love.[27]

Although this passage is a reflection of the colonial stereotypes of the Arab as incorrigibly "Oriental" and an essentially sexual being, it also suggests a juxtaposition of the modern, rational, mature Westerner against the traditional, emotional, childlike "Muslim" who is essentially duplicitous. More implicit is the notion of Algeria as an erotic, sexual space. A notion that would be internalized by the *pieds-noirs,* who not only saw themselves as hardworking, virile, and productive but believed that their "roots" in a land, burned by the sun and washed by the sea, made them so.[28]

In Rhaïs' first novel, Saâda, a Moroccan woman from Fez, moves to Blida in Algeria with her husband, Messaoud, after the departure to the front of his French employer leaves him unemployed. Messaoud had grown used to "the jovial good nature, frankness and gentleness of his Roumi (Algerian Arab term for European) [employer]" in Fez, where he knew he could not find a similar position so he decided to try his luck in French Algeria.[29] In this 300-page novel, Rhaïs introduces her readers to the ethnic tapestry of Algerian society. Like many of her works, it is the tale of deception and betrayal, and the eventual downfall of the heroine, who transgresses the social boundaries of her society. In this case, Saâda, finding herself uprooted to a land that is not her own, responds to her dislocation and impoverished circumstances by taking to a promiscuous lifestyle, thus ruining herself and the honor of her husband and family. Its exotic eroticism is at once alluring and disturbing. The attractions of the Orient are personified in the nubile Saâda, but these same attractions lead to her downfall. It is a cautionary tale of what awaits a woman, who violates familial norms and espouses sexual freedom. In this, and in many of her other stories, which I have described elsewhere, Rhaïs responds to anxieties about the modern, liberated woman by suggesting that tranquility and happiness come from toeing the traditional gender line.[30] As one critic put it: "Could it be that [this tale of] the Orient of the Orientals, [presented] in a different guise, but with the same anxieties, was the obsessive face of the universal modern social question."[31] Exotic women were laudable; disruptive women were not. But the exotic for Rhaïs, is also the overtly feminine. For all her oriental splendor, Rhaïs' exotic woman is ultimately compliant and responsive to male desire. Rhaïs' "authenticity," her understanding of "indigenous" society, so vaunted by her French male critics, was in fact an endorsement of stable gender frameworks; one of the representational tropes associated with nostalgia that she contributed to developing.

The more familiar form of nostalgia, engendered by dislocations of space and culture, also features in the novel. Coming from Fez, renowned for its Islamic architecture, Saâda is shocked by the banality and Westernization of Blida, " with its one storey European buildings that were slowly replacing the tiny Moresque houses . . . it seemed ghastly to her that the mysterious past and the soulless present should be in the same vicinity, rubbing shoulders only to reinforce their discord."[32] Although the passage highlights some of the difficulties arising when two different cultures live side by side, an ambiguous message is embedded in the fact that Saâda eschews modernity as represented by a French urbanism that eradicates or marginalizes traditional Arab living space. On the one hand, it reinforces colonial stereotypes of the "indigenes" being beyond the French Pale; on the other it vaunts Arab culture, thus reflecting contemporary preoccupations about colonial policies with regard to the populations in French North Africa. Rhaïs' heroine is from Morocco, which, at the time the novel was published, had been a French protectorate for seven years. General Hubert Lyautey, who was Resident-General in Morocco from 1912–1924, championed Islamic culture and made a conscious effort not to upset local sensibilities on the scale they had been disrupted in French Algeria. Lyautey's refusal to continence an influx of low-income settlers, of the sort that had colonized Algeria and marked it with what he considered their vulgarity, created a debate in both colonial territories. The paradox of the situation lies in the creation of Saâda as a Moroccan from Fez, a seat of Islamic learning and culture, whose downfall occurs among the ugly, soulless "modernity" of Blida, Rhaïs was endorsing the Lyautey line on the one hand and enforcing her own literary credentials as an authentic voice in tune with indigenous sentiments and behavior, thus providing a twist in the complex colonial relationship between visions of modernity and tradition.

Many of Rhaïs' works reflect contemporary issues in this way. I have shown elsewhere how *La Riffaine* (1929), uses symbolism to foreground the Rif War (1920–1926) or how *La Fille des Pachas* (1922) and *Les Juifs, ou la fille d'Eléazar* (1921) raise the issue of French, Arab, and Jewish relations.[33] Animosity between Jews and Muslims and between Jews and the French reflected reality in both France and Algeria. Settler instigated anti-Semitism was particularly virulent during the Dreyfus Affair and again in the 1930s.[34] But accuracy is not what Rhaïs is after. In *La Fille des Pachas* the married heroine, Zoulika, falls in love with a French army officer, who is a Jew but whom she believes to be a Christian. He keeps it to himself knowing that while Muslims were "indifferent to Christians, they hated the Jews."[35] When the affair is discovered, the officer is beheaded and Zoulika is condemned to death for adultery. Before the execution of the sentence she pleads for his life and it is then that she discovers that her lover is a Jew. Enraged at the deception, and insulted that she had been linked to a Jew rather than a Christian, she recoils in horror, instructing the executioner to get on with his job as she would no longer be a Muslim, if she were to live.[36] The misrepresentation lies in the fact that in strict Muslim practice a Muslim woman is considered defiled if she marries any non-Muslim, whatever the religion, and is punished accordingly. Rhaïs again provides an ambiguous message. On the one hand, the antagonism between Jew and Muslim is highlighted while the compatibility of Christian and Muslim is implied. On the other hand, there is no *deus ex machina* in the form of the French colonial state to stop the execution of a French officer for transgressing a tenet of Islamic law. Such a situation was, in reality, most unlikely but by presenting the denouement in this way Rhaïs implies the impartiality of the French state, when the needs of justice were being served. The Muslims, Jews, and Europeans (Christians) could live side by side but harmony could only be achieved by respecting the tenets of their respective cultures. It was an endorsement of the politics of Association. By focusing on the violent reaction of the Muslim Arabs to the transgression of cultural taboos by Zoulika and her lover, Rhaïs was also occluding the French refusal to accept the Arabs on par with themselves.

In her stories, Rhaïs typically inclined to resolving tensions between French and Arabs by creating the illusion of relative harmony. Harmony would of course be the logical outcome of a society where all its members were equals. In *Le Mariage de Hanifa* Miss Mathieu, the teacher from France, who manifests her "kind French generosity" by telling her multi-racial class that "[w]e are all equals, my dears."[37] Rhaïs emphasizes French values of equality and tolerance through the mouthpiece of her characters, but in the situational content of her tales she is usually clear about the social hierarchy. The civilizing mission of the French is endorsed through the allegiance of her leading Arab characters to the French cause, thus counterbalancing the grumblings of the minor characters about French occupation.[38] Rhaïs' fiction implicitly or explicitly advances the notion of the primacy of French civilization, while underscoring its desire for social harmony. Here again, then we have the development of an image of the colony, where the presence of France as a progressive [implicitly modern] force is coupled with a message of stability along traditional lines, whether it is gender stability achieved by the female compliance to male domination or social stability achieved by compliance to the colonial status quo.

Understanding the sexuality of the "native" was a key to Rhaïs' "authenticity" and an important dimension of her contribution to the creation of the post-independence nostalgic image of colonial Algeria. Although I have discussed the question of sexuality in colonial fiction elsewhere, the subject is worth revisiting briefly in order to emphasize its importance to the *pied-noir* image of themselves. Sexuality and violence are often closely linked in Rhaïs' tales. In *La Riffaine*, for example, the heroine, a rebellious beauty from the Rif mountains, informs the pro-French pasha in graphic detail, that she sexually enticed one of his lieutenants, sent against Abd-el-Krim (the leader of the Rif rebels). Provocatively leading him on, she declares: "To love a man and allow him to penetrate me, I have to know his heart and his secrets." When he was "mad with desire" she whips out her dagger and cuts off his penis *(et tandis qu'il était tout étourdi de désir, je lui tranchai le sexe!).* [39] The juxtaposition of sex and violence, which is supposed to be a portrayal of what the French officer in the book describes as "the curious nature of the Orientals, in whom charm and delicacy can be allied with violence and cruelty," forms a part of the attraction of Rhaïs' work, obliquely suggesting the pleasures of sado-masochism.[40] Violence as a sexual stimulant is reintroduced at the end of the novel when the rebellious heroine, now subdued, is brought " . . . ready for love . . . half naked under her veils" to the pasha who, prior to seeing her, had been imagining the way he would torture her. On seeing her thus prepared, his desire is heightened.[41] Fantasized violence connected to sexual ardor is of course erotically suggestive, which no doubt was one of the appeals of Rhaïs' work. The symbolism of the pro-Riffiane heroine being subdued by the pro-French pasha may also have added to its attractions. But it is Rhaïs' image of a land, where sex and violence were closely associated, that indicates the way in which nostalgia was being written. The sexuality of the Arab may have been Rhaïs' focus, but she was also speaking to the *pied-noir* community's image whose ardor and virile masculinity was not only connected to the land, but was also deemed to be responsible for its fertility.

What "Oriental" romance would be complete without the presence of the harem? As a well-known trope of Orientalism, which functioned both to titillate and to reinforce the notion of male supremacy, it featured in many of Rhaïs' novels. The harem, according to Rhaïs, was full of beauties, eagerly awaiting their turn for love. There they dwelt, "tossing on their couches, their bodies protected by gauze-like silk, [which if] torn revealed a black star shining in between two resplendent thighs. (*une étoile noir se decouvre entre deux cuisses resplendissantes*) *Ouf,* sigh these lovelorn women (*amoureuses*), our turn is so slow in coming."[42] This totally inaccurate portrayal of the harem suggests a high-class brothel. In fact the word means women's quarters in Arabic, and few were "full of beauties, eagerly awaiting their turn." In the limited number of harems in which there were numerous women the existence of most was monotonous. Indeed some women were even overlooked from a sexual point of view, having entered the harem for reasons other than marriage. The image of sexual compliance in the harem, as described by Rhaïs, is certainly in the Orientalist genre and belies the "authenticity" of her "insider" knowledge. By using the male gaze in her descriptions of female sexuality, furthermore, she is also promoting the male oriented vision of a compliant female as eminently attractive. Finally, she is departing from the usual method of implicit sexuality, usually used by women writers of romantic fiction at the time, by explicitly describing the body in sexual mode. While she herself is assuming the masculine erotic gaze, she is presenting traditional gender relations as desirable, and in the process adding to her own erotic charm as a woman who understands the needs of male sexuality.

Rhaïs was certainly a paradox, which added to her mystique. Her false Muslim identity and the overt sexuality in her stories, a sexuality that any Muslim woman would have kept very carefully under wraps, suggested the modernity that the French were advocating for their Muslim women subjects; in other words, a French education and an ability to interact successfully with French men and women, thus eschewing "Muslim tradition." Here was a "Muslim" woman whose depictions of sex and violence not only broke Muslim taboos but whose engagement with sexuality placed her among exotic figures such as Josephine Baker. A "modern" woman who moved from the private into the public sphere yet whose narratives, for all their exotic eroticism were essentially conservative in her approach to gender relations.

The reassuring quality of Rhaïs' tales whereby the rebellious desires of women, which were potentially disruptive to gender relations, were resolved to the advantage of the established order that promoted an image of harmony achieved. Rhaïs' work may have titillated sexually, but it was ultimately reassuring in a world where matters of gender were causing social anxiety. In 1982 the Algerian born journalist and author Jules Roy dubbed her "the George Sand of Islam" and summed up her impact in an article entitled *Le mythe d'une Algérie heureuse,* which appeared in *Le Monde*:

> Her books were redolent of cinnamon, henna, camel dung and spicy sauces, jasmine and absinthe. Elissa Rhaïs was deeply rooted in the people [of

Algeria] . . . She sang of all we loved and left for a more bitter and larger place
[*un ailleurs plus âpre et plus vaste*] she was . . . marvellously old-fashioned
[*suranné*] . . . she *incarnated* [my emphasis] the myth of Algeria as a happy
place, irreplaceable in our hearts.[43]

Rhaïs' tales, evocative, titillating, exotic, spun a web creating and entrapping
a nostalgia that would be intrinsic to so many post-independence memoirs.

Magali Boisnard was the flip side of the Orientalist coin. Her writing
career predated that of Rhaïs, and her style and personality were very different. She was hailed not for her exoticism but for her erudition with
regard to Islam. According to the critic(s) Marius-Ary Leblond, "She was,
of all the women [writers], the most richly gifted *(richement doué)* and best
informed French writer that Algeria had produced."[44] Doumic published her
poems in the *Revue des Deux Mondes,* and she was encouraged by the likes
of Pierre Mille, Gyp, and Jean Richepin.[45] Following the publication of her
first historical novel, *La Vandale,* in 1907 she was praised for her lively style,
for being erudite with modesty and for the way she excelled at presenting
the essence of things, environments, and landscapes. *(traduire le sentiment
des choses, milieux et des paysages).*[46] She lectured in the scholarly societies
of Algeria and then in Paris where, in 1909, *L'Echo de Paris, Le Temps* and
Le Figaro, hailed her easy-going eloquence and the depth of her ideas and
style. Following the publication of *Les Endormies,* she lectured on women in
Muslim society at the Alliance Française in Paris, in the salons of the feminist
newspaper, *La Française,* and at the Sorbonne, where she added a plea for
assistance to alleviate the famine afflicting the Arabs. Her lectures and con-
ferences were reviewed or reported on in leading French papers, and even
found their way into the Arabic press in Tunis.[47]

Boisnard's novels were more sophisticated than Rhaïs' even if they too
were firmly anchored in a colonial thematic. Her scholarly interest in Islam
and her close relationship to the literary personalities rooted her work in a
movement that would posit Algeria as a region of France, while looking to
past Mediterranean civilizations from whose springs the writers of North
Africa, as one writer put it, "owed their eternal youth."[48] Greece, Rome,
but also those of the southern shores of the Mediterranean, such were the
traditions from which "a magnificent *Algéro-Saharienne* literature" was
emerging.[49] Boisnard wrote three novels in the twenties, *Mâadith (1921), La
Kahena (1925),* and *Le Roman de Khaldoun* (1930), all connected in some
way to the Berbers.

Mâadith is the story of a young Kabyle (Berber) woman from the Djur-
jura mountains who joins a convent, converts to Catholicism, but is drawn
back into the Berber fold.[50] It is a complex novel in which Boisnard juxta-
poses colonial ideological discourses of gender, race and historical allusion,
with themes that foreshadow postcolonial concepts of cultural hybridity and
multicultural angst. When Mâadith enters the convent, she declares that her
"ancestors were certainly Christians and, by the grace of God and of the Holy
spirit. I have been restored to the Truth."[51] This statement mirrors a colonial

belief that the Kabyles may once have been Christians. It is Mâadith's passionate nature that draws her to Christianity and her sensuality that leads her back to her Muslim roots in her mountain home. Christianity provides her with a temporary space, where she sublimates her passions but she is eventually seduced by the "orient." Of course, Mâadith's temporary conversion to Christianity symbolizes the cultural assimilation that the French were purporting to introduce in the colony, and her return to her "native" roots is indicative of the prevalent idea that Muslims could never really become French. But, it is of note that Boisnard does not contrast the secular with the non-secular but rather Christianity with Islam, bringing both past and present into play. Unlike colonial ideologues who, by looking to Algeria's Roman past, envisioned the French oeuvre as a way of reclaiming Algeria for the West, Boisnard was suggesting that Algerians had multiple ideological pasts and even if Mâadith's ancestors had once been Christian, it was the more recent Islamic past that was critical in defining her identity.

There is a further ambivalence to the novel, which, although connected to the tug-of-war between the two cultures, transcends colonial discourse. When Mâadith enters the convent she takes the name Cécile. From this point in the novel until she leaves the convent definitively, Boisnard's preferred appellation for her is Mâadith-Cécile. Although the hyphenated name, with the Arab name preceding the French name indicates that Boisnard is implying that the Arab identity takes precedence over the French, it is also symbolic of the cultural hybridity that the colonial situation created but which would only be defined more clearly in the postcolonial (in both senses of the term) era. Like all hybrids, Mâadith-Cécile feels that she is "an outsider . . . pariah of two races. Hers because of her renunciation, and her adopted race because of her origins."[52] Mâadith's cultural alienation, represented by religion in the novel, is akin to that felt by both Maghrebi authors in the period immediately before and after decolonization, and by many second and third generation French Muslims of Algerian origin in France today.[53]

La Kahena, Boisnard's second novel of the twenties, focuses on the seventh-century woman of the same name who achieved mythical status over the years as a powerful symbol of Berber resistance.[54] Dubbed the "Joan-of-Arc of the Aurès" (a mountainous region and home to another Berber group, the Chaouia) she initially resisted the Arab invasion of the time but was finally vanquished and captured. Boisnard's interpretation of the story emphasizes the Kahena's expertize in both war and love but whereas her skills in the former lead to her glory, her skills in the latter lead to her downfall. Although Boisnard is embellishing the stereotype of the "oriental" woman by adding "Amazonian" qualities to her exotic appeal, the message that prevails is that however "exceptional" the woman, she will eventually revert to form by slipping back into her prime role of satisfying male desire. Boisnard, however, adds a twist in this case insofar as the male in question is an Arab, suggesting that such a reversion is in fact a betrayal. While this suggests Boisnard's own ambiguities about gender roles, it is the Arab/Berber conflict of the novel that reproduces colonial narratives. Whether this was the myth of Berber superiority over the Arabs, which developed in the nineteenth century due to French championing the Berbers over the Arabs, or whether it was the notion of the "usurping Arab," the narratives the novel endorses became part of the canonical colonial discourse. Quite apart from its positive reviews, a measure of the contemporary significance of *Le Roman de la Kahena* to the colony is the fact the novel was touted as a work that all French children should read.[55] It was an example of the type of Algerian literature "whose rays in all their splendor should penetrate [the] primary school classroom."[56] For its colonial messages, to be sure, but also for its historical content, for if French children were being taught about "nos ancêtres les Gaulois" or historical figures of mythical stature like Vircengetorix or Joan of Arc, so too should they be taught about such figures from Algeria, which was, as far as the French and the settlers were concerned, a province of France.

In *Le Roman de Khaldoun,* a historical novel about the famous Arab historian, Ibn Khaldoun, Boisnard suggests the connections between the various regions of the Mediterranean through both the genealogy and peregrinations of her main character. Khaldoun, she writes, had an "unusual (*rare*) and complex" personality, the result of a double heredity of "an Andalucian father and an African mother."[57] It was these different cultural traditions that made him such "a diplomat and peregrinating courtier" and led him to become "secretary, ambassador, confident, judge, master of eloquence ... minister."[58] His peregrinations across the territories of what was, in Boisnard's time, French North Africa (Morocco, Algeria, and Tunisia) underscored the connections between the three, and suggested that Khaldoun's ability to negotiate his way through the political upheavals of the different regimes was due to his patience, wisdom, and understanding of their respective political and social cultures. The novel may well have been intended as an object lesson for the French, but by means of its lyrical descriptions of the beauty of France's North African territories, in particular Biskra and the surrounding Berber areas, it also evoked their enchantment. Boisnard's exoticism was associated with the land and its people rather than a romanticized sexuality. In fictionalizing the colony's Arabo-Berber past, in works such as *La Kahena* and Le *Roman de Khaldoun,* and later in the *Sultans de Touggourt,* Boisnard was helping to popularize the interest in the colony's past that preoccupied and would continue to preoccupy colonial and metropolitan scholars throughout the colonial period. An increased interest in an area that had always elicited scholarship of some sort was hardly surprising given that the territory was now under French control. French scholars from all disciplines were working from within contemporary political, social and cultural frameworks, as most scholars do. Boisnard's chosen genre, which wove historical fact and colonial fictions together in symbolically suggestive ways, reached a much wider audience than the works of scholars who were her contemporaries. In doing so, Boisnard was writing a different sort of nostalgia from that of Rhaïs. It was restorative, in the sense that Boym uses the term, for it was using an imagined past to recreate a historical present. In other words, Boisnard appropriated an Arab-Berber past and reformulated it as part of the history of a settler colony. Historical fictions they may have been, but they were also formative fictions of a colonial present.

There is, however, a question relating to the persona of these two women that needs answering, namely what do the different colonial reactions to the cultural transgressions of Eberhardt, Rhaïs, and Boisnard signify? Why was Eberhardt reviled during her lifetime but Rhaïs accepted, and Boisnard championed? The interwar period as apogee of colonial Algeria was symbolized by the fanfare of the centenary celebrations of 1930. As settler society grew in assurance, demarcations within the society appeared to blur. Acculturation was beginning to occur on both sides of the racial divide. Appropriating "indigenous" customs or dress signified a cultural tolerance that was symbolic rather than real. The acceptance of such behavior, however, was limited. A token European, such as Magali Boisnard, could act as a symbol of tolerance and equality in an essentially unequal society. Symbolic tolerance and (or) equality were delusional tactics that responded to French Republican ideals. Isabelle Eberhardt had been castigated for her "Arab" ways and profligate behavior by a settler society that was unstable and in its formative stages. Elissa Rhaïs appeared on the literary scene in the aftermath of World War I. Algerians had fought on the side of the French, but had been given little else but medals and military pensions. Rhaïs became a symbol of what France could "do" for the compliant "indigene." Never mind that Rhaïs was not Muslim at all; she responded to a need both in France and Algeria: escapism in the former, symbolic equality in the latter. Boisnard was different from Rhaïs in that her work was considered more serious and more literary. Furthermore, the height of her career coincided with the development of the Algérianiste movement (see Chapter 5) whose manifesto stated that its aim was "to create an intellectual climate in Algeria common to the races living there and formed from their union."[59] The movement was unsuccessful in its aims and did not last long, but its rhetoric suggested that settler society was more egalitarian than it actually was. By the time Boisnard had created her literary persona, therefore, her sartorial and lifestyle transgressions were considered to be an extension of her writer's personality and their acceptance a sign of French tolerance toward the "indigenous" peoples.

NOSTALGIA AS "THE CALL OF AFRICA"

Florence Riddell and Nora Strange both experienced colonial life in India (Strange was born there) before moving to Kenya, where they worked.[60] Strange, who lived in Kenya for six years from 1913 to 1919, was the first woman to be employed in a business office in British East Africa. Riddell arrived just after World War I, but spent only four years in Kenya as her husband died while she was on leave in England and she did not return. During her Kenya years she tried her hand at a number of jobs, for she declared "I like starting new careers and I like making my own money and being independent of everybody—even of a quite satisfactory husband!"[61] She ended up running a school for the last two years she was in Kenya.

Riddell and her husband had been attracted to Kenya thanks to: "articles written by a certain English nobleman who was then busily advertising Kenya." They were thus "led to believe that anybody could start coffee-farming there on a capital of five hundred pounds and find [themselves] quite wealthy before many years had passed."[62] She was a feisty woman who, as she attests, wanted her financial independence, but Kenya did not prove to be the economic Eldorado that Lord Delamere's advertisements made it out to be. Like many couples, who went to Kenya hoping to make their fortunes, they ended up pumping their savings into what turned out to be the bottomless pit of their import/export business. Riddell's earnings from her Kenya "careers" went the same way as the couple's savings, so her independence proved to be morale-boosting rather than economically profitable. Nonetheless, her Kenya experiences primed her for the literary career that followed. The colony was an essential space for the creative writer she was to become.

When Riddell returned to Britain she found that she was no longer in tune with her fellow citizens: "Like many other returned travellers, I found myself sadly out of touch with the things which interested the Home people. . . . Everybody I know who has come back to England after living for years 'out East' . . . found themselves in the same position. We get 'out of touch' and cannot get into it again."[63] She decided to write about Kenya when she realized that her stories about Africa bored her friends and family, the "Home people" (she always capitalized Home when she referred to Britain), as much as she was bored by the pedestrian accounts of their lives in Britain. Her first novel, *Kenya Mist*, was serialized in the *Daily Mail* as "Love and the Lions," before being published in Britain and the United States in 1924.[64] The novel is notable as much for its colonial themes as for those of gender. It is a tale of the tribulations and romances of Michaela (so named because her parents had wanted a boy) Dundas and Glenison Ross, two cousins who go to Kenya when their partners desert them to live "in a mist of work and happiness" that would completely "shut off the misery" of their immediate past.[65] As women settlers they find themselves in good company for, as the novel explained, "the lone woman settler is rapidly becoming a common feature of Britain's youngest baby, Kenya Colony, where she lived cheerfully beating out an existence from her scant acres—coffee, corn, poultry, vegetables, all adding to her meagre store."[66] With the help of African labor—syces to tend their horses, and " house boys" to see to the domestic chores—the two women oversee the 600 acres that make up their farm, Kenya Mist, and bond socially with settlers whose interests, "coffee, [c]attle, natives and shooting," they share.[67]

As Glen would have it, the two women have put "men, marriage, misery" behind them for Kenya Mist is now "our man, our mate forever."[68] But Michaela's determination to remain independent and single is destabilized by the desire for a child. Although she laments that women cannot have "children without bringing men into the business" and rues the fact the "very destiny of a woman lie in the hands of a man?" she believes that "[t]o love a child of her own body is the meaning behind every woman's creation." It was not, she explained to her cousin "the common sexual craving, the craving of a lonely spinster," for the strenuous open-air life they led purged their minds and bodies "of such taints."[69] For she goes on:

> Men are ill at ease when one woman makes of him the hunted. It is his busi-
> ness to love many, and I doubt if . . . .Nature designed him even to know his
> own children. How then can he know Love? But, civilisation has perverted
> the instincts of womanhood and she showers too much affection, bestows too
> much thought on him who, after all, was planned merely as an instrument for
> her maternal happiness, who can never know love in its deeper sense, and then
> to her comes pain. False gods, Glen, false gods!"[70]

To achieve her maternal ends, Michaela seduces Carr, an upright English-men who believes that his kind must "uphold the honour of their country" otherwise "fairness and straight dealing will soon be a thing to be sneered at by [the] poor heathens."[71] When Michaela discovers she is pregnant she is delighted, but her female friends, including the woman doctor who exam-ined her, try to persuade her to marry the father, to which she replies "it was the baby I wanted . . . The man does not count."[72] Michaela has her child but keeps Carr in ignorance as to his paternity. After many vicissitudes, however, during which time Glen gets married, Carr does find out and the novel ends with his marriage to Michaela.

In much the same way as Rhaïs, Riddell presents her audience with an independent woman, a fighter who initially bucks society's conventions but is eventually brought into line with society's gender norms. Although such a denouement is to be expected from novels in the romantic genre, there are differences worth noting between those of Rhaïs and Riddell. The settings of both the authors' novels were certainly chosen with popular appeal and potential sales in mind, but they also picked up on the emerging metropole image and the attraction to what was exotic about each colony.[73] Exoticism inevitably had its sexual dimension and whereas in Algeria it was linked to the harem and the perceived eroticism of the Orient, in Kenya it was associated with the excitement of the pleasures offered by a game-filled "wilderness." To this could be added a fascination with the hedonistic antics of the Happy Valley social set, a small group of epigones of the British aristocracy resid-ing in the "white highlands," whose sexual activities and over-indulgence in stimulants of various sorts gained them a reputation in the interwar period and acquired legendary status after the murder of Lord Erroll, a prominent member of the set, in 1941.[74] Whereas the image of Happy Valley added to the mystique of Kenya as an aristocratic playground, the behavior of its mem-bers was a negation of the family and the inherent stability it implied. The sexuality in *Kenya Mist* is not, therefore, of the Happy Valley sort, even if it does suggest the sexual agency of a liberated woman. By having sex Michaela is not indulging hedonistic inclinations but maternal desires. In marrying Carr, whose fidelity and stalwart character mark him out as a desirable mate, not only is she finally accepting the "true" role of women, and thus aligning herself with staunch middle class values, she is also marrying a full-blooded male who knows both his duty to his country, his class, and his race. "I am a man," he tells his friend Mayne when they are discussing the question of inter-racial sex, "and I have felt at times all the wild desire of my manhood. But there is something about the smell of a black skin that would turn my passion from fire to ice!"[75]

Ann Stoler, among others, has pointed out the way in which inter-racial sex held the potential of the loss of dignity and respect and the resultant perceived danger to the social hierarchy[76]. As Mayne tells Carr:

> Many a poor little memsahib straight from Home, wonders why black ladies sitting at her garden gate snigger every time she passes, and many a native "boy" nowadays casts an eye on her fairness and cogitates "He took the women of our race, why should I not" So we white men deliberately introduce a new element of danger to the many dangers already surrounding our own women.[77]

The perceived danger to colonial women was a masculine fantasy, geared to camouflage and control inter-racial sexual attractions rather than a fear shared by both sexes. Colonial women were, on the whole, confident of the protective aura of racial superiority. Riddell, for one, declared in the autobiography of her travels: "I have never been nervous of natives. Few white women are, for there is something in our white blood which gives us a feeling of superiority over black blood."[78] Nonetheless, the perilous nature of interracial liaisons was a common theme in the narratives of all colonial novels. There was, however, a notable difference in approach between the novels coming out of Algeria and Kenya in the 1920s. In the case of Algeria, although such liaisons were destined to failure, suggesting their social undesirability, there was an implicit acknowledgement that the allure of the Orient made them understandable, if not acceptable. But for women writing in Kenya interracial sex was depicted as sordid and socially a taboo.

The characters in Riddell's novels are blatantly racist in their attitudes toward Kenyans. Whereas Rhaïs and Boisnard create an image of racial harmony through the benevolent paternalism of "understanding of the native," racial "harmony" in Riddell's novels is maintained through British superiority and the respect it engendered in the Africans. Indeed Riddell believed that working for Europeans was a sign of prestige in African eyes and she was irked when she imagined that white women were behaving in such a way as to "lower themselves in the eyes" of Africans.[79] The romantic novels set in Algeria, thus, projected the perception of a more racially tolerant environment, whereas those set in Kenya emphasized both the racially segregated nature of the British colonial environment and the need to keep it so. These differences were also manifested in French and British approaches to the acculturation of the "native" population to their respective cultures. As Riddell has one of her characters explain:

> The sooner you can talk to the boys in their own language the better it will be. Never let a boy speak English to you if you can help it . . . Treat them as

children . . . Don't let them come up to your level by allowing them to speak a single word of English to you. Go down to theirs by giving every order in the vernacular. They will respect and admire you all the more for it.[80]

Strange has a similar episode in her novel, *Imperial Mountain*.[81] Language is a potent means of control and in early twentieth-century Britain, how one spoke defined class and was an invisible barrier to social mobility. In the colonies, how one spoke English mattered less as national solidarity trumped that of class: "As you journey up and down the Colony . . . you may put in a night or two under the management of a couple whose names figure in Debrett, while you spend the following week-end in an establishment run by a little Cockney who is homesick for the sound of Bow Bells."[82] Class difference certainly played a role in the colonial social scene and, as we saw in the previous chapter, was deemed to determine an individual's behavior toward the Kenyans, but speaking down to the Africans was as much a way of ensuring that they did not acquire the wherewithal to progress as it was a way of maintaining their distance. The patronizing attitude that the characters in these novels so openly expressed was a quasi-universal sentiment among Europeans, no matter how well they treated the Africans, or how differently their inherent racism was performed. Knowing "how to behave" toward Africans implied an even-handed approach with African employees, treating them as faithful retainers, but the language of race was something in which few settlers did not indulge. Eventual equality, which may have been mooted as a long-term goal in the context of the republican ideology in 1920s Algeria, was not a consideration in Kenya.

The racism of Riddell's characters took a variety of forms, from emphasizing that Africans were "only one generation away from a state of utter savagery" to referring to them as "black brutes," "kukes," (for the Kikuyu) or other derogatory terms.[83] Although Riddell counterbalanced her malevolently racist characters by stalwart types whose benevolent paternalism toward Africans implied that she endorsed equitable inter-racial communication, there was no hint of condemnation of settler attitudes, however they were presented. Riddell's depiction of racism was not restricted to the colony, however. In her 1927 novel, *Kismet in Kenya*, she opens the novel with a portrait of British middle class ignorance of, and racist views on, Africa. When the heroine, Virginia Ann Stanhope, considers going to Kenya to take over the farm that has been willed to the family by a distant relative, she elicits the following reaction from her London-based relatives: "And what the Kike-you-yous are, heaven only knows—It sounds like a sort of little monkey . . .go out among a crowd of unclothed blacks! . . . are you quite mad?"[84] Although this is certainly an exaggerated metaphor for Riddell's conviction that her "Home" connections were as disinterested in colonial activities as colonialists were of those of the "Home" people, it is probably not an exaggerated portrayal of the racism often expressed in the middle class circles in which she moved.

In the same novel, when a bevy of Stanhopes from London arrives at the farm, what seems to shock them most is African nudity, in particular that of women: "the way these native women run about the farm half-naked is positively disgusting! It is degrading to us all."[85] Riddell depicts a sexual antagonism toward the African woman that does not exist in the women's writing from Algeria. The clothed "indigenous" woman, who was sequestered by her husband, and whose sexuality could therefore so easily be fictionalized—did not engender the same sexual anxiety as the nude African woman seen to be "parading" her sexuality for all to see, thus potentially provoking a sexual reaction among white males.

Among the prevalent themes of these early Kenya novels is that of the farm, as a site of emotional healing. Even when the plot does not revolve around the activities of farming, as in *Kismet in Kenya*, the farm—Nyumba-heri or Happiness House—serves as a stabilizing anchor for the characters in the novel, creating a sheltered space in which the multiple emotional and relational problems of the Stanhope family are resolved. Similarly, in her 1925 novel, *Out of the Mist*, the farm is both haven and home. Petronia, who marries Roy Baxendale because he is weak and needs her, "loved every stick and stone" of their farm, Shambara, and "the never-ending mystery of the lonely veld."[86] Inevitably she is engulfed in "the ravening flame of tragedy," but attains healing (both emotional and physical) in the haven of the farm, and the novel ends with it bathed in the colors of a glorious sunset.[87] The farm is a pivotal trope in the image of the harmonious colony. No matter how hard the work, or how acute the tribulations the return to tranquility that the site of the farm provided, privileged an agricultural setting over an urban one. The farm was not, of course, depicted as a modest homestead where a pioneer couple struggled to eke out a living but a sizeable agricultural domain with squatters, who provided labor when needed; an agricultural throwback to the pre-twentieth century squirearchy.

Nora Strange wrote over two dozen romance novels (fig. 4.2). In line with other works in the genre, Strange shares similar plot lines and gender themes with Riddell. I shall not waste time discussing these similarities, but rather focus on the differences in Strange's perspective on the colony. For both women the colonial space was a potential marriage market, but Strange expressed it in a much more forthright manner than Riddell. Her novel, *An Outpost Wooing*, first published in 1924, opens with the orphaned Joan Harvey being sent to India, on the understanding that she had to become engaged within a year. "From morn until eve, the more worldly-wise of her relations had preached the doctrine of social success. No girl ever landed in Bombay so thoroughly drilled as to her matrimonial plan of campaign."[88] Joan achieves her goal, and then breaks off her engagement to the consternation of her relatives. Having failed in one colony she moves on to another, Kenya, where she is more successful. Promoting Kenya as a site where the marriage potential was high was not just a variation on the sub-plot of the marriage stakes common to so many romantic novels. In the aftermath of World War I the number of single women in Britain rose as young war widows or single women who had lost their fiancés, brothers or fathers, found themselves bereft of male support (either emotional or financial, or both).

Figure 4.2   Nora Strange. Reproduced with permission from the National Portrait Gallery, London

The colonies were obvious sites for those whose lives had been disrupted by the war. Whereas the government introduced the soldier settlement scheme to attract veterans to the colony, the gendered bias of the scheme meant that hardly any women qualified for it. In an unofficial capacity, therefore, the romantic novels of Strange and Riddell, both of whom had experience of Kenya, strove to redress the imbalance of post–World War I male-oriented settler schemes by promoting the attractions of the colony as a propitious site for finding a partner. Of course it is impossible to claim, let alone ascertain, that these novels actually did attract women to the colony but that is beside the point here. What both writers did achieve, was to create an image of Kenya where the women who successfully settled there were adventurous, resourceful, and tough. If the colony was considered to be "a man's world" where traditional gender relations were valued, there was nonetheless plenty of room for adventurous women to participate in that world on par with men.

Strange's novels provide a broader picture of white Kenyan society and its politics than Riddell's. In *A Wife in Kenya,* published in 1925, Pierce and Beryl Napier go to Kenya for a year to run her uncle's farm and try to sort out their troubled marriage. At a Farmers' Association Meeting in Nairobi, Pierce represents his district and tries to calm the settlers whose attitudes toward the Indian question, their rage at the Colonial Office, and their anxieties about socialism have given rise to an unruly atmosphere and calls for action. In an appeasing tone he calls for moderation and states:

> We are units of the British Empire. We are practical men out here to make a living for ourselves and families . . . We know exactly what little good and what a lot of harm the Indian has done to the Colony. We also know that he is only out for himself and the moment he makes any money back it goes to India . . . it is no good crying murder and cursing the C. O. [Colonial Office], which is somewhere between the devil and the deep sea. On one side they have the agitators in India, who for their own ends, are making capital out of the question, and on the other, the Socialist element, who are out to make trouble whenever they can find a loop-hole . . . We have *got* to wait and see how far the canker of socialism has bitten into the constitution. It may be just a surface blight, but if it goes to the core, well then, we have a remedy, the same remedy that Italy found.[89]

During the early twenties the main focus for the increased antagonism between the Colonial Office and the settlers was due to the question of rights for the Indians but more generally there was the conviction that administrators in Britain had no idea how to handle problems in the colony. At the same time in Britain, the early twenties marked the beginning of the eclipse of the Liberals by Labour. Strange accurately portrays settler reactions to these events. The suggestion of a pro-fascist element among the settlers is also near the mark. Mussolini's brand of fascism was attractive to a minority of conservatives who admired the authority, order, and regimentation that the Italian regime represented. Indeed it was in the aftermath of the 1922 March on Rome that Rotha Linton Orm, the daughter of a British Army officer, formed the British Fascisti, later absorbed in Oswold Moseley's British Union of Fascists. A handful of the aristocracy also flirted with fascism.[90] In the colony the most notable "fellow-traveller" was Lord Erroll. Indeed Strange's description of the Farmers' Association meeting in her 1925 novel is a rowdier version of Nellie Grant's description of a similar meeting held at the Njoro Club in 1934, when Joss Erroll explained British Fascism to his fellow settlers:

> There was [*sic*] 198 people there, and a very good-tempered meeting, as everyone cheered to echo, whatever anyone said. Joss led off by explaining that British Fascism wasn't in the least like any other. It meant super-loyalty to the crown, etc., no dictatorship, complete religious and social freedom and "Insulated Empire.[91]

The fascism of the Erroll variety was of course linked to the desire to maintain order and discipline through the regimentation of a racial hierarchy. Settler resentment of Colonial Office personnel and socialists was connected to their condemnation of settler treatment of Africans, and what was deemed by the settlers to be undue interference in inter-racial policies by members of these groups. As the exasperation of Alan Gresham, reflecting on his term with the King's African Rifles, indicates in the opening pages of *Imperial Mountain*:

> He, for one, would never ask to command finer fighting material . . . he'd never want to handle, whether on the parade ground or on patrol duty, a better drilled and disciplined body of men. Even though his British regiment held his traditional allegiance, he had learnt during his two terms of secondment to the K. A. R. to appreciate the qualities of native troops. Between officer and men the colour bar didn't exist. *That* was the answer he gave, more often refrained from giving, since it was a waste of breath, to theorists. How he hated the intellectual breed! Fatuous, long-winded, self-opinionated individuals, from whose mental equipment common sense was lacking, yes . . . it was a waste of breath attempting to argue with them.[92]

Naturally enough, in a military regiment, the color bar would appear non-existent. A white officer commanding an essentially African regiment meant that due to the hierarchical structure of the military as an institution, the racial hierarchy would be maintained. Officers and men, whether in an all white regiment, or in a black regiment commanded by a white officer, were segregated socially by rank, so the racial separation would be maintained everywhere but on the battlefield. The operative phrase in the passage is "better drilled and disciplined" for whether the Africans were in a military force or in a labor force, the idea that the man/woman with colonial experience knew how to "drill and discipline," in other words to handle the African without the advice and interference of those lacking such experience.

When it came to inter-racial relations, therefore, Strange's novels differ little from Riddell's. Going native was unpardonable. As Pierce explains to Beryl (*A Wife in Kenya*) after she discovers she has been talking to a European who occasionally assumed a Masai identity: "he had no business to speak to you. When a man goes native, it should cut him off from knowing a decent white woman. Most of his kind have the gumption to know that."[93] Here again there is a clear distinction between the approach to masculine sexuality and to inter-racial sex in the writings of colonial women in Algeria and Kenya. If, for the women writing about Algeria such relationships are unfortunate; for the British they are squalid. Does this suggest that the fear of miscegenation was much stronger among the British than among the French? Perhaps. But it is possible to complicate the picture somewhat. Whatever French practices may have been, exclusion for the French was about the culture of Frenchness, a culture that, according to republican meritocratic ideas, could theoretically be acquired through education or socialization. An "understanding" that such relationships could occur was a nod to the republican values of equality and suggested a flexibility toward race, which in fact rarely existed. The British on the other hand, were not interested in assimilating the Africans into their culture. The more liberal minded settlers might well respect African cultural customs, but they did not want to turn them into British clones. Maintaining social and administrative distance was essential for the success of indirect rule and inter-marriage could undermine that distance.

If Strange's views about inter-racial sex were the same as Riddell's, the language of race of her characters was more muted. In *Imperial Mountain*, Strange describes the attitude of Mrs. Stroud toward her squatters as "that of a strict, but benevolent matriarch."[94] Mrs. Stroud's strictness was much the same as Gresham's well-drilled discipline. Benevolent paternalism was the predominant thread, a reflection too of Strange's view that "the average native is a curiously likeable individual. Likeable in the sense of being a mixture of an exuberantly cheerful schoolboy, a vain child with a child's love of dressing up, and a savage with all a savage's potentialities for good and evil."[95] When Strange returned to Kenya in the early 1930s, she was struck by the fact that "[t]he African native has taken kindly to European clothing and astonishingly well he looks in it. In some instances he is as well turned out as his master."[96] In the gamut of racial behavior of the time, paternalism of this sort, which was devoid of the egregious racist excesses, such as "nigger hunts" and collective lynching, associated with the behavior of white supremacists in the United States, served to palliate the segregationist mentality that formed part of white settler society and reinforced the nostalgic view of an essentially fair-minded society that knew how to treat its "natives."

Among the most important tropes representing colonial society were those associated with game and hunting. In both their novels and their memoirs, Riddell and Strange emphasized the fascination with big game and the attraction of the hunt. On arrival in Kenya, the dislocated Riddell "found compensation in the enormous horns and heads which decorated the rooms. They thrilled me. All these things had been killed in East Africa . . . and I was going up country to live in places where I should see numbers of them still roaming the plains alive."[97] Game became an intrinsic part of the colony's settler identity. As Strange explained, "The height of hospitality in Kenya is to show a visitor a lion either by day or night."[98] As we saw in Chapter 1, Kenya provided the opportunity to transgress both the class and gender boundaries traditionally associated with the hunt as an aristocratic male pastime. But, whereas, in the early days of Kenya settlement the emphasis had been on the kill and the collection of trophies—a restorative throwback to the trophy-lined walls of the baronial hall—by the 1930s "the indiscriminate slaughter" was no longer permitted.[99] The 1930s saw the establishment of game reserves to encourage the developing tourist trade. They would add to the "spell" of Kenya, which was such a prominent theme in the novels of both women.

However "cruel" Kenya was considered to be, however difficult the life of the characters in the novels was, the enchantment was never snuffed out. As the following exchange between two of Riddell's characters in *Wives Win* indicates:

> You are one of those whom Mother Africa makes her slaves for life . . . She gets our very souls from the beginning and always her grip grows tighter. She tortures and scourges us, but still we go on worshipping her no matter how

she treats us. And, if we ever settle in colder kinder lands again, till the end of our days we throb to that luring call she sends us to return to her.[100]

Or as, Strange put it when she returned to Kenya in the 1930s:

The call of the wild has become vulgarized by excessive use as a film caption, but it was, is and always will be the most potent lure of Africa.[101]

CONCLUSION

Whether endorsing traditional gender frameworks or extolling the beauties of the colonies in which they were writing, women's narratives of nostalgia-in-the-making were important to the settler community's image of itself. In Algeria colonial women writers contributed to creating an image of a multi-racial society where, for all the existing tensions, an understanding of indigenous society prevailed. Whereas the narratives of modernity, in the guise of the civilizing mission, were manifestations of the attempts by the settlers to impose their minority culture on that of the majority, the patterns that were incorporated into nostalgia came from the two-way acculturation that was most obvious in the way in which ethnic and religious identities were so often performative. Rhaïs' investment in a false Muslim identity sustained her in Paris and on the French literary scene, whereas Boisnard's Berber costumes added to her image of a hybrid identity: a French woman with an Arab soul. The representational tropes in the narratives of women writing about Kenya that were to form nostalgia were connected to the call of the wild, where the farm was a salutary haven and the land beguiling in the beauty of its flora and fauna. Unlike Algeria, the African in the novels of Riddell and Strange was kept at a distance. Racial equilibrium was maintained not by "understanding the native" or by a show of acculturation, but by instilling an "understanding of the racial divide" and maintaining a show of the master/servant relationship. If in Algeria assimilation was from the top down, in Kenya it did not exist at all. And yet women in both colonies were acculturating to their new setting insofar as they were creating tropes and images that arose from the colonial space.

As in chapter three, in both Algeria and Kenya, women's narratives reflected preoccupations engendered by World War I. Women had taken part in the war effort in an unprecedented way but in its aftermath there was a backlash as domesticity was once more vaunted as the correct path for women to take. Colonial women's novels mirrored this dynamic: the colonial setting—whether it was Algeria or Kenya—provided opportunities for freedom loving women but they inevitably reverted to "true" gender form.

CHAPTER 5

WOMEN'S FICTIONS OF COLONIAL REALISM

. . . no person of one race and culture can truly interpret events from the angle of individuals belonging to a totally different race and culture.

Elspeth Huxley, Red Strangers

. . . une race est pire qu'une mère nourrice . . . on retrourne fatalement à sa race . . .

Lucienne Favre, Orientale 1930

The 1930s saw a shift in emphasis in the writing of colonial women from the romantic genre to a more realistic style. The depression dampened spirits, and the rise of fascism and Stalinism focused attention onto political and moral issues. The "frivolities" of the twenties gave way to a more sober, even sombre, mood. Colonial literary "realism" was a question of perception but, as Valentine Cunningham has rightly pointed out in another context, what is perceived to be a reality is "as much a part of the truth, the reality of the time, as what 'actually' happens."[1] The urban expansion that was set in motion after World War I increased steadily throughout the interwar period. In Kenya, Nairobi grew from a "collection of huts" to an embryonic modern city, while in Algeria more settlers moved from the country to coastal cities and towns of Algiers, Oran, Bone (present-day Annaba), and Bougie (Béjaia) or to inland centers such as Constantine and Tizi-Ouzou.[2] As urban centers grew so too did the service sectors in them, providing employment opportunities for women. Women in both colonies attained higher profiles in the public sphere, culturally and politically. The growth of the cities and towns, coupled with continued land expropriation, caused displaced Africans and Algerians to drift into these centers in search of a livelihood. More often than not they ended up as manual laborers, although a minority did enter the service sector. As a result the nature of interracial contacts changed, and tensions in the two colonies increased as Africans and Algerians found a voice and labor started to organize. Relations between the settlers and administrators from the metropole were exacerbated as the latter tried to introduce measures that would improve the lot of the local population and forestall what seemed inevitable to all but the settlers, namely protests and violence that the racial inequality would ultimately engender.

ALGERIA AND KENYA: 1930

The events of the summer of 1930 in both Algeria and Kenya were to shape the future development of their settler societies by entrenching the exclusion of the "native" population from the political and territorial rights to which they should have been entitled. In Algeria the centenary celebrations of the 1830 conquest, in preparation since 1923, were held with great pomp. Coupled with the 1931 Colonial Exhibition in France, which ran from May to November, it thrust Algeria into metropole limelight and highlighted the importance of French colonialism.[3] The triumphalist tone of the centenary, which glorified settler "achievements," must have been offensive to most Algerians, whose token presence in the celebrations was emblematic of their position in settler society.[4] If the settlers were oblivious to the sentiments of the Algerians, officials in the metropole were not. As early as November 1928, former Governor of Algeria, Maurice Viollette, submitted a deposition of the Chamber of Deputies urging its members to avoid the concept of conquest and to emphasize that of fraternity and unification of spirit between French and Muslims. He advocated the creation of Centenary schools and hospitals, the abrogation of the hated *indigénat,* and the introduction of equality in military service.[5] Echoing Viollette, in April 1929 the Deputy for the Saône-et-Loire, Vice-President of the *Commision des Colonies,* Georges Nouelle, published an article in the *Annales Coloniales,* warning of the possible dangers of unrest and stating that the celebrations should emphasize that the French conquest was not undertaken for territorial gain, but to win over indigenous souls *(la conquête des âmes indigènes),* a goal that, the deputy believed, had been achieved.[6] As for the Algerians, those who espoused the notion of assimilation and hoped for a "pact of fraternity and progress" with the French and saw the centenary celebrations as their "14th of July, that is to say the triumph of legality and liberty *(du Droit et de la liberté)* over despotism," were disappointed.[7] The settlers had no intention of accepting a situation that held the potential of power sharing, however limited.

In the same year as the colonial exhibition, the National Council of French Women organized a two-day (May 30–31, 1931) international conference, the *États Généraux du Féminisme,* in Paris to discuss issues of concern to women and, as the President, Avril de Sainte-Croix, declared, "most particularly, the situation of indigenous and metropolitan women in our colonies."[8] As far as the "indigenous" women were concerned, Henriette Célarie, one of the representatives from the colonies, lamented that in Algeria although "there was much good will and devotion on the part of the [French women] who organized [good works], they were very often confronted with extreme ignorance, with total incomprehension of the advice given, [or] with the apathy inherent in their race."[9] Two issues of real concern with regard to Algeria were the question of mixed marriages and the situation of medical achievements that benefited women. In spite of the fact mixed marriages were very rare, anxiety about them was such and the issue preoccupying enough to elicit a condemnatory presentation.[10] In contrast, positive emphasis was placed on French medical achievements in an exposé presented by Dr. Abadie, a female physician who had been practicing in Oran for 20 years.[11] Over and above the various exposés and debates that took place at the conference, what is significant in the context of this study is its timing. Holding it at the same time as the colonial exhibition and so soon after the centenary celebration, it thrust colonial women and their issues into the metropolitan limelight.

In the summer of 1930 in Kenya two governmental White Papers created an outcry in the colony. One was on *Native Policy in East Africa* and projected the introduction of "an equal franchise of a civilization or educational character open to all races," the addition of another member of the Legislature to represent "natives," and the announcement (following the memorandum of 1923) that Kenya is "primarily African and that the interests of the African natives must transcend those of all immigrants, whether European, Indian or Arab."[12] The other, on *Closer Union in East Africa,* proposed the appointment of a High Commissioner "with jurisdiction over Kenya, Uganda and Tanganyika in respect of certain transferred services, including railways, harbors and customs."[13] Both papers threatened the position of the settlers; the first by suggesting that educated Africans should have the same rights as the settlers and the second by thwarting settler desires for increased autonomy. Of the two papers, it was the first that created the most widespread settler discomfort. As one member of the Kenyan Legislative Council, the Honorable T. J. O'Shea, put it:

> ...it is obvious that the authors of this Paper think it possible to stimulate the intellectual and moral advancement of the native so rapidly that in the course of a period of time of which we may at present take account he can participate in the intellectual life of the Colony . . . I regard that as an altogether false assumption . . . due to thinking in terms of mechanical industrial development whereas in actual fact it should be thought of in terms of biological development . . . I cannot conceive of anything more calculated to provoke antagonism to the Government in this country by the settler community.[14]

In short, as far as the settlers were concerned, the White Paper was "an astonishing combination of academic idealism and smug ignorance of facts," ignoring "every claim of the European settler in Kenya to have his welfare considered."[15]

Colonial women in Algeria and Kenya took an active part in countering attempts to increase the rights of the indigenous populations. In Kenya, women responded to the two White Papers by holding a conference at the end of June in Memorial Hall in Nairobi under the auspices of the East African

Women's League. The meeting, convened by the President of the League, Mrs. R. B. Turner, comprised some 79 representatives from all "sections of the European community." The women vociferated against "His Majesty's Government," taking exception to the projected reversal of the more limited communal franchise for Africans introduced in the 1920s, expressing "resentment at the insinuation . . . that the British settlers in Kenya were not to be trusted to deal fairly with the natives," and stressing that the "endeavours [of the Africans] to become efficient artisans, traders, and clerical assistants" was hindered due to the Asians, whose presence prevented the advancement of the "natives."[16] A number of resolutions were passed unanimously at the meeting, which were sent to the Secretary of State for the Colonies and handed to the press. That the women believed their position as settlers was threatened is evident in the following extract from their resolution:

> While agreeing that native interests must be safeguarded, as they have been in the past, this Conference considers that conclusions and the memorandum indicate a strong tendency on the part of the present Imperial Government to destroy in practice, if not in theory the policy, which has been in force for many years, of encouraging white settlement, which was initiated and has been fostered by former British Governments, and therefore constitutes a threat, both to the future security and stability of the white community whose members have made their homes in Africa.
> . . . any attempt by the British Government to force a policy on these Territories which is not generally acceptable to the white community will seriously retard the peaceful and ordered progress of the Colony as a whole.[17]

The resentment of the Government's proposals underlines the colony/ metropole antagonism, which was a feature of both colonies.

In Algeria the possibility of extending the franchise to select groups of the Muslim population was mooted as of the end of World War I, and after extensive parliamentary debate the 1919 Jonnart Law had enfranchised 421,000 Muslim men.[18] Viollette's deposition and the centenary celebrations brought the question to the fore once again, a question that was especially vexing to colonial women as they did not have the vote themselves. In May 1930 a front-page article appeared in the French feminist paper *La Française* in which the secretary-general of the Algerian chapter declared that it would be "very sad for us, French women of Algeria, if the politicians representing our nation, considered giving the vote to the *indigènes* of our colony, and refused the same rights to their mothers, sisters, wives and daughters. The *indigènes* do not seek naturalization and claim that naturalization leads to a loss of esteem and 'family honor.'"[19] The latter sentence was certainly true, as the only way they could obtain French citizenship was to renounce their Muslim personal status, which was in effect apostasy. "We are *furious (nous enrageons)*," the article continued, "to see the coarsest of our indigenous workers placing their ballot in the urn without even being capable of deciphering the name of the candidate, whose name was placed in their hands with a 5 franc note."[20] The spotlight placed on Algeria, due to the centenary celebrations, prompted colonial women to organize their own chapter of the *Union fran-çaise pour le suffrage des femmes* (U.F.S.F.) with offshoots in the main towns of Algeria.[21] If *La Française* used the situation in Algeria to further its own agenda of obtaining the vote for women in France, settler women in Algeria actively supported the paper's stance for their own reasons.[22] They may well have wanted the vote and, suffragists apart, many women probably did, but they also wanted to maintain their dominant position in society and granting more Algerian males the vote would not only create political problems for the settlers as a whole, it would also jeopardize women's position in the social hierarchy of race. Given settler anxieties about the colony's demographic imbalance, it is a measure of the prevailing machismo that the male settlers did not on the whole support granting the women the vote, a measure that would have doubled the European electorate.[23]

The events of the summer of 1930 in Algeria and Kenya heralded the intensification, which was to take place over the decade of the thirties, of the hierarchical stratification of their respective societies as the settlers sought to maintain their dominant political, economic, and social position. The inability of the settler majority to grasp the extent of potential unrest among the Africans or Algerians was due as much to a conviction that a rejection of the modernity they were seeking to impose was a sign of ignorance and recalcitrant backwardness as it was to their self-interested arrogance. The realist style of the women's novels, which emerged from both colonies during the thirties, conformed to literary trends in Europe, but the novels also readjusted the representational patterns that created the discourses of nostalgia in culturally specific ways.

LITERARY DEVELOPMENTS IN ALGERIAN AND KENYA

In interwar Algeria colonial literature came into its own and, although women writers participated in its expansion, there was a gendered quality to this literature. Women authors, who were deemed to be more in tune with the emotions than men, were inclined to emphasize the social rather than the political. Whether this was because women had interiorized the prevalent belief about their emotional acuity or whether by adopting this line they were more likely to get into print is hard to determine. Whatever the reason, colonial women continued to write about interracial relationships and their denouements with a "realism," which, on one hand, perpetuated the trope of "understanding the native" but, on the other, contributed to maintaining the distance of the racial divide. In France, as a result of the increased interest in the colonies engendered by the centenary celebrations and the various colonial exhibitions that were held in Paris and Marseilles, colonial authors moved onto the interwar literary scene, although, more often than not, their novels were classed in the colonial or exotic categories.[24] For colonial women there was the additional category of "feminine" novels.[25] This literary categorization was, of course, the cultural expression of extant power structures, whether they were those of metropole-colony or those of gender.

Regionalism was a feature of a certain type of interwar literature in France and Algeria, deemed to be the extension of France across the Mediterranean, created its own brand of literary regionalism.[26] The two styles associated with colonial literature: the exoticism associated with Pierre Loti and the "new" colonial realism elicited a debate as to what was truly representative.[27] The concept of colonial realism was based on the conviction that authenticity was indispensable for the colonial writer wishing to convey authoritatively the colonial space and its peoples.[28] Depicting the "reality" of colonial society rather than a "romanticized fantasy" allowed for a subtler introduction of the colonial agenda. After all, if reality was being depicted, what scope was there for polemics or flights of fantasy?

Colonial (read settler) realism was first expressed in the *Algérianiste* move-ment whose members appropriated the term *Algérien* as a regional signifier for a native son *(le fils d'une petite patrie)* corresponding to French provincial appellations such as *Bretons, Berrichons,* or *Flamands.*[29] As mentioned above the *Algérianistes'* professed goal was to create an intellectuality with which all races could identify,[30] an imaginative but inappropriately expressed goal. They saw themselves as children of the land *(les fils du sol)* writing about *their* land. For all their claims regarding a common intellectuality of race, they sought to privilege the *colon* position over that of the *indigene.*[31] (Boisnard's historical novels were an exception.) Although the novels of the movement were relatively successful, its ideology was not, and it was overtaken by the *École d'Alger* whose narrative centered on the importance of the Mediter-ranean and whose star was Albert Camus.[32] In spite of its avowed intention of creating a discourse relevant to all races in the French Mediterranean territories, it too remained essentially Eurocentric in its literary privileging of the settlers and of the Romance languages of the area.[33] The increase in women writers during the interwar period enabled a few of them to adhere to these movements. In 1921, the *Association des Ecrivains Algériens* created the *Grand Prix Littéraire de l'Algérie* to encourage colonial authors and put Algeria on the cultural map as a regional literary space.[34] In its second year the prize was awarded to Maximilienne Heller (nom de plume for Maximilienne Fenech) for *La Mer Rouge,* a novel with a Judeo-Maghrebine theme. Written in the realist mode, it foreshadowed the realism that colonial women were to develop throughout the thirties. The awarding of prize to a woman so soon after its inception was an indication, too, of the importance attached to the social (as opposed to the political) realism that women were considered predisposed to portray.

In Kenya there was no literary scene to compare with Algeria. Settler society was at an earlier stage of development, and few women had the incli-nation to write novels. The few who had the aspiration or the confidence to write found their spare time limited by their involvement in farming or trying to keep their farms solvent. For some, such as Eleanor (Nellie) Grant, letters were the preferred means of expression. For others, the attrition in the colonial community, as would-be-settlers failed to make a go of their Kenya venture and left, provided aspiring women writers with the opportunity, once back in Britain, to use the colony as a focus for their fiction. In fact all the female novelists in the interwar period wrote their principal works after they had left Kenya. The difference between the colonial novels of the twenties and the thirties was that novelists such as Riddell and Strange, who started to write in the twenties, had only limited experience of the colony. They had lived there, to be sure, but they had left before the end of the decade. Their vision of colonial society was narrowly limited to settler concerns. Even those novels written by them at a later date were stamped with the experiences of their brief sojourns in the twenties, where there was little place for the Africans unless in the guise of servant or laborer.[35] By the 1930s there was a generation of women who had grown up in Kenya and had had an altogether different type of contact with the Africans than the likes of Strange and Riddell. Many had had African playmates while growing up, and although most were packed off to boarding schools to be "civilized" and socialized into the British class system, having grown up surrounded by Africans, they felt that they "knew" Africa in a way that people who had not grown up there did not.[36] They were familiar with the different tribes and their customs, and although their vantage point was from that of the dominating class, the understanding of the Africans they felt they had acquired endowed those inclined to write with credentials of an authentic understanding of African society. Of the women who had grown up in Africa, only one, Elspeth Huxley, emerged as an important voice in thirties Kenya, but other women such as the "Happy Valley child," Jaunita Carberry, and the aviatrix and horse breeder Beryl Markham, who were part of the same generation, would write memoirs or publish stories at a later date.[37] Having grown up in Africa the sentimental roots of these women were in Kenya. They had a similar sentiment of proprietorial connection to the colony as the settlers in Algeria. Added to this, in the thirties, Africans, many of whom had been educated in missionary schools and had therefore been introduced to egalitarian concepts and Western ideas of liberalism, started to make their voices heard politically in a sustained manner. Literary realism provided a way of engaging, however tangentially, with political issues. The published work of the thirties, whether fiction or nonfiction, had a political dimension that the novels of the twenties did not.

Karen Blixen's *Out of Africa* was, in many ways, the novel that bridged the divide between the writing of the twenties and thirties. Written with hindsight, as were the novels of Riddell and Strange, it was a highly romanticized view of Africa, which did not sit well with the more realistic approach of the thirties. Unlike the works of Riddell and Strange, it was a serious work of literature considered by many as a masterpiece. Whereas the Kenya novels of the romantic genre had served as amusement value for the settlers, who had not been challenged by their content, but had either appreciated their caricatural dimension or dismissed them as lightweight fluff, Blixen's work set a much higher standard, demanding more serious attention. Blixen's lyricism, with its nostalgic themes, was appreciated, but among settlers her lack of realism in portraying them and *their* society was not. Nellie Grant, writing to Elspeth in 1938 after she had finished reading *Out of Africa* agreed with her daughter that the "beginning part [was] really marvellously good, and the imagery-writing <u>wonderful</u>" (Grant's emphasis), but faulted the book for its inaccuracy and self-consciousness.

> She gives one no impression at all of Berkeley's [Cole] and Denys' [Finch-Hatton] characters—they only appear as they affect <u>her</u>, as do also the Somalis, and the absurd scene with Kinanjui . . . the latter bits about Ingrid L. [Ingrid Lindstrom was a close friend of the Grants] are just unintelligible. They don't make sense . . . don't think it is the last word in African books. Good god, you can do better than that! She hasn't the remotest conception of Aldous Huxley's term "non attachment" . . . No, you mustn't think it is a great book.[38]

Although Grant was certainly trying to reassure Huxley, who had embarked on her writing career by then, her sentiments also point to the importance to the settlers of the thirties of having a "sensible" literature that recorded an "objective reality" of settler society rather than a personalized romance with the colony. Nonetheless, Blixen's work was an essential component of the way in which colonial literature was configured. It was no doubt her fine literary sense of allegory and metaphor that led her to choose the title *Out of Africa*, yet in so doing she captured the essence of what it meant to be a woman writer from Kenya and introduced what became a dominant trope of the colonial period. "Out of Africa," in both its literal and metaphorical sense, exemplified what it meant to be a colonial woman novelist: women who wrote once they were out of Africa and yet whose voices were forged in and rose out of Africa.

LITERARY REALISM IN 1930S KENYA : IN AND OUT OF AFRICA

As a "child of Africa" Elspeth Huxley's was the dominant female literary voice of interwar Kenya. She was a prolific writer of both fiction and non-fiction.[39] Although she was brought up in Africa, and is best known for her works with an African focus, as a young woman she was eager to leave her parents' farm[40] (fig. 5.1). Perhaps because she felt overshadowed by her mother, as she later explained in a *Sunday Times* interview:

> I don't think I was repressed in childhood, but I had a dynamic, witty and laughter-loving mother who sparkled in company, with the unintended result that I knew myself to be by contrast a boring grub instead of a resplendent dragon-fly. Perhaps I still am, but whereas in my youth I minded terribly, now I don't mind at all.[41]

She went to school in Kenya, where she impressed her classmates with her eclectic interest in her surroundings:

> Elspeth Huxley (née Grant) was at school with us for quite a long time, until she was sent overseas. Of course, she always excelled at composition, essays

Figure 5.1 Elspeth Huxley. Reproduced with permission from the National Portrait Gallery, London

and was very clever at most subjects. She always carried a box Brownie camera about with her, snapping photographs of all manner of subjects.[42]

On leaving Kenya she studied agriculture at Reading University and went on to Cornell University for a year, during which time she contributed to the *Cornell Daily Sun*.[43] Her agricultural training therefore equipped her to write about the concerns of the settlers from both a political and an economic standpoint, a fact that endowed her work with considerable stature. Once she had left Kenya, she never returned there to live. Like Blixen, therefore, she wrote from a distance, but unlike Blixen she returned at regular intervals and was therefore able to reimmerse herself in settler affairs and gauge political developments in the colony from the settler viewpoint.

Unlike Blixen's *Out of Africa*, which is viewed as a colonial fantasy and part of a larger oeuvre of literature most of which was not set in Africa, Huxley's work, nearly all of which is focused on Africa, is seen as an apology for colonialism, which it was. Huxley believed that British colonialism was a progressive enterprise that would, in the long term, benefit the Africans. Most of her postcolonial critics have labeled her a racist, but by the standards of the day she was considered to have liberal ideas regarding the Africans. Literary scholar Phyllis Lassner faults her critics for wanting to relegate her to the dustbin of history, arguing that occluding colonial voices such as

Huxley's creates as skewed an image of the times as the occlusion of African voices by the colonials:

> To erase the colonial voice in order to hear that of the colonized . . . repeats the conflict between them . . . More dangerously, to vilify the colonial writer's representations of her experience is to erase that Other with whom she shares her narrative and historical space.[44]

In the context of this study, Huxley's voice is important not only for the way it depicts colonial society, but also for how it reformulates the patterns of nostalgia in realist form, and for its trajectory of change, evolving from believing wholeheartedly that Kenya was a White Man's Country to realizing that in fact it was not. For all her liberal views, colonial Kenya got under her skin and she was unable to rid herself of the reputation of spokesperson for the settlers, a position she adamantly disputed. "It puts me in a false position," she wrote to author and Nuffield College Fellow, Margery Perham (1895–1982), in 1942. "I can lay no claim to such a distinction," and continued somewhat disingenuously, "I don't know the present views of the settlers on any of the issues we may discuss and I daresay that in many respects they're quite different from mine."[45]

There is little doubt that Huxley, like her mother Nellie Grant, believed in the superiority of the British and was, in the interwar period, influenced by the ideas on eugenics that were current in both Britain and the colony. Certainly, eugenicist terms appear in some of her early novels.[46] Chloe Campbell has demonstrated the importance of eugenics in Kenya during the interwar period and has argued that Grant's interest and faith in "the progressive nature of science, particularly biology," suggest "a typically eugenic espousal of a materialist, biological pragmatism."[47] The same could apply to Huxley. But as Campbell has also pointed out, the members of the Kenya Society for the Study of Race Improvement (KSSRI), which was founded in 1933, were a mixed bunch with different ideas and agendas, both liberal and reactionary. What they all seemed to agree on, however, was the potential value of eugenics to Kenyan society.[48] The Kenyan eugenicists, Campbell declares, "were on occasion quick to rebut statements by settlers that attempted to co-opt the research on race and intelligence into the canon of arguments used to defend European supremacy."[49] In fact most of the Kenya eugenicists were more interested in race improvement of the white population rather than the Africans, in much the same way as eugenicists in Britain focused on the working class. Poor whites were especially irksome to the class-oriented genteel settler, who deplored what they considered their propensity to breed. As Grant wrote to Huxley (her only child) in 1935: "I wish some day you'd do research in Kenya on poor whites, and how to stop them. The amount of babies arriving in N'ku Hospital is terrific and to what end?" Citing the case of a clerk, one Noble, who had one child and whose wife was expecting another, Grant continued, "[T]he Sullivans know them and say they are completely feckless . . . and they go on breeding. All most worrying."[50]

In Christine Nicholls' opinion, although Grant was a member of the KSSRI, she did not approve of eugenics.[51] This appears to be a contradiction, but in fact it suggests that Grant was certainly more interested in the theories than in the more radical methods of their implementation such as sterilization and enforced selective breeding.[52] Regardless of the extent to which Grant and Huxley were involved in the eugenics movement (Huxley did not belong to the KSSRI), they were certainly willing to flirt with its ideas. The notion of sticking to one's own kind, when it came to marriage, was the internalization of the notion of selective breeding. Eugenics was as much about class or status as it was about race.

The anxiety among the settlers of Grant's class about poor whites, especially the Afrikaaner poor, was linked to fears that Kenyan society would develop along the lines of South Africa, where poor whites were much more numerous. Such anxieties increased as the Depression bit into the Kenyan economy and farms went bankrupt. Schemes were devised to attract "suitable" settlers or to try and alleviate those who decided not to leave, all of which elicited debate both in the colony and in Britain. A proposal to create small farms was opposed by some settlers "on the ground that they might lead to the growth of a class of poor whites without capital to farm and unable to obtain employment such as [was] appropriate to the dominant white race."[53] It was a question of good "breeding" and this would depend on the type of education given to "European children who grew up amidst a black population."[54] The characteristics of the ideal settler were "his native qualities as an Englishman— his ingenuity, his inventiveness, his determination," who would of course "be all the better for a little more knowledge of farming."[55] Settlers who did not make a "go of it" and complained were also undesirable.

It is no coincidence that Huxley's first major work was the two volume *White Man's Country: Lord Delamere and the Making of Kenya*. Entrusted by Gladys, Lady Delamere, to undertake her husband's biography it was published in 1935, four years after Delamere's death. Written both as a tribute to Delamere and to record the history of the establishment of the colony whose founders, according to Huxley, were "too preoccupied with pioneering to keep many records," it was enthusiastically received in the colony and by the metropole press.[56] Huxley wrote well and researched thoroughly, but she espoused the colonial line, even if within its perimeters she tried to be even-handed. In the early thirties, World War I still cast its dark shadow over society, both metropole and colonial. Huxley saw it as an ideological and political watershed in the affairs of the colony arguing that prior to World War I, the "inherent conviction," which the pioneers carried with them to Kenya, "that civilisation in itself was good . . . and savagery was bad," was universally believed. In wanting "the African to become civilised [t]hey never doubted that they were doing right in trying . . . to detribalize him. Tribalism was something reactionary, stubborn, and opposed to progress and to Western ideas of individualism."[57] The African would be considered truly civilized when he was "able to design an engine, not only to run it; to create literature and not only to read it. Until he could do these things as well as a European . . . the white man must be paramount . . . To suggest that the interests of the natives were paramount would have seemed to that generation a mere contradiction in terms." This paternalistic altruism, Huxley believed, was shattered by the war and changed the attitudes of the "ordinary Englishman towards colonisation and the colonial policy of the Imperial Government." The gulf between pre- and post-war attitudes was "most marked in [the] question of policy in Africa."[58] The war demolished the belief in the inherent excellence of civilization, and led to the beginning of a more vociferous anticolonial lobby and a more acrimonious relationship between the settlers and British officialdom. "Behind the almost fanatical manner in which many African questions are approached today," Huxley wrote, "lurks the feeling that we who so obviously and so tragically fail to manage our own affairs in Europe should not meddle in Africa."[59] Huxley was acutely aware of the rising tide of fascism, a theme she touches on in *White Man's Country* and picks up in her interwar fiction. "Why train him [the African] to democracy," she continues in describing attitudes in Britain, "when country after country is discarding its principles, or tell him to abandon tribal raids when we are preparing for a far more brutal and devastating form of warfare? And how can we teach him precepts which we ourselves have learnt to doubt."[60] It was, she believed, due to this loss of faith in Britain that misunderstanding and bitterness had developed between the settlers and their rulers. The difference in outlook between the English and the settlers meant that the settler felt betrayed, and "cut off by a post-war tide of disillusion from the shore which he so confidently left, and gazing with puzzled and aggrieved expression at the unfamiliar and defeatist sea."[61]

A strong strain of nostalgia hovers over the justificatory passages and the well-researched details of the economic and political situation in the colony. Huxley, who was seven years old when World War I broke out, and had spent a year in Kenya before returning with her mother to Britain for the war's duration, had her father at the front, an uncle killed in action, and another paralyzed for life. Many of the Grants' pioneer friends were also casualties of the war.[62] She was therefore acutely aware of its impact, first from a personal and later from a societal point of view. Like so many of her generation, the prewar years came to signify all that was lost: values, a deferential class system, "civilized" behavior which had, it seemed, together with the millions of dead and missing, disappeared on the battlefields of the various fronts. The nostalgia inherent in the above passages was not just about the loss of vision regarding the European role in Africa, the book also obliquely endorsed the quality of African/European relations that she felt had developed in Kenya, and which in her later work she would see as having splintered. In her chapters on the War and its impact in Kenya, Huxley stated that the nervousness about leaving their wives and farms that settlers felt when they went off to war was unjustified:

> Many had felt nervous about leaving their women folk unguarded, fearing that natives might seize the chance to raid the farms, carry off stock and perhaps

threaten the safety of isolated women. It was an ideal opportunity for natives suffering from grievances to pay off old scores. But their fears had been groundless. In spite of this sudden exodus of the majority of the able-bodied males in settled areas, the preoccupation of the officials and the complete defencelessness of the farms, no European estates were raided, no women harmed and no native outbreaks occurred. This spoke well for the relations existing between settler and native.[63]

Unlike other parts of Africa, such as Nyasaland (present-day Malawi), "which [in 1915] was on the brink of revolt," Huxley implies that relations between the Europeans and the Africans in Kenya were sufficiently equitable not to have led to such as pass.[64]

Like Blixen's *Out of Africa,* therefore, Huxley's *White Man's Country,* was an examination of a slice of colonial life that was past. Whereas Blixen's work was individualistic in so far as it centered on a personalized vision of what that life was like, Huxley's was collective in so far as she used Delamere as a foil to examine the early development of settler society, a biography with a definite political message. Writing from *out of Africa* she could be "objective" by providing both settler and metropole points of view and thus negotiate the fraught relationship that had developed in the postwar period between settler and official in the hope of enabling them to reach an understanding. For all her objectivity, her admiration of Delamere was also an admiration for the type of "feudal" system he believed in and strove to recreate. Although scholarly reviews were mixed, *White Man's Country* elicited great praise from leading lights in the colony and from the press in Britain and established Huxley's reputation in much the same way as Blixen's *Out of Africa* established hers.[65] Having demonstrated her credentials as a writer of biography, Huxley switched to fiction publishing four works in the thirties: three detective novels and an "anthropological" novel about the disruptive impact of white colonization on Kikuyu society.[66] Both genres shed light on her political views and the strategies she pursued to establish herself as a metropole writer rather than merely a colonial one.

When *Murder at Government House,* the first of her murder mysteries, was published in 1937 the detective genre in Britain was undergoing a renaissance, thanks to the rising star of Agatha Christie. Christie, who started her career as a detective writer in 1920, had published 22 detective novels by 1937 and was already a best selling author. Huxley must have been aware of her successes and indeed those of the other women who formed part of what is now called the golden age of detective fiction.[67] Huxley's choice of the detective genre allowed her to present colonial society in an innovative way to a wider audience, to air her political anxieties about both colony and metropole, and to use a popular genre to enter the literary mainstream. Like Hercule Poirot, Christie's Belgian detective, Huxley's detective, Superintendent Vachell, is an outsider. A Canadian, who could view the inbred conflicts and tensions of settler society with the objectivity required of a good detective but who, coming from an area that was still a Dominion, was familiar with British political and legal structures. The choice of a Canadian allowed

Huxley to use her experience of American life acquired during her year at Cornell University, to create a North American character who was convincing in both speech and action. In all her detective novels, Huxley highlights the antagonisms between the settlers and British officials. At the dinner party that opens the action in *Murder at Government House,* Donovan Popple, who had been "farming and trading in Chania [Huxley's imaginary African colony] for twenty-five years" had spent "most of his spare cash and all of his spare time in fighting the farmer's battles with the Government."[68] Government bureaucrats were equally sour about the settlers. On being informed that the Governor of Chania, Sir Malcolm McLeod, has been murdered, the Secretary of State for the Colonies declares: "Good God! I knew these bloody settlers would be up to something soon, but this is too much!"[69] Huxley uses the investigation to highlight the inherent racism of the local bureaucracy. Major Armitage, the Police Commissioner of the colony, immediately suspects an African and settles on a discontented "Swahili" [Huxley's designation] as the possible culprit, but the murderer turns out to be Victor Moon, the Secretary for Native Affairs, a "self-made man," who "knew more of native customs and languages, [and] had a better understanding of native psychology" than most men in the colonial service.[70] Huxley entices the readers up a number of false paths before it finally dawns on Vachell who the murderer is. He is able to do so, thanks to Silu, an African elder, who gives evidence in the form of a riddle. "It was the fool riddle that put me on the trail. I got to puzzling over it . . . and suddenly I saw it."[71] Huxley is thus suggesting that African culture should be respected, and the racism of the likes of Armitage is totally misplaced. Furthermore, by making both murdered and murderer members of the colonial service Huxley was allegorizing the inherent corruption that personal ambition engendered among government officials. Moon was trying to cover his tracks for the murder, committed long ago, of the Governor's brother. In the end Armitage grudgingly acknowledges Vachell's success in finding the true villain and exits musing on the fact he had always had "doubts about whether he [Moon] was really a pukka sahib."[72] Moon was, after all, a self-made man and expert of native affairs, which, to the race and class conscious Armitage, explained his aberrant behavior. If, as author, Huxley was distancing herself from the class and race consciousness of settler society, the focus of her critique was the bureaucracy and not the settler as such. Furthermore, the escapism inherent in her choice of genre undermined the situational realism of her descriptions.

Huxley's concerns regarding both colonial and international politics are also evident in the novel. On the one hand, the backdrop of colonial politics in the novel is the Chania-Totseland federation scheme, an imaginary reflection of the Closer Union White Paper. On the other hand, Huxley's anxieties about the rise of fascism are deflected through denigrating remarks about the emerging fascist leaders in Europe. Shortly before the murder takes place, Popple expresses his dislike of the Governor by labeling him a "damn fool pocket Mussolini" and, toward the end of the novel, Vachell declares that a promotional report, forged by Moon, "reads like Dr. Goebbels' opinion of

Adolf Hitler."[73] Huxley expressed her anxiety about the political situation in Europe in a letter to her aunt, Vera Campbell Grant, in 1935:

> The situation is pretty menacing, don't you think? Mussolini will get away with it now, of course, but that only makes war in Europe a certainty as soon as Germany is ready. So get ready to go to Kenya. Ma is rather agitated as she seems to think that Mussolini will attack Kenya, but has no convincing reason in support of this!"[74]

Huxley's anxieties were also reflected in *So This is Kenya!*, a 1936 memoir by Evelyn Brodhust-Hill, who came to Kenya with her husband Charles on the *New Mayflower* as part of the Soldier Settlers' Scheme :

> In 1934 we heard that British Fascism was to be given a start in Kenya: many of its theories and plans excellent [sic], but on the whole possibly a doubtful blessing with Fascist Italian Jubaland on our northern frontier, and the Germans in Tanganyika all out for Nazism—and Nazi propaganda of a very peculiar description going the round in our colony. British Colonial Fascism would never be sufficiently militaristic to form the ham in such a sandwich!"[75]

If the reaction to fascism in the colony was ambiguous, the rise of Hitler was keenly felt. The thirties saw an influx of Jewish refugees into the colony. In 1934 Josceline Grant, Huxley's father, informed his sister that a German "girl," who was a trained agricultural chemist and botanist had visited them. "She gave us the most terrible account of things in Germany. Amongst the many who had been shot was a cousin of hers . . . she said all the best jobs are now held by Hitlerites, many of them completely illiterate young wasters."[76] But by the late thirties the refugees had created a wave of anti-Semitic feeling in the colony. Writing to Elspeth in 1938, Nellie Grant declared:

> I don't much like the idea of Jew refugees swarming into Kenya as per that b.f. [bloody fool] Ld. [Lord] Winterton's proposal. In principle one is pro Jew, but there are so many implications for the future in letting them in to this country and if water is going to be found for them round Voi etc. why shouldn't it be found for more Africans. I wish I knew more about Jews and why there is this age-long and world-wide fear of them—for such hatred can only be based on fear.[77]

The nuances of anti-Semitism and the way it was played out during this period have been captured in Stephanie Zweig's bestselling autobiographical novel about growing up in Kenya as the child of German-Jewish refugees.[78] Nellie Grant's attitudes in the early years of the war certainly confirm some of Zweig's fictional representations of her experiences. When in 1941 the question of bringing British bombed babies into Kenya to be fostered, Grant who had mixed feelings about the scheme felt that "it is a very good idea to get some British babies to counteract the hordes of Jew refugee babies that are swarming into the Kenya world. But . . . they might be a poor white threat, and do no one any good. Everything is in a muddle."[79] Writing to a friend a few weeks earlier she complained that: "My Jew [who was doing some work for her] walked out on me, as they do. I hope the whole lot get pushed"[80] Anti-Semitism in Huxley's novels does not extend beyond the occasional stereotype about Jews and money for she is much more concerned with the menace of Nazism.

The third novel in the Vachell series, *The Death of an Aryan* focuses on a Nazi Bund in the colony and the murder of one of its members, Karl Munson. The title, which was probably an ironic reference to Hitler's ideas on Aryanism (Munson was too objectionable a character for her to be using it in a positive eugenic sense), was changed to *African Poison Murders* when it was issued in the United States. Although it was published in 1939 it was of course written while Hitler was flexing his prewar muscles, and reflects Huxley's preoccupation with the influence of the Nazi menace in East Africa. As Lassner suggests in her analysis of the novel, Munson's death was probably meant to be "poetic justice for his heinous politics."[81] But the novel is about more than retribution or even the creation of an allegory of a wished for end to Nazi power. The colony harbored a number of fascist sympathizers, in the shape of the likes of Lord Erroll, who admired the order, discipline, and hierarchies inherent in the ideology, but Mussolini's invasion of Ethiopia and Hitler sabre rattling in Europe had made even those settlers with such sympathies fearful of the territorial claims one or the other might make.[82] The ambiguity is captured by Corcoran, the naturalized British nephew of the murder victim: "[A]lthough I have a lot of sympathy for the Nazis, I'd hate to see them taking over this country. That would mean the push for any one who isn't actually a German, including me."[83] The novel also touches on settler uneasiness about the possibility of the loss of the colony to the Axis powers in the event of a war that went badly for the British.

Africans make appearances in all Huxley's detective novels. An African is usually the first suspect in Huxley's murder mysteries, but the choice always turns out to be an error of judgment on the part of colonial officials (but not on the part of Vachell), suggesting a criticism of prejudicial behavior among officials and settlers. The "natives" are ever present as laborers, household staff, or members of the lowest echelons of the colonial administration. Huxley uses their tribal denominations when she wants to emphasize a particular cultural or social trait of the group in question. Taking place in the thirties, British influence (usually missionary) had introduced "progress," which her African characters have, in varying degrees, espoused. Such progress is not always welcome, however, as in the case of the League of Plain dwellers, which features in *Murder in Government House*. According to the African chief, Kyungu, the League was "very evil" and its members were "young men, with a knowledge of white men's ways."[84] The corrupting influence of Western ideas on Africans was as much a settler concern as it was a generational irritant in African society. The "evil" was therefore synonymous with disruption, disruption of African social norms and of colonial civilizational hierarchies. In her detective stories, therefore, Africans are certainly present, but they remain in the background and the story line revolves essentially around settler issues.

Africans may not have been the most important players in her murder mysteries, but they nonetheless featured prominently on her literary landscape as evidenced by her 1939 novel *Red Strangers,* which focuses on three generations of a Kikuyu clan. The success of *White Man's Country* prompted Nellie Grant to encourage her daughter to write a book about Africans. Extensive research, a course in anthropology at the London School of Economics (LSE) from Bronislaw Malinowski, and her own childhood proximity to the Kikuyu enabled her to take up the challenge and create a sympathetic tale of three Kikuyu brothers and their families who, during the period 1890–1937, responded differently to the advent of colonialism. In spite of her avowal in the foreword that she was not an anthropologist and had neither adopted anthropological methods nor could make a claim to scientific exactitude, she produced what was in effect an anthropological novel in its attention to detail and its in-depth understanding of Kikuyu ceremonies and customs. Reading *Red Strangers,* I was struck by the similar story line with the Nigerian author, Chinua Achebe's novels *Things Fall Apart* (1958) and *Arrow of God* (1967); an irony given that Achebe was one of Huxley's most pointed critics. In much the same way as *Red Strangers* depicts the disruptive impact of British colonialism on the Kikuyu, Achebe's novels portray colonialism's disruptions on the Ibo of Nigeria with the resultant clash between tradition and modernity. Given the fact Huxley is writing at the height of the colonial period, and Achebe as British colonialism was falling apart, the tone of the two authors is obviously very different. Furthermore, Achebe is voicing an African viewpoint whereas Huxley disclaims "any intention of speaking for the Kikuyu people or of putting forward their points of view" being well aware that "no person of one race and culture can truly interpret events from the angle of individuals belonging to a totally different race and culture."[85] It is this that bestows the novel with its anthropological quality. Huxley sees the upheavals caused by the advent of Westernization as the inevitable side effects of a traditional society being exposed to modernity and progress, first through the medium of Christianity and then via the channel of capitalism. In her interpretation of the "clash of cultures," the Africans are as culturally surprised as they are culturally shocked. When confronted by the invading British, the elders' council is perplexed: "How could a man conquer an enemy and take no cattle? The very lack of purpose in such an action made them uneasy."[86]

Red Strangers is a saga covering three discrete periods 1890–1902, 1902–1919, and 1919–1937. Each revolves around one of three brothers, Muthengi, Matu, and Karanja as they interact with the red strangers (the British colonials) of the title, who make their appearance at the very end of part one of the book. The first section describes the customs, rituals, and rites of passage of the Kikuyu. Among the most important rites of passage for Kikuyu women and one of the central cultural institutions of construction of gender identity was female circumcision.[87] Huxley's detailed description of the ritual of circumcision, male and female, and her refusal to cut the more graphic passages, led to a rejection by the first publisher

(Macmillan) to whom she submitted the manuscript.[88] Her inclusion of the ritual was part of her anthropological approach to describing Kikuyu society, but she also wanted to present Kikuyu customs to the British public, "[A]s it is, not as certain people in this country would like to think it is, whether some aspects are abhorrent or not is beside the point."[89] Far from wanting to spare the British the squeamishness that the editors at Macmillan believed they would feel when reading the passages on circumcision (and especially clitoridectomy), Huxley wanted to confront them with the full force of a practice that most Europeans found abhorrent when inflicted on young women. Female clitoridectomy was a topic of heated debate in Kenya and had provoked a crisis in 1930 in what came to be known as the circumcision controversy.[90] The initial storm coincided with the declaration by the Labour government of native paramountcy in the colony, but the controversy continued. Jomo Kenyatta, Kenya's first president after independence appropriated the ritual as an essential component of what held the Kikuyu nation together and, hence a potent symbol of Kikuyu nationalism.[91] Huxley hinted at this development at the end of the book, when she drew attention to the rite's anticolonial potential. Describing the reaction of the Kikuyu elders to the proposed law outlawing the practice, she wrote that they saw it as "part of a plot to destroy the Kikuyu people so that the Europeans could seize the land." Girls who were not circumcised, they believed, "could not be true Kikuyu . . . All would be barren and then [the Kikuyu] race would cease to exist."[92] Whatever the Kikuyu elders may have felt about the intrusion of the British into their age-old customs, by the end of the novel the younger generation was critical of the older men and their traditional beliefs. When Karanja refers Crispin, the son of Muthengi, to the council of elders to decide about the collective land that Crispin is claiming as his own, Crispin brushes the suggestion away: "The council is made up of old men who do not understand modern customs!"[93] When it comes to land holding, Huxley implies, colonial modernity suits the African too.

With regard to interracial relations, Huxley does not shirk from describing the ills that the British colonial system brought with it, whether it was political manipulation or economic exploitation. In one of the early passages on the confrontation between the British and the Kikuyu, the "red stranger" tells Muthengi:

> I have come to govern the country with justice on behalf of my leader, who is a very great ruler indeed and has conquered many peoples besides you . . . if you will keep peace between your warriors and me, I will make you a leader in your own country and you shall help me to rule. But if you resist, then I shall bring followers who kill as you saw your warriors killed, and there will be much bloodshed and suffering, and you yourself will be captured and sent far away from your own people to live alone in poverty.[94]

Huxley captures the tactical use of fear and the carrot and the stick approach, both important tools of political manipulation, deployed by the British from their earliest encounter with the Africans. Just how disruptive to tribal customs the British incursion was, is expressed by Matu:

> At first I thought these strangers would go, but now I know they intend to stay . . . the power of the elders is broken like the bones of a goat beaten before the council. Men steal and evade punishment, for thieves need no longer pay compensation. Instead they are taken to Tetu to work for strangers. What sort of justice is this? Is it not in itself a kind of theft? The country is like a swarm of bees when the queen is dead."[95]

Huxley's portrayal of the Kikuyu was extremely sympathetic, eliciting praise from Margery Perham, with whom Huxley was to carry on a lengthy correspondence (see chapter 6). Perham considered *White Man's Country* to be "the best apologia for white settlement that has been written"; *Red Strangers*, on the other hand, was "an astonishing exercise of sympathy and imagination on behalf of the Africans."[96] According to Christine Nicholls, the archaeologist and naturalist, Louis Leakey felt that "it was the best book on the Kikuyu he had ever read."[97] As much as Leakey may have liked Huxley's book, his unmitigated endorsement probably had as much to do with his antagonism toward Kenyatta as it did with his admiration for Huxley.[98] Kenyatta's *Facing Mount Kenya,* published a year before *Red Strangers*, was an anthropological portrait of Kikuyu society in which he defended the practice of clitoridectomy. The apparent paradox of Huxley's ability to write with such sympathy from both sides of the fence is explained by her biographer as a sign of the evolution in her ideas.[99] To be sure, when in Britain, Huxley came into contact with educated Africans in a way she probably did not growing up in Kenya. Kenyatta, for one, was Huxley's classmate in the LSE Malinowski seminar. She also was exposed to a much wider range of political ideas on colonialism. Although Huxley's ideas about the colony certainly changed over time, there is nonetheless a thread that links both *White Man's Country* and *Red Strangers*, namely the nostalgia for a past when society had not been disrupted by outside events: the class values of white society by the war and age-old customs of African society by the whites. Modernity in its different forms, Huxley is suggesting, played havoc with the agrarian systems that both societies valued and sought to preserve. Thus the nostalgia of *Red Strangers* is, as Renato Rosaldo has stated in another context, "mourning for what one has destroyed."[100] Ambiguity and nostalgia, two sentiments that so often go hand in hand in unsettled times.

One of the notable features of Huxley's interwar fiction is her choice of different genres for her portrayal of the two components of colonial society, settlers and Africans. The choice probably had something to do with saleability. As mentioned above, the detective genre was a popular one, and it is difficult to imagine how in that period a white author could produce a serious minded novel about Africans, if it did not have an anthropological bent.[101] Healthy sales were important for the royalties they would bring. Not only did she have her own farm in Britain to run, but she also sent regular sums to her mother and father in Kenya, who struggled constantly—and not very successfully—to keep afloat. But there was another dimension to the choice of different genres. Although it may have been unconscious, Huxley was in effect compartmentalizing the settlers and the Africans into separate spheres in much the same way as each group lived. Even if African and settler did on occasion come together, the color bar was practiced "with vehemence in schools, hospitals, hotels, trains, and the allocation of land for business and residential purposes."[102] Huxley and her fictions may have been emblematic of the "tolerance and understanding" of the good settler, but it was nonetheless from the vantage point of a racially segregated framework. As Margery Perham was to put it when writing to Huxley in 1942: "To you the conflicts of racial interest seem to be like passing shadows on an otherwise fair and open landscape."[103]

Huxley was not the only published author in the interwar period. In addition to *So this is Kenya!* Evelyn Brodhurst-Hill published *The Youngest Lion* (using the pseudonym Eva Bache) in 1934.[104] Both books were about her experiences as a farmer's wife in Kenya and were pro-colonialist is a way that Huxley's were not. Whereas Huxley sought to understand the viewpoints of the Africans, settlers and colonial officials, even when her opinions differed from theirs, Brodhurst-Hill did not. Her sentiments were adamantly pro-settler. Her opinions of the Africans were stereotypically racist and she had no faith in African goodwill and cooperation. "A curious feature of native reports," she wrote, "if by any chance there is any foundation for them, is that they are nearly always brought too late to be of any use." As for their capacity to work, she opined that the "African does not work if he can possibly avoid it. His object is to do as little as he can and that little badly, and if he has a specialized job, such as driving a team of oxen, cooking or gardening, he is usually quite content to acquire the rudiments of it and has no ambition to excel."[105] Both Brodhust-Hill's books were reactions to outside criticism of settler attitudes and behavior toward the Africans: "There is something strangely upside-down in the mentality of thinkers who would fain *uplift* backward races by showing how little they value white civilisation . . . and who deliberately bring white people down to the level of those who have no value for the laws of sanitation, cleanliness and health. If the natives are to be *raised*, it is no good trying to do it by lowering Europeans in their eyes."[106] In the 1930s settlers felt threatened by the economic situation in the colonies, which was dire; by the rising tide of African nationalism; by the political situation in Europe; and by the criticism of settler methods by left-wing politicians and intellectuals, in particular members of the Fabian Society.[107] Colonial women felt the need to defend themselves against what they saw as an anticolonist onslaught as much as men and the easiest way to do so was the memoir. *So this is Kenya!*, which is dedicated to "Kenya, the land we love" uses the trope of the farm to emphasize the qualities Brodhurst-Hill saw as inherent in settler mentality: hard work, stoicism in the face of adversity and the struggle to "civilize" the land and its peoples and to ward of criticism. Another settler woman Marion Cran commenting on Simpson's *The Land That Never Was*, (see chapter 3) in her own memoir, *The Garden Beyond*, reacted as follows:

> The book will probably do Kenya a very good turn since it may prevent people like the writer from going out there. It is a remarkable self-indictment. The myopic and the parochial, those without humour, the grumblers, the lazy and the self-absorbed, are best off in Europe where they can get lost in the crowds. The glaring light that beats upon the pioneer is too cruel for them.[108]

Both Brodhurst-Hill and Cran were amateur naturalists, so their books contained the sort of engaging details of the colony's flora and fauna and the unfamiliar yet picturesque customs of the "natives" that appealed to the British public. To the trope of the farm, writers such as Brodhurst-Hill and Marion Cran elaborated the trope of Kenya as a garden, as an Eden where flora and fauna flourished and were cherished and tended by the settler.[109] The patterns of nostalgia persisted, but they were redefined by edginess about the settler position that was evidenced by self-justification or, even worse, by racism. The call of Africa to preserve and maintain its flora and fauna, which would become a predominant literary theme and ecological preoccupation of post-independence Kenya, was starting to take shape.[110] Who, but the settlers, could ensure that such a luxuriant paradise was not lost?

LITERARY REALISM IN 1930S ALGERIA

In spite of experiencing a similar economic turndown, there were important differences in the situation in Algeria from that in Kenya. The well-developed literary scene in Algeria, due to its longer existence as a colony, meant that there were many more women who published fiction and nonfiction than in Kenya.[111] There was, therefore, more scope for critical voices to develop. A significant number of Algerian men were also writing works of fiction and nonfiction at the time and were doing so in both Arabic and French.[112] Although some of these men still had faith in the ideal of assimilation, others were critical of a regime they saw as bent on maintaining the second-class status of the "indigenous" population. The political situation in Algeria was also more fractured and fractious than in Kenya.[113] But like Kenya, settlers and colonial officials were usually at loggerheads and both colonies wanted more autonomy from the metropole. Furthermore, the political scene in France was more ideological and therefore more volatile than in Great Britain. The extreme right in France, under the banner of political movements such as the *Action Française,* was bent on putting an end to the Third Republic and what it saw as the corrupting influence of French democracy. Street riots, anti-Semitism and political fears, of Bolshevism on the right and fascism on the Left, found echoes in Algeria. Unlike Kenya, where anti-Semitism was not physically violent, in Algeria it was. The worst incident of the interwar period was the 1934 pogrom in Constantine, which claimed the lives of 25 Jews and 2 Algerians and injured many more.[114] In early 1935

Jeanne Alquier, archeologist and President of the Constantine branch of the U.F.S.F., wrote to Cécile Brunschvicg explaining why delegates from Algeria were not going to attend the Conference of the International Women's Alliance, which was to be held in April 1935 in Istanbul, Turkey:

> Beware of speechmakers and newspaper articles. The situation [here] is very serious. What we have witnessed to date is only a prelude. We must be resolved to face the truth. It is not about [the] secular anti-Semitism of the Muslims, nor the economic crisis, nor the desire to participate more fully in the political life of France; these are only pretexts. The real reason for the present turbulence is a latent Francophobia that has existed since the conquest and which is exploited by indigenous social climbers (*arrivistes*), French politicians and foreign nations.[115]

The Algerian newspaper, *La Dépêche algérienne,* interpreted the situation somewhat differently. Under the banner headline "A plot against State security in Algeria," the newspaper stated that the head of the right-wing league, the *Croix de Feu,* had uncovered a communist plot inciting the "indigenous" population to rise up against France.[116] Anticommunist feelings ran, particularly, high in the lead up to the 1936 elections. The advent in 1936 of the Popular Front in France changed the life of the working classes in France, by shortening the work week and introducing paid holidays, but attempts to improve the political and economic situation of Algerian workers met with resistance in the colony. The tension in the colony was such that shortly after the Spanish Civil War broke out, *La Dépêche algérienne* was led to wonder whether Algeria too would know "the horrors of civil war."[117] These developments impinged on the lives of colonial women. Certainly the most important political and social issues that underpinned women's "realism" of the thirties was the question of who should take precedence in obtaining the political and social rights that were the focus of thirties debates: French women or "indigenous" men. The main issue was of course the vote, but workers' rights and access to a decent education for the Algerians were equally prominent. The decade was thus circumscribed by the 1930 centenary celebrations, at one end, and the 1936–1939 Popular Front, at the other. Metaphorically speaking it opened with a display of colonial fireworks and ended with their extinction, although in 1939 the settlers did not see it that way. Settler obstruction of the Viollette-Blum bill, the last pre–World War II effort to widen the franchise for Algerian men introduced during the Popular Front, convinced all but the most pro-French Algerians that they would never obtain parity. During this time women continued to move into the public sphere, expressing themselves in both fiction and nonfiction, to lay claim to what they felt were their rights. As a result in the colony gender and race became politically, socially, and culturally enmeshed in ways different from Kenya.

As we have seen, even in the early twenties the question of the vote for Algerian men caused concern among French women and those French men who felt that women should be granted the vote. Feminists and pro-suffragist women in Algeria took advantage of publicity surrounding the centenary celebrations to promote their agenda and establish branches of the U.F.S.F. in towns that had hitherto had none.[118] As Cécile Brunschvicg of *La Française* proclaimed, "[T]o this propaganda, which serves as an example to all our departments, our friends in Algeria have added an active social propaganda, and the Algiers group, with the blessing of the Administration, has made serious efforts to establish a section sponsoring children in need (*enfants assistés*)."[119] Algerian branches of the U.F.S.F were active throughout the thirties receiving delegates from France, and taking their own initiatives to try and persuade their local representatives of the importance of giving women the vote.[120] In 1933 Violette Marchal, a lawyer at the court of appeal in Algiers, wrote to *La Française* in the name of the French women living in Algeria who were originally from France. Highlighting the fact that "indigenous" men, who were not required to renounce their personal statute, could vote in municipal elections, a privilege denied to French women. It was, she said, a particularly shocking and humiliating situation, as French women were largely responsible for the education of the indigenous population. Furthermore, *néo-French* men [mostly of Spanish and Italian origin] could also vote, whereas French women from the metropole could not, and, she continued:

> It gets better: if néo-French women had kept their nationality of origin, they would be eligible to vote in their own countries but as they have become French they have lost a part of their position, their rights and their independence: they have been deprived of their right to vote and do not even have the right of an opinion (*droit de regard*) on the public affairs of their country of adoption.[121]

The article went on to reprint and reiterate the demand in the petition that had been sent from the Financial Delegation of Algeria to the French president in 1931. Among the justifications they provided for the request was that French women had contributed in great measure to the colonization of Algeria, even regularly replacing men in their work.[122] The injustice of the disparity in voting rights between the "indigenous" man and the French women was the more common justification of settler women in their own demands; the use of the *néo-French* argument was far less common, and in spite of its all encompassing claim, it really only applied to the "neo-French" of Spanish origin. (Of the three Mediterranean countries from which most "neo-French"originated, Spain granted women the vote in 1931, Italy in 1945, and Malta in 1947.) The nature of the colonial social hierarchy, which is inherent in these justifications, occurs repeatedly in women's fiction.[123] Equally important, though, is the use of women's prominent role in the colonizing process as a justification for being granted the right to vote.

In April 1935 the novelist Lucienne Jean-Darrouy, in her capacity of head of the Algerian federation of the U.F.S.F., headed a delegation to the Prefecture of Algiers to present a petition to the prefect:

> The French women of Algeria who have, as mothers and workers, contributed to the prosperity of the colony, are worried about the dangers that at present

threaten their country, and fervently desire to be asked to collaborate (*être appelés à collaborer*) with the [voting] citizens to assist in the necessary task of moral, economic and social recovery.

They are expressing this wish to the President of the Council to urge him to insert the right of vote for women in the State programme of reform.[124]

A few months later Blanche Icard, Vice-President of the Oran sector of the U.F.S.F., published an article in *La Française* again tying the call for the female franchise to women's achievements in the colony. Signing herself a paysanne *algérienne* she wrote:

The settler (*colon*) has suffered . . . suffered, with "his woman" (*sa femme*) at his side. Thanks to the settler, Algeria has become a beautiful country, envied (*convoité*) by all and now are you, woman, (*femme*), going to allow it to collapse, even to disappear! What good are all the sacrifices made by the blood of our ancestors . . . Rise up women farmers (*femmes paysannes*), and all you workers who pay taxes, you must unite, because in Algeria by raising up agriculture, the mainspring (*pivot principal*) of the country's activity, commerce, and industry will regain their momentum, unemployment will disappear, life will be less cruel and famine will disappear. Women, it is imperative to restore to France her prestige and guide her to resurrection.[125]

Women in Algeria therefore used both their position in the social hierarchy and their performance in the colonial enterprise to campaign for franchise parity with men. In Kenya British women had the vote and, in theory, had equal political rights. Such demands as they made were related to more colony specific concerns, whereas interwar Algeria was an arena for the larger debate about women's vote in France. Nor did feminists in France and Algeria lose sight of the importance of the Algerian woman to the civilizing mission. At the Congress of Mediterranean Women, held in Constantine in 1932, Marie Bugéja was lauded for her "veritable ministry" for the amelioration of the lives of "indigenous" women.[126] The presence of "large numbers" (*très grand nombre*) of educated Algerian women at the conference, one of whom spoke of the "spiritual osmosis" of French culture in Algerian circles, was a call to the feminists to campaign for the education of Algerian women. The settler feminists resolved to ensure the "raising up of the indigenous women and to spread the word that the various branches of the feminist cause in Algeria was at their disposal to help them in every way they could "to improve their lot, the lot of their children and of the whole indigenous family."[127]

Colonial women's preoccupations with the vote, the status of the "neo-French" and the political turbulence of the thirties played itself out in women's fiction in a number of ways. It is impossible to cover all the novels that were published during the decade, or indeed all the authors. The authors mentioned in previous chapters continued to write novels and short stories, but the decade saw the emergence of a number of women writers three of whom, Lucienne Favre, Lucienne Jean-Darrouy, and Jeanne Faure-Sardet, reflected the preoccupations of the thirties in different ways. All were also awarded the *Grand Prix Littéraire de l'Algérie,* which had as much to do with their status as representatives of the colony as it did to any literary merit.[128] They came from dissimilar backgrounds and presented visions of settler society that reflected different facets of women's fictional representations of political concerns and colonial society.

Lucienne Favre (1896–1958) was born in Paris of modest parents. She emigrated from France to Algeria, married there, and was widowed during World War I at the age of 19 with a small child in tow. She took up writing out of economic and probably therapeutic necessity, publishing her first novels in 1923.[129] She was introduced to the French literary scene by Colette, who published *Dimitri et la Mort* in a series she edited.[130] She had a successful literary career and was appreciated both in the colony and abroad. Her plays *Prosper* and *Isabelle d'Afrique,* the latter coauthored with Constance Coline, were performed in Paris at the Théâtre Montparnasse and an English arrangement of *Prosper* was performed in New York.[131] Her novel *Mourad* (also published as *Mille et un jours: Mourad)* was translated into English and German.[132] The author and critic Pierre Mac-Orlan considered her to be "singularly independent" and a friend, who embraced life wholeheartedly and was always ready to provide succor if needed. She was, he declared, "a man's image of camaraderie."[133] Writing about her work, the critique John Charpentier stated that she had "a remarkable talent for satirical observation and a streak of Moliéresque gaiety, [that was] quite rare for a woman."[134] Lucien Descaves, a less patronizing critic of her work, placed her "in the leading ranks of today's women of letters."[135]

Lucienne Jean-Darrouy, who was born in the colony, was better known outside of Algeria for her feminist activity than for her novels, all of which were staunchly pro-settler and, as such, were well received in the colony.[136] She was a journalist and the music critic for *l'Echo d'Alger,* a contributor to *Notre Rive* and founder of the Algiers paper *Femmes de Demain.* As a member of the Algiers branch of the U.F.S.F. she attracted over 1000 women to the municipal theater in Oran when she took part in the conference "Should women vote." It led to the founding of a branch of the U.F.S.F. in that city in 1930.[137] Throughout the thirties she campaigned in leading cities of Algeria for women's suffrage and for access to commercial courts in the colony (women had been granted the right in France in 1931, but not in Algeria). Not only did such a state of affairs discriminate against women, but it also discriminated against the colony. "Algeria," she declared was "once more being treated as the poor relative."[138] Her political stance reflected the resentment the settlers felt at being "misunderstood" and "marginalized" by the metropole.

Jeanne Faure-Sardet who was born in Oran, the daughter of primary school teachers. She had a degree in Arabic, and was the wife of a senior colonial administrator *(haut fonctionnaire).*[139] She wrote a number of novels and a meditation on Tipasa, an important site of Roman ruins in North Africa and a signifier of settler identity.[140] Her novels were hailed in France as fine examples of literature from the colony. Marie-Louise Armand, reviewer for *Minerve,* declared that the "divine" poetry of *Fille d'Arabe,* (analyzed below) and the profoundly human nature of the tale, classed Faure-Sardet among "the greatest of women writers from Algeria."[141] All three women, therefore, brought a different perspective to colonial women's literature.

Of these three women, two published novels to coincide with the 1930 centenary celebrations: *Orientale 1930* by Lucienne Favre and *Le marriage de Mademoiselle Centhectaires* by Lucienne Jean-Darrouy.[142] Although it was Jean-Darrouy's first novel, Favre was already a published author and had obtained or had been runner up for two prizes, winning the *Grand Prix Littéraire de l'Algérie* a year later.[143] Both women certainly planned the publication to coincide with the centenary, but the appearance of these particular novels at the same time was emblematic of a number of tensions: the political, between metropole and colony; the sociological, between the urban and the rural, and the ideological, between the reservedly pro-colonial and the unabashedly pro-colonial. Like all Favre's novels about Algeria *Oriental 1930* had an urban setting, where the interactions of the different ethnic components were shaped by their physical proximity and socio-economic variety that was lacking in the rural novels of Jean-Darrouy, where the predominant social hierarchy was European landowner and Algerian worker. Favre's urban roots in Paris, the experiences of her own background and the fact she had, at one time, worked in a factory, enabled her to write with confidence about those members of society, who were at the lower end of the social scale. *Orientale 1930* was an account of Algiers society as seen through the eyes of Fathma, an Algerian servant working for a French woman writer from France, whom she greatly admired, as she shuffled back and forth each day between two worlds, the Algerian and the French, the Casbah and the European sector.[144] By choosing to narrate the novel in the first person, Favre—as Fathma—viewed the triangular relationship between the "true" French, the "neo-French" and the Algerians from both inside and out. Fathma was the generic name by which the French referred to all servant women, in the same way as Mohammed was the generic name used for Muslim men. In the opening pages of the novel, Fathma explains that she will tell her story to her mistress "who is as wise as a *marabouta,*" adding that "only a woman is capable of understanding another woman's truth."[145] She goes on to state that: "A photograph of me veiled will appear on the cover with her name underneath. Thus, nobody will know who I am or be able to shame me. She will split her earnings with me. I think she will do so honestly because she is a real Frenchwoman from France."[146] Both women, French author and Arab "heroine," appear on the cover, but not on equal terms. The Arab woman is anonymous, hidden from view, unidentifiable beyond the ethnic category of Muslim-Arab in much the same way as the Algerian population is effaced by settler marginalization. While the contents of the book counteract the anonymity of the cover, by unveiling the Arab woman's life, it occurs in the presence of a French woman from France, not one born in Algeria. The passage underscores both the social hierarchy of the colony with the "true" French in the most esteemed position and suggests the self-imposed distance of the French from the settlers or *pieds-noirs,* a distance the latter resented.[147]

One of the advertisements for the novel appearing in *Les Nouvelles Littéraires* declared: "In all simplicity, [a portrait of] a poor Muslim woman. Here is the true document on the conquest of Algeria."[148] The advertisement is a bald statement of the master-servant relationship encoded in colonial domination. Furthermore, it alludes to the "benevolent" paternalism of the novel's tone and to the way Favre contrasted the cultural differences between what she perceived as a traditionally hidebound "indigenous" culture and the materially and ideologically progressive French one, thus calling attention to the potential benefits of France's civilizing role. Favre's novel was not, however, a whitewash of colonialism in the colony. Coinciding with the fanfare of the centenary, the realism of the novel "maliciously mocked," as the critic John Charpentier put it, the romanticism that enveloped the 1830 conquest.[149] Like all the colonial writers of the period, Favre was obviously not interested in advocating an end to colonialism; her preference was to highlight its shortcomings, which were invariably put down to the behavior of the "neo-French." Her work certainly had a satirical streak, but if she poked fun at the foibles of the "neo-French" and presented her readers with a portrait of what Charpentier, labeled "the degenerate Muslim world" *(le monde musulman abâtardi),*[150] (paraphrasing Louis Bertrand) by "realistically" representing their thoughts and speech, she was really intent on emphasizing that it was only proper French values that would make colonialism a success. Far from offending the settlers, her interpretations of urban life were well received. In an article on Isabelle Eberhardt and the literary scene in Algeria, fellow novelist Jean-Darrouy stated that, in spite of being born outside of Algeria, Favre's vision of life in the different districts of Algiers was both powerful and true.[151] With her urban sensibilities and sympathies for the laboring classes, Favre was able to take the pulse of a society where ethnicity substituted for class in the social hierarchy.

In contrast, Jean-Darrouy, who was born and bred in Algeria, chose to write about a rich *colon,* Monsieur Rousselot. Told in flashback, it is the tale of a peasant from the Ardèche, who came to Algeria as a young man and fell in love with the country. He is, Jean-Darrouy writes, "a man of the land and the land is his thing."[152] She uses sexual imagery to emphasize the close tie between Rousselot and his land:

Him and Her! *(Lui et Elle* [la terre]*)* They are producers, the primary source, the origin of provisions *(origine des vivres).* Allies, they are an inseparable supernatural couple *(époux surnaturels).* The *colon,* willful, harsh, and armed, came to her with desire, the lazy, female, [the] inert and cruel land, who refused to give herself up. He had to be firm to catch her. And now she was subdued *(dompté).* Instead of standing naked as before, she lies, plump, harmonious, draped in shades of green.[153]

Through "hard work and steely will," Rousselot turned his farm into a lucrative enterprise. The sexual imagery that Jean-Darrouy uses was a staple of the language encoding domination, whether it was explorers penetrating "virgin" country or "virile" colonizers taming wild spaces, but Jean-Darrouy was also metaphorically alluding to the rampant sexuality that was considered to be the badge of honor of the *colon* of Algeria. Rousselot's virility was not only evidenced by the manner in which he rendered the land fertile, he also produces a daughter, Edmée, who was "sturdy, beautifully trim and blooming" (*bien-planté, taillé strictement et florissant*).[154] Jean-Darrouy's use of the metaphors of nature tie Edmée to the land of her birth and make her the perfect example of the Algerian-born settler woman: beautiful, healthy and, above all, fertile. Rousselot pampers and educates her and she turns out not only to be beautiful but also to be a "winner in the stakes of elegance, luxury and wealth."[155] She spends her summers at a fashionable spa, (an allusion to Vichy, which was a health Mecca for colonials[156]) and is "insulted" by the familiarity of acquaintances, who knew the family when they were still struggling: "guardians of a humiliating past," who "stubbornly continue to remain old friends."[157] In contrast to the farm in the Kenya novels, which was owned and run by settlers whose roots were in the upper crust of British society, the farm in Algerian novels was a site of social mobility. The effort expended in cultivating and transforming the land was also the route to personal improvement. To be sure, the transformative factors of enterprise, perseverance, and endurance that ensure this mobility are also the perceived attributes of the successful Kenyan farmer, for like the fictional farm in Kenya it represents the arena where modern capitalist order is imposed on backward subsistence chaos. As Rousselot explains:

> It is we, who have ploughed with oxen, who, in the fields, have suffered from the summer sun, thirst and fever. So, since we have cared for the land, as we would a sickly child, if it then rewards us and endows affluence and rest . . . we have not stolen it.[158]

The transformation of the land inevitably entailed the transforming of the laborer, a fact that irked the settlers and added to their anxieties:

> The grape-harvester! They are the bane of today's settlers. When I first arrived, one could see them as of July, skulking about the farms, ragged, poor, asking to be employed for a few pennies and a bunch of grapes. This year, they had to be fetched from the roads of the South, to persuade them, they had to be promised good salaries and transport by bus.[159]

The availability of cheap labor was always a preoccupation for settlers, whether it was in Kenya or Algeria. In Algeria the settlers were aggravated by the fact Algerian workers emigrated from Algeria to France, where the post-World War I labor shortage guaranteed them work. In France workers came into contact with trade unions and the Communist party, institutions that were better organized and more developed than their offshoots in the colony. Fearful that they would lose the cheap source of labor, the settler lobby tried to slow the emigration by introducing measures to control quotas. But Jean-Darrouy's depiction of settler exasperation, as voiced by Rousselot, is also an expression of the ambiguity of the settler mantra of colonization's endowment of progress. On the one hand, they vaunted the way they were modernizing the country, on the other they deplored the benefits that modernization could bestow on their labor force.

The literary careers of both women flourished in the thirties: Favre's mainly as a novelist and dramatist and Jean-Darrouy's as a novelist and journalist. I have analyzed a number of Favre's novels from a racial and gender perspective elsewhere, so will not go over those again here.[160] Like all colonial novels they contain their share of the prevalent themes and stereotypes of the genre. The reader encounters failed interracial relationships, violence, lasciviousness, and sexual double standards perceived to be inherent to the personalities of Arab men, and allusions to the seriousness with which the French regard their civilizing mission and educational role.[161] Nonetheless, two interconnected features of Favre's work distinguished her from other women writers in the colony at the time. She used the first-person Algerian voice in two of her novels, Fathma in *Orientale 1930* and Mourad in the novel of the same name; by doing so she sought to bring a critical approach to the tensions and conflicts of the various groups of colonial society. As Mourad explains in the opening passage of the second of the two novels:

> My ambition is to offer the world an account of my country, of the people of my race, and of their relations with our conquerors—an account less false and less perfunctory than those hitherto published by professional writers during the century of French occupation.
>
> So I shall not use the themes of the *caid's* fatal love for the colonist's daughter, nor of the non-Muslim's *(roumi)* love for the fair Fatima. Such things are not common here, between people of different races and conflicting mores.[162]

Her desire to set the social record straight extended beyond highlighting the tensions between the "conquered" and the "conquerors." Thus the French from France, the "neo-French," the Jews, and the Algerians (Arabs and Berbers) are all examined in her different works. Her critique of the "neo-French" stems from her perception that on the whole they did not share the "civilized" behavior and values of the French.[163] They thus hinder cultural and social harmony; the former by unsettling the cultural unity necessary for a successful "civilizing" process and the latter by their lack of social discrimination.

In Favre's last novel of the decade, *Le Bain Juif,* she broaches interracial politics that was plaguing the colony as well as raising colonization's corrupting influence. Unlike writers who implied that this corruption was a result of the colonial space as a site of domination, Favre perceived it as the result of a negative type of acculturation, which she believed arose when two ethnicities rub shoulders.

> The Algerian *colon* is readily extravagant. His life-style and lack of thrift bears no resemble to the French farmer *(paysan)*. He has appropriated some of the

Arab vices, for the Arab is generally prodigal. When the *colon* sells his wine at a high price, he spends on his wife and mistresses without counting the cost (the harem of a wealthy Christian is no less numerous nor less costly than that of a Moorish chief, even if more clandestine).[164]

But at the heart of the novel is the issue of anti-Semitism in the colony. The wariness of the Algerian Jews toward other ethnic groups is due to the memory of past violence they suffered, in particular at the height of the Dreyfus Affair:

> the anti-Jewish troubles . . . lasted from 1895 to 1905; ten abominable years. They beat people in the street, who were suspected of having bought wares in Jewish shops . . . A Jew in a theatre found a crushing majority demanding his immediate expulsion. The tenor and the soprano stopped singing until the intruder was expelled . . . and then they sang the Marseillaise!
> A Jew of whatever age of social station, circulating in the European town during the day risked being thrashed or lapidated without any form of trial.[165]

Such memories led Rachel, the matriarch of the family in the novel, to refuse to respect Christians in any way, never to touch a Christian hand or ever to smile at a Christian child. Only an anti-Semite, Favre declares, could understand such a sentiment of racist repulsion.[166] The implication is that social assimilation is a pipedream; a recurring theme in her novels. *Le Bain Juif*, which was published in 1939, was written at a time of resurging anti-Semitism in France and the colony. In the novel, Favre mentions the Stavisky affair and the ensuing crisis of February 6, 1934 in France, followed six months later in Algeria by the anti-Semitic riots of Constantine.[167] The turbulence of the colony was compounded by the arrival of refugees from the Spanish Civil War, who Favre deemed to be the most disruptive of influences, who were "[m]onarchists from Castile" and "so-called republicans from Andalucia," whose internecine struggles created problems. So too did the "groups of natives *(bandes d' indigenes)* who travelled up and down the countryside carrying red banners and inciting illiterate agricultural laborers." Such activities alarmed the *colons*, who knew that if the immediate result of such incitement was "a few ravaged fields," the situation could easily spin out of control and end "in the burning of farms and the harvest and the massacre of women, children and the elderly."[168] Favre's novels depict the identity politics of race and ethnicity as well as what she sees as the shortcomings of a colonial situation directed by settlers who have lost, or never had, their true French moorings. The constant of the "realism" in all Favre's novels was hierarchy of values and race with the French and their republican ideals lodged firmly at the top.

The third person in this trilogy of women writers, Jeanne Faure-Sardet also focused on interracial tensions and discrimination, albeit with a different approach. In her 1935 novel, *Fille d'Arabe*, the plot revolves around a Muslim Arab, Chaalal, his Christian Spanish wife Carmen, and their only child, Meriem. Chaalal, scion of a wealthy Arab family, is an *évolué* whose father

educated him to "spare him the troubles" of his own trade as a cloth merchant. Chaalal's French education allows him to become a legal interpreter
and acquire French ways, although to the chagrin of his wife Carmen, he
continues to wear a fez; a sartorial signifier of incomplete assimilation.[169] In
spite of his intelligence and Western demeanor, Carmen's family disapproves
of the match, her brother initially going as far as repudiating her. Nonetheless, they marry but not before Carmen elicits a promise from Chaalal that
their children will be brought up as Christians. Chaalal agrees, but he secretly
"decides to break his promise should [the child] be a son."[170] As it happens, their only child is a daughter and she is duly brought up as a Christian.
Chaalal's female relatives think it should be otherwise, however, and when
the opportunity presents itself, they assure her that she is "more Arab than
Spaniard, Muslim rather than Christian. We will bewitch you" they continue,
"we will possess you; our magic will infiltrate your blood with an irresistible
love; in our midst you will glorify Islam."[171] In spite of these predictions Meriem falls in love with Jean Renaud, a young French student of the prestigious
École polytechnique. As a Catholic, Jean is the guarantee that she will maintain
her commitment to Christianity (and acquire true French identity); the match
is thus encouraged by Carmen. Jean returns Meriem's affections with equal
ardor, but his mother is horrified at the idea of a union "my Jean . . . the
husband of Meriem? My heirs, Muslims, Arabs, wogs *(des bicots)?* A drop of
black blood in our veins, perhaps? Horrors!" She spirits Jean back to France
to finish his studies and, she hopes, to forget Meriem. Although originally in
great favor of the match, Carmen consoles her desolate daughter: "the devil
take the Renauds and their Jean. Jean? You are not made for him, because you
are like me . . . Jean, gentle, sensitive, a Frenchman from France, you will tire
of him: at a certain time in your life you'll need a Spaniard or an Arab for a
husband . . . Your eyes are made of fire, your mouth a burning red pepper"[172]
Faure-Sardet thus contrasts the virile sexuality of the Algerian-born with the
more sexually docile French-born; a prominent trope in the colonial literature
of Algeria.[173] In the end Meriem marries an Arab, Hamdane (who does not
wear a fez) and is "courteous, tender, respectful [of her] and caring."[174] She
has a son whom she names Mohammed; thus indicating that she has returned
to the fold of Islam. Jean makes an appearance, too late and concludes that
"destiny has betrayed love."[175]

Vient de Paraître enthused that it was "yet another well-managed *(bien-
mené)* novel of great literary merit, which presented [the reader] with the
wrongs caused by racism."[176] The observation about racism is certainly true,
but Faure-Sardet perpetrates certain stereotypes, even as she destabilizes
others. Carmen and Chaalal have a happy marriage, a departure from the
usual unhappy denouement of mixed marriages in similar novels. But then
Carmen is not of French, but of Spanish origin; a "neo-French" woman,
even a *mauresque* given the Moorish past of southern Spain from where
she originated. In spite of the religious difference between husband and
wife, Faure-Sardet is suggesting a cultural proximity between Spaniard and
Muslim-Arab that distinguishes them from the French and makes for better

compatibility. In short, even if Carmen never fully joins the Islamic religious fold, as does her daughter, she nonetheless is attracted to it culturally and joins it socially. Faure-Sardet is stressing the liminality of the Spaniards, the indeterminate nature of their Frenchness, which set them apart. Favre uses cultural racism to emphasize the ambiguous relationship between the settlers and the mainland French, and in doing so turns the usual image of the racist settler and the non-racist mainlander on its head. On the one hand, Faure-Sardet portrays the settlers of non-French origin as seeking to acquire the aura of Frenchness, which brings with it social advantage and is most easily achieved through marriage.[177] On the other hand, she depicts the mainland French as snobbishly incomprehensive of the colony and its inhabitants. The importance of French cultural identity is therefore under-scored, but the behavior of mainlanders toward the colony is condemned. Unlike the French-born Favre, who was inclined to place racism at the door of the settlers and in particular the "neo-French";[178] for the Algerian-born Faure-Sardet racist behavior was more pronounced among the French, and in particular the French woman, than it was among the settlers. Race, there-fore, becomes a tool of condemnation for if Jean's mother in *Fille d'Arabe* is overtly racist, by being so she is also anti-assimilationist and discrimina-tory. Faure-Sardet therefore extends the trope of "understanding the native" to one of "successful co-habitation with the native," which in France is never understood. In spite of a more relaxed attitude toward mixed mar-riage, Faure-Sardet's novel reinforces the notion of the intransigence of the Muslim religion. The characters in these colonial novels that stray from the Muslim fold or who are, like Meriem, of dual heritage, inevitably return to Islam. In *Fille d'Arabe,* Meriem's Christian mother is out-maneuvered by her Muslim in-laws; it is the paternal line that is the ultimate arbitrator of Meriem's cultural and religious future. Faure-Sardet may be condemning racist behavior; but by reflecting French legal structures by which French identity (citizenship) is bestowed through the male line, she is also caution-ing against the pitfalls of marrying a Muslim, however *évolué* he might be.[179] Miscegenation as a theme in these women's novels is often linked to class. When an intercultural relationship occurs, whether it is successful or not, it usually does so among members of the lower echelons of the social scale.[180] In the hierarchy of the colony, settlers of Spanish origin were more likely to be on the lower rungs of the social ladder.

CONCLUSION

If the common denominator of women's writing in the thirties in Kenya and Algeria was the fact it reflected both local politics and international events, its distinguishing features were shaped by the socio-economic structure and interracial preoccupations of the colonies themselves. The urban settler cul-ture, more developed in Algeria than Kenya, meant that there was the neces-sary literary space and incentive to write fiction from within the colony. Not only was the cultural scene livelier, but the network of presses and publishing houses of Algeria was also largely absent in Kenya. This meant that colonial women in Algeria had the cultural space that encouraged them to write and the means by which to get published there, if they were unable to find publishers in France. The absence of this type of space in Kenya meant that whatever networking women had to do to get into print could only be done in Britain. Furthermore, the rural nature of the lives of most settlers in Kenya meant that the severe economic crisis of the thirties, which had a devastating impact on colonial agriculture, engulfed the lives of most women who were either too preoccupied with farm business or too distracted mentally to write fiction. Colonial women who wrote while in Kenya wrote memoirs and letters; those writing fiction wrote from the outside looking in—or looking back. The colonial situation of each colony shaped the way women's writing was practiced as much as it did what women wrote about.

Race was a feature of both the structure and content of women's novels in the two colonies. Huxley used different genres to segregate the races, writing an "anthropological" novel about the Africans and biography or detective fiction about the European settlers. The accuracy with which Huxley depicted Kikuyu society in *Red Strangers,* which was lauded at the time, had the inevitable effect of exoticizing the African for a British lay audience who were presented with a "realistic fiction" of "darkest" Africa. Huxley's choice of a biography of Lord Delamere, as her first foray into serious writing, reveals her commitment to the settler cause and her desire to justify it to a wider public. Using the modern detective novel, a particularly popular genre, as the literary site for the representation of settler life was an extension of her desire to engage a wider audience with colonial issues. In Algeria, Favre compartmentalized the different groups of Algerian society—French, "neo-French," Algerian—in a more subtle way by focusing each novel on the life and activities of a character from each group.

In both colonies the farm was a trope, whether in women's memoir or in fiction, which became the tool by means of which modernity was imposed on a backward looking society. Western values of hard work, strong will, and perseverance were deemed the motor that drove the tool forward and distinguished it from what it was replacing, thus taming the land and making it flourish. Modernity in colonial women's writing, fictional or nonfictional, was a paradoxical concept. Women writers promoted the binary of the modernity of colonization versus the traditionalism of the local society. The ambiguity of their use of the concept escaped them, however. For, if colonization sought to impose a modern economic and political framework on the colonies, its social structure with its class-like or caste-like rigidity was not modern, even by the standards of the day. Furthermore, what colonial writers could not appreciate, however close they felt they were to the local population, was that African or Algerian traditionalism that was perceived to be too entrenched for real change (i.e., modernization), was by the thirties, often a conscious maneuver of resistance representing the desire to maintain African or Algerian cultural integrity and hence identity in the face of the onslaught of colonial culture and practices.

Gender and sexuality were the features that most differentiated the writings of colonial women in Algeria and Kenya. French women's continuing struggle to obtain the vote added to the shaping of gender structures in the colony and reinforced the racial divide by pushing women to campaign against granting Algerian men the vote. Denying women the vote subordinated her to the enfranchised male population in the colony, a very small percentage of which was Algerian. Additionally, the maintenance of settler women in their traditional nonpolitical role belied the modernity by which they were held up to colonized women as models to emulate. The racial tensions, which denying the vote to women helped to exacerbate, are transposed in women's fiction in gendered and sexual terms, as is the natalism that was a feature of interwar France. The fecundity of settler women and the virility of settler men were expressed positively, whereas similar traits in the "indigenous" population were treated with far less respect. The most flagrant difference between the fictional texts coming out of Algeria and Kenya was the question of miscegenation. In Algeria it was a possibility, even if its usual outcome was negative; in Kenya it was not.

The extension of the franchise in Britain to women over 30, immediately after the war and to women over 21 in 1928, meant that colonial women in Kenya did not have the same sort of political recriminations. British segregationist tendencies and the preoccupation with theories of eugenics in the colony meant that interracial tensions were not expressed by means of gender and sex. Rather they were framed in terms of economic, political, or cultural development. In other words, unlike the Algeria novel where the potential of equality is presented through the interracial relationship, the role of the African in the Kenya novel is one of subordinate to the settler in every way. The potential of equality, if acknowledged at all, is situated in an almost unforeseeable future.

Finally, to the patterns of nostalgia that had developed in the previous decades, was added a new settler nostalgia born of the political anxieties and economic distress of the thirties. Colonial women in both Algeria and Kenya looked back to the struggles of the early days of colonization as an affirmation of settlers' raison d'être. The declaration of war in 1939 and the collapse of France in the summer of 1940 slowed down women's output. When the dust settled at war's end, the settlers in both colonies found themselves embroiled in struggles that called into question that very raison d'être.

PART III

IMPERIAL DECLINE AND THE
REFORMULATION OF NOSTALGIA

NATIONALIST ANGER; COLONIAL ILLUSIONS: WOMEN'S RESPONSES TO DECOLONIZATION

It was not justice the settlers wanted; it was retribution and they didn't much care how they got it.

> *David Anderson* Histories of the Hanged

I came back to Paris and summed up my impressions for Francis: All Saint's Day is not an incident.

> *Colette Jeanson*

The upheavals to settler society in the two colonies caused by World War II were compounded in its aftermath by a noticeable change in the tone of Algerian and Kenyan nationalism. Prior to the war the majority of Algerian and Kenyan activists had been more concerned with obtaining equal political, economic or social rights, but by the end of the 1940s, demands for independence from colonial rule were added to those for rights. In the interwar period settlers in both colonies had either chosen to ignore their "subjects" demands completely or had implemented palliative measures that failed to address the political, economic, and social inequalities in their societies. Militant frustrations were compounded as a result of the war, during which Algerian and Kenyan troops fought on the side of the French and British, respectively. Any expectations that their war service would be rewarded at armistice with more than medals were dashed as settlers, fearful of the political implications of the colonies' demographics, continued to block the type of reform that would have granted their "subjects" the degree of political and economic participation they wanted. The extensive alienation of land by the settlers had also created problems for the local populations that would come to a head in the 1940s: in Algeria migration to urban centers and to

France; in Kenya the squatter problem and, to a lesser extent, urban migrants to Nairobi, which now qualified as a developing city.[1] In both Algeria and Kenya the political and economic inequalities between the settlers and the local population caused the hardening of the nationalist line and a push to capitalize politically on the alienated groups in their respective societies.

In Kenya, settlers had responded to the 1930s depression by switching to beef-farming and high-grade dairy produce. Squatter owned cattle, not subject to veterinary controls, held the threat of disease and settlers attempted to introduce legislation restricting the number of cattle squatters could own. Their efforts met with success in 1940, although they did not act on the law until 1945. When it was enforced, it was a serious blow to the squatters, most of whom were Kikuyu. To make matters worse, the demand for agricultural produce increased during the war enriching white farmers but pauperizing the Kikuyu. Not only did the average annual income of a squatter family drop from 1400 shillings in 1940 to 300 in 1946, but the 1940 cattle legislation made it impossible for squatters to redress their unfortunate economic situation.[2] During the forties, therefore, Kikuyu discontent greatly increased providing the more radical militants with an opportunity to induce the squatters to rally to their cause. The campaign to obtain reform started in the Rift Valley in 1946. Militants demanded the full support of the squatters in the form of an oath of loyalty.[3] The original aim was "to unite, discipline and foster political consciousness among the Kikuyu."[4] The increase in oath-taking ceremonies, occurring during this period, was the first sign of the emergence of the Mau Mau movement, the British response to which was "the Emergency."[5] Initial squatter resistance to oath-taking led to intimidation and manhandling of resisters, some of whom complained to their European employers about the violence they suffered at the hands of the militants.[6] As a result the British construed Mau Mau as essentially a movement of Kikuyu hard-core activists, who used their societies' cultural practices to baneful ends. The initial response in the colony was to try and outwit the Mau Mau at their own game by introducing counter-oathing ceremonies. Spearheaded by the archaeologist and ethnologist, Louis Leaky and pro-British African chiefs and elders, the campaign accelerated the spiral of violence that led to the deaths of more than 1800 African civilians at the hands of the Mau Mau (as opposed to only 32 settlers deaths), the hanging by the British of 1090 Kikuyu, and the detention of tens of thousands more in special camps.[7] As Anderson explains, "[A]t no other time in the history of British imperialism, was state execution used on such a scale . . British justice in 1950s Kenya was a blunt, brutal and unsophisticated instrument of oppression."[8] State executions far exceeded the number carried out by the French against convicted militants in Algeria, and yet there were certain parallels in the way the situation developed in both colonies.

In 1954, two years after the declaration of "the Emergency" in Kenya, the French started what they termed as operations to preserve order *(Operations de maintain d'ordre)* in Algeria, in response to the beginning of what was to escalate into a bitter war of independence.[9] In fact, in much the same way as in Kenya, part of the psychological groundwork for the transition from the demand for rights to the demand for independence was laid in the closing years and the immediate aftermath of World War II. The presence of Allied troops in Algeria, following Operation Torch of November 1942, and the ensuing marginalization of the pro-Vichy colonial government was an indication to the Algerians of the weakness of the French and an additional sign, if such a sign was needed, of the wrong-headedness of the colonial regime.[10] But it was not just the Algerians that were affected by the Allied presence. The presence of members of the Women's Army Corps and the inevitable fraternization between the Allied rank and file and the Algerians perturbed the gender and racial norms of the colony.

The point of no return on the road to independence for Algeria was reached at about the same time that the Mau Mau oath-taking was getting underway in Kenya. On May 8, 1945 demonstrations by Algerians in the town of Sétif degenerated into clashes between the demonstrators and the gendarmerie leading to an Algerian rampage in the surrounding area in which several women were raped and 103 settlers were killed.[11] The colonial repression was out of all proportion to the initial events, searing into the minds of ordinary Algerians and reinforcing the determination of the pro-independence militants to achieve their ends, whatever the cost.[12] Furthermore, it was not just the forces of order that were implicated; settler militias were also involved in the massacres.[13] The violence triggered at Sétif, served to polarize Algerian society in much the same way as Mau Mau oath-taking did in Kenya. If, as Anderson rightly states, the "disruption wrought upon Kikuyu society by the Emergency was almost unimaginable," the war in Algeria not only disrupted Algerian society in an unimaginable way it also traumatized the warring parties and led to long-term political, social, and cultural effects.[14]

Both the Kenya Emergency and the Algerian War of Independence created serious fissures within the societies of the colonized peoples as violence against Kenyans and Algerians recalcitrant to the appeals of the militants escalated into purges of anyone suspected of pro-colonial sympathies. In Algeria the victims of such measures surpassed those in Kenya, with the greatest bloodletting occurring in 1957–1959, particularly in Wilaya III, and in the months immediately following independence, when the *harkis* (Algerians who had served in the French army) were killed.[15] In both colonies incidents against civilians, such as the massacre of 300 Algerian villagers in Melouza carried out by the National Liberation Front (FLN) in June 1957 or the Lari massacre of 75 Kenyans carried out by the Mau Mau in March 1953, set off protracted internecine struggles that served the propaganda purposes of the settlers and colonial authorities, who highlighted the events as evidence of the barbarity of the rebellious elements in the colony.[16]

The punitive responses by the two colonial regimes to their respective insurgencies had judicial and extrajudicial dimensions. On the one hand, the implementation of a special judicial infrastructure to try and condemn militants provided a veneer of legal normalcy to activities that were not only far from normal in more senses than the mere legal, but whose violence matched or surpassed that of the insurgents.[17] Judicial executions in Kenya may have exceeded those in Algeria, or in any other British or French colony for that matter, providing a legal justification for the excessive use of state-violence, but they also deflected attention from extrajudicial violence, such as sustained harassment and torture, although there was certainly an awareness that such activity existed. Eileen Fletcher, a Quaker who spent 14 years in British government posts and worked in Kenya as a rehabilitation officer in the detention camps, wrote in the British Pacifist Journal, *Peace News*, that she had gone "to Kenya in December 1954 to work in Mau Mau camps because I was concerned at the accounts in English papers of atrocities by the Mau Mau and by certain British people in suppressing them."[18] Victims of harassment were not just militants or suspects, however. Trial lawyers in both colonies were willfully obstructed in their endeavors to prepare and present their briefs in defense of militants.[19]

Torture became an issue during the Algerian War in a way it never did during the Emergency and has since been the object of both scholarly and media attention.[20] Just why this is so is difficult to pinpoint, although there are a number of factors in the Algerian case that may have contributed to this development. Perhaps the most important of these, and relevant to what follows, is the fact that the Algerian war was both a national/nationalist war, between Algeria and France, and virtual civil war on each side. The fissures of war did not just occur in Algerian society. Existing antagonisms between the settlers and mainland French became blurred and morphed into quasi-civil war between those who were for maintaining Algeria French and those who were for Algerian independence. Rosa Serrano, a settler of Spanish origin and member of the local communist party (PCA—*Parti Communiste Algérien*), was arrested in 1957. Released, while awaiting trial she found that "[m]y French neighbors, people with whom I had grown up" [in the Bab-el-Oued district of Algiers], avoided even bidding me good morning. The Algerians who came to the house were pleased; they embraced me."[21] Later these same French neighbors threatened her, making her fearful for her life and that of her family. Elyette Loup, another woman militant of settler origin, was arrested in the same year and tortured. Although her tormentors told her that they "were going to throw her into the drink (*la flotte*)" she was spared, remaining in prison until 1960 when she was sent back to France.[22] Another PCA militant, Jacqueline Guerroudj, came to Algeria from France to teach in a rural primary school and joined the independence movement at the outbreak of hostilities. She transported arms and liaised with her compatriot, Fernand Yveton, who was caught, tortured, and then executed by the French.[23] Guerroudj was imprisoned in the notorious Barberousse prison, "a nightmare" of a place where "executions occurred at dawn once or twice a week . . . we used to hear noises at dawn and we then knew there would be . . . executions, it was truly horrible. We couldn't sleep . . . the days that followed."[24]

The line between judicial and extrajudicial execution was more blurred in Algeria than in Kenya. According to Paul Teitgen, General Secretary of the Algiers police prefecture during the war, at the height of the Battle of Algiers, in January and February 1957, 3,024 people disappeared; most were dropped from helicopters into the sea.[25] Victims of torture and other extra-judicial activities were singled out irrespective of race and gender. In Kenya no white women was tortured nor did any join or help the Mau Mau in the way women assisted Algerian militants, whether it was by taking part in F.L.N. activities or by drawing attention to the atrocities being carried out in Algeria by the French. Colette Jeanson, Hélène Cuénat, and Cécile Marion, for example, were members of the Jeanson network, the most renowned of the pro-F.L.N. networks dubbed the *porteurs de valises*.[26] The defense lawyer, Gisèle Halimi and the author and feminist, Simone de Beauvoir, brought the case of Djamila Boupacha, an Algerian women tortured by the army, to the attention of the French public in 1960.[27] In an article published in *Le Monde* on June 3, 1960, de Beauvoir reported on the trial and stated that on learning of de Gaulle's outlawing of torture, the army officer dealing with the Boupacha case responded: "De Gaulle can call the odds back home but we are masters here."[28] The war in Algeria turned the French against the French in a way the Emergency in Kenya did not with the British. Certainly there were critics in Britain of what was going on in Kenya, including women such as the author and specialist of Africa, Margery Perham and the Labour politician, Barbara Castle, but Britain never came to the brink of civil war. Neither did Kenya during the Emergency become a pawn in the Cold War to the extent that Algeria did during the war of independence, even if there were concerns about keeping it in the Western camp.[29] It had no oil; nor was it connected in any relevant way to the politics of the Middle East. Furthermore, the judicial apparatus in Emergency Kenya was perceived as proof that justice, the corner stone of British values, was being maintained whereas in Algeria French Republican values, especially those of human rights were being transgressed and betrayed. The perception of legality that allowed the British to transgress human rights in Kenya with relative impunity was absent in Algeria. This inevitably shaped women's involvement and responses, whether through their activities or their writing.

Wᴏᴍᴇɴ's Wʀɪᴛɪɴɢ ᴀɴᴅ Dᴇғᴇɴsɪᴠᴇ Nᴏsᴛᴀʟɢɪᴀ

The 1942 Allied landings in North Africa and the 1947 granting of independence to India by the British cast shadows respectively over Algeria and Kenya. In Algeria the Allied presence transformed Algiers from a pro-Vichy stronghold into, as one writer put it, "the capital of [free] France" and for "one year . . . France was, in a way, embodied in Algeria."[30] Whatever the pro-Vichy settlers may have thought of the Allies, the importance of Algiers to the eventual liberation of mainland France reinforced, in settler perceptions, the bond of Algerian regionality in relation to France and accentuated resistance to any dilution of what they deemed to be the colony's French-ness through the acceptance of the Algerians as legally, politically, and socially French. In Kenya, on the other hand, the granting of independence to India, Britain's prize colony, sent an undeniable message. No matter how complacent about their situation the Kenya settlers may have been, decolonization—hitherto envisaged as too remote to contemplate—had been fast-forwarded into real time. In Algeria and Kenya, for those settlers who would not accept the inevitability of majority rule, nostalgia became one of the defensive responses to a situation that was both unsettled and unsettling. In both colonies an initial reaction to the anxieties and disturbances of the postwar situation was to reissue the works of women writers whose writing was perceived as having captured the essence of the colony in print. The reissuing of novels written in an early period was in itself a form of nostalgia as they were originally penned at a time when the permanence of settler society was not deemed to be in question. The reissued editions also marked a transition from prewar to postwar thematics in colonial women's writing.

ALGERIA: NOSTALGIA AS DEFENSE; NOSTALGIA AS ANGER

In 1943, *Mourad,* of one of the novels comprising Lucienne Fave's *Mille et un jours* series was reissued, the first of a number of her works to be so.[31] It was subsequently translated into English and German, suggesting that its reappearance was as much a response to the role of Algiers in the war as it was a sign of the perceived merit of her work.[32] The American presence in Algiers had put Algeria onto the American radar screen and, in the colony, called attention to French and American differences with regard to gender relations and race. Furthermore, in 1948 oil had been discovered in the Sahara adding to settler fears of foreign interference.[33] Favre's writing career had peaked in the interwar period, and she wrote virtually nothing after the 1940s. Nonetheless, as the translations of her novels imply, she had by then acquired a national if not an international reputation. Favre's focus on urban settings and her choice of socio-economic themes had enabled her to illustrate the intermixing of cultures and pinpoint racism as a colonial rather than a French phenomenon, and as the inevitable friction caused by the two radically different approaches to religion and secularism among the colony's inhabitants. The racial ideologies of the pre-War period were discredited due to the horrors of the Holocaust and in response to their disrepute, the French made political and juridical concessions to the Algerians in an attempt to counter accusations of racism and create equality, illusionary though the latter was.[34] Racism did not disappear from colonial society nor did its fictional portrayal. Colonial women writers were still concerned with portraying the hierarchical complexities of colonial society, but their novels were threaded through with social and political anxiety that was not merely a response to racial fears spawned by the demographic imbalance of ethnicities, but also responded to the international attention that was being focused on the colonies and in particular to the pressure to decolonize.

In 1953 Jeanne (Jeannine) Montupet (1920–?) published the first of a trilogy of novels, collectively entitled *La Fontaine Rouge,* a trilogy that was dubbed the "Gone with the Wind of Algeria."[35] The novels, which were translated into German and English and became best sellers, related the saga of three generations of the Vermorel family.[36] The founder of the settler "dynasty" had originally gone to Algeria in 1837 to "awaken Africa to life, [to] restore it to Christianity, [to] continue, with the hoe and the crucifix, the conquest France [had] begun with weapons"[37] and had acquired *Haouch Aïn el Hamra- La Fontaine Rouge*, a property near Boufarik in the Mitidja, which he bought from an old Turkish janissary. The novel traces the vicissitudes of the family in Algeria throughout the nineteenth century. Once settled, Simon, the paterfamilias, helped to persuade the government to drain the Mitidja swamps for his fellow settlers and by the third generation, the hardworking Vermorels felt their presence in the colony to be entirely justified.

> We have cultivated this land: we are now the new Algerians. Compatriots, but not Frenchmen . . . we have brought our own freedom, our own needs, our own independence with us. That was our capital. And therefore Algeria will never become France. It remains a land to itself, our land, the land of our love and our tears.[38]

Montupet, whose family first settled in Algeria in 1838, was born in 1920 in Oran where she spent the first 15 years of her life after which she moved to Paris with her family. She married there and spent much of her life between France and the United States, eventually settling in Arizona. Although there are certainly autobiographic elements to her saga of the Vermorels, what is more important than the actual plot is its timing. The three novels, which were published at yearly intervals on either side of 1954, when hostilities first broke out, reiterated the themes of the hardworking pioneers whose attachment to the land made them inseparable from it. By 1955 when the third of the three novels was published, a backlash against the war had already developed.[39] In October of that year the *Union des femmes françaises de la Seine* published a tract under the headline, "All women, All Mothers want the return of all the young soldiers sent to North Africa" in which they not only demanded the return of their young men, but they also laid out the injustices of colonial society where the majority was made up of second class citizens. "One cannot forcefully stifle the desire of a people for dignity, justice and well-being," they wrote.[40] Colonial women's literature in the fifties, which emphasized the agricultural achievements of the *colons* and the "melting pot" inter-ethnic familiarity of urban life, was a response to the national and international rumblings against colonization in general and the more pointed criticisms of Algerian settlers in particular.

In her 1958 novel, *Un Feu d'Enfer*, Catherine Lerouvre traces the lives of a family of *petits-blancs* of Spanish origin in Algiers, during the Second World War. Although the novel reiterates the theme of racism through the lens of gender relations, the American (as opposed to the Allied) presence allows her to complicate the picture somewhat. The anti-hero of the novel,

Sauveur, is upset by the presence of the young American WACs, whose allure makes them only "good for stealing the husbands of others."[41] Woman as a seductress disarming the innocent male was a staple of *pied-noir* gender dogma. Women, Sauveur opines, "should stay at home" and, admitting that he agrees "with the position of the Muslims," he adds that any apparent anti-Arab hostility on his part was due to the fact he wanted "to be like everyone else."[42] On the other hand, Sauveur's headstrong wife, Conception, has no problem with disliking the Arabs and has little time for the submissive and stay-at-home colonial wives, who, "through living so long in Algeria have become like the Mauresques who never answer back to their husbands."[43] Independent though she may appear to be, Conception does not move beyond her own settler prejudices. When she is confronted with a successful Algerian woman assistant at the local health center, instead of seeing this as a step in the direction away from the "stay-at-home" woman, she declares confidently that if the young woman has been placed in such an exalted position "it is solely to show the Americans that [the settlers], at least, do not have racial prejudices."[44] The novel appears to be thematically in line with those of the prewar in its iteration of neo-French racial antagonisms and endorsement of orthodox gender relations, but it makes no mention of the anti-Jewish measures of the war or of the pronounced anti-Semitism of the settlers most of whom were pro-Vichy. The theme of the disruptive American presence signals postwar anxieties not only about gender and race, but also about the international response to four years of what all but the French called a colonial war. John F. Kennedy's 1957 speech to Congress, in which he stated that he believed Algeria was not an integral part of France, but was a colony and that imperialism was the greatest enemy of man's desire to be free and independent, greatly upset the French and, in spite of the initial negative reaction of many members of Congress, signaled the eventual change in U.S. policy toward Algeria from a pro-French to a pro-independence stance.[45] By 1958, therefore, the settlers and pro-*Algérie française* elements in the metropole were on the defensive. The advent of de Gaulle may have swept such anxieties aside but it was a momentary reprieve. It was the first signs of what Geneviève Baïlac was to call the settlers' "abandonment of Algeria complex" ("*le complexe d'abandon de l'Algérie*").[46] By that time too, the role of women in the Algerian war had taken on added importance for both sides. Yacef's "girls" had planted bombs in the European heart of Algiers causing devastation.[47] French women, such as Germaine Tillion and settler women like Lisette Vincent were actively involved in supporting the Algerians, either by their critique of torture and capital punishment as in the case of Tillion or by espousing the cause of the F. L. N. as in the case of Vincent, a choice for which she was imprisoned in Barberousse.[48]

Gendering and gender issues were not however just features of colonial fiction. Gender was used as a tool in colonial politics and linked to the beneficial impact of French civilization. Picking up on interwar activities to "modernize" Algerian women, the wartime regime in Algeria spearheaded a campaign to "emancipate" Algerian women, freeing them from the "shackles" of Muslim male domination.[49] Echoing interwar beliefs, the colonial regime saw Algerian women's emancipation as a means of accessing the Muslim family and, in the context of the war, placing the F.L.N. in the awkward position of either having to agree with the notion of women's rights and, hence acknowledge the progressive colonial state or show itself to be reactionary by opposing reform.[50] On May 16, 1958 there was an extraordinary episode of fraternization between the Algerians, the *pieds-noirs* and the army, which included the unveiling of a mass of Algerian women in central Algiers.[51] Historians differ as to the degree of spontaneity of the occasion, but whether it was entirely or partially orchestrated, it convinced the settlers of the "devotion" of the majority of the Algerian population to the settler cause.[52] It was, as one press article put it: "the 'Algerian miracle' of the days following May 13th . . . the great reconciliation of hearts for an ardently desired French peace by the whole community *(par tout une peuple)*," but, the article continued, there was more to the occasion than patriotic fraternization; "there was the enormous hope of Muslim women [and] French women [who were] tired of having the inferior condition [of Arab women] in a modern Algeria, which was as open to progress as all French territories the world over."[53] For the *pieds-noirs,* it was when the "neo-French and the Muslims were reconciled and the good-natured racism, which had occurred on occasion, had disappeared *(le racisme bon enfant qui pouvait y régner parfois a disparu).* It was the perfect idyll."[54]

The theme of fraternal coexistence was picked up in two other works, which appeared in the same year as Lerouve's novel: Geneviève Baïlac's play, *La famille Hernandez* and her novel, *La maison des soeurs Gomez.* Baïlac, who was born in Algiers in 1922 of Franco-Spanish parents, won first prize at the Algiers Conservatory for both acting and the harp. In 1947 she created the *Centre Regionale d'Art Dramatique d'Alger* (CRAD), an important cultural institution of post-World War II Algiers. Both her play and her novel were portraits of what Baïlac termed "neo-French" families, those "humble, poor families who formed the majority of the European population of Algeria and who had developed a very specific character *(et en forgeaient le temperament)*."[55] The novel had a limited success in comparison to the play, which was first performed in Paris in 1957 at the Charles de Rochefort theatre. Baïlac's professed aim in producing the play was "to create a dramatic style specific to Algeria, this land of cohabitation where so many diverse groups *(communautés diverses)* French, Spanish, Italian, Jews, Arabs have been rubbing shoulders and exhibiting their peculiarities, their customs and their mores for 130 years."[56] The actors were a collection of amateurs from a variety of professions, who had been given a plot outline and told to adlib, using the *pied-noir patouete* and neo-French humor.[57] It was, in fact, a *pied-noir* sitcom at a time when television hardly existed in France, let alone sitcoms.[58] To the surprise of the actors involved, it was a runaway success. The original engagement of two weeks stretched into months and the play was performed throughout Europe. Satire is often the mask for tragedy and whatever the original intentions of Baïlac and her players, *La Famille*

Hernandez became, in Baïlac's words "the symbol of a suffering people."[59] In spite of Baïlac's declaimers that there was no political message, comedy creates figures of fun and whether or not the audience relates to them on a personal level, the harshness and violence or discomfort of any given situation is dissipated in laughter.[60] Furthermore, the self-deprecating humor of the characters in the play captured the audience's sympathy and helped to erase negative preconceptions. *La Famille Hernandez* recreated an image of a society where such racial antagonism as did exist was merely a manifestation of normal frictions and human interaction rather than of an exploitative, violent society portrayed by the critics of colonialism. *La Famille Hernandez* cannot be categorized as a "myth" of social harmony; the inescapable and ever-present violence of the war had encroached too far into the lives of the settlers and, thus precludes such an analysis. Rather, it is an example of defensive nostalgia insofar as it was a reaction to the violence with which it was unable to come to terms, a wished for the harmony from an imagined and longed for tranquil past.

The other novel published in 1958 worth mentioning at this juncture is Anne Durand's *Idir et Thérèse*. Anne Durand was the pseudonym for George Cezilly (1904–?), a pharmacist and close friend of Ferhat Abbas, who wrote the preface to the 1981 edition.[61] The novel takes place in a small town of the Sahel and traces the lives of the daughter of a wealthy settler, Thérèse, and a French educated Algerian, Idir, who ends up being employed in the pharmacy of one of Thérèse's friends, Lucienne. The novel begins by describing the "profound unity of a country where all the races of the Mediterranean had merged together" and ends in its disruption by the war.[62] Idir, who as far as Thérèse and her friends are concerned, is above reproach, is arrested, and tortured by the French paratroopers, but eventually killed by the F.L.N. The novel is well written, and evokes the way war fractures allegiances and ends friendships.[63] But in this context, the content is less noteworthy than the fact Cezilly made the unorthodox move, for a male writer at the time, of choosing a female pseudonym. Unlike most of the other European male writers who wrote about the war, Cezilly did not focus on the exploits of battle or the politics of the war in which Algerians were either occluded or marginalized as the enemy. Rather, he focused on the close interactions and friendships between Algerians and the settlers told from the viewpoint of two women, Thérèse and Lucienne. Although it is impossible to state with any certainty why he made such a choice, it does suggest that Cezilly, who was concerned with presenting an "authentic" portrait of a disintegrating society, felt that a portrayal of the emotional bonds of interracial inter-gender friendships would be perceived as more authentic by an Anne Durand than a George Cezilly, thus harping back to the interwar notion that women were better equipped to describe the social, rather than the political intricacies of colonial society.

If the first four years of the Algerian war gave rise to novels in which a defensive nostalgia of equitable "family" relations between the various elements of colonial society attempted to trump the reality of the colonial situation, by the end of 1960 it had become clear to all but the most obdurate that the demise of French Algeria was imminent.[64] Algiers was crawling with metropole and foreign (mainly American) journalists.[65] What was not yet clear was the shape the new state would take. Women's novels published in the early sixties reflect these uncertainties as well as the social anxieties and political divisions engendered by the war.

In *Ces forêts d'orangers* Marie Sils (1914–1982), who was not of settler origin but nonetheless used the colonial *zeitgeist* to good commercial effect, employs themes of loss and regeneration to capture the atmosphere of the war. The novel, which was published in 1962, focuses on the final years in the life of Théodore, whose grandparents left Alsace in 1870 and settled on 300 acres of "uncultivated, quasi-virgin land" in Kabylia turning it into a money-spinning orange and olive producing domain. They had not chosen the spot, Sils tells us, for its beauty but rather for its fertility.[66] What Sils does not mention is that most of the French immigrating to Algeria in the 1870–1871 wave acquired land expropriated in the aftermath of the 1871 Kabyle rebellion. In the novel, then, Kabylia is the site of loss and regeneration: the post-1871 loss for the Kabyles and regeneration for the Alsatians, who had lost their moorings in France; in 1954–1962 loss for the French Théodore but regeneration for the Kabyles, who were at last able to reclaim their land.

Théodore is a rough diamond; "savage and brutal" like the land he loves so well.[67] He is in love with Damienne, a beautiful but frivolous woman who is young enough to be his daughter. She leads him on, agreeing to marry him, but then spurns him. Two threads of loss run through the novel, over-lapping symbolically: the loss of Damienne and the loss of the "Domaine." Dada, his affectionate name for Damienne, represents the woman as much as Théodore's beloved land. His ruminations after he leaves Algeria for France, at the end of his life, revolve around these dual meanings. For all his brutality and savagery, his relationship with the Algerians is portrayed as ambiguous. Early in the novel, his servant of long-standing, Tassadit, comes to him to intercede with the authorities on behalf of her son and his childhood friend, Kader, who has killed his daughter for showing her face to a man. When he hesitates, telling her that the law must take its course, she admonishes him: "You are fair, Mr. Théodore, you are our father, you understand that a daughter can be killed to preserve her honor. And yet, you observe *(tu respectes)* your laws. But one day you will suffer for it . . . One cannot . . . defend two sets of laws."[68] She is in fact warning him of the rebellion that is about to erupt in 1954. He refuses to intercede on behalf of Kader but does not report him, going instead to visit him in his mountain hideout. Kader also warns him of the forthcoming rebellion and urges Théodore to join him for his safety. In the end, Théodore loses his domain but survives, protected by Kader and Tassadit. The beautiful Damienne does not, hacked to death with the rest of her family. As Théodore tells Rosalie, the young girl who cares for him in France in his final days:

Damienne is dead, and my Domain, and my country: vanished in a single morning. I lost . . . lost without understanding why, without admitting

how . . . Damienne and my Domain, a woman and a few hundred hectares.
That day I lost my whole life.[69]

The loss felt by Théodore exemplifies the loss felt by the 1.2 million *pieds-noirs* who left Algeria precipitously in the summer of 1962. By closely asso-ciating Damienne to Théodore's "Domaine," Sils genders the loss in the novel and renders it more poignant by associating it with a further loss: that of youth. The novel has strong currents of nostalgia: of Théodore looking back to his past life; of the loss of Algeria; of the loss of love. The hacking to death of Damienne, who symbolizes Algeria in its settler prime, provides an unmistakable message. Sils is pointing to the mercilessness of the Algerians and eliciting sympathy for the pointless death of the youthful Damienne. By sparing Théodore, whose relationship to the Algerians is of a hard taskmas-ter, and killing off the shallow Damienne and her family, the novel captures some of the ambiguities of the war: the futility and seeming irrationality of its violence and the unpredictability of its human relations. Théodore, who engaged with the Algerians on a relational level, albeit in often a harsh one, is spared; Damienne, who had little to do with Algerians, is not. Although this denouement seems somewhat of a paradox, in fact it symbolized the resentment felt by the Algerians at having been occluded from colonial soci-ety for so long. The final image the reader is left with is that of a broken old man reminiscing about the loves he has lost. His nostalgia, that of a loss of identity as much as a loss of what he has loved, signals the form *pied-noir* nostalgia will take in the post-Algerian war period.

The symbolism of the novel is evident in Sils' choice of focus: the rich *colon* and his milieu rather than the neo-French urbanites, who made up the majority of the settler population. Generally speaking, there was not much love lost between the two groups, the urbanite being indifferent to the colon "in much the same way as Parisians were of inhabitants of the French coun-tryside," but as a result of the war the fact that the *colon* was considered to have borne "the brunt of F.L.N. ferocity for six years made him the foremost *(premier)* soldier of France" who "had earned everyone's respect" *(le droit au respect de tous)*.[70] In much the same way as the *colon* had been, at the time of the centenary celebration in 1930, the symbol of the hard worker who had transformed a backward terrain into a modern agricultural miracle, the *colon* was once again conjured up as a symbol; this time to represent the loss of that modernity.

More men than women chose to focus exclusively on the war, but one of the few women to do so was Anne Loesch.[71] Loesch was born in Bab-el-Oued in 1941 and finished her education at the Algiers Conservatory of Music.[72] Her 1963 autobiographical docu-novel *La valise et le cercueil* was a defense of the activities of the O. A. S. (Organisation armée secrète) in which she was actively involved and to which, she declared, most *pieds-noirs* adhered.[73] Written as extracts from her journal (a journal which she actually kept) and a fictional one of her partner, Jean Sarradet, Loesch's avowed aim was "to demystify an organization which was born of *pied-noir* patriotism,

without ever sharing French ambitions."[74] The book, which covers the
period October 1961 to July 1962, traces her activities with Jean Sarradet
until their departure from Algeria. A post-scriptum reprints newspaper
accounts of his accidental death by carbon monoxide poisoning in Beaune,
near Dijon, in December 1963. Loesch was motivated as much by anger and
bitterness as she was by the sense of loss—the loss of all she had loved—for
she declared that it had been "genocide" of the settlers that had occurred
in Algeria. "One does not only kill a people by eliminating them physically,
their assassination can be accomplished even better by tearing them away
from all they had created, from the very reasons for life."[75] The title, which
paraphrased the F. L. N. slogan *la valise ou le cercueil*, implies that for the
pieds-noirs it was not in fact a choice of one or the other, of leaving or of
death, but was both: in leaving the *pieds-noirs* symbolically died. Although
the journal entry for June 19, 1962 states that they left Algeria "without
regret as it had become so dismal *(lugubre)* due to all the bad memories," an
entry at the end of July 1962 states that "past memories had gained a new
light *(un éclat nouveau)*, the worst moments seemed full of an intensity that
engendered a love of them *(une intensité qui vous les fait aimer)*," because
in the final analysis they had called forth the best in the *pieds-noirs*. She
continues with the following appeal: "in an unstable and uncertain present
let us idealize that which we have left behind and which seems from every
angle preferable to boredom and exile."[76] Loesch's call to idealize their
memories of the past was picked up by countless *pieds-noirs* in the ensuing
decades. Loesch and Sarradet, like nearly all the *pied-noirs* who flooded into
France, were disappointed with what they found in the French countryside:
poverty, dirt, and abandoned villages.[77] After having compared "the riches
we left behind to the penury of the French countryside," she incited her
fellow exiles "to *colonize France, [for] she is dying*." Rather than remaining
"in the asphyxiating and castrating atmosphere of the cities *(devirilisation
des grandes villes)*," she urged them "to take over empty lands and places . . .
and transform them . . . so that the Tarn, the Périgord and the Poitou will
become flourishing oases where cleanliness and light reign . . . this will show
the [metrople] French, what it was, what it can still mean to be French.[78]
This notion that the *pieds-noirs* would regenerate France was a throwback
to one of the early staples of colonial ideology, first elaborated by Louis
Bertrand in the fin-de-siècle, that the virility and hard work of the settlers of
Algeria would regenerate a diminished France.[79]

Two years later Loesch published a much more nostalgic novel, *Le tombeau de la chrétienne*. It was a lament for the loss of "her land" and, according
to Stora, with Marie Elbe's 1963 novel, *Et à l'heure de notre mort*, launched
the genre of *Nostalgérie*.[80] In fact Francine Dessaigne's *Journal d'une mère
de famille pied-noir* and *Déracinés!*, both of which were written for the *pied-
noir* community in the early 1960s, were as significant.[81] Dessaigne, who was
actually born in France, a fact that may account for Stora's omission, spent
most of her life in Tunisia and Algeria, first with her civil servant parents and
then with her husband and was greatly affected by the war of independence.

"The Pieds-Noirs" [her capitalization], Dessaigne states, "who found their memories and their reactions [to the events of the war] alive on each page of my earlier work [Le journal . . .], asked me to write the sequel"[82] They were exiles whose "memories were small painful roots indissolubly linked to a lost land. They [the memories] arise from all and from nothing, from a state of mind, from the weather at a given moment, even from smells."[83] Nostalgérie would be steeped in every aspect of the "exiles" life.

The defensive nostalgia of colonial women's novels and memoirs can also be seen as a response to the emergence of an Algerian voice, in the literature of the colony. In the fifties and sixties authors such as Mohammed Dib (1920–2003), Kateb Yacine (1929–1989), Mouloud Mammeri (1917–1989), to name just a few of the most renowned, started to write about the existential angst of the Algerian people and about the impact of the war.[84] The importance of their writings lay not just in their themes but also in the fact that they were writing in French, were published in Paris, and were influencing a section of the French public. Their counter-narratives presented a portrait of a society where French influence was a disruptive rather than a civilizing force. In much the same way as Baïlac, Loesch, Dessaigne and others became the spokespersons of a dying community, the Algerian writers became the spokespersons of a dying colonialism, but whereas the former looked with nostalgia to the past, the latter looked with hope to the future.

KENYA: NOSTALGIA AS REALITY?

The state of colonial women's writing in Kenya, and hence the range of responses, was more limited than in Algeria. Nonetheless there were certainly similarities due to the fact that women's writing in the post-World War II period was, like that of Algeria, responding to the deteriorating situation in the colony and the mounting criticism of colonialism nationally and internationally. The self-questioning in Britain about the future of her Empire had started well before the end of World War II. As Nellie Grant put it in 1941, "[T]here is a tremendous tide of public opinion at home working against the settler community in Kenya, and at the same time, a great awakening of the public conscience to Imperial responsibilities towards the 'backward peoples' of Africa."[85] If the question of what was to become of its empire was beginning to plague the British, it was also "being asked in no uncertain terms from America."[86] As historian Michael Howard recently put it, "throughout the war the United States consulted her own interests . . . and these did not extend to helping Britain either to remain solvent or to retain any part of her empire once the war was over."[87] The publication in 1944 of the eighteen-month correspondence between Elspeth Huxley and Margery Perham was an initial response to this British soul-searching. The two women met in 1941 in Oxford at a Colonial Conference organized by Perham, who was the first woman fellow of Nuffield College and had been instrumental in developing colonial studies as an accepted academic discipline. She was also an influential lobbyist and adviser on colonial affairs. The correspondence, which began on Perham's invitation, was meant to be a discussion of the "tangled problem of Kenya and its future."[88] It was Huxley's hope that by profitably discussing the problems of Kenya, "a glimmer of light might be thrown on to the wider question of the colonial empire as a whole."[89] The choice of Kenya was due as much to Huxley's knowledge of Kenya as to the fact that "[f]or many years [the] colony had been a minor storm-centre of controversy and discussion." Its "very name seems to send people's temperature up," Huxley wrote.[90] At the root of the discussion was the question of racial relations for, as Perham replied, the attention Kenya attracted both in the British government and among members of the British public was a result of their awareness of developments in Southern Africa, where the fear of being submerged by Africans led Europeans to vaunt their superiority by denying Africans the sort of economic and political advancement they were achieving in other parts of Africa "where they did not have a white colony sitting on their heads."[91] As for Kenya, Perham stated that having "watched the first similar endeavours of a much smaller minority in Kenya, and because the attempt here is being made in a restricted highland area in the heart of black tropical Africa it has still less justification and it is unlikely to achieve even that measure of temporary success which is possible in the South."[92]

The two women exchanged letters on a monthly basis from March 1942 to November 1943, and although their discussions covered a wide range of political, economic, and legal issues the core question and the basis for their disagreement was whether or not "the ideas and ambitions of white and black can be reconciled."[93] Although Huxley declared that she supported equality, and envisaged a gradual evolution toward that goal, as Perham put it toward the end of their correspondence:

> I feel that as you . . . look at the future your attention is drawn always to that little band—to which you yourself belong—of highly civilised whites, whom you see leading and leavening the vast backward masses of other races. The whites are the important people, the *élite, they* must be given more understanding, sympathy, and security. *They* can make or mar Kenya . . . I see the same scenes but the high lights fall differently. My gaze is riveted upon a huge African population . . . I admit their backwardness and disunity now, but I believe that the powerful modern administrative and educational techniques could be used . . . to bring them forward . . . the settlers . . . all through their history, and even in very recent times . . . [have] with a strong and united voice claimed the right to rule the other races . . . how can we image that this handful of our own countrymen will be able, in the midst of this great indigenous electorate of the future, to maintain its present superior position?[94]

Unlike Huxley who, for all her understanding of Kikuyu culture and her belief in encouraging equitable racial relations, supported the idea of the Highlands remaining in the hands of the settlers, Perham believed that Africa was for the Africans even if she did not envisage independence until they had been properly groomed to take control. Many of the settlers were riled by Perham's views and endorsed Huxley's. In a letter congratulating Huxley on "the splendid way [she] handled her part of the correspondence, Francis Scott wrote: "[t]he Europeans are here for keeps, and must increase in strength both *[sic]* numerically, economically and politically . . . However much in a minority of numbers we may be, our ideas will always be the dominant ones. This is what our British race has proved throughout the ages."[95] Huxley's subsequent publications in the period leading up to the Emergency were a guarded defense of her position. She had settled in Britain prior to the war but she maintained close contact with settler society and kept a hand on the pulse of its attitudes, thanks to her regular correspondence with her mother. Indeed, as we shall see below, Grant's descriptions of Mau Mau activities and the settlers' response to them greatly influenced, *A Thing to Love,* Huxley's fictional account of the Mau Mau period.[96]

Four years after the publication of her correspondence with Perham, Huxley published *The Sorcerer's Apprentice: A journey through East Africa.*[97] In a review in the *Times Literary Supplement* it was commended for its good politics, the author's objectivity, accuracy, liberal generosity, and balance as well as its entertaining style.[98] In the book Huxley reflected on the question of whether one race could pass on its experience to another. If she approached the situation from the settler viewpoint, she was nonetheless acutely aware of the coming storm.[99] In discussing the general strike in Mombasa and the evidence given in the subsequent tribunal, she wrote that, "[a]t no point in the evidence did any glimmer of the notion break through that reward must be linked to output. The African's dreams and not his needs or, still less, his economic value, were the only criterion. Pinioned by print [in the local newspapers], these dreams look tawdry—a mere caricature of our own sense of values at its least civilised."[100] The situation in Kenya was full of danger, Huxley believed, because the African coveted the goods of his richer masters, had no idea that money earned depended not on the organization of discontent, but on the work of labor, and felt excluded from what she termed the "esoteric circle."[101] She may have admitted that inequality was at the root of the trouble, but she also believed that the problem was African covetousness and inability to work to the rhythm of modernity, rather than settler exploitation and land control. Huxley's choice of title for this work is an interesting one. *Der Zauberlehrling,* Goethe's poem by the same name is too well known, and Huxley was too well read to shrug it off as mere coincidence. Was she the apprentice? If, so who was the sorcerer who would put to rights the problems she was evoking? Was it East Africa, peopled with apprentices to those sorcerers of modernity, the Europeans? A more likely possibility, as suggested by her introduction, in which she declares that it was not about the old vanishing Africa that she had chosen to write, but about the new: "eschewing lions, I talked with the clerks—less splendid, but more potent in this turbulent and groping age which is rolling over Africa."[102] On the whole Huxley was indeed describing the Africa of the 1940, but there were also flashes of nostalgia as in the passage on an agricultural project in Makueni for the Africans. Having visited the project, Huxley and her party went off in search of lions and other wildlife. "No sign of human life intruded, no smoke of fires, no homing goatherd. This was Africa as it used to be and soon will be no longer, lonely, magnificent and alive with secrets. Away stretches the world forever, as it seems, into the sunset; empty, as you think, or all life, fresh from the hand of God"[103] The notion of a vanishing Africa, of an Africa which implicitly suggested the halcyon days of the pioneers, would become a recurring trope in post-independence writing.

Huxley's exposure to the liberal currents of the metropole had led to the reformulation of her own ideas to make them acceptable to an audience much larger than that of East African settler society, but her unease about the political situation in Kenya was not merely a result of having been exposed to metropole liberalism. The more liberal minded settlers, also took steps to try and ease the rising racial tensions in the colony. Nellie Grant, for example, suggested in 1945 to the Njoro Settlers' Association that the settlers "had better know a bit more about the African than [they] did and the best was to meet a real one." The time the meeting was to be held led to much discussion for, she wrote, "[I]t couldn't be [held] in the Club House at 6 p.m. as was usual because it wouldn't do for the educated African to see European ladies in the Bar (really 'cos J. Beeston etc. thought they might get landed in the position of having to offer 'a bloody nigger a drink'). I longed to ask why an educated African couldn't see this as a long succession of uneducated African bar boys had survived the spectacle." [104] A year later Grant wrote to Huxley enclosing a memorandum on the *Problems of Racial Relation in the Settled Areas. A Possible Aid to their study,* which reiterated the danger posed by the deteriorating relations between European employers and African employees and set out a series of suggestions on how to improve relations. This was to be done by a series of study groups run by committees of three Africans and three Europeans.[105] For all its good intentions, the scheme, known as the Maswali Matatu League, never amounted to anything; not surprising really as any attempt to placate Africans by addressing the problem of race relations had more to do with settler self-interest than with an attenuation of inherent racism. In the letter enclosing the memorandum to Huxley, who was temporarily sharing lodgings in Cairo with a young woman, Grant wrote: "A small room with a Jewess sounds too foul, and very bad for the carnations."[106]

Whatever their sentiments, the fraught situation encouraged most settlers to dig in their heels. Nor did the problems discourage settlement. With the end of World War II a wave of new settlers descended on Kenya, some with as many as five children, to the apparent surprise of Grant. "We hope to get through the present acute crisis with demobs from the Army" she wrote.[107] At about the same time the East African Women's League composed a letter to women who were planning to make their lives in Kenya. "We are anxious to give all the help we can to intending settlers," the letter stated, "and if you have not yet decided to come to Kenya it may help you to a decision."[108] There was a measure of desperation to this desire to swell the ranks of the settlers, and the old adage "to close the stable door after the horse has bolted" seems particularly apt.

By 1948 it was clear to Huxley, if not to the settlers, that the ideal of a white dominion of Kenya, let alone the whole of East Africa, was a pipedream.[109] In addition to *The Sorcerer's Apprentice,* her reaction to this eventuality appeared in two other works published in that year: *The Settlers of Kenya,* a history of white settlement, and *African Dilemmas,* a pamphlet on the possibilities of self-rule for Britain's African colonies.[110] *The Settlers of Kenya* starts with an anecdote, whereby a "young educated African of political leanings" informs an old settler that he and his like are intruders in Kenya. The settler replies: "But why . . . After all, I have lived here much longer than you." The response startles the young African for, Huxley states, "it was a new idea to him that a European might have lived longer in Africa than he, an African had done." By compressing the history of Kenya to the lives of two men, an old settler and a young African, the implication is that African history is no older than that of British settlement. "The point," Huxley continues, "is that, whether we like it or not, settlers are among the peoples of Kenya, and to a large extent they give the country its present character and shape it history." [111] The rest of the short book sets out the achievements and vicissitudes of the settlers who made a success of farming in Kenya. Settlers, Huxley writes, "were encouraged in their belief that autonomy on a white basis was the country's destiny by the grant of self-government to Southern Rhodesia in 1921." Lord Delamere was the standard bearer for self-government for "his vision was of a white dominion stretching from the Kenya Highlands to the Southern Highlands of Tanganyika—prosperous, loyal to the Crown, offering to men and women of the British race new outlets for the spirit of adventure, and to Africans the example of industry and leadership to conduct them from primitive tribalism . . . to a more civilised and improved form of existence."[112] After describing the past and present economic and political situation, Huxley looks to the future. The real task for the settlers was, she believed, "to find a way of carrying over into his relations with the new generation of Africans that easy and friendly atmosphere which so happily, as a general rule, surrounded his dealings with the old."[113] Huxley admitted that the notion of racial superiority that had characterized the behavior of the settlers would have to disappear, but she concluded that "the European will have to prove his right to leadership, just as the African will have to prove his fitness for citizenship, by justice, toleration and a spirit of generosity and give-and-take."[114] What she was not yet prepared to envisage was that no matter how equitable racial relations became, European leadership in Kenya could not go on indefinitely.

In *African Dilemmas,* Huxley argues that African colonies were being pulled in two directions. On the one hand, by the colonizers who needed "a new world to cultivate, if not to conquer; a need sharpened by withdrawal from the East and by the pinch of the dollar famine," an allusion no doubt to the huge debt Britain needed to repay the United States. On the other hand, was the gathering tide of self-determination, which "sucks African hope and effort away from British mastery, as from all European hegemony."[115] Written in the wake of Indian and Burmese independence and couched in the language of political and economic rationality, the pamphlet is an appeal to delay the independence of African colonies for as long as possible. The hardest dilemma of all, Huxley writes, is whether the rulers can inspire the ruled with the resolution to master their surroundings and remake their world a loftier place. It can be done with good leadership but that leadership is "impotent' without the trust and love, of a good relationship. She continues

> Those who knew Africa during the first half of our half-century of rule affirm that trust then flowered; it was in fact the trust, indeed the love, so widely felt between white and black that sweetened the white man's struggle with sickness, isolation and discomfort that would otherwise have disheartened him. And it is of the decline of this trust, this love, that they are thinking when they tell you that the golden days in Africa are over. The pattern then was simple, the just master and the faithful man. On both sides there were derelictions, but the aim was clear. That simplicity has vanished.[116]

She admits that the master/man relationship is outdated, but the task in hand was "to build a new relation between white and black as happy as the old"[117] Huxley's economic, political and agricultural knowledge of Africa provided the measured tone of *The Sorcerer's Apprentice* and *The Settlers of Kenya,* so vaunted by Huxley's contemporaries both in the colony and in Britain. But for all the knowledgeable information imparted in *African Dilemmas,* its tone was tinged with bitterness. Collectively these three works were a defensive reaction to the impending unraveling of life in Africa as Huxley knew it. Written in different genres, the three works exemplify the types of nostalgic writing that would emerge in the post-independence period: nostalgia as travel to sites of a vanished past; nostalgia as the epic pioneering past; nostalgia of what could have been or could be.

By the 1950s Huxley had acquired a reputation for serious informed opinion on Africa and she worked ceaselessly to publicize her views. Her novels were reviewed on both sides of the Atlantic, she was often interviewed on radio and television, and her articles had been and were published in leading newspapers and weeklies, including the *New York Times.*[118] In a series in the latter paper, she argued that there was a choice for the white man to make in tropical Africa, either to let them continue in their own ways or to modernize; "whether to stand by and see irreplaceable topsoil destroyed in the name of freedom and democracy, or whether to step in and compel people, perhaps even with the aid of rifles, to farm intelligently and to save themselves." For all their qualities—and she enumerated a long list of them—Africans needed organization and discipline, for the discipline of the tribal system was waning and the younger generation was inclined to idleness, lack of purpose, spiritual discontent, and work-shyness.[119] At the root of Huxley's ambiguity toward the Africans was the duality inherent in her existence as a second-generation settler. She had grown up in close proximity to the Kikuyu on her parents' farm and she knew their culture and mores almost as well as she knew her own. But she was most comfortable with those Africans, who were of the same generation as the pioneer settlers and not the younger generation of Africans, who had been introduced to Western ways and education, and who, as a result, were better able to challenge the colonial system. The loss of tribal discipline, she so lamented, was a form of nostalgia for the paternalism of the well-ordered past, where the deference implicit in British class values held sway. There is an irony in the fact that the modernity the settlers declared they were bestowing on Africans as justification for their settlement in the prewar decades, was now seen as one of the causes for the growing tensions in the colony.

While Huxley was responding to the evolving situation in Kenya and Africa from Britain, colonial women were reacting to developments within the colony. In 1948 the *Kenya Weekly News* started a column entitled "The Distaff Side" to which the "Women of Kenya" were invited to contribute each week "their views and comments on life as they find it today."[120] Journalism and letters were women's main channel of communication with the outside world, but a number of women kept journals throughout the fifties. Letters and journals were mechanisms of reassurance in a rapidly deteriorating situation. Letters provided a channel of reassuring contact with the outside world, whereas journals served as self-reassurance insofar as they recorded the illusion of a calm and measured response to critiques from overseas and the increasing violence in the colony. As Mary Casey (1915–1980), one of the journal-keeping women, put it: "this odd habit of writing a journal is simply a matter of choosing what I wish to remember, an idealizing of the days, a poetizing of woes, and enhancing of blisses."[121] Casey, who was well read, knew numerous languages including Chinese and Greek and spent some of her spare time translating classical texts with her husband, kept a voluminous journal.[122] Often self-conscious in tone it starts, symbolically, with a description of the rising dawn and until October 1952 when the governor proclaimed a state of emergency, it was full of romantic but evocative descriptions of nature interspersed with her opinions on philosophy, literature, and the translating she did with her husband, Gerard. There was, Casey noted, "a marked effort to tone down the news," although reading between the lines she realized "that the arrest of 98 . . . Mau-Mau leaders was only just in time to prevent a general massacre of Europeans, or at any rate a grave insurrection."[123] To counteract fear and to avert a race war, it was essential to be patient, remain calm, and as much as possible to continue life as usual.[124] Three months later, however, she was stating that "the air [was] full of fear and rebellion," and that some settlers "talked of going to Nairobi . . . deposing the governor and setting up a government of Kenya Europeans."[125] Casey was nonetheless aware that the troubles were due in some measure to settler attitudes. "However much we are to blame, it must be admitted that the government is slow and does almost nothing to protect us. If a man or woman fails to defend him or herself, he or she is murdered in as horrible a manner as may be."[126] Casey reflected settler sentiment that it was government ineptitude and Kikuyu "vindictiveness" that created and maintained the perilous situation. In April, Casey complained that "there was talk of an amnesty with the Mau-Mau" a frightening prospect that made her lash out at the government for their weakness in dealing with the troublemakers. It was, she concluded, rather like suggesting "an amnesty with a rabid dog or a plague."[127]

Nellie Grant's letters to her daughter were in much the same tone. "Kenya is in a very poor way," she wrote: "whenever the powers that be most madly announce in the press that the situation is contained or improved, or in hand, something worse than ever quickly happens. On Tuesday poor old Waruhiu got murdered and that has created a stink. Last week it was 1 headman murdered per day for 3 days, and another European woman stabbed to death making the 2nd in a fortnight."[128] Security was "so hopeless" that she had decided to get lessons to load her revolver from the police. "If I am told to keep it loaded, she concluded, I shall live at the far end of the house from it; how I hate firearms."[129] Two weeks later she was informing Huxley that the general opinion among the settlers was that on the farms it was certain that "all Kukes have taken the oath but some at least hope most fervently they will never be called upon to do anything drastic about it, but if terrorism does go on they can't help themselves."[130] By the end of November, Grant declared, "the daily murders of loyal headmen and informers goes on in a crescendo . . . They [the colonial authorities] now talk of public hangings as a bit of the "Psychological warfare."[131] Throughout the Emergency her letters to Huxley are a record of the incidents that happened, the measures taken to combat the situation by a government, which she felt was inept, and publicity for the settlers, which she believed was totally lacking. The real tragedy as far as Grant was concerned was that the Emergency was going "to sink Kenya economically."[132] As time progressed settler suspicions increased and their trusted retainers, the "houseboys" were seen as potential killers. Michael Blundell, one of the leading settler spokesmen, suggested that all Kikuyu houseboys be sacked, or locked out of settler houses after 6 p.m. Grant thought it was a hysterical response. "What DOES he mean?" she wrote to Huxley, "One doesn't come in till 6.45, and in lots of houses you can't even boil up a kettle INSIDE your house, so surely stumbling about outside in the dark would be lovely for the Mau Mau who could then pounce out of every corner without having to bother to go into the house."[133] By December 1954 the veneer of settler patience and calm had worn thin. Grant wrote *Operation Uncomfortable,* a memorandum on her views on how to end the emergency, which she sent to Huxley. By this time her moderation toward the Africans had evaporated:

> It is all very well but lots of moderates like myself have "had it" and are convinced that the velvet glove is just all wrong for their psychology, which is close to the beast as ours is too when roused. They just DON'T understand the gentleness. Besides everything else, I honestly do think that unless and until they are CONQUERED there is no hope of ever making a people of them.[134]

Grant's letters are useful as a record of the attitudes of a section of settler society, but in the context of this study equally significant is their importance as a source for Huxley's novel about the Mau Mau.

Mau Mau/Settler conflict of the Emergency was the subject of, or background for, a number of novels, two of which were written by women: Huxley's, *A Thing of Value,* and M. M. Kaye's *Death in Kenya*.[135] The two novels are different in genre and reflect the differences in colonial background of the two women as well as their different personal and literary agendas. Unlike Huxley, Mary Margaret ("Mollie") Kaye (1908–2004) was brought up in India and only got to know Kenya during the Emergency, when her husband was posted there with his regiment to fight the Mau Mau. Kaye is mainly remembered for her 1978 best-seller, *The Far Pavilions,* a historical novel set in India, but she started writing before World War II publishing her first novel in 1940.[136] *Death in Kenya*, which was originally published in 1958 under the title of *Later than you think*, was the fourth in a series of mystery novels that was published between 1953 and 1960. The venue of each reflected the military postings of her husband; mainly colonies or ex-colonies. Kaye was enthralled by Kenya and "despite some hair-raising moments . . . enjoyed practically every minute of [her] stay."[137] The novel is set by Lake Naivasha, the spot where Kaye had lived while in Kenya, although *Flamingo*, the house in the estate at the center of the novel, was based on those built by the early settlers. In the author's note at the beginning of the novel, she states that the opinions of her characters were "taken from life and at first hand. For though the Wind of Change was rising fast, very few of the Kenya-born settlers would believe that it could possibly blow strongly enough to uproot them from a country that every single one of them looked upon, and loved, as a '*Land where my fathers died, Land of the pilgrim's pride*."[138] The plot revolves around the DeBrett family, the matriarch of which, Lady Emily DeBrett (Em), had with her husband been among the first settlers in the Rift Valley. On her arrival in Kenya she had "taken one look at the great golden valley . . . and had fallen in love with it as some women fall in love with a man." She immediately decided to make it her home and never leave it. When her grandson, Eden DeBrett, was born in *Flamingo* she congratulated herself on founding "a Kenya dynasty, which in one hundred, two hundred, even three hundred years would still be living and farming on her land."[139]

The novel takes place immediately after the Emergency and opens with a description of Eden's wife, the timorous and fearful Alice who is not of settler origin. Her fear of Kenya, which to her was "a savage and uncivilised land full of brooding menace" was the lingering fear of the Mau Mau but also a portent of imminent murder. She dislikes settler society and is horrified by "[t]he casual attitude of most women towards firearms and the sight and smell of blood," and all she wants is to leave the colony.[140] The novel is not about the Mau Mau per se, rather Kaye uses the Mau Mau as a devise to ratchet up the suspense by creating a crescendo of violence that simulates episodes of African violence during the Emergency. The Emergency may be over but fear and suspicion of the Africans are not. The breakage of valuables in the DeBrett home sets in motion a series of mishaps that lead to Alice's murder, the first of several. When the household guard dog is poisoned, mimicking the way in which the Mau Mau started their anti-settler campaign by attacking the settlers' animals, the already terrified Alice becomes panic-stricken. The methods by which the series of murders are committed initially suggest that they are the work of Africans, renegade Mau Mau who have taken to the forests, but as the plot progresses it becomes obvious that the situation is much more ambiguous. Although, Kaye references various incidents that occurred during the Emergency, such as the Lari massacres, the novel is really about the dissolution of settler society. Kaye emphasizes the anxiety of the settlers, both with regard to the Africans and with regard to international criticism. Mau Mau-oathing disrupted the master/ servant relationship in those households where the employees were Kikuyu and the settlers were now wary of all Africans. As Lady Emily's manager informs a group of her friends, when she stalwartly continues to protect her staff from police interference: "[I t]old her years ago she should throw out all her Kukes. But Em's always fancied she knew better than anyone else. 'Treat 'em right and they'll be loyal.' *Bah*! There's no such thing as a loyal Kuke. We've learned that—the hard way!"[141] It would seem that the aristocratic Lady Emily's sense of entitlement toward her land and her behavior toward her "retainers" is very much that of her class, the pioneer aristocracy of Kenya. The reiteration at various points in the novel, of her refusal to deny her servants' loyalty also emblematizes an inability to admit that the Africans could actually dislike the settlers and their regime. Settler anxiety of international pressure to decolonize and, hence lose their place in Kenya is best expressed by the male love interest of the novel, Drew.

> I was born here and this is as much my home as Sendayo's [his employee]. I want to stay here, and if that is immoral and indefensible Colonialism, then every American whose pioneer forebears went in a covered wagon to open up the West is tarred with the same brush; and when the U.N.O. orders them out, we may consider moving![142]

The reference to the United States is, of course, a response to American criticism of British colonialism, which the settlers saw as the pursuit of American interests, rather than the altruistic desire to encourage the self-determination of colonized peoples; an estimation, which with the hindsight of the twenty-first century, was not far off the mark.

In the denouement of the plot the reader discovers that it is not the "Kukes" that are to blame for the murders but Lady Emily herself. Kaye, therefore, challenges the concept of the courageous aristocratic, who cares for and is loyal to her African staff, by showing that Lady Emily's behavior was one of self-preservation rather than any affectionate loyalty to the African. The novel can be read in two ways: as a straightforward detective story with the added "spice" of a tropical setting or as an allegory of the

demise of settler society, whose leading lights are as depraved as the Mau
Mau were accused of being by the settlers.

Huxley's *A Thing to Love*, published four years earlier than Kaye's and
written at the height of the Emergency, is a very different type of novel.
Although there are certain similarities to *Death in Kenya* in its presentation of settler attitudes, it is essentially a political novel and, hence more
complex. The action takes place during the Emergency and Huxley sets out
to illustrate the politics and progression of events from both points of view.
She introduces the main settler and Kikuyu characters in her first chapter
and alternates subsequent chapters between developments on the Kikuyu
and the settler sides. In each case she demonstrates the tensions within each
group as well as the violence inflicted by each on the other. The authenticity of the Kikuyu voice is suggested by the extensive use of Kikuyu parables
and riddles in the dialogues between the main African characters, whereas
that of the settler voice comes from her settler roots, her familiarity with the
settler community and, naturally enough, from her correspondence with her
mother and other settlers.[143]

The main characters of the plot are the settlers: Sam Gibson, Patricia
Foxley, and her parents, and the Africans: Gitau, Georges Rutinau, Josiah-
Kimani, and the Spokesman— presumably meant to be Jomo Kenyatta—as
the supreme leader. Huxley rightly situates the roots of the problems in
Kenya as land and political inequality: "Scratch a Kikuyu and you find a
grievance about land; talk to one for five minutes and you're on to politics,"
Sam reflects to himself in the opening chapter after Gitau has told him that
he is landless.[144] At the first gathering of the Kikuyu leaders, all of whom
were educated in Britain, Georges Rutinau reflects that to gain freedom it
was necessary "to unite his people in a great revolt against that smug superiority, that intolerable arrogance . . . Only the Kikuyu could bring that off in
Kenya, for only the Kikuyu had the intelligence, the courage, and the unity
to right all the wrongs."[145] By juxtaposing settler arrogance with Kikuyu
arrogance, Huxley undercuts potential sympathy for the Kikuyu cause. She
reminds her readers through the musings of the spiritual and mild-mannered
Pat Foxley that "a conspiracy founded on hatred by seekers after power, and
built up by intimidation, couldn't be the answer" to Kenya's problems.[146]
The problem as Pat saw it was the city, which stifled people and made them
rot inside. "[S]omething like that was happening to many of the Kikuyu
she had grown up among and loved . . . once they left their mountain and
its green shoulders for the hard cities and alien farms, something in them
withered . . . and some among them turned rotten, sterile and dangerous . . .
The power to create died . . . and they had in them only the power to
destroy."[147] Pat's dilemma was a reflection of Huxley's own: how to reconcile childhood memories of equitable and trusting relations between African
and European with the mistrust and anger of the present. The nostalgia for
this lost tranquility is implicit not only in Pat's reflections as she takes in the
beauty of her rural surroundings, but also in her father's anger at what he
sees as the credulity of the simple African "lads from the farms," who were

being radicalized by agitators and a subversive press. He puts it down to a "form of racial conceit," for it was "a great mistake to suppose that Europeans were the only ones to practice racial arrogance."[148]

As the violence in the novel against the settlers escalates from the destruction of the prize, cattle of the Foxley's former farm manager, Piet Hendrik, to the eventual killing of Pat's parents by their servants led by their headman, Raphaelo, Huxley parallels the progression with details of the growth of the Mau Mau movement. Shortly after the evisceration of Piet's cattle, when Pat raises the question of the Mau Mau with Raphaelo, who has known her since she was a baby and with whom she has always had excellent relations, he claims he has never heard the word. In fact, in exchange for all his life's savings the Kikuyu leaders have promised him the Foxley farm and all its land once Kenya is free. As they explained to him "there would come a morning when no European in Kenya would wake up to see the sunrise. Each of these well-fed, ill-mannered men would expect his morning tea to come as usual, but a sword or a panga would bring in his tea. For weren't the Kikuyu in every European house and farm?"[149] Even the most "faithful" Kikuyu is not trustworthy, therefore. If Africans like Raphaelo, cannot be bribed to join the Mau Mau, they are intimidated. Huxley describes the violence the Kikuyu inflicted on their fellow tribesmen and women to force them to take part in the Mau Mau oath-taking rituals. Once taken, the oath bound them to maim and kill if required to do so. But she also raises the violent interrogation methods of the police. "Hatred was catching," Pat realized when confronted with Piet's initial reactions to the loss of his cattle, and it is Piet who is involved with the police in trying to force captured Africans "to vomit out everything [they] know" by "pouring bitter medicine down [their] throats."[150] That Huxley chooses to make Piet, the only named person in her reference to torture, an Afrikaner and originally of lower social status than her British characters, reiterates settler ideas about the brutality and inferiority of the Afrikaners. The confession extracted by Piet provided the names of the other conspirators and, as Sam tells Pat, "we shall get most of them, and they'll hang," to which she replies, "[i]t would be better news if we could understand what had got into them and how to cure it. Hanging people doesn't get you very far."[151]

Huxley illustrates the divisions within the Kikuyu community by focusing on Chief Kimani and his two sons, Josiah and Matthew. Whereas Josiah Kimani is part of the Mau Mau elite, Matthew and his father remain loyal to the British. For Matthew the Emergency with its arrests and violence has turned "the whole country upside down" and he feared that "far from ending the trouble, the emergency would intensify it. The leaders of the conspiracy would leave Nairobi and bring their evil and their wild intoxicating notions with them like an infection, to spread far and wide," and he hoped that the "leaders of his generation" would be able to find a way to "repel this plague of the mind."[152] By using the African voice to express settler beliefs that the Emergency was going to do more harm than good and that the Mau Mau was a plague, Huxley adds ballast to them. The grisly end at the hands of the Mau Mau of Chief Kimani and Matthew reinforces the ideas even further. The problems during the Emergency are compounded by generational differences and tensions within the two separate communities. The Kikuyu elders feel that members of the younger generation who join the Mau Mau are "bad men because they mock the customs of our fathers."[153] Settlers, on the other hand, are wary of liberals and the metropole British. Again Huxley uses the African voice to make her point. Some British M. P.s, Josiah tells a Mau Mau supporter, "do not like these Kenya Europeans any more than we do and wish to destroy them. When they make speeches, the Governor [of Kenya] is afraid."[154]

The Mau Mau leaders of the novel may have appreciated the liberals of Britain but they were wary of those in the colony, in particular women like Pat who supported and were friendly toward the Kikuyu. "The Europeans who . . . bark like jackals and hit people when they are angry . . . [t]hey keep hot the hatred of the European, as a smith's bellows heats his fire. They will send the young men to the forest for us, and teach them not to care for their lives. But the soft Europeans, who try to win us round with smiles and medicines, they are dangerous."[155] For Huxley, therefore, the racism, violence, and excessive behavior of some die-hard colonials, most of whom are not part of the settler upper crust, helps to fuel the rebellion and unravel the benefits that colonialism has bestowed on the Africans. The novel, however politically and ethnographically accurate it was—or is—deemed to be, is a lament; a lament for what could have been but wasn't. The racism of uncouth settlers, the corruption of the urban space, the loss of respect for traditional order and social hierarchy, whether it was that of tribe or class; these were the things that had led to the pass in which Kenya found itself. But the novel was certainly also designed to instruct the British public in the horrors of the Emergency; a novel on the Mau Mau being much more digestible than a political treatise on the subject. Indeed throughout the postwar period until her death, Huxley kept up a steady stream of articles and letters in the British press on developments in Kenya particularly and Africa generally, the output of which matched that of her published fiction and nonfiction.

The period from the end of the Emergency in 1959 to independence in 1963 was an anxious time for the settlers, who were fearful of the inevitable loss of power independence would bring. By 1960 "extreme and utter gloom" had descended because, Grant stated:

> More and More and More [was] being given to Black Brother and no one seeming to be making an effort to get any form of security whatever for anything not black; perhaps they know it wouldn't be worth the paper written on. It really is extraordinary how all the politicians (except of course poor Briggs) seem to think their blue-eyed though black skinned playmates at the Conference are really men of utter integrity, sincerity and every Christian virtue.[156]

Whatever the settlers may have thought, they were unable to reverse the march toward independence, which was being hurried along by Iain Macleod, Secretary of State for the Colonies from 1959–1961. Christine

Nicholls informed me that in an interview he gave to the Colonial Records Project, he said that had the settlers caused obstruction he would have given in to them.[157] It seemed a curious departure from his stance when he was Secretary for the Colonies.[158] Indeed a perusal of the manuscript showed that he had in fact only been concerned about the support of the moderate settlers, led by Michael Blundell. Such a loss of support would have slowed down the progress to independence, not halted it altogether.[159] By his own admission, Macleod's firm belief was "that the best future for the Europeans [in all African territories] was to stay in an African-run country."[160] A memory lapse or nostalgic wishful thinking on Nicholls' part? A bit of both, perhaps. When independence was finally granted, whatever her mother may have thought, Elspeth Huxley had come around to the fact that it was indeed time to give Africans the responsibility for their country whatever it would mean for European enterprises in Kenya and those Africans that depended on them.[161] Huxley's shift in perspective is significant. Unlike her counterparts in Algeria who wrote with the settler's voice and had a much harder time coming to terms with their loss, she accepted the inevitable. This did not mean that nostalgia would be kept at bay, but it did mean that it would not be as virulent.

CONCLUSION

Apart from the pressures of national and international politics, the most important factor that shaped the differences in women's writing in the two colonies during the conflicts of decolonization was the socio-economic make-up of the settler population and its relationship to the metropole. The fact that the majority of settlers in Algeria were urbanites, who had come from countries along the northern shores of the Mediterranean, meant that they were doubly immigrant in the sense that on arrival in the colony they belonged neither to the culture of the dominating French nor to that of the dominated Algerians. Although they had acquired French citizenship along the way and with it a veneer of Frenchness of varying thickness, they had forged a settler culture sui generis: "the Mediterranean melting pot." Whether or not this identity was chimerical is immaterial, it was not as closely linked to the metropole as the settler identity in Kenya was to Britain. Algeria was, of course, near enough for those who could afford it to be able to slip over to France on a regular basis, but even so France and its culture was, for the majority, more of an imagined ideal than a lived reality. As one of Baïlac's neo-French characters put it: "France? I never go there, only to fight if there is a war." Furthermore, nearly all settler children were educated in Algeria up to and including university, at least for those who qualified. There was therefore a cultural disconnect between colony and metropole, which meant that the relationship of the *pieds-noirs* to the metropole French was lived and experienced differently from the relationship between the Kenya settlers and metropole British.

The majority of settlers in Kenya were of British origin and, although those who had settled in the Highlands and other premium areas saw themselves as permanent fixtures in the colony, they remained stalwartly British. The Indians and the Afrikaners, who formed the largest groups of non-British settlers were kept, or kept themselves, both socially and hierarchically apart. It was the British settlers who formed the political and social elites and kept British culture entrenched in colonial society. Furthermore, their Kenya-born children, often as young as 6 or 7, were sent to boarding schools in Britain to be educated and socialized into the British way of life. Prior to World War II, when air travel was not yet the standard means of travel, this usually meant seeing their parents once a year, sometimes even less. When they returned to the colony they considered themselves to be British, and not part of a mixed-ethnic melting pot. The perceived incomprehension of the metropole for the colony, which existed among the settler populations of both Kenya and Algeria, was compounded for the settlers in the latter by a much greater cultural disconnect than was the case in Kenya. Not only did this mean that settler allegiances during the decolonization conflicts were much more fractured in Algeria than in Kenya, but it also meant that the "melting pot" mentality in Algeria prompted some settlers to ally themselves with the Algerians of the F. L. N. In both Algeria and Kenya anxiety at the impending loss of a way of life characterized women's writing at the time of decolonization and pointed to the type of nostalgia that would emerge in the post-independence period, but in the case of Algeria it would be conjoined to a disorienting loss of identity.

CHAPTER 7

Happy Families, *Pieds-Noirs*, Red Strangers, and "a Vanishing Africa": Nostalgia Comes Full Circle

De l'épopée veritable à l' épopée mythique, la marge me semble bien moins grande qu'il pourrait en paraître

Geneviève Baïlac, Les absinthes sauvages

I remembered the Swahili proverb: he who has tasted honey will return to the honey pot.

Elspeth Huxley, The Mottled Lizard

Algeria gained its independence in 1962; Kenya in 1963. Immediately following the Evian peace accords of March 1962, 1.2 million *pieds-noirs* left Algeria for France; many with little more than a suitcase. This mass migration became embedded in *pied-noir* memory as "the exodus," a term with quasi-religious connotations. On July 5, 1962, the day independence was officially declared, Algerians in Oran indiscriminately killed Europeans, while Algerian police and the French army, under orders from de Gaulle not to assist O. A. S. (Organisation armée secrète) sympathizers or anyone who protested the Evian accords, looked on. The figures for the massacre vary and are impossible to verify, but the event became part of the lore of victimhood.[1] (Oran had been the enclave of the O. A. S. whose members had committed over 500 assassinations of which over 400 were of Muslims.[2]) The bitterness that settlers in both Algeria and Kenya felt at decolonization was compounded in the case of Algeria by these events and a keen sense of betrayal, which was focused primarily on de Gaulle.[3] Furthermore, on arrival in France the Algerian settlers were greeted with hostility by the metropole French, many of whom had lost relatives in a war, the length of which they believed was due to the intransigence of the settlers.[4] The defensive mechanism of the *pieds-noirs*, against both the metropole French and the loss of their former identity, was to coalesce into a tight-knit community of "exiles." This notion of exile was to give rise to a very specific form of nostalgia, which although sharing some of the attributes of what one thinks of as colonial nostalgia, was unique in its long-standing bitterness and cohesive potential.

In Kenya there was no mass exodus, thanks in large part to the pragmatism of Jomo Kenyatta. Six months before independence, on June 1, 1963, he was appointed Prime Minister. In August of that year, in Nakuru, he made his now famous "Harambee" speech in front of 400 white Kenya farmers, when he called on the peoples of Kenya to forget the past and work toward a prosperous and united future, regardless of race. As *The Times* put it:

> Mr. Kenyatta, who introduced himself as 'a farmer like yourselves,' went on to appeal to them for mutual forgiveness for past wrongs. He suggested that Kenya could show that white, black, and brown could work together in harmony and 'make this country great.' He went on 'We can show other people in various parts of the world that different racial groups can work together.' . . . We want you to stay and farm well in this country.[5]

When he finished his speech "the white farmers roared . . . 'Harambee' and Lord Delamere, the leader of the farmers declared the event to be "unique and historic."[6] As a result, many settlers chose to stay and some eventually opted for Kenyan nationality. The die-hard supremacists sold up and moved to Rhodesia or South Africa. A few settlers moved to other countries. Eighty-year old Nellie Grant, for example, went to Portugal where she bought a *quinta* in Burgau on the Algarve. Kenyatta's success in dissipating settler anxiety and the fact that those who chose to return to Britain, were not confronted with the sort of harsh reception that precipitates feelings of victimhood, meant that the forms nostalgia would take would be less strident and devoid of the intense bitterness that was to characterize so much of *Nostalgérie,* especially in its early manifestations.

ALGERIA: "HAPPY FAMILIES" AND *PIEDS-NOIRS:* NOSTALGIA AS IDENTITY LOST OR IDENTITY REGAINED?

"Non et non, je n'irai pas!" (No and no, I will not go!) are the evocative opening words of Francine Dessaigne's *Déracinés!. . .* (Uprooted), for if the *pieds-noirs* left Algeria physically, the majority was never to do so mentally. Published in 1964 *Deracinés* is divided into two parts; the first is in journal form starting with an entry for May 1962 and ending with one for April 1964, the second is a short story. Together they form cameos of nostalgia insofar as they evoke the "lost" lifestyle, customs, and happiness of these "orphans of the sun" who had been "wrenched from their province" *(notre Province nous a été arrachée).*[7] Describing a gathering of 40 repatriated settlers in November 1962, Dessaigne writes: "They feel good together but their pleasure lacks joy, their jokes are feeble. They have suffered too much not to be weary in their leisure time. Despoiled *(dépouillés)*, they are now only a group of disparate, exhausted beings, united in a pagan worship of their nostalgia."[8] Like Anne Loesch, Dessaigne sympathized with the O. A. S. In her entry for September 1962 she describes her children and their friends playing a new game, that of the O. A. S. preparing to blow up the post office. Later, the children decide to play at parading down the Rue Michelet. They march down the alleys around their new homes, draped in flags, banging on saucepans with wooden spoons to the 5 tone beat of *Al-gé-rie Fran-çaise*. One of the young mothers, Dessaigne declares, bursts into tears.[9] By reducing the events of the final paroxysms of settler Algeria, when the O. A. S. was on the rampage, to children's games not only does Dessaigne dissociate them from their true violence and destruction, but she also demonstrates that *pied-noir* memory would be kept alive and passed down across generations. As she explicitly states in another section of the journal: "We will never lose the yearning for our lost shores. We will never be like others. Our nostalgia resurfaces at each instant . . . But we must make a place for our children. They will adapt. Through us, they will keep alive the memory of the Province which was snatched from us *(notre Province arrachée)* and of those who suffered for it."[10] Needless to say she also evokes the trope of the civilizing impact of the settler community: "That land, which when it has gripped you makes you love it even to its rags and vermin *(jusqu'aux haillons et à la vermine)* which would have required a thousand years of patient love to get rid of. The rags have won; the vermin spreads."[11]

If anger and bitterness were the terms in which this first wave of nostalgia was couched so too was the theme of betrayal. In the short story that ends *Déracinés!* . . . Marie is the anxious, weary wife of an O. A. S. sympathizer, Jacques, with whom her marital relationship has cooled. When an old friend, André, now a policeman, arrives from France, Jacques breaks up the friendship. The lonely Marie nonetheless takes up with André, and when André arrests a member of the O. A. S. cell, Marie, who is in fact innocent, is suspected of betrayal and shot. That Marie is not even given a chance to defend herself, underlines the fact that the mere act of fraternizing with a French official is in itself a betrayal that merits the loss of life, an erasure of a perfidious identity. Marie's loss of life in the last sentence of the book becomes a mirror image of and a retribution for the metaphoric loss of life of the *pieds-noirs* that Dessaigne repeatedly stresses in the first part of the book.

The metaphor of the settlers' death and victimhood was elaborated in Marie Elbe's 1963 novel, *Et à l'heure de notre mort*.[12] Elbe, the pseudonym for Janine Plantié-Bromberger, was born in Boufarik in 1926 and taught in primary school in the Algiers Casbah. She was also a journalist for Radio Alger and a reporter for the *Dépêche Quotidienne* and *l'Echo d'Alger*.[13] Her novel, which starts on the quayside of Algiers harbor on June 17, 1962, opens with the sensationalist sentence "They have just slit the throat of a 15 year old kid."[14] The action takes place over two days and, by means of the conversations and reminiscences of the departing *pieds-noirs*, catalogues their deaths and despair. The tone is again angry and bitter; the message it imparts

is of betrayal by the French government and the political and religious similes and metaphors Elbe uses create an image of the settlers as martyrs and
victims. The events of the Rue d'Isly in March 1962 become "the Saint-
Bartholomew of the *pieds-noirs,*" the siege of Bab-el-Oued, its "Budapest"
and of course their final departure is the "Exodus."[15] The importance of the
book lies, not so much in its plot as in the fact it put in writing what many
pieds-noirs felt in 1962 and thus concretized the sentiments of victimhood
that would underpin so much of *pied-noir* nostalgia.

In 1972, at the 10th anniversary of the loss of Algeria, Geneviève Baïlac's
Les absinthes sauvages: Témoignage pour le peuple pieds-noirs appeared with a
preface by Robert Aron, the author and elected member of the *Académie
française*.[16] In it, Aran declared that 10 years after they had left Algeria, the
pieds-noirs were still "an ardent community full of dynamism".[17] For Baïlac,
however, "[h]istory had thrown the community far from its native shores to
a land where it had been badly treated, misunderstood and ill-loved."[18] In
her short introduction, Baïlac lists a series of questions, the most tantalizing
of which for her is what would have happened to Algeria had the "*pieds-noirs*
won their fight." Right from the start, therefore, she introduces a dreamlike
thread into her reminiscences. "Maybe," she admits, "by undertaking the
history of my people, I am only embarking on the recitation of my dreams.
But everyone knows today, that dreams are closer to profound truth than any
reality *(n'importe quelle réalité)*.[19]

The opening sentence of her first chapter refers to the "tranquil ruins of
Tipasa," the ideological site of *pied-noir* identity.[20] Baïlac declared that she
belonged to a quintessential "creole" family of Algeria forged from a cultural
melting pot of races, so gloriously described by Louis Bertrand.[21] Throughout the book Baïlac refers to the creoles/*pieds-noirs* as "my people," who,
she emphasizes at intervals, are exiles. On one occasion she even uses the
word *proscrits* with its dual meaning of exile and outlaw, hence alluding to
their "marginalized" status in France.[22] By the 1970s the anger of the first
wave of nostalgic memoirs had dissipated, but the bitterness had not. It had
morphed into a distancing mechanism that stressed the differences between
the *pieds-noirs* and the French and the unscrupulousness of U.S. Cold War
politics.

In contemplating what exactly epitomized "her people," Baïlac acknowledges her debt to the character Cagayous, the creation of Auguste Robinet
(Musette). Cagayous was the archetypical Bab-el-Oued *pied-noir* without
whom, Baïlac states, many "[European] Algerian writers would not be who
they were." The *pieds-noirs* were a people, she continued, who proudly
adopted French nationality but were totally united *(sans clivage)* in their
beliefs and attitudes. "The French flag, and with it French glory, [French]
culture and with it the French language, were theirs without being tinged
with the least nostalgia for a native land. *(une patrie d'origine)*."[23] In other
words, whatever their country of origin and their degree of espousal of
Frenchness, their only allegiance was to Algeria. In 1955, she states, these
modest *pieds-noirs* "were prepared to lay down their lives not to save their

privileges in Algeria, which they didn't even think about, but for the honor of France."[24] By placing the onus of their struggle in Algeria on France rather than their self-interest, Baïlac rescues the *pieds-noirs* from the injustices of colonialism and their inability to accept the Algerians on an equal footing with themselves. Indeed, like so many writers of *pied-noir* origin, she sees pre-independence Algerian society as one big happy family. The last manifestation of this togetherness, she believes, occurred on May 16, 1958, when "one hundred thousand people, Europeans and Muslim standing shoulder to shoulder, sang the *Marseillaise* . . . [while] astounded foreign journalists cried 'We've never seen anything like it in our lives!.'"[25] If the *The Times* of London and *The New York Times* are anything to go by, Baïlac's interpretation of events had more to do with wishful thinking than the reality on the ground.[26] The journalists may have felt they had seen nothing like it in their lives, but it was not the result of any manifestation of solidarity between Europeans and Algerians, but rather to the impending crisis between the politicians in France and the military in Algeria, whose machinations threatened civil war; a situation which would be temporarily deflated by de Gaulle's accession to power.

Coinciding with the 1958 crisis in Algiers, Nikita Khrushchev promised Gamal Abdel Nasser full cooperation in his bid to unite the Arab peoples.[27] Cold War fears and the promise of access to Algerian oil led the United States to change its policy toward Algeria from backing France to supporting the struggle for independence.[28] Baïlac expresses *pied-noir* bitterness at United States pressure on France to decolonize: "It is well to remember that American propaganda against the French presence in Algeria was among the most efficient." She goes on to deride American hypocrisy by reminding her readers that "the American people owes its existence to the nearly complete extermination of its native peoples . . . The grand children of the colonial exterminators [i.e., the U.S.] were unable to contain their criticism of the grand-children of the truly civilized colonizers [the *pieds-noirs*] who did not annihilate their indigenous population but helped to develop their lives."[29]

In much the same way as Camus, Baïlac had dreamed of reconciliation between the Europeans and the "Muslims" in Algeria, between the "Occident and the Orient." That it did not happen was due, not to settler intransigence or ill-will toward the Algerians, but to "French and Algerian nationalisms." Of these two she asked herself as her parting question, "[W]hich is the most dangerous."[30] The idea that it was a combination of the evils of nationalism, U.S. propaganda, and French betrayal that had disrupted the possibility of reconciliation gave rise to the "happy family" as a trope of nostalgia. *La Famille Hernandez,* she asserted, "was the symbol of an authentic Franco-Muslim fraternity."[31] Indeed the 1979 edition of *La Famille Hernandez* was published with the subtitle *L'Algérie heureuse.*[32]

The fear that *pied-noir* memory would be lost permeated the writings of the early post-independence period and led, in 1973, to the founding of *Le Cercle algérianiste,* whose objective was "to safeguard the cultural patrimony of the French presence in Algeria."[33] Its journal *L'Algérianiste,* together with the local branches of the association, were the vehicles by means of which information was disseminated to promote an understanding of the *pied-noir* presence in France and to prevent the disintegration of the community. Among its methods was the publication of "testimonies of those who had labored in North Africa and thus provided to all interested in the past the essential elements of the history of **our** country."[34] Ten years on from independence and in spite of a relatively successful integration into French society, the *pieds-noirs* still imagined Algeria as their land. The *Cercle's* ideological *raison-d'être* was expressed in its manifesto, entitled "Because We Love Algeria." The association was created, the manifesto stated: "to protest against the official history of the French presence in Algeria, which was written by those who had forced *(acculés)* us into exile . . . [and] to preserve from oblivion what little remains of our magnificent and cruel past."[35] A second association, the *Centre de Culture, de Recherche et Documentation historique sur l'Algérie* was established in 1974, in Aix-en-Provence. Now known as the *Centre de Documentation Historique sur l'Algérie*, it is a *pied-noir* initiative but claims complete objectivity in collecting personal and cultural material ranging from before the conquest to the present.[36] The flood of *pieds-noirs* fiction and nonfiction that ensued the establishment of these two institutions is a measure of the seriousness with which their members sought and still seek to provide a counter narrative to mainstream interpretations of the French episode in Algerian history.[37]

It was a woman, Marie Cardinal (1929–2001), whose fiction broke through the barrier of mainstream French literary disinterest in *pied-noir* colonial concerns.[38] Cardinal's first novel, *Ecoutez la mer* was published in 1962, winning her the *Prix International du Premier Roman*. Her 1975 novel *Les mots pour le dire* brought her international fame, earning her the 1976 *Prix Littré* for the best novel about a medical condition and transforming her into a feminist icon. Cardinal was born in Algiers, and educated at religious institutions there before going on to university in Paris, where she obtained a philosophy degree at the Sorbonne. She taught in Salonika, Lisbon, Vienna, and Montreal before embarking on a journalistic career, contributing to magazines such as *L'Express* and *Elle*, which eventually led to a successful literary career.[39] With few exceptions, Cardinal's fiction alludes to or is about her experiences growing up in Algeria. As she herself admitted, Algeria was a "world about which she wanted to write and about which she never stopped writing."[40] Much of her fiction has a strong allegoric element. In her autobiographical novel *Les mots pour le dire,* for example, the plot deals with the process of psychoanalysis and liberation of the mentally ill and "mute" Cardinal from the trauma and pain of her mother's overbearing influence: a "Clytemnestra, Electra and Iphigenia, all in one."[41] Her biological mother, to be sure, but also mother-Algeria, for the healing process that Cardinal undergoes can also be read as an escape from settler society and the regaining of her equilibrium after the dislocation associated with Algerian independence. It is a novel of personal and political decolonization: from the colonizing presence of her mother and the colonizing of her body by the restrictive socializing she received at the hands of a machismo settler society, on the one hand, and as a reflection of the trajectory of the country's decolonization, on the other. Toward the end of the novel, she describes a "nightmare" in which her ambiguous feeling about Algeria is symbolized by two rooms of a house in which she finds herself, one containing three members of the F. L. N., the other a group of women. "I was, she writes, 'for an independent Algeria; my mother knew it but I did not understand her terror [at the thought of it].' "[42] She tries to go toward the F. L. N. room but cannot.

> My mother and the other women held me back. I was bound to them in an incomprehensible way. I wasn't their prisoner; it was fate that attached me to them in an absurd way, which I did not question . . . Little by little I retreated until I found myself shut up in the room with these women. Mediterranean women dressed in black, mumbling their prayers . . . crossing themselves and whispering "aie, aie, aie . . . my God my poor child . . . Their fear became my fear, I perspired, I trembled like them . . . There we all were, squeezed together . . . fear in our bellies and terrible stories in our heads, stories of women, raped and disembowelled.[43]

The words to say it of the title are the words she eventually finds to express what had hitherto been taboo: her sexuality, the intimacies of the female body, and the politics of the war. Like Algeria, Cardinal finds her independence. Unlike her mother, who at the age of 60 loses "her universe" when she finds herself in alien surroundings and prefers to die; Cardinal manages to exorcise the past and is "reborn."[44]

It would be a mistake to think that unlike other *pied-noir* writers, Cardinal had, through psychoanalysis, rid herself of the ghosts of her colonial past. In another of her semi-autobiographical novels, *Amour . . . Amours,* the protagonist, sixty-five year old Lola sits in her garden and daydreams about her past life in Algeria, where her identity is rooted. On leaving Algiers after the war she gazes at the disappearing city and realizes that "she will never again be at home *(chez elle)* . . . in those streets, in those gardens, where her soul had emerged, where her mind had been formed, where her body had developed."[45] As she thinks back on her childhood, she envisages the past as one of family happiness. Not so much with her biological family, who were often arguing, but with her Algerian family, whose food, hospitality, and warmth she misses. "Her mothers were called Daïba, Zorah, Fatmina; her fathers Barded, Aoued. Kader. She had lots of brothers, sisters, cousins, uncles and aunts." [46] The concept of Algeria as an extended "happy family" is a recurring theme of *Nostalgérie*. As in this instance, the happiness is usually defined by a paternalistic master/servant dynamic, but the image is complicated when it concerns childhood reminiscences. Colonial ideology, whatever the colonizing power, emphasized the paternalism of its system by claiming that the colonized were children to be cared for and raised to adulthood by the colonizers. By making the beloved family the extended family of her real family's Algerian servants, Cardinal reverses the power dynamic making the parents the colonized rather the colonizers. Such nostalgia is not only a yearning for the apparent tranquility and happiness of a conflict-free childhood, but also a nostalgic yearning for what had never actually been; a society free of racialization and social hierarchies.

In *Autrement Dit*, the sequel to *Les mots pour le dire*, Cardinal declares, "I often dream of returning to Algeria and I imagine that it would be exactly as it was when I was a child." [47] The book, which is in the form of an extended conversation between Cardinal and the feminist, Annie Leclerc, is as significant for its feminist content as it is for its nostalgia about Algeria. Indeed, Cardinal became a prominent figure in the French feminist movement. In 1973 she edited a collection of the writings of the Tunisian born feminist lawyer and activist, Gisèle Halimi, under the title *La Cause des Femmes*.[48] Published two years after *Les mots pour le dire*, Cardinal's reminiscences in *Autrement Dit* elaborated what she had already stated elsewhere in less explicit terms. The relation between the sexes was a con-game *(attrape-couillon)*, she declared. Women were hemmed in by the need to respond to men's desire to be surrounded by beautiful women. Citing the example of Margaret Mead, who, in spite of her plainness "had always been listened to and taken seriously in her country," Cardinal continues, "[i]magine such an ugly women in France stating the things she did. Nobody would listen to her or else she would remain in the wings . . . Do you know of a really ugly woman who succeeded in making her voice heard in France? I certainly don't."[49] But beauty alone was not enough, she adds, for "beneath the beautiful exterior a woman had to be a good fucker, a good cook, thrifty, a mother, wife, nurse, needlewoman and washerwoman." These were the attributes that had been "inculcated in us from birth."[50] Cardinal's feminism flourished during the wave of 1970s French feminism, but her critique of the machismo of French society had its roots in the phallocentrism of the colonial society in which she grew up. Indeed, she links the paternalism of the colony to the paternalism of the family unit. "I always compared colonization to the traditional couple . . . the family . . . Why was it that as a child I was ashamed of colonialism when it was presented to me as natural, even blessed? . . . with the clarity of a child I realized that it did not practice what it preached."[51] As demonstrated by her description of Margaret Mead, whom she actually categorized in the above-cited passage as "ugliness incarnate," *(la laideur incarnée)*, Cardinal was not as liberated from the gendered assumptions of her colonial past as she implied. Her ambiguous sentiments toward her colonial past and intense nostalgia coupled with selective repudiation enabled her to carve out a creative path that led her into the mainstream of the metropole cultural scene. It is interesting to compare Cardinal to two other post-independence "stars" of the *pied-noir* firmament, who were of her generation, Hélène Cixous (b.1937) and Jacques Derrida (1930–2004). Like Cixous and Derrida, Cardinal's works extend beyond the narrow confines of her Algerian past to address larger philosophic concerns, yet unlike them she engages explicitly with her Algerian past in nearly all of her texts.[52] Cardinal's nostalgia was more nuanced than most of her *pied-noir* compatriots, who had taken to writing about Algeria during the 1960s and 1970s, but it still manifested itself as a loss of identity. There is a certain irony in the fact that the modernity of gender relations, that the settlers had tried so hard to instill into "indigenous" women throughout the colonial period, and in particular during the 1954–1962 war, was called into question by one of their own.

Post-independence nostalgia for Algeria and things Algerian as not restricted to *pied-noir* angst about lost identity and lost land, however. During the 1980s and 1990s, although works of *pied-noir* nostalgia continued apace, becoming a veritable cottage industry, a nostalgia for the exoticism associated with the colony also emerged.[53] It focused mainly on two women, Elissa Rhaïs and Isabelle Eberhardt. On May 7, 1982 Bernard Pivot, French literary pundit and mediator of the popular cultural program, *Apostrophes,* introduced the author Paul Tabet (b. 1942) as one of his guests. Tabet's book *Elissa Rhaïs, un roman,* had just appeared in the bookstores. (The qualification *un roman* was later dropped and the book assumed the status of biography.[54]) Tabet was head of the French Cultural Service in Rome at the time and is a relative of Rhaïs. In his portrait of Rhaïs, he contended that she was virtually illiterate. Her amanuensis had been a young nephew, Raoul-Robert (Tabet's father), whom she had taken under her wing and then made her lover and virtual prisoner. Rhaïs had been a beautiful woman in her youth, who, according to Tabet, had been married off to an older Arab man and incarcerated in a harem. There she had first been fêted and then totally neglected. Her husband's death liberated her and enabled her to create a new life for herself. Resentment of the years lost in the harem and the anger at her treatment by her late husband had stirred up feelings of revenge against humanity in general, and men in particular, which led to her pressuring her nephew to become her lover and scribe. According to Tabet, in 1939 Rhaïs had been considered but passed over for the *Légion d'honneur,* her illiteracy being the reason for this rejection.[55] The shock of having her deception uncovered was so great, according to Tabet, that she passed out in the Ministry office where she had been summoned, and died eight months later, in August 1940, without ever regaining consciousness.[56] Within days of the program, a controversy started in the French press over the authenticity of Tabet's claims.[57] Taking part were the few remaining members of Rhaïs' family and friends as well as literati of *pied-noir* origin, such as Jules Roy and Bernard Henri-Levy, who had in fact first promoted Tabet's book.[58] Pivot was declared to be the target of a hoax. Rhaïs' supporters denied her illiteracy and the use of her nephew in the scurrilous way implied by Tabet. As Jules Roy wrote in *Le Monde:* "It seems incredible . . . Could she have tricked the esteemed publishers, Plon, [as well as] Colette, Mallarmé and M. Paul Morand?"[59] Tabet defended himself by saying his biographical portrait of Rhaïs accorded with the account of events his father related to him before he died, adding somewhat cryptically that given her assumption of Muslim identity she would have wished it to be so.[60] In 1996 in a preface to the reedition of Rhaïs' novel *Le Sein Blanc,* Tabet again defended his position against his critics, the most significant of whom were now dead.[61] It is impossible to judge the veracity of Tabet's account, as Jean Déjeux has pointed out.[62] The accuracy or fallacy of Tabet's account is immaterial in the context of this study. Its pertinence lies in the fact the exoticism of Tabet's tale of colonial Algeria was an excellent marketing ploy, which thrust a figure of the heyday of colonialism in the limelight. The debate his book produced regenerated interest in Rhaïs and her world, and resulted in the reissuing of some of her novels and short stories and the production of a television film, *Le Secret d'Elissa Rhaïs,* directed by Jacques Otmezguine.[63] The nostalgia for the exoticism and mysteriousness of colonial Algeria, thus extended *Nostal-gérie* beyond the *pied-noir* community to the wider public.

Isabelle Eberhardt was even more important to this process. Unlike Rhaïs, by the post-independence period, Eberhardt was already something of an icon. Her independent nature, her trans-gender persona, and her determination to pursue her writing career at all costs, to say nothing of her repudiation by colonial society during her lifetime, combined to make her a figure from the colonial past worthy of respect. The process of Eberhardt's acquisition of iconic status started almost immediately after her death and continued throughout the colonial period. In 1947, when Lucienne Jean-Darrouy wrote an article reclaiming Eberhardt as a notable and influential figure for Algerian literature, she glossed over her maltreatment at the hands of the settler community. Jean-Darrouy emphasized those attributes that had made her an outsider during her lifetime, namely her nonconformist nomadic existence, but it was the freedom of her errant lifestyle and her romantic heritage that made her so compelling. Eberhardt, she opined, had influenced a generation of writers in the colony and this in spite of having lived in Algeria for only 10 years. She "had a greater knowledge of the country and its flavour, its beings and its soul than the more organized writers *(producteurs bien organisés)* who came after her . . . romanticism was part of this women, like an intoxication."[64] Articles such as that of Jean-Darrouy appeared sporadically throughout the 1950s and early 1960s, but her reputation received a real boost in the post-independence period. Renewed interest in Eberhardt among scholars was certainly due to the emergence of post–World War II feminism and with it the disciplines of women and gender studies. Equally noteworthy, however, was the interest generated in the wider public, with Algerians appropriating her persona with the same enthusiasm as the French. Two articles, which appeared in the newspaper *L'Action,* one in 1974 by Mahmoud Bouali and the other in 1976 by Abdelmajid Chorfi, picked up the themes which had been used about Eberhardt during the colonial period by Algerian writers and set the tone for the articles that appeared in the 1980s and 1990s.[65] For Chorfi, Eberhardt had found her true homeland in Algeria *(sa vraie patrie).* "She was not an agent of colonization . . . she hated Europe (at least the Europe that exported its "civilization" and not the Europe of art and thought) . . . she was drawn by pure affinity of temperament to a people enamored *(épris)* with independence . . . [and] proved that riches were born of admiration and exchange and not contempt."[66] Chorfi was writing at a time when North African immigration was beginning to be perceived as a "problem" in France. In late 1960s and early 1970s over one million North Africans, mainly Algerians, emigrated from the Maghreb to France creating tensions that led to the tightening of immigration policies and, in the 1980s, to the emergence of Le Pen and his anti-immigrant politics. Not only was he appropriating Eberhardt's legacy for Algeria, but he was also implicitly calling for the acceptance and tolerance of Islam that Eberhardt had personified. A similar article in 1984 by Mohamed Hamouda Bensaï compared her exceptional character to that of Louise Michel and Séverine, and reminded his readers of the fact "she was the true sister of the 'destitute' ("*misereux*") of this Algerian land when it was prey to the exploitation of an inhuman regime . . . she loved our country passionately . . . and should therefore never be forgotten."[67]

Throughout the 1980s and 1990s, Algerian journalists continued to write articles in this vein.[68] The notion that Eberhardt belonged to Algeria was reiterated by the Algerian film director, Farouk Beloufa, in an interview he gave about the possibility of making a film about Eberhardt. "She is an absolutely fascinating character," he said, "who haunts one and from whom it is impossible to escape. She permeates you, bewitches you, pursues you. One can never break away from her . . . It is important that we, Algerians, make this film, because Isabelle Eberhardt belongs to Algeria."[69] Beloufa never made his film, probably due to lack of funding, but others did. In 1988 artist and director Leslie Thornton made the impressionistic *There was an unseen cloud moving* for Women Make Movies. Two years later, Ian Pringle directed a Franco-Australian version of Eberhardt's life entitled simply, *Isabelle Eberhardt*, with Peter O'Toole in the role of Major Hubert Lyautey (later Field Marshal), and in 1993 Djafar Djamardji directed *Errances (ou Terre en Cendres)*.[70] As the dates of these films suggest, the 1980s and 1990s were decades where interest in Eberhardt reached new heights. It is an interest that has not yet abated.[71]

In addition to the film, she was a focus of a number of theatrical performances and her writings were reissued in a variety of editions and translated into a number of languages.[72] Articles in both the Algerian and French press also continued to appear. One writer compared her to Rimbaud and wondered whether she was "a spy or a marabout, depraved or mystical," another saw her as emblematic of the fascination for Islam.[73] There was even a graphic story about her life, entitled "Mektoub."[74] Whatever the individual conclusions drawn by these writers, journalists and film directors, they agree that Eberhardt had achieved "legendary status." There is a nostalgic dimension to the attraction of figures, whose posthumous stature is so much greater than that of their lifetime for their past has been mentally airbrushed of its unattractive elements. The admiration and desire they elicit can become a romance with the past.

Since the summer of 1962, *Nostalgérie* has taken different forms and has evolved over time, but the *pieds-noirs* or French-Algerians as some prefer to be called, have remained militantly nostalgic. The colonial archives in Aix-en-Provence now has a special section to assist former settlers or their progeny with genealogical research and the Association du Centre de Documentation Historiquesur l'Algérie is a repository for *pied-noir* documents and memorabilia. The Sainte Claire convent in Perpignan is slated to house a substantial *pied-noir* museum, an intriguing choice of venue given that there is even religious dimension to their nostalgia in the form of two yearly pilgrimages, the first by the *pieds-noirs* of Oran at Ascension to the cathedral of Notre Dames et Saint Castor at Nimes, and the second by *pieds-noirs* and *harkis* on May 1st to the basilica of Notre Dame de la Victoire at St. Raphaël (Var), which looks out to Algiers.[75] In 2007 a Wall of the Disappeared was erected in the courtyard of the Sainte Claire convent, which lists the names of 2,700 *pieds-noirs* who disappeared during the war. *Pieds-noirs* or their descendants have moved into politics, particularly in the south of France, and continue to lobby for museums and other sites of remembrance, an ongoing struggle to keep the notion of victimhood alive.[76] Just how seriously they take this quest was expressed by the Deputy Mayor of Perpignan, Jean-Marc Pujol, when he told *The New York Times* reporter, Michael Kimmelman, in 2009, "We are a country that took 50 years to say we bear responsibility for what happened to the Jews during World War II, [o]ne day I think we will have to take responsibility for what happened to the pieds-noirs."[77] If the *pieds-noirs* feel slighted by history, they have no compunction at erasing their own excesses during the colonial period. In Denise Morel's, *Sétif de ma jeunesse,* published in 2001, for example, the only mention of the 1945 incidents at Sétif and Guelma, with the horrendous repression that ensued, is a chronological entry as *"Le 8 mai, révolte à Sétif par les Arabes."*[78] Responsibility, it would seem, is a one-way obligation.

KENYA: RED STRANGERS AND A VANISHING AFRICA

The themes of betrayal, bitterness and anger that characterized *Nostalgérie*, and in an attenuated form still do, are largely absent from post-independence writings on Kenya by women. To begin with, there was no O. A. S. type organization whose tactics of violence and hatred disrupted the possibility of a peace settlement that might have accommodated the settlers in the way that Kenyatta did in Kenya and which, through its rumor-mongering and anti-Muslim/anti-liberal propaganda, managed to rally much of the *pied-noir* community to their cause, contributing to the post-independence acrimony. Secondly, the move of the more reactionary settlers to Rhodesia and South Africa removed the element that could potentially have reacted with the anger and bitterness that was prevalent among the *pieds-noirs*. Thirdly, the fact that some of the leading settler families of Kenya, such as the Delameres, chose to stay in Kenya meant that the nostalgia of the post-independence era was not written in terms of bitter loss, but rather in terms of a glorified past characterized by adventure, grit, and aristocratic behavior. Fourthly, the geographic and topographic differences of the two former colonies shaped the pioneer nostalgia that features in post-independence writing. Whereas in Algeria the pioneers were considered to have made barren or swampy areas flourish, in Kenya the pioneers were deemed to have tamed a wild Eden. It was the sun and the sea that filled the reminiscences of Algeria; it was the magnificent flora and fauna those of Kenya. Finally, in France there was little official attempt in the early years to help the *pieds-noirs* preserve their colonial legacy, whereas in Britain, the Oxford University Colonial Records Project was established to assemble together as many privately owned documents and material relevant to the colonies as possible.[79] The project, which was started in 1963, was the brainchild of Margery Perham and A. F. Madden, who was the director of the Institute of Commonwealth Studies at the time. They were concerned that the documentary evidence of the British colonial period was at risk due to the rapid dismantling of the Colonial Service and the prevalent anticolonial atmosphere at the time.[80] The historical worth of the documents collected may have been the main aim, but there was also a nostalgic element inherent in the project insofar as the participants who responded represented only around 10 percent of those approached.[81] This suggests that those who did reply were not only interested in leaving a trace of their own colonial experience, but also in preserving a colonial memory devoid of its more unpleasant aspects. But, in much the same way as in Algeria the colonial nostalgia associated with Kenya was characterized by different stages, shaped by distance from independence, and prevailing political concerns.

The 1959 publication of Huxley's most famous work, *The Flame Trees of Thika, Memories of an African Childhood,* marked the first wave of Kenyan nostalgia.[82] She was aware, when writing it, that it was only a matter of time before Kenya received its independence.[83] The book is a paean both to a happy childhood and to a "vanished Africa," and is therefore unabashedly a work of nostalgia. Huxley resisted her publisher's suggestion of the subtitle "A Fictional Autobiography" and did not want to include any illustrations so as to avoid a suggestion of nonfiction.[84] She had fictionalized the names of her parents as Tilly and Robin and invented some of the neighbors who feature in the book. In much the same way as Blixen's *Out of Africa,* therefore, Huxley's "fictionalized" memories of her life in Kenya are an evocation of what it was about Kenya that the settlers so loved. The comparison with Blixen is not an idle one. Huxley did not share her mother's misgivings about Blixen. Rather she admired her work and had it in mind to emulate and even to better her.[85] *The Flame Trees of Thika* was the result. Like *Out of Africa* it became a bestseller. It was first serialized on the BBC for Women's Hour in May 1959, read by the noted actress, Fay Compton, and repeated in 1978 on BBC Story Time, read by Virginia McKenna.[86] In 1981 it was turned into a television series and shown in Britain on Thames TV and then in the United States on Mobile Masterpiece Theatre, introduced by Alistair Cooke.[87] What was it that made it so popular and set it apart from other such memoirs? It was, of course, very well written. Furthermore, Huxley knew Kenya well and had established a reputation for herself as an analyst of African affairs. To be sure her sympathies were with the settlers, but she was pragmatic enough to accept the demise of colonial Africa, whatever her true feelings regarding decolonization may have been. In spite of Huxley's insistence on the fictional quality of *The Flame Trees of Thika*, it was soon being treated as a real memoir packaged as fiction. Its credibility came from Huxley's reputation as an Africanist and from the fact she was perceived to be, as Laurens van der Post stated in his review of the book, "the missing link between humanity and the most Blimpish settlers at one extreme and, at the other, the worst globetrotting left-wingers."[88] She was a moderate with expert knowledge and as such was deemed to be in the best position to describe what Kenya had been about. Authenticity thus trumped fiction and made it a powerful vehicle of nostalgia.

Unlike Blixen, who did not present *Out of Africa* as fiction, or even as glorified memoir, Huxley's insistence on the fact *The Flame Tress of Thika* was a fictionalized account, exempted her from the sorts of accusation of inaccuracy that had been leveled at Blixen by settlers, such as Nellie Grant and Ingrid Lindstrom. The fictions of Huxley's work were not merely the calculated name changes and the additions of nonexistent neighbors. They were also lodged in the mind of the child narrator, who could and did describe the material hardships of the family's establishment in Kenya, but could overlook the political and socioeconomic implications of colonization for the Africans, as any child would.

The *Flame Trees of Thika* is a bewitching book, in much the same way as *Out of Africa* is. Huxley managed to evoke the sights and smells of Kenya suggesting their indelible dimension. In describing the sunset over the Rift Valley, for example, she writes:

> . . . the crimson sky, the golden light streaming down the valley, and then its obliteration by the dusk, as if some great lamp had been turned down in the heavens, filled me with the terrible melancholy that sometimes wrings the hearts of children. It was as if the day, which was unique, had been struck down and would never come again . . . as if something in each one of us had died with it, and could never be recalled. I felt it desperately important that the moment should be halted, the life of the day preserved, its death indefinitely postponed, and the memory of every instant, of every fleck of colour in that tremendous sky, should be branded on my mind so as to become as much a part of my existence as an eye or hand.[89]

It is hard to image that anyone, settler or metropole Briton, reading the passage in the 1960s , when decolonization was a political reality, would remain unaffected by its evident nostalgia or fail to equate it with the imminent demise of colonial Kenya. The narrator may be Huxley as a child, but the "terrible melancholy" that she described was written by a 50-year-old Huxley and the understanding of settler society is that of Huxley the adult. It is in the relationship with the Africans that the child narrator is of particular use. The child understands the Africans (Kikuyu) in a way the adults do not. She knows their legends and proverbs, she appreciates their company, and she understands their behavior, which to adults could seem aberrant. When a neighbor's "houseboy" is accused of theft, Elspeth reflects:

> The Kikuyu were perfectly honest with each other: crops grew unplundered, homesteads were fortified only against evil spirits, if a women left a load of millet by the path-side, or a man a snuff-horn or spear, it would be found intact on its owner's return. But Europeans were outside the ordinary stream of living and their property, therefore, exempt from ordinary laws; it sprang up like grass after rain, and for a Kikuyu to help himself was no more robbery than to take the honey from wild bees.[90]

The ability of the child to be able to relate to the African as an equal in a way the adult could not—to be on a par with Africans—implicitly underscore the colonial conviction that the Africans were children. Unlike *pied-noir* childhood reminiscences of their relationship with Algerians, Huxley does not consider the Africans to be her "real" family or even part of an extended or generalized happy family, but rather as potential equals in understanding the nature and spirit of Africa. It is an equality that is eventually outgrown even if the affection and respect remains.

As for the relationship between the adults of the novel and the Africans, in much the same way as British adults were expected to set the right example for their children, so too they felt it necessary to set an example to the Africans, "even if it's only a matter of soap and water, and clean houses, and rudimentary hygiene, and properly clothing and—well—decency."[91] Huxley presents a nuanced picture of settler attitudes from differences in degrees of racism to attitudes toward their presence in the colony. Whereas, Tilly believes that once the British have "knocked a bit of civilisation into them, all this dirt and disease and superstition will go and they'll live like decent people for the first time in their history," an acquaintance, Alec Wilson, is more forthright about his motives. "I didn't come to civilise anyone. I came to escape from the slavery one has at home if one doesn't inherit anything. I mean to make a fortune if I can. If that helps to civilise anyone I shall be delighted, but surprised."[92] The civilizing pretense that was such an important part of settler ideology in Algeria was not nearly as strong among settlers in Kenya, if indeed it existed at all. Like the Algerians, the Kenyans were kept at a distance politically and economically, but also at a personal distance to ensure "proper respect." The feeling of personal betrayal and/or loss that often permeates the *pied-noir* pioneer novel is largely absent. Post-independence, Kenya nostalgia is devoid of the bitter overtones prevalent in so much of *Nostalgérie*.

The Mottled Lizard, sequel to *The Flame Trees of Thika*, was published in 1962. It picks up the story after the World War I as Tilly and Elspeth are about to return to Kenya, covers the move from their farm in Thika to the one in Njoro, and ends with Elspeth leaving for university.[93] Huxley continues to relate the personal and economic trials and tribulations of the settlers and emphasizes the way in which her circle of settlers reproduced the behavior and values of the British gentry, whether it was in their relationship to the Africans they employed or, as the following passage suggests, when they were "at play":

> When it was neither too wet nor too dry, and the farm was running well, Tilly and Robin would drive to a place called Makuyu . . . where an affluent sports-man named Mervyn Ridley had started not only a small [Polo] club, but a hunt complete with imported English foxhounds . . . To hunt with the Makuyu hounds we got up in the dark, dressed by the light of a smoky safari lamp and emerged as dawn began to fill the sky above the plains . . . we hurried to the meet before the sun broke over the straight horizon and flooded a limpid sky with gold.[94]

They hunted the jackal or small buck rather than the fox, and they rode through the bush rather than over the downs or the vales, but the goal was the same; not just to create a corner of Britain in the wilds of Africa, but also to reinforce class structure and ties, epitomized by the hunt.

The importance of animals to the nostalgia of Kenya is suggested throughout the two books of Huxley's "memories." As a child she had a menagerie of animals, as did many settler children. Most were foundlings or the unweaned offspring of animals that had been shot, like Huxley's cheetah cub, Rupert, or her wild cat, Genet. The fauna and flora of Kenya were an essential element of Kenya nostalgia, most especially when the two were closely associated, as illustrated by a passage that describes Elspeth's sadness at leaving the farm at Thika for the family's new acquisition at Njoro:

> . . . all the animals [pets and domestic] would come with us . . . But not the twisted erythrina on the edge of the *vlei* where doves always cooed. Not the *vlei* itself with its fighting wild fowl, not the pool below the waterfall where pythons lived, . . . not the bluff across the river where reed-buck lay concealed, not the grenadilla creeper over the lizard-sheltering wall, not the hillside sham-bas where guinea fowl cried after tea . . . nor the old grass house whose walls rustled with white ants.[95]

In 1984 Huxley devoted a whole book to the evocative beauties of Kenyan wildlife, entitled *Last Days in Eden*. Illustrated by the wildlife photographer, Hugo van Lawick, it is, as its title implies, a look at a Kenya that was feared might be vanishing.[96] Game parks in Kenya were first established during the colonial period and one of the anxieties leading up to, and in the years following independence, was what would happen to them in the future.[97] The pressures of unchecked population growth and intensive poaching were the primary concerns, for more people meant less wild space, and "when the habitat goes, the wild animals go too."[98] In her chapter entitled "Eden under Siege?" Huxley asks, whether animal sanctuaries and national parks can in fact survive and highlights the importance of conservation. "Conservation has become one of the great issues of our time . . . We are all conservationists now—in theory. In practice, and with few exceptions, battle after battle to preserve one or other of the earth's natural resources has been lost . . . Year after year, the threat intensifies."[99] Huxley's was by no means the first book concerned with conservation.

The centrality of animals to the settlers' existence and, in particular, their importance to women during the colonial period has been discussed above. But the connection between women and wildlife continued as evidenced by the number of books that appeared in the 1960s. Works on animal research apart, the most popular were certainly those of Joy Adamson (1910–1980).[100] Adamson was Austrian by birth whose second marriage was to Peter Bally, a Swiss botanist, who worked at the Coryndon Museum (now the National Museum of Kenya). Accompanying him on his expeditions, she sketched the specimens he collected, a pastime which, thanks to the encouragement of Lady Muriel Jex-Blake and Louis Leakey, would lead to the production of 500 paintings and a book on East African plants and flowers.[101] By her own admission, she had a difficult time adapting to the British code of self-control. "In Austria, emotional outbursts were quite acceptable . . . but here they were regarded with distaste," she wrote.[102] In any event by 1943 she had adapted sufficiently well to remarry an English game warden, George Adamson. When he brought back the three cubs of a man-eating lioness he had shot, the saga of Adamson and her lions began. *Born Free,* Adamson's first book on the lions was written up from notes on watching Elsa, the first lioness she tracked. It was an instant success, was translated into numerous languages and was made into a Hollywood film in 1966.[103] At independence Adamson had been very concerned about the future of Kenya's game reserves and parks. By the time the film was released she had already committed herself to the conservation of wild animals, whose well-being had become a primary concern.[104] In 1963 the Elsa Wild Animal Appeal Trust was established to raise money for her cause and thanks to the funds acquired, she was able to make a considerable contribution to wildlife conservation in Kenya. Her Elsa and Pippa books were also a boost to her preservation campaign, for they "made many people the world over aware of the disastrous plight of wild animals and of the continuing efforts needed to save them from extinction," and led to worldwide travel.[105] As her role in conservation increased she became more involved in research and, until her murder in January 1980 not far from her camp in the Shamba reserve, she was involved in numerous research projects leading to more publications.[106] As of the 1960s, therefore, wildlife conservation and research developed into important post-independence activities in Kenya.[107]

More recently, nostalgia in women's memoirs of Kenya has also taken a form in which personal loss, nostalgia for a past that the author never knew personally, and conservation, became linked. Kuki Gallmann's *African Nights,* a follow-up to her successful *I Dreamed of Africa,* is a collection of stories chronicling some of her experiences in Kenya after the death of her husband Paola and her son, Emanuele. "When I first came to Africa," she writes in her opening sentence, "the people addressed me as Memsaab. In time, they baptized me Nyawera. The One Who Works Hard. Now they call me Mama, because I have chosen to stay, and because I belong."[108] Gallmann, therefore, situates herself firmly in Kenya and does so through reference to acceptance by the Africans with whom she is in daily contact. Loss permeates the book and Gallmann's stories are lyrical in their nostalgia. Whether she is evoking the remaining white highlanders or the flora and fauna, her love of the country seems tied to images of the vanished or vanishing.

In the story *Looking for Sandy*, she describes the search for white highlander Sandy's plane following his disappearance, and evokes the close-knit community of the white highlanders and their upper-class bearing. "Here the solidarity and friendship that unites the people of the Highlands once again prevailed," she writes, "and everyone who had a plane or could hire one went looking for Sandy . . . I respected his courage and leadership . . . he was one of the few remaining old soldiers of bygone days, with the soul of a poet, the manners of a gentleman."[109] In several of her stories she alludes to her friendships with the scions of the pioneer "aristocracy," as in the following passage about Hugh Cole (descendent of Berkeley and Galbraith Cole), whom she admires for their connection to the values and adventurous spirit of the past:

> Like the sons of the Delameres, of the Longs and the Powys families, and of a few others, Hugh had been brought up to farm one day the vast family estates on the Kenya Highlands. They were families who belonged to Kenyan history, and to that earlier generation of eccentric, adventurous or aristocratic Kenyan pioneers who had walked their way through Africa against all odds.[110]

The importance to Gallmann, of the adventurous spirit coupled with a love or understanding of "the wild," which was an essential part of the nostalgic image of the pioneer, is evident in her love affair with Aidan, the man with whom she eventually forms a partnership after the death of her husband. When he left her temporarily in much the same way as Finch-Hatton used to leave Blixen, she describes him as having "the subtle poetry and inexplicable appeal of the solitary nomad, the adventurous man who walked alone and to whom the wild was familiar. Aidan had no fear in the bush. His confidence came from his knowledge and love of things untamed, of plants unknown and of paths not yet trodden by human feet. I missed him with a longing to which I could give no name."[111] Unlike Finch-Hatton with Blixen, however, Aiden eventually returns and stays.

In addition to Gallmann's connections to the families of the "pioneer aristocracy," she also had close ties with members of the white "conservationist aristocracy," such as Joan Root, Iain and Oria Douglas-Hamilton, and Mirella Ricciardi, Oria's sister.[112] To begin with, in the case of the latter two women, this was no doubt due to their shared Italian heritage but eventually to their shared loved of the flora and fauna of Kenya. After the death of her husband, Paolo, and her son, Emmanuele, Gallmann's loss is expressed in a two-pronged nostalgia associated with wildlife that anchors her identity in Kenya and memorializes her loss. Wild animals evoked what Kenya signified to Gallmann. Hence, of a sheep-killing leopard she had trapped, she writes: "How deep had been his bronchial roar. How much its sound had been for me the voice of Africa and of all the unknown, untamed world around me."[113] Is her choice of the past tense a mere reference to the animal's demise or is it part of the nostalgia for a wildlife vanishing nobility, in this case of the great cats? It can be read either way. The untamed world around her is one she wants to preserve. The inspiration as to how to do so came, she writes, while "[w]alking alone on the hills and in the valleys of this place [Laikipia] he [Emmanuele] had loved above all, I decided to open its door to other young people like him: enthusiastic, fond of the wild, with a sense of purpose, so that they might learn to understand, and so to respect, Africa."[114] The result was the Gallmann Memorial Foundation, established in memory of Paolo and Emmanuele. Gallmann turned her cattle farm in Olari Nyiro into a 100,000 acre conservation area, whose mission statement was to promote "the coexistence of people and nature in Africa through harmonizing the protection and the creative sustainable and ecological utilization of the natural resources." The Gallmann Conservancy, an offshoot of the foundation, followed later to promote cultural, educational, and environmental research.[115] Through these efforts, Gallmann became a leading light in the "conservationist aristocracy" of Kenya, whose life's work is to arrest the "vanishing of Africa's Garden of Eden." This was an "aristocracy" of plucky adventurers in much the same vein as the aristocratic pioneers of the past. Kenya, she believes,

> with its unbounded space and spectacular landscapes teeming with wild animals . . . its savannah, forests and windswept Highlands, attracts people of unusual quality, who regard risk and challenge as an intrinsic part of the *safari* of existences. They fly with the moonlight and land in the dark; they hunt alone for lion and buffalo in thick bush, or for crocodiles, wading waist-deep into rivers and lakes . . . they defy malaria, yellow fever and tropical disease; they approach dangerous animals to study or film them. They gaily court danger.[116]

There is also among some of these "people of unusual quality," the urge to educate (it is tempting to use civilize) the African in the etiquette of conservation and environmentalism by showing them what makes their country "great" for, Gallmann writes, "the drama of Africa's environment, the loss of identity of the African people, the reason why the environment is not safe" is because "local people in Africa cannot afford even to see their own wildlife. As if in Italy we could not afford . . . to be inspired by our monuments . . . to experience the art which makes Italy great."[117]

There is a strong element in Gallmann's books of mimicry or, to put it more precisely, nostalgia as mimicry. She reproduces the representational similes, tropes, and themes that characterized the works of the earlier women writers of Kenya, in particular Blixen and Huxley. It is not just the lyricism of her evocations of Kenya that reflect those of Blixen and Huxley— Kenyan landscapes certainly merit lyrical description—it is in the way the book is structured. There is no doubt affection and even friendship for the Kenyans, and yet they remain at a distance. Most Kenyan characters in the stories are in her employ or are casual connections. When she does focus on an African who was not in her employ or with whom she had more than a passing relationship, much like Blixen did in *Shadows in the Grass* for her servant Farah, she dedicates a story to them.[118] Like Finch-Hatton's enchantment with Blixen's story-telling, Aiden is enchanted with Gallmann's. "I like to hear your stories" he tells her, which sets her off: "gathering a shawl about me, under a sky bejewelled with stars, listening to jackals far away, I close my eyes. From the treasure chest where my past sleeps . . . memories unfold."[119] There, too, is the same streak of self-centeredness that is often evident in writings of personal loss, which is in itself an important element in the nostalgia associated with "yesterday's self."[120]

The "updating" of Blixen's world is a constant in the memoirs of several post-independence women, who live or have lived in Kenya. Mirella Ricciardi (b.1930), now a world-class photographer who no longer resides in Kenya, is a case in point.[121] In her photographic memoir, *African Visions,* she writes: "I am a child of Africa. I grew up in a kind of sophisticated wilderness and took for granted all that Karen Blixen so eloquently described in her writing. The star-filled sky was my roof at night and the rising sun my early morning call. Nature was my teacher."[122] Blixen's words, she writes, "like Circe's song, awoke the sleeping adventurer and beckoned him into the unknown; fearless, confident and unaware, towards the Garden of Eden."[123] Ricciardi's Franco-Italian parents emigrated from Europe to Africa in 1927 and like the Blixens, family wealth enabled their successful implantation in Kenya.[124] Ricciardi grew up in Naivasha in the Highlands during "the era of the Happy Valley set" and had "an unusual upbringing—a mixture of sophisticated fantasy and wilderness freedom. We played with animals instead of toys and were looked after by a bevy of smiling Africans."[125] Like many children who were brought up in Kenya she had always been surrounded by Africans, but the relationship remained an uneven one, as she admits. "I had basically always liked the Africans and got on well with them, deluding myself that because I had grown up with them, there was an affinity between us . . . that I had somehow established a more meaningful contact with them than that of master and servant."[126] Whatever her real relationship with Africans, in her photographic works her gaze is not of a participator but rather of an observer capturing fleeting images for posterity. *African Visions* is a photographic compilation of the histories of her family, of renowned white settlers past and present, and of shots of Africans, who she writes "seemed unaware of the implications of photography and looked straight into my camera with the uninhibited curiosity of children."[127] A technologically savvy sophisticate photographing the innocence of Africa. Whatever her focus was, the concept of a vanishing Africa runs throughout her work. "My own love affair with Africa . . . was not love at first sight and everlasting [like Blixen's], but a gentle and progressive ripening of many summer fruits which slowly soured and fermented into fetid waste . . . [i]t became one of unrequited love with all its ensuing torment that tore me apart and left me aching."[128] Whether she is writing about her own disillusionment, the "vanishing tribes" of Africa as in, *Vanishing Africa*, her earlier work that catapulted her to fame, or the white Kenyans who stayed on because they "know nowhere else and because Kenya was *once* (my emphasis) the Garden of Eden," the underlying nostalgia is palpable.[129]

In 2005 Christine Nicholls published *Red Strangers. The White Tribe of Kenya*, a less romanticized vision of Kenya's settler past.[130] Nicholls grew up and went to school in Kenya before going on to the University of Oxford. She sets out on what she rightly states to be the unfashionable pursuit of evaluating the settlers' contribution to Kenya.[131] Part history, part settler resurrection and achievement, Nicholls attempts to provide a "balanced" view of the settler past. She was 19 at Kenyan independence and has therefore spent most of her life in Britain, so her vision is one shaped by the politics and events of the intervening years. Although the book is essentially about the white settlers, she does touch on the African response to colonialism and in her chapter on "the final years" she raises the question of racism and the color bar, a measure she states was "enforced by custom alone rather than by law."[132] It was the enclave mentality, common to all colonies that encouraged the idea of never-ending white domination. As Nicholls puts it, the perception that the whites would remain the dominant class in Kenya was reinforced by cultural activities that excluded Africans."[133] When the settlers scattered at independence, those who returned to Britain initially had difficulty adjusting both materially and psychologically and in her description of their problems, Nicholls points a finger at the British government for misleading the settlers and at the settlers for naively believing "the British adage that 'my word is my bond' when governments pronounced that . . . the highlands were to be kept white."[134] Nicholls' work differs from that of the above-mentioned writers and doesn't fall comfortably into a nostalgic genre. Can one therefore call it a work of nostalgia? If one considers that nostalgia is an essential element in the identity recreation of the displaced, whether they are exiles or immigrants, then this work certainly qualifies.[135] By categorizing them as Red Strangers (the name the Kikuyu gave to the early pioneers) and qualifying the category as the "White Tribe of Kenya," Nicholls has created an identity for a disparate group of individuals now scattered around the globe. In presenting the pioneer saga in empirical rather than romanticized form, she has given them a history that is not purely hagiographic. Is it an apology for colonialism? One can certainly read it that way. In fact Nicholls' history is much like Huxley's writings on the settlers, albeit written from a twenty-first century vantage point.[136] Indeed Nicholls' admiration of Huxley shines through her text, not that she concentrates on Huxley above the other settlers, she protectively describes—she has done that elsewhere—but rather in her style: well-written, empirical, pragmatic, and cautious in her plaudits. Nostalgia for Kenya comes in many forms.

CONCLUSION

In her book on nostalgia and the immigrant identity, Andreea Decíu Rítívoí suggests that immigrant adjustment to the host society "can be defined as reconciliation, requiring that the immigrant find a bridge between cultures and the potential identities that are acceptable and necessary in each culture."[137] The former settlers from Algeria and Kenya were not immigrants in the strict sense of the term, for whether they left their former colony or whether they remained, decolonization had not usually been their choice and the resultant dislocation of identity that occurred and made of them quasi "immigrant" or "exile" type personalities was predicated on diminished political and in some cases social status. Their identities were fractured and their adjustment to their host society, whether it was the metropole or the ex-colony, can be defined in terms of reconciliation—or lack of it—to the bifurcated sense of self that comes of permanent displacement. In much the same way as the spontaneous affinity that the *pieds-noirs* claim links them together, so too there is an affinity that links the *red strangers*. The difference between the two is in their response to the inevitability of their changing status. Ricciardi, who came of age during the period leading up to decolonization, describes it thus:

> But this was not white man's country and as I became an adult the winds of change began to blow; the land from which our three generations drew life became threatened, dark clouds gathered on our horizons and gradually infiltrated the light, until the Africa we had been born to became hardly recognisable . . . When you have been born in Africa you are marked by Africa and wherever you go, you are a displaced person, for you have two identities; you are a white man with a black man's soul. When you meet a kindred spirit you recognise one another, for you have both drunk from the magic chalice whose mysterious alchemy creates a bond that sweeps aside unnecessary prelude.[138]

The proprietorial dimension that characterized the relationship of the colonizer to the colony was dissipated or greatly attenuated in the case of the Kenya settlers, but remained strong in the case of the *pieds-noirs* who still refer to "my Algeria" or "our Algeria."[139] These differences are partially shaped by the size and territorial situation of the two communities. Whereas the bulk of the much larger community of former Algerian settlers and their progeny settled in France, the much smaller Kenya settler community is divided between its members who are still in Africa and those who are in Britain, or elsewhere. Furthermore, the anger and bitterness that was so prevalent, and still occasionally is, among members of the *pied-noir* community has often acted as a restraint from willingly returning either spiritually or physically—or both—to post-independence Algeria. In the case of Kenya, on the other hand, those settlers and their progeny who did not chose to continue to reside there have always been able to return, whether they have actually done so or not. The personal rupture was potentially gradual and the resultant nostalgia less strident. Although there were certain settler associations that formed in the aftermath of independence, as the former settlers grew older, the associations shriveled. There was no determined effort to maintain a memory of victimhood as there was among *pieds-noirs* from Algeria. Finally, the "Lost Eden" of the Kenya settlers suggests a loss of innocence deflecting the intensity of blame the *pieds-noirs* leveled and often still do at the French government. But the concept of a "Lost Eden" also suggests entry into a harsher world from which looking back can only be rose-tinted, and here it meets up with *pieds-noirs'* nostalgia or indeed most any form of nostalgia colonial or otherwise.

CONCLUSION

European women settled in the colonies of Algeria and Kenya for a variety of reasons. Whether from a sense of adventure, to escape economic or social pressures in France or Britain, or because they followed their spouses; once there, they became part of a society that sought to emulate the metropole and yet was very different from it. The dislocation in moving from a familiar social environment to an alien one induced them, either consciously or unconsciously, to create an image of the colony that intertwined what they loved best about the social and national spaces they had left behind with what they loved most about the space they had come to inhabit. Whatever the proportional relationship of one to the other, nostalgia was present. Nostalgia, therefore, was inherent to settler society and was shaped and reshaped throughout the colonial period. In the process definite topoi with representational images and tropes developed that would define post-independence settler nostalgia. It is pertinent to reiterate the need to distinguish between nostalgia for empire or imperial nostalgia, which connotes a loss of world power and territory and is therefore a post-independence phenomenon, and colonial nostalgia, which is emblematic of the loss of a certain life-style and is embedded in the colonial period as a mental survival strategy of recuperation as much as it is in the post-independence period. Whereas the former is usually written in national terms, the latter is written in personal terms. Colonial nostalgia, therefore, is not a monolithic category encompassing the imperial loss(es) in general, but is as varied as individual colonial societies are one from the other and of the settlers that peopled them. Women's lives and the narratives that emanated from these colonies were factors in this development.

The similarities that linked settler women in Algeria and Kenya were those associated with colonialism in general; the differences that separated them were specific to the place and time during which the women had settled there. Women's lives in both colonies were shaped by theoretical and practical structures of colonialism and the mental pressures and exigencies of permanent or semi-permanent expatriation. Settler women in Algeria and Kenya, whether they were novelists, memoirists, or just letter writers, created the homes—in both the individual and collective sense—out of which the narratives flowed. Women were powerful vectors of colonial or national discourses and narratives insofar as they were the leading players in socializing their children and new arrivals into settler culture and attempting to do as much with the women and children of the local populations of the colonies in which they lived. Novelists and published memoirists extended the narrative net beyond the confines of the colony to national and in some cases international audiences. They were, therefore, instrumental in creating, defining, and popularizing the image of the colony; an image that was fine tuned as circumstance and events dictated.

In 1900 Algeria had been occupied by the French for 70 years and had been constituted as three French departments for 52 of those. Kenya, on the other hand, was in its infancy as a colony. Whereas in Algeria the majority of the settlers were urbanites, congregated mainly in the towns and cities along the Mediterranean coast, Kenya was still in its "pioneer" infancy with no urban dimension at all. The ethno-cultural and social diversity of the Algerian settlers, most of whom were *petits-blancs,* was in contrast to the ethnic and relative social homogeneity of the European settlers of Kenya, most of whom in the early years had aristocratic pretentions, real or imagined. Algerian settler society was ethnically exogamous and with few exceptions religiously endogamous, thus creating the concept of a white/European "melting pot" and making the attainment of a colonial version of "Frenchness" the ultimate criterion of acceptance and successful integration. The aspiration to acquire the cultural, social, and political trappings of this Frenchness whatever one's ethnicity, race, or religion, was constituted as a move toward modernity. Settler society in "pioneer" Kenya, on the other hand, was purely endogamous making the criterion for acceptance and successful integration British upper class values and behavior. Continental Europeans and non-aristocratic Britons could understand the niceties of British class behavior and adhere to its principles, thus allowing for social mobility but, as far as many of the settlers were concerned, Kenyans could never really do either. The "gift" of British modernity to the Kenyans had little to do with its social culture and everything to do with its economic, technological, legal, and administrative cultures.

By 1900 the image of Algeria as the "exotic" extension of France was well developed. Women, who had been writing about the territory from the mid-century, had contributed in various ways to this image, even though most were travelers, or other migratory types. But it was a palimpsest image of French culture written over and across the culture of Islam. In Kenya, which had not yet even acquired its name in 1900, the image was that of a wild and beautiful Eden—a pristine space onto which Britishness could be written in spite of, or around, the "primitives" or "noble savages" who peopled it. Women who settled there initially were mostly spouses with a sense of duty or adventure or both. Their sense of the exotic was environmental rather than cultural. Writing the exotic in Kenya was a pastoral romance with the veld; writing the exotic in Algeria was an eroticized romance of intercultural relations.

The way in which women writers lived and experienced the exotic in each colony was shaped as much by colonial ideological tendencies as by the personal proclivities of the individual women in question. In Algeria, where values of equality and fraternity were foundation stones of republican ideology, women could and did transgress the racial divide sartorially, thus suggesting a two-way acculturation that reinforced the idea of assimilating the local culture into that of France. In Kenya, where hierarchical gradations were significant and sartorial choices were a signifier of class or hierarchy, women did not dress as Africans. Rather they hunted, and oversaw farm management, thus overtly situating themselves as part of the dominating structures of the colony.

Modernity, the carrot and stick of colonization, was also envisaged in different terms: in Algeria as imposing French culture and civilization on a "hidebound" and "archaic" society; in Kenya as imposing British administrative and economic order on a wild terrain and its "primitive" peoples. The concept of the modern settler woman, furthermore, was shaped by the colony rather than the metropole. When held up to the values and behavior of the "new woman" of the metropole, settler women in both colonies (the Happy Valley minority apart) were, more often than not, traditionally minded with regards to gender relations and family "ideology," but were positioned as exemplars of modern womanhood in relation to the colonized peoples. It was one of the paradoxes of their lives. The hallmarks of female modernity for settler women themselves, however, were the adventurous and enterprising spirit and the desire to contribute to the success of colonization; whether it was by civilizing the "native" as in the case of Algeria or by taming the land (and its peoples) as in the case of Kenya.

All societies have emblematic personalities from the past around whom admiration of one sort or another coalesces. In the case of women it is very often those who have gone against the class, race, or gender grain of society to distinguish themselves in some way. Eberhardt and Blixen were two such women. The emblematic stature of these two women was tied in with the way their respective colonies were romanticised—erotic allure and the mysteries of the desert for Algeria and an Edenic aristocratic playground for Kenya—but also to concepts of female modernity, not as conceived by their contemporary societies, but rather based on post-independence notions of independent behavior and adventurous spirit. Their literary merit certainly helped to elevate their images. So too did their status as "foreigners," which placed them outside the narrow confines of settler mentality and endowed them with a singular and exceptional presence. Their purposeful delineation from the mainstream of settler society, either by bucking colonial conventions

altogether, as in the case of Eberhardt, or by packaging them in a suitably
original manner, as in the case of Blixen's adopted lifestyle, made them icons
worthy of posthumous (in the case of Eberhardt) and post-independence
admiration and emulation. Unlike Huxley, Boisnard, or Rhaïs, they wrote
from the colonial periphery and not from its core. Their works were individualistic and self-absorbed in that they were concerned with creating an
airbrushed image of themselves and the colony. They did not respond to the
colonial exigencies of a particular moment as did the other writers discussed
in this book, but rather to their own personal vision of how life should have
been rather than how it was. In this they were personified emblems of colonial nostalgia.

The interwar period in both Algeria and Kenya was one of attempted
colonial consolidation in response to the disruptions caused by World War I,
and the desire for more settler autonomy from France and Britain respectively. In the immediate aftermath of the war, women writing about the two
colonies indulged in an escapism that reflected postwar anxieties and colonial
policies. In Algeria the fiction of Rhaïs was in line with the erotic overtones
of the escapism that characterized twenties' Paris, while serving to reinforce
the magnetism of the colony as beguiling. The fiction of Riddell and Strange
described the attractions of Kenya as an escape from the conventions of the
homeland and the traumas of a war that had skewed the gender ratio by
the enormity of its male casualties. Kenya in their novels became a site both
of adventure and of potential marriage. The fact that Rhaïs was writing in
Algeria; whereas Strange and Riddell were writing out of Kenya reflected
demographic differences of size and space. A larger settler population concentrated in the urban centers of Algeria was in contrast to a smaller settler
population scattered around the agriculturally and climatically strategic spaces
of Kenya. Whereas the former had developed a lively artistic community with
its own publishing houses and connections to those of France, the latter had
not and publication was only possible in Great Britain. In both cases, however, women's publications were read in both colony and metropole, thus
serving to anchor and disseminate the settler self-image and the tropes about
the colony that were part of post-independence settler nostalgia.

In the case of Algeria, the images of ethnic-cum-racial interaction, however positive or negative, were a prevalent feature of colonial women's writing. Whether Rhaïs, Godin, Boisnard —Robert Randau's constellation of
"romancières esquises"[1]—or the more prosaic Bugéja penned them, they
reflected the convictions of, and the anxieties engendered by, the ideology
of assimilation and the republican values of equality and fraternity. Thus,
Boisnard's historical fictions attempted to assimilate the precolonial history
of Algeria into French intellectual space, and Godin raised the possibility that
acculturation could be a two way process, thus hinting at fraternity; whereas
Bugéja's writing, fictional and nonfictional, reflected the assimilatory anxieties of the "civilizing" mother toward her culturally "problematic" children.
The urban *petits-blancs* milieus of Algeria, the favored setting of so much of
women's fiction, were spaces where the demographic (as opposed to sexual)

promiscuity of races and ethnicities trumped racial intolerance, which was deemed to be a mere symptom of such promiscuity, thus enforcing the image of French assimilation. Even though, as was usually the case in such fiction, these efforts were counteracted by what they believed to be the recalcitrant mores of the Algerians. Whatever the approach women chose to take in their writing, the focus was colonial society in its diversity.

Although Kenya lagged behind Algeria in the colonizing process and its settlers were still concentrating on carving their identity onto the land, it was not the length of colonization that shaped its colonial writings, but the relative homogeneity of settler society and the ideology of the dual mandate. Whether it was fiction or nonfiction, women's writing focused on settlers and their concerns sidelining most Kenyans to positions of servant and laborer. Unlike Algeria, therefore, it was *settler* society and not *colonial* society as a whole that was the focus. Class, with its behavioral rituals and activities, was of the essence in Kenya and the worlds women created were framed within its concepts. African characters of distinction—loyal and respected chiefs, *askaris* and minor Kenyan officials—when they were present, were an implicit confirmation of the successful functioning of the dual mandate. With no urban culture to speak of, it was the diversity of the veld with its extraordinary wild life, either to be hunted or tamed, that featured prominently in women's writing of this period. Together with the importance accorded to "aristocratic" or "gentlemanly" behavior, it became an essential factor in the settlers' self-image.

Political tensions marked the interwar period in both colonies. Riots and anti-Semitic violence in Algeria and anti-Indian agitation in Kenya were compounded in each colony by the emergence of nationalist movements; slower to develop in Kenya than Algeria, but present all the same. The question of political representation for the colonized, which was at the core of interwar nationalism, was complicated in Algeria by the fact that French women did not have the vote. As a result settler women found themselves in a paradoxical situation. On the one hand, they were seen and saw themselves as harbingers of modernity, as the "civilizers" and "educators" of Algerian women and, by extension, Algerian society, a role that they had assumed and continued to practice with enthusiasm. On the other hand, they resented the possibility of Algerians being granted the vote from which they, as women of French nationality, were excluded. Women's narratives reflected their ambivalence insofar as characters representing French modernity and cultural largesse were nearly always in counter-position to Algerians who, however enlightened, were depicted as eventually succumbing to the traditionalism and illiberality that the majority of the settlers considered innate to their culture.

In Kenya, particularly in the thirties, the tensions created by local politics combined with anxieties about the international situation to produce works like Huxley's murder mysteries that used popular fictional genres to offer an oblique critique of aberrant behavioral practices of the settlers and issue warnings about international developments; in Huxley's case the rise of National Socialism. That strictures of class and race functioned in tandem is evidenced by the fact members of the Kenya eugenics movement were as concerned, if not more so, about the class implications of "rampant breeding" to the colony as the racial ones. For Huxley, in particular, the dual mandate also functioned in symbolic terms. Her major works of the interwar period, *White Man's Country* and *Red Strangers,* both nostalgic in tone, were focused respectively on settler and African society, thus reinforcing the image (and ideological concept) of two societies developing in tandem at their own speed rather than as an amalgam, as in Algeria. Separate spheres were more aptly related to race than to gender in Kenya. Politics and race apart, women's writing and activities continued to reinforce the image of an Eden nurtured by the settlers and women's role in it. Amateur naturalists such as Evelyn Brodhurst-Hill or Marian Cran, or animal lovers such as Joy Adamson and Beryl Markham were the public faces, but many settler women, whether they wrote or not, acquired wild animals of some sort which they tended and tamed or tried to tame. Their role in wild animal nurturing was an initial step in the direction of wildlife preservation to which a number of women would dedicate their lives in post-independence Kenya.

World War II was as much of a milestone in the trajectory of the two colonies as was World War I, even if the nature of that milestone differed. Throughout the interwar period nationalism in both colonies gained force, and by the war's end France and Britain were faced with demands for independence. By granting independence to India and Burma almost immediately after the war, Britain appeared to acknowledge that the independence of all its colonies would come sooner than later. British women writing from or about Kenya realized this, even if they did not like or accept the idea. The supreme confidence in empire that had been the hallmark of British imperialism for so long had been shaken by World War I, but was shattered by World War II. Even though France's position as a world leader was under threat, or perhaps because of it, there was much more resistance to the eventuality of granting independence to its overseas territories as events at the war's end as events in French Indochina demonstrated. The fact that Algeria had, for the period of Allied occupation, served as the free capital of France bound it to the liberated metropole and reinforced in the minds of the settlers the colony's inalienability from the nation. The U.S. presence in urban Algeria unsettled racial and gender norms insofar as *pieds-noirs* found themselves, for the first time, confronted on their territory with a non-French culture that was not perceived as inferior by them. Furthermore, the Allied presence in what had for long been a Vichy stronghold, created ideological and power imbalances in favor of the Allies that disquieted the settlers whose only real *bêtes noires* to date had been French liberals and politicians, who had tried to reduce the disparities of power between the settlers and the Algerians.

In the years immediately following the end of the war, nationalism in both colonies shifted into a much more violent mode. The events of Sétif and Guelma in 1945 Algeria and the beginning of Mau-Mau oathing in Kenya, which started at about the same time, frightened the settlers who became, to paraphrase Henry Rousso, "ensnared in memories of their own."[2] Whereas women like Huxley and Grant engaged in the postwar debate as to how and when to grant independence to Africans in general and Kenya in particular; in Algeria few women writers broached the possibility of independence for Algeria until after the outbreak of hostilities in 1954. Although Huxley was intelligent enough not to play the card of African ingratitude for modernity bestowed, she believed that Africans were not yet ready for independence. It was as much a defensive reaction as was that of women in Algeria, such as Lerouvre, who continued to reiterate the cultural disparities between the French and the Algerians, while stressing their fraternal coexistence. In both Algeria and Kenya the "classics" of colonial women's writing of the interwar period were reissued, a nostalgic glare in the face of social disruption and impending loss.

The legal and technological "modernities" of decolonization in the two colonies: force of modern weaponry; internment camps and judicial executions in Kenya; torture, napalm, and the jettisoning of prisoners from helicopters in Algeria, made the flight into nostalgia a face-saving imperative. In addition to the reissuance of prewar novels and writing, women produced a spate of works looking back to the early days of the colony, works that even if they did not whitewash the settlers completely nonetheless presented an anodyne portrait of colonial society. Works such as *The Flame Trees of Thika* and its sequels for Kenya or the *Red Fountain* trilogy for Algeria provided detailed portraits of the evolution of pioneer families in each colony, without undue emphasis on the political or economic impact on the societies of the local populations.

The big difference between Algeria and Kenya during the decolonization was the actual role women played in the conflicts. Whereas in Kenya no settler woman supported, let alone became affiliated to, the Mau Mau movement, in Algeria not only did some women support the F. L. N. efforts, but a few were even tortured for their pains. The Algerian War of Independence was one of the most sustained paroxysms in contemporary times of the Franco-French wars that have flared up with relative regularity during the course of the country's history. Its aftershocks are still being felt in France and Algeria. This meant that the way the war was remembered and the way in which settler nostalgia was written was initially more complex than in Kenya. The *pieds-noirs'* conviction that they were losing French territory, and not a colony, made their sense of betrayal at the hands of the metropole much more acute and their bitterness more pronounced than in Kenya. The mass exodus from Algeria of the *pieds-noirs* at the war's end and the lamentable fate of the *harkis,* Algerians who had fought on the side of the French, created a fraught atmosphere in France that led to a legacy of memory that is as divisive today as the war had been. For Algerian settlers loss was written through narratives of anger, betrayal, and disillusion, whereas for Kenya loss was written in terms of "realistic" regret at a "modernizing mission" interrupted, hence unaccomplished, and distress at the impending loss of what they considered to be an environmental paradise. The anger and bitterness of Kenyan settlers was dissipated by Kenyatta's invitation to the settlers to remain and help rebuild an independent Kenya. Those settlers who could not envisage a life where they were not the top dogs of the pack, migrated to South Africa and Southern Rhodesia, as it was then, taking their bitterness and anger with them. Those who returned to Britain opted out of the colonial lifestyle, whether by choice or by force of circumstance.

The different colonial structures and frameworks of the two colonies, which had created the representational tropes of Algeria and Kenya, and manner in which the decolonization conflict was experienced and remembered (or forgotten), formed the basis of the nostalgia that emerged in the post-independence period. The fact that most of the settlers who left Algeria ended up in France meant that they were able to coalesce into a community of "exiles" allowing for the transmission of colonial nostalgia from generation to generation. The Kenya settlers who chose to leave the colony were scattered more sparsely and, although many joined associations for overseas personnel, such as the Overseas Service Pensioners' Association or the Overseas Service Pensioners' Benevolent Society, they never formed a tight-knit community like the *pieds-noirs*. Had it not been for the Oxford University Colonial Records Project, their colonial memory may well have dried up altogether. The *pied-noir* community of France continues to frame its nostalgia in terms of traumatic loss, the most eloquent example of which is the work of Marie Cardinal but the output is as prolific today as it was in the years immediately following the war. Being much larger and less scattered than the settler community of Kenya, it has sought to maintain its distinctive *pied-noir* identity and anchor that identity in the metropole landscape through sites of memory in the form of publishing houses, exhibitions, memorials, associations, archives, and most recently a museum. It has also become a political force in the way the Kenya settler community in Great Britain has not.

For both Kenya and Algeria, women contributed and continue to contribute to a literature that strives to set the colonial record straight. Christine Nicholls, *Red Strangers, The White Tribe of Africa*, Juanita Carberry's *Child of Happy Valley*, which depicts a not-so Happy Valley, or the collection edited by Joan Considine, *Childhood Memories from Colonial East Africa*, are all nostalgic looks at colonial Kenya that seek to debunk the idea of settler life as one of easy living and unfettered exploitation. As for Algeria, the picture books and memoirs, which have been published since 1962, are legion. Works such as Denise Morel de Marnard's, *Sétif de Ma Jeunesse*, or Marie Cardinal's *Pieds-Noirs*, express modernity bestowed through pictorial images of European-style buildings, classrooms, hospitals, and industry emphasizing all the while the intermingling of the races and their cultures; the "happy family" in all its splendor. Writing colonial nostalgia is not, of course, restricted to women and in the case of Algeria, men have been as prolific as women in desiring to assert their *pied-noir* identity as a distinctive form of Frenchness, another difference with Kenya.

In the post-independence period the main difference between Algeria and Kenya with regard to the writing of nostalgia is that women narrating Kenya-colony nostalgia were as often as not writing from within Kenya as they were from out of it. Women like Gallmann and Ricciardi did not suffer the loss of territorial lifestyle that writers like Cardinal or Baïlac did. Rather they were (or still are) in situ and, thus embrace the "aristocratic" imagery of the past through reference to its leading personalities such as Blixen or Delamere. Unlike the reflective nostalgia of the Britain-based former settlers or the *pieds-noirs* in France, theirs is a restorative nostalgia, which replicates the activities of the colonial period in a late twentieth century mode. The photographic safari, where the trophies are live animals rather than dead ones, simulate the hunting safaris of the past, whereas wildlife preservation, elevates the caring of wild animals from a personal to a national scale. Women involved in these activities today echo those of settler women such as Karen Blixen, Lady Macmillan, or Helen Cleland Scott. If wildlife preservation reverses the bagging of trophies of the past by protecting rather than killing its prey, it nonetheless reflects the earlier urge to tame the wild through the imposition of order and it does so by creating designated spaces that cordon off wild animals and encourage economic activity, in this case tourism.

The post-independence period brings colonial nostalgia full circle. The *pied-noir* community in France has been more militant about their memories and the shaping of their nostalgic vision of Algeria than the Kenya settlers. It is true the Oxford project institutionalized their nostalgia in archival form in Rhodes House, where many women's unpublished memoirs and letters are included in the colonial archives, but nothing like the veritable industry of *Nostalgérie* has developed, with even the French government buying into the "benevolence" of colonialism as expressed in the now repealed article 4 of the law of February 23, 2005. Nostalgic writing about Kenya is more individualistic. Kuki Gallman's memoir, *I Dreamed of Africa,* on the trials and tribulations of her life in Africa or Mirella Riccardi's photographic tribute to the Masaai in *Vanishing Africa* both contain strains of personal nostalgia for relations lost or space destroyed. But whether writing out of Kenya or from beyond Algeria, the nostalgia of post-independence women's works is structured by the representational tropes and nostalgic patterns that developed and were laid down by women writing in earlier periods.

To end, I should like to reflect briefly on the concept of colonial nostalgia and its metaphoric significance. The term nostalgia was first introduced into the medical lexicon as a serious pathological disorder. In its trajectory from the seventeenth to the twenty-first century, the concept morphed from a medical condition to a psychological one and a metaphorical one. In the colonial context it is pertinent to revisit its medical connotations in terms of metaphor. It is possible to argue that imperial nostalgia is a wound of empire, resulting from the loss of world status and economic or political power. In the context of this study, where I have argued that colonial or settler nostalgia is different from imperial nostalgia, I believe the more appropriate metaphor is the cancer of colonialism; a cancer whose growth started in the colonial period and metastasized over time, reaching high points in the post-independence 1980s and 1990s, and again in the early twenty-first century. Like a cancer there is no real cure, only remission. It can be cut out or eliminated temporarily, but it reoccurs at times of anxiety, social dislocation, or existential unease, forever attached to the body of the metropole.

NOTES

INTRODUCTION

1. Judith Thurman, *Isak Dinesen: The Life of a Storyteller*, 1st ed. (New York: St Martin's Press, 1982), 232–61, 33.
2. Patricia M. E. Lorcin, "Decadence and Renascence: Louis Bertrand and the Concept of Rebarbarisation in Fin de Siècle Algeria," in *New Perspectives on the Fin de Siècle in Nineteenth- and Twentieth-Century France*, ed. Kay Chadwick and Timothy Unwin (London: Edwin Mellen, 2000); Patricia M. E. Lorcin, "Women, Gender and Nation in Colonial Novels of Inter-War Algeria," *Historical Reflections/Reflexions Historiques* 28, no. 2 (2002); Patricia M. E. Lorcin, "Sex, Gender and Race in the Colonial Novels of Elissa Rhaïs and Lucienne Favre," in *The Color of Liberty: Histories of Race in France*, ed. Tyler Stovall and Susan Peabody (Durham, NC: Duke University Press, 2003); Patricia M. E. Lorcin, "Mediating Gender, Mediating Race: Women Writers in Colonial Algeria," *Culture, Theory & Critique* 45, no. 1 (2004).
3. Jean Déjeux, *Littérature Maghrébine de Langue Française: Introduction Générale et Auteurs*, Littératures (Sherbrooke: Naaman, 1973); Jean Déjeux, *La Littérature Algérienne Contemporaine*, 1. ed. (Paris: Presses universitaires de France, 1975); Guy Dugas, *Algérie: les Romans de la Guerre* (Paris: Omnibus, 2002); Peter Dunwoodie, *Writing French Algeria* (Oxford: Clarendon Press, 1998); Peter Dunwoodie, *Francophone Writing in Transition: Algeria 1900–1945* (Oxford: P. Lang, 2005); Seth Graebner, *History's Place: Nostalgia and the City in French Algerian Literature* (Lanham: Lexington Books, 2007); Philip Dine, *Images of the Algerian War: French Fiction and Film, 1954–1992* (Oxford: Clarendon Press: New York, 1994). An early exception is Sakina Messaadi, *Les Romancieres Coloniales et la Femme Colonisé: Contribution à Une Étude de la Littérature Coloniale en Algérie Dans la Première Moité Du Xxe Siècle* (Alger: Entreprise nationale du livre, 1990).
4. Jenny Sharpe, *Allegories of Empire: The Figure of Woman in the Colonial Text* (Minneapolis: University of Minnesota Press, 1993); Dunwoodie, *Francophone Writing in Transition*, Chris Bongie, *Exotic Memories: Literature, Colonialism, and the Fin de Siècle* (San Francisco: Stanford University Press, 1991); Carolyn Burdett, *Olive Schreiner and the Progress of Feminism: Evolution, Gender, Empire* (New York: Palgrave, 2001); Antoinette M. Burton, *Dwelling in the Archive: Women Writing House, Home, and History in Late Colonial India* (Oxford: Oxford University Press, 2003); Laura Chrisman, *Rereading the Imperial Romance: British Imperialism and South African Resistance in Haggard, Schreiner, and Plaatje* (Oxford: Clarendon Press, 2000); James Eskridge Genova, *Colonial Ambivalence, Cultural Authenticity, and the*

Limitations of Mimicry in French-Ruled West Africa, 1914–1956, Francophone Cultures and Literatures, Vol. 45 (New York: Peter Lang, 2004); Philip Holden and Richard R. Ruppel, *Imperial Desire: Dissident Sexualities and Colonial Literature* (Minneapolis: University of Minnesota Press, 2003); Paula M. Krebs, *Gender, Race, and the Writing of Empire: Public Discourse and the Boer War* (Cambridge/New York: Cambridge University Press, 1999); Simon Lewis, *White Women Writers and Their African Invention* (Gainesville, FL: University Press of Florida, 2003); Cristina Lombardi-Diop, "Writing the Female Frontier: Italian Women in Colonial Africa, 1890–1940" (PhD, New York, New York University, 1999); B. J. Moore-Gilbert, *Writing India, 1757–1990: The Literature of British India* (Manchester: New York, 1996); Panivong Norindr, *Phantasmatic Indochina. French Colonial Ideology in Architecture, Film and Literature* (Durham: Duke University Press, 1996); LeeAnne M. Richardson, *New Woman and Colonial Adventure Fiction in Victorian Britain: Gender, Genre, and Empire* (Gainesville: University Press of Florida, 2006); Anindyo Roy, *Civility and Empire: Literature and Culture in British India, 1822–1922* (London; New York: Routledge, 2005); Hsu-Ming Teo, "The Romance of White Nations: Imperialism, Popular Culture, and National Histories" in *After the Imperial Turn: Thinking with and Through the Nation,* ed. Antoinette M. Burton (Durham: Duke University Press, 2003), 280–92; David McDermott Hughes, "The Art of Belonging: Whites Writing Landscape in Savannah Africa," in *Conference paper presented to the Program in Agrarian Studies* (New Haven: Yale University Press, 2006).

5. An example is: Saad Noah Ahmed, "Desert Quest: French and British Writers in Arabia and North Africa, 1850–1950" (PhD Thesis, University of Illinois at Urbana-Champaign, 1983).

6. George Steinmetz, *The Devil's Handwriting. Precoloniality and the German Colonial State in Qindao, Samoa, and Southwest Africa* (Chicago: University of Chicago Press, 2007).

7. According to Robinson and Gallaghar, British occupation of this territory was a strategic necessity due to the perceived need to forestall a French advance into the area or some other unfriendly power (Germany or Belgium) threatening the interests of Britain in India. Ronald Edward Gallagher, John Robinson, and Alice Denny, *Africa and the Victorians: The Official Mind of Imperialism,* 2nd ed. (London: Macmillan, 1981), Chapter 11, especially 308–29.

8. For development of society Algiers and Bone, see Julia Clancy-Smith, "Exoticism, Erasures, and Absence. The Peopling of Algiers, 1830–1900," in *Walls of Algiers. Narratives of the City through Text and Image,* ed. Zeynep Çelick, Julia Clancy-Smith, and Frances Terpak (Seattle: University of Washington Press, 2009), 19–61; David Prochaska, *Making Algeria French: Colonialism in Bône 1870–1920* (Cambridge/New York: Cambridge University Press, 1990).

9. For a recent analysis of the civilizing mission in Algeria see Osama Abi-Mershed, *Apostles of Modernity: Saint-Simonians and the Civilizing Mission in Algeria* (Stanford: Stanford University Press, 2010).

10. For a discussion of French and British ideologies of Empire and colonial policies, see Raymond F. Betts, *Assimilation and Association in French Colonial Theory, 1890–1914* (New York: Columbia University Press, 1961); Michael Crowder, *Senegal: A Study of French Assimilation Policy,* Rev. ed.

(London: Methuen, 1967); Margery Perham, *Colonial Sequence 1930 to 1949: A Chronological Commentary Upon British Colonial Policy, Especially in Africa* (London: Methuen, 1967); S. E. Stockwell, *The British Empire: Themes and Perspectives* (Oxford: Blackwell, 2008). For contemporary works on the subject, see Frederick John Dealtry Lugard, *The Dual Mandate in British Tropical Africa* (Hamden, CT:. Archon Books, 1965), First published 1922; Hubert Deschamps, "Et Maintenant Lord Lugard?" *Africa. Journal of the International African Institute* 33, no. 4 (1963); Jules Harmand, *Domination et Colonisation* (Paris: E. Flammarion, 1910); Léopold de Saussure, *Psychologie de la Colonisation Française, Dans Ses Rapports Avec les Sociétés Indigènes* (Paris: F. Alcan, 1899); Stephen Henry Roberts, *The History of French Colonial Policy, 1870–1925* (London: Cass, 1963), first published 1929.

11. See Patricia M. E. Lorcin, *Imperial Identities: Stereotyping, Prejudice and Race in Colonial Algeria*, Society and Culture in the Modern Middle East (London: I. B. Tauris; New York: Distributed by St. Martin's, 1995); Lorcin, "Decadence and Renascence: Louis Bertrand and the Concept of Rebarbarisation in Fin de Siècle Algeria"; Patricia M. E. Lorcin, "France and Rome in Africa: Recovering Algeria's Latin Past," *French Historical Studies* 25, no. 2 (2002): 295–325. See also Seth Graebner, *History's Place: Nostalgia and the City in French Algerian Literature*, After the Empire (New York: Lexington Books, 2007); Jonathan K. Gosnell, *The Politics of Frenchness in Colonial Algeria, 1930–1954*, Rochester Studies in African History and the Diaspora, Vol. 14 (New York: University of Rochester Press, 2002).

12. Julia Ann Clancy-Smith and Frances Gouda, eds., *Domesticating the Empire: Race, Gender, and Family Life in French and Dutch Colonialism* (Charlottesville: University Press of Virginia,1998); Clare Midgley, *Gender and Imperialism* (Manchester: Manchester University Press; New York: St. Martin's Press, 1998); Carolyn Martin Shaw, *Colonial Inscriptions: Race, Sex and Class in Kenya* (Minneapolis: University of Minnesota Press, 1995); Ann Laura Stoler, *Carnal Knowledge and Imperial Poser, Race and the Intimate in Colonial Rule* (Berkeley/Los Angeles: University of California Press, 2002).

13. "With the wives came the clubs and the social colour bar." Roland Anthony Oliver and J. D. Fage, *A Short History of Africa*, Penguin African Library (London: Harmondsworth, 1962).

14. Dea Birkett, *Spinsters Abroad: Victorian Lady Explorers* (Oxford, UK: New York, NY, 1989); Alison Blunt, *Travel, Gender, and Imperialism: Mary Kingsley and West Africa*, Mappings (New York: Guilford Press, 1994); Indira Ghose, *Women Travellers in Colonial India: The Power of the Female Gaze* (Delhi: Oxford University Press, 1998); Sara Mills, *Discourses of Difference: An Analysis of Women's Travel Writing and Colonialism* (London: New York, 1991); Kumari Jayawardena, *The White Woman's Other Burden: Western Women and South Asia During British Colonial Rule* (New York: Routledge, 1995).

15. A few exceptions are Messaouda Yahiaoui, "Regards de Romancières Françaises Sur les Sociétés Féminines d'Algérie, 1898–1960," in *Regards Sur les Littératures Coloniales Afrique Francophone*, ed. Jean-François Durand and Jean Sévry (Paris: L'Harmattan, 1999).

16. Mary Jo Maynes, Jennifer L. Pierce, and Barbara Laslett, *Telling Stories: The Use of Personal Narratives in the Social Sciences and History* (Ithaca, NY: Cornell University Press, 2008), 16–17.

17. See, for example, Helen Callaway, *Gender, Culture, and Empire: European Women in Colonial Nigeria* (Urbana, IL: University of Illinois Press, 1987); Margaret Strobel, *European Women and the Second British Empire* (Bloomington, IN: Indiana University Press, 1991); Nupur Chaudhuri and Margaret Strobel, *Western Women and Imperialism: Complicity and Resistance* (Bloomington: Indiana University Press, 1992); Margaret Strobel, "Gender, Sex and Empire," in *Islamic & European Expansion: The Forging of a Global Order,* ed. Michael Adas (Philadelphia, PA: Temple University Press, 1993), 345–75; Jayawardena, *The White Woman's Other Burden: Western Women and South Asia During British Colonial Rule*; Anne McClintock, Aamir Mufti, and Ella Shohat, *Dangerous Liaisons: Gender, Nation, and Postcolonial Perspectives* (Minneapolis, MN: University of Minnesota Press, 1997); Clare Midgley, ed. *Gender and Imperialism* (Manchester: Manchester University Press, 1998); Antoinette M. Burton, *Gender, Sexuality and Colonial Modernities* (London/New York: Routledge, 1999); Ann Laura Stoler, "Carnal Knowledge and Imperial Power: Gender, Race and Morality in Colonial Asia," in *Gender at the Crossroads of Knowledge: Feminist Anthropology in the Postmodern Era* ed. Micaela di Leonardo (Berkeley, CA: University of California Press, 1991); Ann Laura Stoler, *Race and the Education of Desire. Foucault's History of Sexuality and the Colonial Order of Things* (Durham, NC: Duke University Press, 2000); Philippa Levine, ed. *Gender and Empire* (Oxford/New York: Oxford University Press, 2004); Angela Woollacott, *Gender and Empire* (New York: Palgrave Macmillan, 2006); Elsbeth Locher-Scholten, *Women and the Colonial State, Essays on Gender and Modernity in the Netherlands Indies 1900–1942* (Amsterdam: Amsterdam University Press, 2000).

18. Clancy-Smith and Gouda, eds., *Domesticating the Empire: Race, Gender, and Family Life in French and Dutch Colonialism*; Rebecca Rogers, "Telling Stories About the Colonies: British and French Women in Algeria in the Nineteenth Century," *Gender & History* 21, no. 1 (2009); Locher-Scholten, *Women and the Colonial State;* Lora Wildenthal, *German Women for Empire, 1884–1945* (Durham, Duke University Press, 2002); Sarah Curtis, "Emilie de Vialar and the Religious Reconquest of Algeria," in *French Historical Studies*, 29 (2006); Stoler, "Carnal Knowledge and Imperial Power: Gender, Race and Morality in Colonial Asia"; Stoler, *Race and the Education of Desire*. An older work on French women in the colonies is Yvonne Knibiehler and Régine Goutalier, *Les Femmes Au Temps des Colonies* (Paris: Stock, 1985).

19. Mills, *Discourses of Difference: An Analysis of Women's Travel Writing and Colonialism*; Blunt, *Travel, Gender, and Imperialism: Mary Kingsley and West Africa*; Ghose, *Women Travellers in Colonial India: The Power of the Female Gaze*; Laura Jane Loth, "Moving Pictures: Gender, Vision and Travel from Colonial Algeria to Contemporary France," (PhD thesis, University of Minnesota, Minneapolis 2005); Messaadi, *Les Romancieres Coloniales et la Femme Colonisé: Contribution à Une Étude de la Littérature Coloniale en Algérie Dans la Première Moité Du XXe Siècle*; Jean Déjeux, *La Littérature Féminine de Langue Française Au Maghreb* (Paris: Karthala, 1994); Yahiaoui, "Regards de Romancières Françaises Sur les Sociétés Féminines d'Algérie, 1898–1960"; Sharpe, *Allegories of Empire: The Figure of Woman in the Colonial Text*. Examples of comparative works are Susan R. Horton, *Difficult Women, Artful Lives. Olive Shreiner and Isak Dinesen, in and out of Africa*

(Baltimore, MD: The Johns Hopkins University Press, 1995); Lewis, *White Women Writers and Their African Invention.*

20. "Women, Gender and Nation in colonial novels of inter-war Algeria" *Historical Reflections/Reflexions Historiques* 28, no. 2 (2002): 163–184; "Sex, Gender and Race in the colonial novels of Elissa Rhaïs and Lucienne Favre," in *The Color of Liberty: Histories of Race in France,* ed. Tyler Stovall & Susan Peabody (Durham, NC: Duke University Press, 2003) 108–130; "Mediating Gender; Mediating Race: Women Writers in Colonial Algeria," *Culture, Theory and Critique* 45, no. 1 (2004): 45–61.

21. Shirley Ardener, *Women and Space: Ground Rules and Social Maps* (New York: St. Martin's Press, 1981). See also Alison Blunt and Gillian Rose, *Writing Women and Space: Colonial and Postcolonial Geographies,* Mappings (New York: Guilford Press, 1994); Gillian Tindall, *Countries of the Mind. The Meaning of Place to Writers* (Boston: Northeastern University Press,1991).

22. See, for example, Albert Memmi, *The Colonizer and the Colonized* (New York: Orion Press, 1965).

23. Peter Fritzsche, "Specters of History: On Nostalgia, Exile and Modernity," *American Historical Review* 106, no. 5 (2001): 1587–1618, 1605.

24. For example, *Chocolat,* 1988, directed by Claire Denis; *Indochine,* 1992, directed by Regis Wargnier; *Outremer (Overseas),* 1992, directed by Brigitte Rouan; *Passage to India, 1985,* directed by David Lean, *Out of Africa,* 1985, directed by Sydney Pollack.

25. See, for example, Alison Murray, "Women, Nostalgia, Memory: *Chocolat, Outremer,* and *Indochine,*" *Research in African Literatures* 33, no. 2 (2002): 235–244; Marina Hung, "The Family Romance of Orientalism: From *Madame Butterfly* to *Indochine,*" in *Genders* 33, no. 2 (1995): 222–258, 21; Mireille Rosello, "Tattoos or Earrings: Two Models of Historical Writing in Mehdi Lallaoui's *La colline aux oliviers* (The Olive Grove)," in *Algeria and France 1800–2000: Identity, Memory, Nostalgia,* ed. Patricia M. E. Lorcin (New York: Syracuse University Press, 2006).

26. William Cunningham Bissell, "Engaging Colonial Nostalgia," *Cultural Anthropology* 20, no. 2 (2005): 215–248, 215.

27. Bissell, 239.

28. Kathleen Stewart, "Nostalgia—A Polemic" *Cultural Anthropology* 3, no. 3 (1988): 227–241.

29. Janelle L. Wilson, *Nostalgia: Sanctuary of Meaning* (Lewisburg: Bucknell University Press, 2005), 31.

30. Fred Davis, *Yearning for Yesterday. A Sociology of Nostalgia* (New York/ London: The Free Press, 1979), 122.

31. Svetlana Boym, *The Future of Nostalgia* (New York: Basic Books, 2001), 26.

32. Boym, xiii.

33. Boym, xvi.

34. See my "Rome and France in Africa . . . " and Graebner, *History's Place.* Graebner examines nostalgia in the colonial literature of Algeria, exploring the concept in relation to place. He deals almost exclusively with male writers.

35. Roxanne Panchasi, *Future Tense. The Culture of Anticipation in France between the Wars* (Ithaca, NY: Cornell University Press, 2009), 162.

36. See for example: Fritzsche, "Specters of History: On Nostalgia, Exile and Modernity"; Davis, *Yearning for Yesterday,* Salman Rushdie, *Imaginary*

Homelands. Essays and Criticism 1981–1991 (London: Granta Books in association with Viking, 1991); Alexander Meena, *The Shock of Arrival: Reflections on Postcolonial Experience* (Boston: South End Press, 1996); Susan Rubin Suleiman, ed., *Exile and Creativity. Signposts, Travelers, Outsiders, Backward Glances* (Durham, NC: Duke University Press, 1998); Mae G. Henderson, *Borders, Boundaries, and Frames. Essays in Cultural Criticism and Cultural Studies*, ed. Mae G. Henderson (New York/London: Routledge, 1995); Linda Marilyn Austin, *Nostalgia in Transition, 1780–1917* (Charlotesville: University of Virginia Press, 2007); William Cunningham Bissell, "Engaging Colonial Nostalgia," *Cultural Anthropology* 20, no. 2 (2005); Seth Graebner, *History's Place: Nostalgia and the City in French Algerian Literature*; Jean Pickering and Suzanne Kehde, ed. *Narratives of Nostalgia, Gender, and Nationalism* (New York: New York University Press,1996); Christopher Shaw and Malcolm Chase, *The Imagined Past: History and Nostalgia* (Manchester: Manchester University Press, 1989); Tamara S. Wagner, *Longing: Narratives of Nostalgia in the British Novel, 1740–1890* (Lewisburg: Bucknell University Press, 2004); Andreea Deciu Rítívoí, *Yesterday's Self: Nostalgia and the Immigrant Identity*, Philosophy and the Global Context (Lanham, MD: Rowman & Littlefield, 2002).

37. Shaden M. Tageldin, "Reversing the Sentence of the Impossible Nostalgia: The Poetics of Postcolonial Migration in Sakinna Boukhedenna and Agha Shahid Ali," *Comparative Literature Studies* 40, no. 3 (2003): 232–261, 33.

38. Rítívoí, *Yesterday's Self: Nostalgia and the Immigrant Identity*, 32.

39. Michael Dorland, *Cadavarland. Inventing a Pathology of Catastrophe for Holocaust Survival. The Limits of Medical Knowledge and Historical Memory in France* (Walthan: Brandeis University Press, 2009), 10.

40. Glenda Riley, *Taking Land, Breaking Land: Women Colonizing the American West and Kenya, 1840–1940* (Albuquerque: University of New Mexico Press, 2003), 13.

41. Romy Golan, *Modernity and Nostalgia. Art and Politics in France between the Wars* (New Haven: Yale University Press, 1995).

42. Antoinette Burton, "The White Woman's Burden: British Feminists and 'The Indian Woman,' 1865–1915," in *Western Women and Imperialism: Complicity and Resistance,* ed. Chaudhuri and Strobel; Antoinette M. Burton, *Burdens of History: British Feminists, Indian Women, and Imperial Culture, 1865–1915* (Chapel Hill: University of North Carolina Press, 1994); Dipesh Chakrabarty, *Provincializing Europe. Postcolonial Thought and Historical Difference* (Princeton: Princeton University Press, 2000); Howard J. Rigby and Nigel Booth, *Modernism and Empire* (Manchester: Manchester University Press, 2000); Phyllis Lassner, *Colonial Strangers: Women Writing the End of the British Empire* (Newark: Rutgers University Press, 2004).

43. Whitney Chadwick and Tirza True Latimer, *The Modern Woman Revisited: Paris Between the Wars* (New Brunswick: Rutgers University Press, 2003), 19.

44. For some recent examples, see Abdelmajid Hannoum, *Violent Modernity. France in Algeria* (Cambridge, MA: Harvard University Press, 2010); Benjamin Claude Brower, *A Desert Named Peace: The Violence of France's Empire in the Algerian Sahara, 1844–1902* (New York: Columbia University Press, 2009).

45. Gertrude Himmelfarb, *The Roads to Modernity: The British, French, and American Enlightenments*, 1st ed. (New York: Knopf, 2004).

46. Jo Burr Margadant, ed. *The New Biography, Performing Femininity in Nineteenth-Century France* (Berkeley, CA: University of California Press, 2000), 2.

47. Diana Holmes, *French Women's Writing, 1848–1994.* (London: Athlone, 1996), 11

48. See, for example, Claudia Roth Pierpont, *Passionate Minds: Women Rewriting the World* (New York: Knopf, 2000); Elaine Showalter, *A Literature of Their Own: British Women Novelists from Brontë to Lessing* (Princeton, NJ: Princeton University Press, 1977).

49. Holmes, 13.

50. The Amrouches, mother and daughter were the rare exceptions. Fadhma A. M. Amrouche, *Histoire de Ma Vie*, Domaine Maghrébin (Paris: F. Maspero, 1968). Fadhma Amrouche (1882–1967) was the illegitimate daughter of a Kabyle widow, who entrusted her to Catholic missionaries to escape the opprobrium of her compatriots. She was thus brought up as a Christian. She wrote poetry, which was published by her daughter, Marguerite (Marie-Louise) Taos Amrouche (1917–1976), and her son, Jean Amrouche. Her autobiography was published posthumously. Taos Amrouche, who was a friend of André Gide and Jean Giono, published a number of works. These include Marie Louise Amrouche, *Jacinthe Noire, Roman* (Paris: Charlot, 1947); Marguerite Taos Amrouche, *Rue des Tambourins* (Paris: La Table Ronde, 1960); Marguerite Taos Amrouche, *L'amant Imaginaire: Roman*, 4th ed. (Paris: Editions Robert Morel, 1975). Her collection of her mother's poems was published as Marguerite Taos Amrouche, *Le Grain Magique. Contes, Poèmes et Proverbes Berbéres de Kabylie* (Paris: n.p., 1966).

51. For a discussion of the education of Algerian women, see Diane Sambron, *Les Femmes Algériennes Pendant la Colonization* (Paris: Riveneuve, 2009), 187–225.

52. For a comparison of the politics of education in Algeria and Kenya, see Elsa M. Harik and Donald G. Schilling, *The Politics of Education in Colonial Algeria and Kenya* (Athens, OH: Ohio University Center for International Studies, 1984).

53. For accounts of Algerian and Kenyan women during colonization, see Sambron, *Les Femmes Algériennes Pendant la Colonization*; Marnia Lazreg, *The Eloquence of Silence: Algerian Women in Question* (New York: Routledge, 1994); Tabitha M. Kanogo, *African Womanhood in Colonial Kenya, 1900–1950* (Athens, OH/Nairobi: University of Ohio Press/East African Educational Publishers, 2005); Luise White, *The Comforts of Home: Prostitution in Colonial Nairobi* (Chicago: University of Chicago Press, 1990).

54. A few examples: Mieke Bal, Jonathan Crewe, and Leo Spitzer, eds., *Acts of Memory. Cultural Recall in the Present* (Hanover/London: University Press of New England, 1999); Maurice Halbwachs, *On Collective Memory*, ed. Donald N. Mevine, trans. Lewis A. Coser, The Heritage of Sociology (Chicago: University of Chicago Press, 1992); Alec G. Hargreaves, *Memory, Empire, and Postcolonialism: Legacies of French Colonialism*, After the Empire (New York: Lexington Books, 2005); Katherine Hodgkin and Susannah Radstone, eds., *Contested Pasts. The Politics of Memory* (London/New York: Routledge,2003); Susannah Radstone, *Memory and Methodology* (New York: Berg, 2000); Susannah Radstone and Katherine Hodgkin, eds., *Regimes of*

Memory, Routledge Studies in Memory and Narrative (London/New York: Routledge, 2003); Paul Ricoeur, *La Mémoire, L'histoire, L'oubli* (Paris: Seuil, 2000); Rushdie, *Imaginary Homelands*; Daniel J. Sherman, *The Construction of Memory in Interwar France* (Chicago: University of Chicago Press, 1999); Michael Kenny, "A Place for Memory: The Interface between Individual and Collective Memory," *Comparative Studies in Society and History* 41, no. 3 (1999).

55. Exceptions relevant to this study and discussed below are Karen Blixen, Nellie Grant, and Isabelle Eberhardt.

56. Seth Graebner's recent book explores the manner historical nostalgia is used to fabricate settler identity in Algeria. Graebner, *History's Place: Nostalgia and the City in French Algerian Literature*. I have also written articles on this subject: Lorcin, "France and Rome in Africa: Recovering Algeria's Latin Past"; Lorcin, "Decadence and Renascence: Louis Bertrand and the Concept of Rebarbarisation in Fin de Siècle Algeria"; Lorcin, "Women, Gender and Nation in Colonial Novels of Inter-War Algeria." See also Lynne Huffer, "Derrida's Nostalgeria," in *Algeria & France 1800–2000, Identity, Memory, Nostalgia*, ed. Patricia M. E. Lorcin (Syracuse: Syracuse University Press, 2006). Peter Dunwoodie and Edward J. Hughes, *Constructing Memories: Camus, Algeria and Le Premier Homme* (Stirling: Stirling French Publications, 1998). Dunwoodie, *Writing French Algeria*; Peter Dunwoodie, "Postface: History, Memory, and Identity—Today's Crisis, Yesterday's Issue," *French History* 20 (2006) 318–332. Lucienne Martini, *Racines de Papier: Essai Sur L'expression Littéraire de L'identité Pieds-Noirs* (Paris: Publisud, 1997); Edwige Tamalet Talbayev, "Between Nostalgia and Desire: L'École d'Alger's Transnational Identifications and the Case for a Mediterranean Relation," *International Journal of Francophone Studies* 10, no. 3 (2007); John J. Su, *Ethics and Nostalgia in the Contemporary Novel* (Cambridge: Cambridge University Press, 2005); Rushdie, *Imaginary Homelands*; Ralph Pordzik, *The Wonder of Travel: Fiction, Tourism and the Social Construction of the Nostalgic* (Heidelberg: Winter, 2005); Brian Herne, *White Hunters. The Golden Age of African Safaris* (New York: Henry Holt & Co., 1999); Marie-Helene Hertaud-Wright, "Masculinity, Hybridity and Nostalgia in French Colonial Fiction Films of the 1930s."

57. Felix Driver and David Gilbert, *Imperial Cities: Landscape, Display and Identity* (Manchester: Manchester University Press, 1999); Zeynep Çelik, *Urban Forms and Colonial Confrontations: Algiers under French Rule* (Berkeley: University of California Press, 1997); Zeynep Çelik, Julia Ann Clancy-Smith, and Frances Terpak, eds., *Walls of Algiers: Narratives of the City through Text and Image* (Los Angeles, CA: Getty Research Institute, 2009); Gwendolyn Wright, *The Politics of Design in French Colonial Urbanism* (Chicago: University of Chicago Press, 1991); Saïd Almi, *Urbanisme et Colonisation: Présence Française en Algérie* (Sprimont, Belgique: Mardaga, 2002); Nezar AlSayyad, *Forms of Dominance on the Architecture and Urbanism of the Colonial Enterprise*, Ethnoscapes (Aldershot: Avebury, 1992); Dana Arnold, *Cultural Identities and the Aesthetics of Britishness* (Manchester: University of Manchester Press, 2004); Joëlle Bahloul, *The Architecture of Memory: A Jewish-Muslim Household in Colonial Algeria, 1937–1962* (Cambridge: Cambridge University Press, 1996); Penny Edwards, "Cambodge: The Cultivation of a Nation 1860–1945" (Ph.D., Monash University, 1999); Seyi Fabiyi, "Colonial

and Postcolonial Architecture and Urbanism," in *Nigeria's Urban History: Past and Present*, ed. Hakeem Ibikunle Tijani (Lanham: University Press of America, 2006); Mia Fuller, *Colonial Constructions: Architecture, Cities, and Italian Imperialism in the Mediterranean and East Africa* (London: Spon, 2003); Mia Fuller, *Moderns Abroad: Architecture, Cities and Italian Imperialism* (New York: Routledge, 2007); Thomas R. Metcalf, *An Imperial Vision: Indian Architecture and Britain's Raj* (Berkeley: University of California Press, 1989); P. A. Morton, *Hybrid Modernities: Architecture and Representation at the 1931 Colonial Exposition, Paris* (Cambridge: MIT Press, 2000); Norindr, *Phantasmatic Indochina.*

58. For some examples of thematic analyses of women discussed in this study, see Frantz Leander Hansen and Gaye trans. Kynoch, *The Aristocratic Universe of Karen Blixen: Destiny and the Denial of Fate* (Brighton, U.K.: Sussex Academic Press, 2003); Annelies van Hees, *The Ambivalent Venus: Women in Isak Dinesen's Tales (Condensed Version of Van Hees' Doctoral Thesis: De Ambivalente Venus in Het Werk Van Karen Blixen)* (Minneapolis: Univiversity of Minnesota Press, 1991); François Cornu, *L'afrique Dans L'oeuvre d'Elspeth Huxley*, Thèse à la Carte (Lille: Atelier national de reproduction des thèses, 2004); Hariclea Zengos, "A World without Walls: Race, Politics, and Gender in the African Works of Elspeth Huxley, Isak Dinesen, and Beryl Markham" (Boston: Tufts University Press, 1989); Jean-Luc Manaud and Catherine Sauvat, *Isabelle Eberhardt et le Désert* (Paris: Ed. du Chêne, 2003).

CHAPTER 1

1. The Berbers of Algeria comprised the Kabyles, originating from the Djurdjura mountains, the Chaoui from the Aurès mountains, the Mozabites from the Mzab in the south and the Tuareg, nomads of the desert. Of these four the Kabyles were the most numerous.

2. See, for example, Julia Ann Clancy-Smith, *Mediterraneans: North Africa and Europe in an Age of Migration 1800–1900* (Berkeley, CA: University of California Press, 2010); Denise Brahimi, *Femmes Au Pays: Effets de la Migration Sur les Femmes Dans les Cultures Méditerranéennes* (Paris: Unesco, 1985); Dominique Valérian, *Bougie, Port Maghrébin, 1067–1510* (Rome: École française de Rome, 2006).

3. Received ideas about the Crusades, the Barbary Pirates, and an Ottoman Empire in decline distorted the image of the area and fed into general anxieties about Islam. The literature of Western perceptions of Islam is extensive. See for example: Norman Daniel, *Islam and the West: The Making of an Image* (Edinburgh: University Press, 1960); Norman Daniel, *Islam, Europe and Empire* (Edinburgh: Edindurgh University Press, 1966); Edward W. Said, *Orientalism* (New York: Pantheon Books, 1978); Robert K. Davis, *Christian Slaves, Muslim Masters. White Slavery in the Mediterranean, the Barbary Coast, and Italy 1500–1800* (New York: Palgrave Macmillan, 2003).

4. Tanzania, formerly Tanganyika, was a German colony until 1918.

5. Other ethnic groups include the Luhya, Meru, Kisii, Kalinjin, Embu, and Kamba.

6. The mortality rates in 1847 were 54.57 percent for every 1000 males and 43.22 percent for every 1000 females. In 1852 the figures were 61.91 percent and 41.97 percent, respectively; in 1853, 48.12 percent and 32 percent and

in 1854, 53.35 percent and 44.17 percent. By 1891 it had dropped to 32.57 percent and 25.30 percent. The lower female death rates were apparently due to better adaptation to the climate, coupled with more strenuous workloads and alcoholism among men. Claudine Robert-Guiard, *Des Européennes en Situation Coloniale: Algérie 1830–1939* (Paris: l'Université de Provence, 2009), 73–74.

7. For a recent work detailing the progression of land appropriation in the early colonial period, see Diana K. Davis, *Resurrecting the Granary of Rome. Environmental History and French Colonial Expansion in North Africa*, ed. James L. A. Webb, Ohio University Press Series in Ecology and History (Athens: Ohio University Press, 2007), especially 27–51. For different aspects of nineteenth century colonial society in Algeria, see Marc Baroli, *La Vie Quotidienne des Français en Algérie 1830–1914* (Paris: Hachette, 1967); Annie Rey-Goldzeiguer, *Le Royaume Arabe: la Politique Algérienne de Napoléon III, 1861–1870* (Alger: Société nationale d'édition et de diffusion, 1977); Claudine Robert-Guiard, *Des Européennes en situation coloniale: Algérie 1830–1939;* David Prochaska, *Making Algeria French: Colonialism in Bône 1870–1920* (Cambridge/New York: Cambridge University Press, 1990); Charles André Julien, *Histoire de l'Algérie Contemporaine. La Conquête et les Débuts de la Colonisation (1827–1871)*, 2 vols., Vol. 1 (Paris: Presses Universitaires de France, 1964); Patricia M. E. Lorcin, *Imperial Identities: Stereotyping, Prejudice and Race in Colonial Algeria*, Society and Culture in the Modern Middle East (London/New York: I. B. Tauris/St. Martin's, 1995).

8. John Ruedy, *Modern Algeria. The Origins and Development of a Nation* (Bloomington, IN: Indiana University Press, 1992), 69.

9. Ibid., 85.

10. For a discussion of colonial ideas on this subject, see Lorcin, *Imperial Identities: Stereotyping, Prejudice and Race in Colonial Algeria*; Jonathan K. Gosnell, *The Politics of Frenchness in Colonial Algeria, 1930–1954* (Rochester, NY: University of Rochester Press, 2002).

11. Robert M. Maxon, *Struggle for Kenya. The Loss and Reassertion of Imperial Initiative, 1912–1923* (London/Toronto: Associated University Presses, 1993), 13.

12. The classic study of settler society in Kenya and Southern Rhodesia is Dane Kennedy, *Islands of White: Settler Society and Culture in Kenya and Southern Rhodesia 1890–1939* (Durham: Duke University Press, 1987). See also Marshall S. Clough, *Fighting Two Sides: Kenyan Chiefs and Politicians, 1918–1940* (Niwot, CO: University Press of Colorado, 1990); Charles Chenevix Trench, *Men Who Ruled Kenya* (London/New York: The Radcliffe Press, 1993); Errol Trzebinski, *The Kenya Pioneers* (New York: W. W. Norton, 1986); C. S. Nicholls, *Red Strangers: The White Tribe of Kenya* (London: Timewell Press, 2005). Although a pro-settler approach to colonial society, Nicholls' work contains useful statistics and demographic information. For discussions of differing settler societies in the British context, see James Belich, *Replenishing the Earth: The Settler Revolution and the Rise of the Anglo-World, 1783–1939* (New York: Oxford University Press, 2009); Robert A. Bickers, *Settlers and Expatriates: Britons over the Seas* (New York: Oxford University Press, 2010); Carl Bridge and Kent Fedorowich, eds., *The British World: Diaspora, Culture, and Identity* (Portland, OR: F. Cass, 2003); Marjory Harper and Stephen Constantine, *Migration and Empire* (New York: Oxford University Press, 2010).

13. Kennedy, *Islands of White: Settler Society and Culture in Kenya and Southern Rhodesia 1890–1939,* 23.

14. Trzebinski, *The Kenya Pioneers,* 63.

15. Ibid., 83.

16. See Maxon, *Struggle for Kenya. The Loss and Reassertion of Imperial Initiative, 1912–1923,* 31–34.

17. The tax was levied according to the number of huts an African possessed, thus targeting wealthier Africans, who owned multiple huts. As the settler population increased so too did the demands for labor. In 1908 a poll tax was introduced, which was levied on every African male over the age of 16 who did not pay a hut tax.

18. Trzebinski, *The Kenya Pioneers,* 15. According to Trzebinski, of the 31,983 Indians who were contracted to build the railway, 6,794 remained on till completion.

19. H. F. Ward and J. W. Milligan, *Handbook of British East Africa* (Nairobi, 1912), 5.

20. In 1905 British East Africa was transferred from the Foreign Office to the Colonial Office. For an account of the dispute, see ibid, 4–5.

21. Kennedy, *Islands of White: Settler Society and Culture in Kenya and Southern Rhodesia 1890–1939,* 24.

22. Ibid., 197.

23. In Rhodesia the settler population in 1901 was 11,000; in 1920 it was 32,620. Ibid.

24. Nicholls, *Red Strangers: The White Tribe of Kenya,* 130. The surface area of Kenya was 137 million acres (55.44 million hectares).

25. As mentioned in the introduction, I distinguish between colonial myths and the themes and activities that I consider inherent to colonial nostalgia.

26. For aspects of this discourse in Algeria, see Patricia M. E. Lorcin, "France and Rome in Africa: Recovering Algeria's Latin Past," *French Historical Studies* 25, no. 2 (2002): 295–329; Seth Graebner, *History's Place: Nostalgia and the City in French Algerian Literature* (Lanham, MD: Lexington Books, 2007); Jean-François Guilhaume, *Les Mythes Fondateurs de l'Algérie Française* (Paris: L'Harmattan, 1992).

27. See, for example, Kennedy, *Islands of White: Settler Society and Culture in Kenya and Southern Rhodesia 1890–1939*; Nicholls, *Red Strangers: The White Tribe of Kenya*; Edward I. Steinhart, *Black Poachers, White Hunters: A Social History of Hunting in Colonial Kenya* (Oxford/Nairobi: James Currey, 2006); John Lonsdale, "Kenya. Home Country and African Frontier," in *Settlers and Expatriates: Britons Over the Seas,* ed. Robert Bickers, 74–111.

28. Raymond Williams quoted by Diana Holmes, *French Women's Writing, 1848–1994* (London/Atlantic Highlands, NJ: Athlone, 1996), xi.

29. For more on feminism and literature, see ibid.; Diana Holmes and Carrie Tarr, *A "Belle Epoque"?: Women in French Society and Culture, 1890–1914* (New York: Berghahn Books, 2006); Mary Louise Roberts, *Disruptive Acts: The New Woman in Fin-de-Siècle France* (Chicago, IL: University of Chicago Press, 2002); Elaine Showalter, *A Literature of Their Own: British Women Novelists from Brontë to Lessing* (Princeton, NJ: Princeton University Press, 1977); Shari Benstock, *Women of the Left Bank. Paris 1900–1940* (Austin: University of Texas Press, 1986).

30. Holmes, *French Women's Writing, 1848–1994,* 18.

31. See, for example, Saree Makdisi, *Romantic Imperialism: Universal Empire and the Culture of Modernity* (Cambridge/New York: Cambridge University Press, 1998); Heather McCaw, *Women on Two Sides of the Divide: Gender, Identity and Colonialism in Jane Eyre and Wide Sargasso Sea* (Columbus, OH: Ohio State University, 2000); Margaret A. Majumdar, *Postcoloniality: The French Dimension* (New York: Berghahn Books, 2007).

32. For more information on Picard, see Georges Hirtz, *Islam, Occident: les Voies du Respect, de L'entente, de la Concorde: Abd El Qader, La Morcière, Aurélie Picard, Si Ahmed Tidjani* (La Roche-Rigault: PSR, 1998); George R. Trumbull IV, *An Empire of Facts. Colonial Power, Cultural Knowledge and Islam in Algeria, 1870–1914* (Cambridge/New York: Cambridge University Press, 2010), 120–123. For romanticized or recuperative narratives on Picard, see Gabriel Camps, *L'afrique Du Nord Au Néminin. Héroïnes Du Maghreb et Du Sahara* (Paris: Perrin, 1992); José Lenzini, *Aurélie Picard: Princesse des Sables* (Montpellier: Chèvre-feuille Étoilée, 2007). For comparative narratives, see Élise Nouel, *Carré D'as . . . Aux Femmes!: Lady Hester Stanhope, Aurélie Picard, Isabelle Eberhardt, Marga d'Andurain* (Paris: G. Le Prat, 1977); Ursula Kingsmill Hart, *Two Ladies of Colonial Algeria: The Lives and Times of Aurélie Picard and Isabelle Eberhardt* (Athens, OH: Ohio University Center for International Studies, 1987). Hart does not paint a very sympathetic picture of Picard, whereas she does of Eberhardt.

33. MSS. Afr.s.1456-East Africa European Pioneer Society, Box 9, binder listing names and information on Kenya pioneers. What is now known as the Limuru Girls' High School was founded in 1922 by Arnold McDonell, who appointed Roseveare as the first head mistress.

34. MSS. Afr.s.2318-Alice Hammond, Kenya Memories, Chapter four.

35. Women caterers, prostitutes and a few officers' wives accompanied the 1830 expedition. For a detailed demographic account of women in the early stages of colonization in Algeria, see Robert-Guiard, *Des Européennes en Situation Coloniale: Algérie 1830–1939*, especially 61–75.

36. Sarah Ann Curtis, "Emilie de Vialar and the Religious Reconquest of Algeria," *French Historical Studies* 29, no. 2 (2006). There is also a discussion of de Vialar in Clancy-Smith, *Mediterraneans: North Africa and Europe in an Age of Migration 1800–1900*, 249–264.

37. On leaving Algeria she went on to found an establishment in Tunis and from there went on to create a network throughout the Levant. She was beatified in 1939 and canonized in 1951.

38. See Sarah Ann Curtis, "Civilizing Habits: Women Missionaries and the Revival of French Empire" (New York: Oxford University Press, 2010).

39. Pauline de Noirfontaine, *Algérie. Un Regard Écrit* (Havre: A. Lemale, 1856); Barbara Leigh Smith Bodichon, *Algeria; Considered as a Winter Residence for the English* (London: English Woman's Journal Office, 1858); Matilda Betham-Edwards, *A Winter with the Swallows* (London: Hurst and Blackett, 1867); Louise (Louise Mesnier) Vallory, *A L'aventure en Algérie* (Paris: Hetzel, 1863). For a discussion of the activities of Gautier and Fromentin in Algeria, see Laura Jane Loth, "Moving Pictures: Gender, Vision and Travel from Colonial Algeria to Contemporary France" (PhD, University of Minnesota, Minneapolis, 2005), 23–157. For Pauline Noirfontaine, Bodichon and other women travellers, see Deborah Cherry, *Beyond the Frame: Feminism and Visual Culture, Britain 1850–1900* (London: Routledge, 2000), 75–100

reprinted in Deborah Cherry, "Earth into World, Land into Landscape: The 'Worlding' of Algeria in Nineteenth Century British Feminism," in *Orientalism's Interlocutors: Painting, Architeture, Photography,* ed. Jill Beaulieu and Mary Roberts (Durham, NC: Duke University Press, 2003); Rebecca Rogers, "Telling Stories About the Colonies: British and French Women in Algeria in the Nineteenth Century," *Gender & History* 21, no. 1 (2009): 39–59.

40. "Letter to Léon Gozlan, July 1849," Noirfontaine, *Algérie. Un Regard Écrit,* 6. Noirfontaine, who also dabbled in poetry, entertained artists and politicians, many of whom were Republicans. See Mrs. Branch Williams, *Mosaics* (Nashville: Southern Methodist Publishing House, 1881), 50–51; René de la Ferté, "Le Monde, les Arts, le Théâtre," *L'Artiste. Revue du XIXe siècle,* no. N° du 1er mai (1868): 300–301; Ibid. 281–307, 300–301; Ibid.

41. The scholarly literature on women's travel writing is vast ranging from edited anthologies to analyses of individual women. Some notable examples are Ali Behad, *Belated Travelers. Orientalism in the Age of Colonial Dissolution,* ed. Stanley Fish and Fredric Jameson (Durham & London: Duke University Press, 1994); Alison Blunt, *Travel, Gender, and Imperialism: Mary Kingsley and West Africa* (New York: Guilford Press, 1994); Jane Fletcher Geniesse, *Passionate Nomad: The Life of Freya Stark* (New York: Modern Library, 2001); Indira Ghose, *Memsahibs Abroad: Writings by Women Travellers in Nineteenth Century India* (Delhi/New York: Oxford University Press, 1998); Indira Ghose, *Women Travellers in Colonial India: The Power of the Female Gaze* (Delhi: Oxford University Press, 1998); Cheryl McEwan, *Gender, Geography, and Empire: Victorian Women Travellers in West Africa* (Aldershot: Ashgate, 2000); Sara Mills, *Discourses of Difference: An Analysis of Women's Travel Writing and Colonialism* (London/New York, 1991); Jane Robinson, *Wayward Women. A Guide to Women Travellers* (Oxford: Oxford University Press, 1990); Michèle Salinas, *Voyages et Voyageurs en Algérie 1830/1930* (Toulouse: Éditions Privat, 1989).

42. Noirfontaine, *Algérie. Un Regard Écrit,* 34.

43. Bodichon considered marriage to be legally detrimental to women and throughout the 1850s, with Caroline Norton, was involved in a campaign to improve women's rights. Their campaign culminated in the Matrimonial Causes Act, which ended divorce by Act of Parliament and implemented divorce through the law courts. Most scholarship on Bodichon concerns her role as feminist and writer. See, for example, Pam Hirsch, *Barbara Leigh Smith Bodichon, 1827–1891: Feminist, Artist and Rebel* (London: Chatto & Windus, 1998); Sheila R. Herstein, *A Mid-Victorian Feminist, Barbara Leigh Smith Bodichon* (New Haven: Yale University Press, 1985). There is much less on her activities in Algeria beyond her painting.

44. See Gerald M. Ackerman, *Les Orientalistes de l'École Britannique* (Paris: ACR Edition, 1991), 40–44; John Crabbe, "Barbara Leigh Smith Bodichon," in *Dictionary of Women Artists,* ed. Delia Gaze (Chicago/London: Fitzroy Dearborn, 1997), 283–286; Cherry, "Earth into World, Land into Landscape: The 'Worlding' of Algeria in Nineteenth-Century British Feminism."

45. Bodichon wrote a number of articles on her impressions of Algeria for the *English Woman's Journal.*

46. Namely from: Eugène Bodichon, *Considérations Sur l'Algérie* (Paris: Comptoir Central de la Librairie, 1845); Eugène Bodichon, *Hygiène à Suivre en Algérie. Acclimatement des Européens* (Algiers: Delavigne, 1851); Eugène

Bodichon, *Études Sur l'Algérie et L'afrique* (Algiers: Chez l'Auteur, 1847). Quotation from the fly-page signed by Barbara Bodichon.

47. I use Algerian in the sense of the population native to Algeria and not the settlers. The distinction during the colonial period was *Algérien* (for settlers) and *indigène* for the population native to Algeria. Rather than referring to the local population as Muslims, which suggests a religious spin and excludes other local groups, I prefer the modern appellation.

48. I hesitate to make assertions about the absence of Algerians in her painting as I have seen very few of them, but in those I have seen such figures that are present, are very small, and blend into the background.

49. I have written about Eugène Bodichon's ideas elsewhere: *Imperial Identities,* 122–127.

50. Bodichon, *Algeria; Considered as a Winter Residence for the English,* 82.

51. Ibid., 92. For comparisons of French and British reactions to Madame Luce's school, see Rogers, "Telling Stories About the Colonies: British and French Women in Algeria in the Nineteenth Century." See also Osama Abi-Mershed, *Apostles of Modernity: Saint-Simonians and the Civilizing Mission in Algeria* (Stanford, CA: Stanford University Press, 2010), 138–142.

52. In Gayatri Chakravorty Spivak, "Can the Subaltern Speak?" in *Marxism and the Interpretation of Culture*, ed. Cary Nelson and Lawrence Grossberg (Urbana: University of Illinois, 1988), 271–313. Spivak suggests that focusing on "barbaric" practices involving women, such as sati, was a question of "white men saving brown women from brown men" (296). Although it is possible to apply such reasoning to the issues of polygamy and child marriage in Algeria, I would argue that the situation in Algeria was complicated by the fact Arab women were seen as potentially symbolic and practical vectors of the civilizing mission.

53. Steven C. Hause, *Hubertine Auclert: The French Suffragette* (New Haven, CT: Yale University Press, 1987), 139–140; Julia Ann Clancy-Smith, "Islam, Gender, and Identities in the Making of French Algeria, 1830–1962," in *Domesticating the Empire: Race, Gender, and Family Life in French and Dutch Colonialism*, ed. Julia Clancy-Smith and Frances Gouda (Charlottesville, VA: University Press of Virginia, 1998), 154–174, especially 67–72. For an evaluation of Auclert's involvement in the imperial debate in France, which builds on Clancy-Smith's work, see Carolyn Eichner, "*La Citoyenne* in the World: Hubertine Auclert and Feminist Imperialism," *French Historical Studies* 32, no. 1 (2009): 63–84. See also Edith Taieb Smith, "Coloniser and Colonised in Hubertine Auclert's Writings on Algeria," in *A "Belle Epoque"? Women in French Society and Culture, 1890–1914*, ed. Diana Holmes and Carrie Tarr (New York: Berghahn Books, 2006). And Joan Scott's chapter on Auclert in *Only Paradoxes to Offer. French Feminists and the Rights of Man*, ed. Joan Wallach Scott (Cambridge, Harvard University Press, 1996), 90–124. Scott concentrates on Auclert's feminist activities and dedicates 2 pages to her Algerian sojourn (115–117).

54. Hubertine Auclert, *Les Femmes Arabes en Algérie* (Paris: Société d'Èditions littéraires, 1900), 31.

55. Ibid., 63.

56. Ibid., 65.

57. See George W. Stocking, *Victorian Anthropology* (New York/London, 1987), 203–205.

58. Ibid., 3. For a more detailed treatment of Auclert's views on Algerian women, see Lorcin, "Mediating Gender, Mediating Race: Women Writers in Colonial Algeria," *Culture, Theory & Critique* 45, no. 1 (2004): 45–61.
59. Auclert, *Les Femmes Arabes en Algérie*, 143.
60. Ibid., 33 [my emphasis].
61. Ibid., 17.
62. Ibid.
63. For analyses of these developments, see Ruedy, *Modern Algeria. The Origins and Development of a Nation*, 80–113; Charles Robert Ageron, *De L'insurrection de 1871 Au Déclenchement de la Guerre de Libération (1954)* Histoire de l'Algérie Contemporaine; T. 2 1st ed. (Paris: Presses universitaires de France, 1979), 39–70.
64. Hause, *Hubertine Auclert: The French Suffragette*, 46.
65. Jean Pommerol, *Une Femme Chez les Sahariennes: Entre Laghouat et in-Salah* (Paris: E. Flammarion, 1900), frontispiece. Pommerol was the author of a number of novels and travel books. Her other works include Mme Jean Pommerol, *Le Péché des Autres, Roman* (Paris: L. Chailley, 1890); *La Faute D'Avant, Roman* (Paris: L. Chailley, 1896); *Scènes Viennoises: Une de Leurs Étoiles, Son Chien, Son Père, Son Secrétaire et Ses Amis* (Paris: P. Lamm, 1897); *Le Crible, Roman* (Paris: H. Simonis Empis, 1897); *Islam Saharien: Chez Ceux Qui Guettent (Journal D'un Témoin)*, Collection Minerva (Paris: A. Fontemoing, 1902); *Le Cas Du Lieutenant Sigmarie* (Paris: Calmann-Lévy, 1907); *Un Fruit et Puis Un Autre Fruit* (Paris: C. Lévy, 1911).
66. From the advertising back matter of the facsimile edition of Henry Fielding's *The Hearts of Men*, first published in 1902. See also the account of her travels and travails in the introduction to her article written "A Lady in the Unexplored Sahara," *The World Wide Magazine* 5 (1900): 54–62, 54–55.
67. Pommerol published a number of fictional and non-fictional works on Algeria. *Islam Saharien* (Paris, 1902), the follow-up to *Une femme chez les Sahariennes*, was serialized in the literary paper, *Minerva* in June and July 1902.
68. Her work was reviewed internationally in journals and magazines such as the *Spectator* (86, 1901, 774), *The Scottish Geographical Magazine* (17, 1901, 212), *Literature* (142–47, 1900, 462), *Book News* (19, 1901, 344), *Bulletin of the American Geographical Society* (32, 1900, 193).
69. Pommerol, *Une Femme Chez les Sahariennes: Entre Laghouat et in-Salah.* 3.
70. Ibid., 26–27. The military remained a presence in the Sahara throughout the colonial period.
71. Ibid., 191.
72. Ibid., 191 and 202.
73. Ibid., 4.
74. Ibid., 21–22.
75. There is an extensive literature on the use of women in this way and the gender implications of this use. See Malek Alloula, *The Colonial Harem* (Manchester: Manchester University Press, 1987); Julia Ann Clancy-Smith and Frances Gouda, eds., *Domesticating the Empire: Race, Gender, and Family Life in French and Dutch Colonialism* (Charlottesville, VA: University Press of Virginia,1998); Inderpal Grewal, *Home and Harem: Nation, Gender, Empire and the Culture of Travel* (Durham: Duke University Press, 1994); Simon Katzenellenbogen, "Femmes et Racism Dans les Colonies Européennes," *Clio, Histoiore, Femmes et Sociétés* 9 (1999); Philippa Levine, *Gender and*

Empire (Oxford/New York: Oxford University Press, 2004); Elsbeth Locher-Scholten, *Women and the Colonial State, Essays on Gender and Modernity in the Netherlands Indies 1900–1942* (Amsterdam: Amsterdam University Press, 2000); Billie Melman, *Women's Orients. English Women and the Middle East, 1718–1918: Sexuality, Religion, and Work* (Ann Arbor, MI: University of Michigan Press, 1992); Clare Midgley, *Gender and Imperialism* (Manchester, UK: Manchester University Press; New York: St. Martin's Press, 1998); Ann Laura Stoler, *Carnal Knowledge and Imperial Power: Race and the Intimate in Colonial Rule* (Berkeley, CA: University of California Press, 2002).

76. Pommerol, *Une Femme Chez les Sahariennes: Entre Laghouat et in-Salah*, 53: "Or, selon moi—sauf exception difficile à clairement concevoir—, il n'y a pas de femmes honnêtes sous ce climat, dans ces races. Il n'y a pas de fiancée chaste. Il n'y a pas de vertu. Car la vertu, l'honnêteté, la chasteté sont la conservation volontaire d'un état de pureté morale et physique. C'est un instinct ou effort qui vient de la personne même, une estime qu'on veut éprouver de soi à soi. Comment l'épouse, la fiancée, la jeune fille arabe du Sud pourraient-elles sentir ou vouloir rien de tout cela? Je les ai—vous le rappelez-vous?—comparées aux gazelles et aux chattes. Vous imaginez-vous une chatte vertueuse? Une chatte pudique autrement que par caprice ou par dedain?"

77. English edition Chapter 4: "A Difficult Chapter." Jean Pommerol, *Among the Women of the Sahara; Uniform Title: Femme Chez les Sahariennes. English*, trans. Mrs. Arthur Bell (N D'Anvers) (London: Hurst and Blackett, 1900), 41–46.

78. See Reina Lewis, *Gendering Orientalism. Race, Femininity and Representation* (London/New York: Routledge, 1996); Melman, *Women's Orients. English Women and the Middle East, 1718–1918: Sexuality, Religion, and Work*; Jill Beaulieu and Mary Roberts, *Orientalism's Interlocutors: Painting, Architecture, Photography* (Durham, NC: Duke University Press, 2003).

79. Trench, *Men Who Ruled Kenya*, 11.

80. C. S. Nicholls, *Elspeth Huxley. A Biography* (London: St. Martins, 2002), 12.

81. Elspeth Joscelin Grant Huxley, *White Man's Country; Lord Delamere and the Making of Kenya* [New ed], 2, Vol. I. (London: Chatto & Windus, 1953), 131.

82. Quoted by Trzebinski, *The Kenya Pioneers*, 91.

83. Kennedy, *Islands of White: Settler Society and Culture in Kenya and Southern Rhodesia 1890–1939*, 46.

84. Eleanor Cole, *Random Recollections of a Pioneer Kenya Settler* (1975), 40.

85. MSS. Afr.S.504-Dobbs, 34.

86. Ibid.

87. Ibid, ii. According to the memoir, C. M. Dobbs was born in 1882 and educated at Trinity College, Dublin. His forebears were apparently of Danish origin, having settled in England after the Danish invasions and ending up in Yorkshire. His was a well-to-do family whose sixteenth-century ancestors included a Sheriff (1543) and a Mayor of London (1551), who had been knighted by King Edward VI, and whose grandson had married a daughter of the Earl of Tyrone. Marion Dobbs, on the other hand, came from Lancashire and although her line was obviously not as "illustrious" as her husband's her mother's younger brother had achieved the rank of Major General and had been knighted for his services. Marion Dobbs learned French and German in Bavaria and taught languages until she went to Kenya, where she continued to study languages but only taught her children.

88. Kennedy, *Islands of White: Settler Society and Culture in Kenya and Southern Rhodesia 1890–1939*, 26.

89. Florence Riddell, *Out of the Mist* (London: Thornton Butterworth, 1925), 175.

90. Interview with Christine Nicholls, July 13, 2005.

91. Ibid.

92. These were: Architect 1; Bakery 1; Café Proprietor 1; Civil Service 1; Education 4; Farmer 8; Hotel Manager 1; Missionaries 6; Nursing 10; Pianist 1; Post Office 3; Prison superintendent 1; Salvation Army 1; Social Work 1; Traveller 2. Data taken from two binders entitled: European Pioneers, East Africa, Biographies A to H and I to Z, compiled by W.G. Beaton (no date). MSS. Afr.s.1456, Box 9.

93. MSS. Afr.s.1558-Margaret Elkington, *Recollections of a Settler in Kenya 1905–1970*, Chapter Five.

94. MSS. Afr.s.1558-Margaret Elkington, *Recollections of a Settler in Kenya 1905–1970*, Chapter Three.

95. Ibid.

96. MSS. Afr.s.1558-Margaret Elkington, *Recollections of a Settler in Kenya 1905–1970*, Chapter Four.

97. For a fine analysis of the importance of gender and race on women's pioneer experience, see Glenda Riley, *Taking Land, Breaking Land: Women Colonizing the American West and Kenya, 1840–1940* (Albuquerque, NM: University of New Mexico Press, 2003).

98. MSS. Afr.s.504-Dobbs, 31.

99. Cole, *Random Recollections of a Pioneer Kenya Settler*, 98–99. On the determination of Nellie Cole, see MSS.Afr.s.1424-Cholmondeley, Letter from Lord Delamere to Glady [his wife], March 27, 1930. Eleanor Cole née Balfour, was the daughter of the 2nd Earl of Balfour and Lady Edith Bulwar-Litton. She married the Hon. Galbraith Lowry Egerton Cole in 1917. She became an active member of the East African Women's League and was appointed its president in 1944, taking up the position in 1946 on her return to Kenya from Great Britain.

100. Quote from: Ward and Milligan, *Handbook of British East Africa*, 6.

101. In 1911 Theodore Roosevelt stayed at Juju House, MacMillan's residence, when he came to Kenya to hunt big game.

102. MSS. Afr.s.1217-Hilda MacNaghten.

103. Micr.Af.585-Cara Buxton, Letter to Desmond Buxton, Kericho, B. E. A., November 6, 1913.

104. Elspeth Huxley and Arnold Curtis, eds., *Pioneers' Scrapbook. Reminiscences of Kenya 1890 to 1968*, 2nd reprint (first published 1980) (London: Evans Brothers, 1981), 38.

105. Gretchen Cron, *The Roaring Veldt* (New York/London: Putnam, 1938), 14.

106. On the topic of hunting, see John M. MacKenzie, *The Empire of Nature: Hunting, Conservation, and British Imperialism* (Manchester/New York: University of Manchester Press, 1988); Steinhart, *Black Poachers, White Hunters: A Social History of Hunting in Colonial Kenya* (Oxford/Nairobi, James Currey, 2006).

107. MSS. Afr.s.1558-Margaret Elkington, *Recollections of a Settler in Kenya 1905–1970*, Chapter eight.

108. Huxley and Curtis, eds., *Pioneers' Scrapbook*, 152.

109. MSS.Afr.s.2018-Miss K.A. Hill-Williams, chapter 2. Hill-Williams parents met in South Africa during the Boer War. Her mother was a "great sportswoman" who hunted, played golf and rowed "in a boat with sliding seat on the Severn," a sport not many women of her day did. They were married in London and had two daughters, Hilda (1904) and "Tuppence" (1906). They went out to East Africa when a friend of Hill-Williams' father asked him to join a big game expedition. Once there they decided to settle.

110. For an analysis of the importance of the club to British identity in India, see Mrinalini Sinha, "Britishness, Clubbability, and the Colonial Pubic Sphere: The Genealogy of an Imperial Institution in Colonial India," *The Journal of British Studies* 40, no. 4 (2001).

111. The Nairobi Club, which was established slightly earlier than the Muthaiga Club, was the haunt of civil servants and officials with whom the settlers rarely saw eye to eye. The Muthaiga Club became the most important settler club. See Nicholls, *Elspeth Huxley*, 29, and Stephen Mills, *Muthaiga: The History of Muthaiga Country Club; Vol. 1: 1913–1963* (Nairobi: Mills Publishing, 2006).

112. Among its founding and permanent members mentioned in this chapter were Eleanor Cole, Lady MacMillan, Helen Cleland-Scott, K. (Tuppence) Hill-Williams, and Hilda MacNaghten. A historical outline of the league and its various branches can be found at: http://www.eawl.org/eawl-early-years.html.

113. Quoted by Janet Seeley, "Social Welfare in a Kenyan Town: Policy and Practice, 1902–1985," *African Affairs* 86, no. 345 (1987): 542.

114. Maxon, *Struggle for Kenya. The Loss and Reassertion of Imperial Initiative, 1912–1923*, 65.

115. Kennedy, *Islands of White: Settler Society and Culture in Kenya and Southern Rhodesia 1890–1939*. See 32 and 151.

116. The Ordinance only came into force after World War I and was amended by the July 1920 law.

117. MSS.Afr.s.540-Dobbs, 146–147.

118. Nicholls, *Elspeth Huxley*, 25.

119. MSS.Afr.s.504-Dobbs, 4.

120. Trzebinski, *The Kenya Pioneers*, 126.

121. "Birch for the Boys. An Evening out with a Pony and Cart," *Eastern Morning News*, September 16, 1911. http://www.corpun.com/ukju1109.htm. Accessed August 1, 2008.

122. Huxley and Curtis, eds., *Pioneers' Scrapbook*, 56.

123. MSS. Afr.s.504-Marion Dobbs, 143.

124. MSS. Afr.s.1217-MacNaghten.

125. MSS, Afr.s.1058-Madeline La Vie Platts, 27.

126. Alyse Simpson, *The Land That Never Was* (London: Selwyn & Blount, 1937), 152–153.

127. Life for the settlers, male or female, was not easy. In the early decades the rate of suicides as a result of failed enterprises or an inability to deal with colonial existence gained notoriety for the colony. See C. J. D. Duder and C. P. Youé, "Paice's Place: Race and Politics in Nanyuki Districe, Kenya, in the 1920s," *African Affairs* 93, no. 371 (1994): 253–278, 53.

128. Simpson, *The Land That Never Was*, 161.

129. Michel de Certeau, *The Practice of Everyday Life* (Berkeley: University of California Press, 1984), 134.

CHAPTER 2

1. Edward Berenson and Eva Giloi, eds., *Constructing Charisma. Celebrity, Fame and Power in Nineteenth-Century Europe* (New York / Oxford: Berghahn Books, 2010), 4.
2. Adhering fairly closely to Max Weber's definition of charisma, Berenson and Giloi argue that it is the attribute of a leader or personality endowed with a sense of mission as well as powers or qualities that are exemplary. Fame, on the other hand, is more closely associated with renown and the famous person is not necessarily a charismatic personality, although of course s/he can be. Both are concepts of long-standing, the former having originated BCE and the latter during the medieval period. Celebrity, they argue is a newer concept, tied more closely to the advent of the print and media cultures. Blixen could certainly be considered charismatic after she left Kenya and reinvented herself as a Scheherazade type storyteller, but it is not that period of her life with which I am concerned.
3. Mary Louise Roberts, "Rethinking Female Celebrity. The Eccentric Star of Nineteenth-Century France," in *Constructing Charisma. Celebrity, Fame and Power in Nineteenth-Century Europe*, ed. Edward Berenson and Eva Giloi (New York/Oxford: Berghahn Books, 2010), 103–116, 10.
4. Ibid.
5. See, for example, Nupur Chaudhuri and Margaret Strobel, *Western Women and Imperialism: Complicity and Resistance* (Bloomington: Indiana University Press, 1992).
6. I have deliberately chosen to use the concept of transgression rather than crossing or transference, concepts used by more recent scholarly works when it comes to crossing boundaries of race or gender, as I feel it is a stronger concept and hence more appropriate for the period.
7. Lesley Blanch, "Isabelle Eberhardt. Portrait of a Legend," in *The Wilder Shores of Love*, ed. Lesley Blanch (New York: Simon and Schuster, 1954), 271–310. Cecily Mackworth, *The Destiny of Isabelle Eberhardt* (New York: Ecco Press, 1975); Denise Brahimi, "A l'ombre chaude de l'Islam," *Sans Frontière*, no. 65, June 4, 1982, Denise Brahimi, *Requiem pour Isabelle* (Paris: Publisud, 1983) Ursula Kingsmill Hart, *Two Ladies of Colonial Algeria: The Lives and Times of Aurélie Picard and Isabelle Eberhardt* (Athens, OH: Ohio University Center for International Studies, 1987); Annette Kobak, *Isabelle: The Life of Isabelle Eberhardt* (New York: A. A. Knopf, 1989); Julia Clancy-Smith, "The Passionate Nomad Re-considered" in *Western Women and Imperialism: Complicity and Resistance*, ed. Chaudhuri and Strobel, Laura Rice, "Eberhardt and Gender" and, Karim Hamdy, "Eberhardt and Mysticism" both in Isabelle Eberhardt, Karim Hamdy, and Laura Rice, *Departures: Selected Writings* (San Francisco: City Lights Books, 1994), Laura Rice, "Nomad Thought: Isabelle Eberhardt and the Colonial Project," *Cultural Critique* 17, Winter (1990–1991), 151–176; Linda Donelson, *Out of Isak Dinesen in Africa: The Untold Story*, 1st ed. (Iowa City, Iowa: Coulsong List, 1995); Susan R. Horton, *Difficult Women, Artful Lives. Olive Shreiner and Isak Dinesen, In and Out of Africa.* (Baltimore: The Johns Hopkins University Press, 1995); Simon Lewis, *White Women Writers and Their African Invention* (Gainesville, FL: University Press of Florida, 2003); Annelies van Hees, *The Ambivalent Venus: Women in Isak Dinesen's Tales (condensed version of van Hees' Doctoral Thesis: De Ambivalente Venus in het werk van Karen Blixen)*

(Minneapolis, Univiversity of Minnesota Press, 1991); Olga Anastasia Pelensky, *Isak Dinesen: The Life and Imagination of a Seducer* (Athens, OH: Ohio University Press, 1991); Olga Anastasia Pelensky, *Isak Dinesen: Critical Views* (Athens, OH: Ohio University Press, 1993); Susan Hardy Aitken, *Isak Dinesen and the Engendering of Narrative* (Chicago: University of Chicago Press, 1990); Diane Simmons, "A Passion for Africans: Psychoanalyzing Karen Blixen's Neo-feudal Kenya," *Scrutiny* 7, no. 2 (2002): 19–32; Frantz Leander Hansen and Gaye (translator) Kynoch, *The Aristocratic Universe of Karen Blixen: Destiny and the Denial of Fate* (Brighton, UK: Sussex Academic Press, 2003).

8. Quoted by Edward A. Apers "The Nineteenth Century: Prelude to Colonialism" in *Zamani: A Survey of East African History,* ed. Bethwell A. Ogot, New Edition (Nairobi: East African Pub. House, 1974), 53, 229–248.

9. Under the Soldier Settlement Act. See Tiyambe Zeleza, "The Establishment of Colonial Rule, 1905–1920" in *A Modern History of Kenya, 1895–1980: in honour of B.A. Ogot,* ed. William Robert Ochieng and Bethwell A. Ogot (Nairobi: Evans Brothers [Kenya], 1989), 35–70, 41.

10. In 1912 five landowners owned 20 percent of the land alienated to Europeans. In the fertile Rift Valley 50 percent of the land was owned by Europeans. Zeleza, 41.

11. Ogot, 254.

12. "Letter to Ingeborg Dinesen, 17 March 1931" in *Letters from Africa 1914–1931,* vol. I (London, Picador, 1986), 416.

13. Eloued, 18 janvier 1901, "Cahiers - Vers les horizons bleus" in *Oeuvres complètes: Écrits sur le sable,* ed. Isabelle Eberhardt Delacour Marie-Odile and Huleu Jean-René, 2 vols. (Paris: B. Grasset, 1988), 83.

14. *Out of Africa* was published in London and Denmark in 1937 and in New York in 1938, where it was sold to the Book of the Month Club.

15. The political nature of much of the early criticism of Eberhardt has obscured the fact her literary merit was also disputed. See Robert Randau, *Isabelle Eberhardt. Notes et Souveniers,* Paris, La Boîte á Documents (first published 1945, 227 & 243. For the political criticisms, see Kobak, *Isabelle. The Life of Isabelle Eberhardt,* 239–245.

16. For example, Lucienne Favre in Algeria, Elspeth Huxley in Kenya. Huxley's work, although immensely popular, never really transcended the colonial barrier.

17. Joseph Chailley-Bert, *L'émigration des femmes aux colonies* (Paris: A. Colin & Cie., 1897), 19–20.

18. Kingsley journeyed to Africa in 1893 and 1895. Her most renowned works were *Travels in West Africa* (London, 1897) and *West African Studies* (1899). Mary Hall crossed Southern and Central Africa in 1904 producing the work *A Woman's Trek from the Cape to Cairo* (1907).

19. Trophimowsky was eager to escape the "pernicious influence of civilization" and farm in Algeria, although he did not in fact remain long enough to pursue this goal; Augustin had joined the foreign legion and was in Bone. See Kobak, 48–49.

20. Eberhardt's belief she was born a Muslim appears to have developed in early adulthood. Kobak, 28–29.

21. Frans Lassen, Introduction, *Letters from Africa,* xxxii.

22. Exports of Kenyan coffee increased from 8.5 tons to 5,328 tons in the period 1909–1920. In monetary terms this signified a jump from £239 to £392,507. Zeleza, 42.

23. Thomas Dinesen, *My Sister, Isak Dinesen* (translated by Joan Tate) (London, Michael Joseph, 1974), 60.

24. The initial investment in 1914 was 300,000 Danish Kroner, which in 1975, was the equivalent of 3m Kroner or approximately $500,000. (Thomas Dinesen, *My Sister...* 53) By today's standards it would be about 6 times the 1975 amount.

25. Judith Thurman, *Isak Dinesen: The Life of a Storyteller*, 1st ed. (New York: St Martin's Press, 1982), 123.

26. Lassen, Introduction, *Letters from Africa*, xxiv–xxv.

27. "Letter to Thomas Dinesen, Ngong, 10 September 1923," and "Letter to Thomas Dinesen, Ngong, 24 April, 1924," in *Letters from Africa,* 168 and 212. A rejoinder to the "tragedy" of her divorce: according to Elspeth Huxley, Blixen treated Bror very badly, turning him off the farm without a penny. C. S. Nicholls, *Elspeth Huxley. A Biography*, 73.

28. "Letter to Mary Bess Westemholz (Aunt Bess), Ngong, 6 May 1928, in *Letters from Africa,* 358.

29. "Heures de Tunis" in *Écritssur le sable,* 1, no. 32 ; See also "Letter to Ali Abdul Wahab. Bône, le 10 septembre 1897," in Isabelle Eberhart, *ÉcritsIntimes. Lettres aux trois hommes les plus aimés* (eds. Marie-Odile Delacour & Jean-René Huleu) (Paris: Editions Payot, 1991), 85.

30. "Réminiscences.Vers les horizons bleus" in *Écrits sur le sable* I., no. 73.

31. For her views on nomads, see: "Au pays des sables" and "Pour tuer le temps. Sudoranais 2e partie" both in *Écritssur le sable* 1, no. 44 & 242.

32. "Printemps au Désert.Vers les Horizons bleus" in *Écrits sur le sable* 1, no. 100.

33. CAOM, 75APOM/38-Arnaud-Randau, VI Premiers contacts avec les gens et les choses de Ténès.

34. "Dernières visions. Sud Oranais 1er partie," in *Écrits sur le sable* 1, no. 203.

35. Eberhardt on Slimène Ehni in her diary, "Marseille, 7 mai 1900" in *Écrits intimes,* 241.

36. Quoted by Delacour in *Écrits intimes,* 245.

37. Ibid., 244. A marabout was a Muslim holy man and mystic.

38. CAOM, Série 23X26, Letter from Ehnni to Augustin Moerder (no date).

39. "Le 12 avril 1901, à Batna. Deuxième Journalier" in *Écrits sur le sable* 1, no. 363. An exception was Eberhardt's friendship with the Sufi woman, Lalla Zaynab (1850–1904). See Julia Ann Clancy-Smith, "The House of Zainab: female authority and saintly succession in colonial Algeria," in *Women in Middle Eastern History: Shifting Boundaries in Sex and Gender*, ed. Nikki R. Keddie and Beth Baron (New Haven, CT: Yale University Press, 1993), 254–272.

40. Richard Kohn quoted by Randau, *Isabelle Eberhardt*, 208–209.

41. CAOM Serie X-31/MIOM/17-Lyautey. Letter from Lyautey to Victor Barrucandd April 2, 1905.

42. Lyautey spent much time sorting through her work and corresponding with Barruccand about it. About half of her manuscripts were intact; the other half was incomplete or damaged. Barrucand pieced together what Lyautey sent him and published it as "Du l'ombre chaude de l'Islam," for which Lyautey expressed "a great satisfaction." CAOM Serie X-31/MIOM/17-Lyautey. Letter to Barrucand, February 19, 1909.

43. Mme Henriette Celairé on Lyautey, quoted by Randau, *Isabelle Eberhardt,* 203 (Africa denotes North Africa).

44. Kobak, *Isabelle: The Life of Isabelle Eberhardt*, 213.

45. Karim Hamdy, "The Intoxicated Mystic: Eberhardt's Sufi Experience" in *Departures. Selected Writings,* ed. Isabelle Eberhardt (translated and edited by Karim Hamdy and Laura Rice) (San Francisco: City Lights Books, 1994).

46. Thurman, *Isak Dinesen: The Life of a Storyteller*, 124.

47. "Letter to Ingeborg Dinesen. M'Bagathi, December 3, 1914," in *Letters from Africa*, 26.

48. "Letter to Ingeborg Dinesen. May 18, 1930" in *Letters from Africa*, 407.

49. "I am Given a Hit by Her Hand," in *Longing for Darkness. Kamante's Tales Out of Africa* Kamante, collected by Peter Beard, San Francisco, Chronicle Books, 1990 (no pagination).

50. "The Goodness of Mrs. Karen" in *Longing for Darkness* (no pagination).

51. Thomas Dinesen, *My Sister, Isak Dinesen*, 59.

52. "Letter to Thomas Dinesen.Ngong, August 5, 1926," in *Letters from Africa*, 270 (my emphasis).

53. "Letter to Thomas Dinesen, Ngong, May 7, 1931" in *Letters from Africa*, 431.

54. "Letter to Aunt Bess. April 1, 1914" in *Letters from Africa*, 4.

55. "Letter to Ingeborg Dinesen.Ngong, July 9, 1918" in *Letters from Africa*, 74.

56. In addition to the Somalis as servants, the Masai were singled out for their intelligence and as excellent warriors. They were, according to one colonial administrator: "more intelligent than, and of a type superior to, the other native tribes around them." D. Storrs-Fox, quoted by Tidrick, Kathryn Tidrick, "The Masai and Masters: A Psychological Study of District Administration," *African Studies Review* 23, no. 1 (1980): 16.

57. Isak Dinesen, "Farah" in *Shadows on the Grass* (New York: Vintage Books, 1974), 15.

58. Ibid., 17.

59. "Letter to Ingeborg Dinesen, Ngong, May 20, 1918" in *Letters from Africa*, 69.

60. For a detailed account of their relationship, see Sara Wheeler, *Too Close to the Sun. The Audacious Lives and Times of Denys Finch Hatton* (New York: Random House, 2006).

61. "Letter to Ingeborg Dinesen, Bogani, April 6, 1918" in *Letters from Africa*, 66.

62. "Letter to Ingeborg Dinesen, Ngong, May 5, 1918" in *Letters from Africa*, 67.

63. "Letter to Thomas Dinesen, October 22, 1926" in *Letters from Africa*, 292.

64. "Letter to Ingeborg Dinesen, April 2, 1923" in *Letters from Africa*, 146.

65. C. J. D. Duder and C. P. Youé, "Paice's Place: Race and Politics in Nanyuki District, Kenya, in the 1920s," *African Affairs* 93 (1994): 253–278; Dane Kennedy, *Islands of White: Settler Society and Culture in Kenya and Southern Rhodesia 1890–1939* (Durham, NC: Duke University Press, 1987), 183.

66. According to Tidrick, one of the Kenya hotels was nicknamed "the House of Lords" for this very reason. Kathryn Tidrick, *Empire and the English Character* (London: Tauris, 1992), 130.

67. For analyses of the significance of hunting to British imperialism, see Edward I. Steinhart, *Black Poachers, White Hunters: A Social History*

of Hunting in Colonial Kenya (Oxford/Nairobi: James Currey, 2006); John M. MacKenzie, *The Empire of Nature: Hunting, Conservation, and British Imperialism* (Manchester/New York: Manchester University Press, 1988).

68. "Letter to Mary Bess Westenholz, Ngong, May 23rd 1926," in *Letters from Africa*, 263.
69. "Letter to Ingeborg Dinesen, Mountain Health Resort, 'Kujabe Hill,' July 14, 1914," in *Letters from Africa*, 13.
70. "Letter to Ingeborg Dineson, Uasha Nyero, 23 August, 1914" in *Letters from Africa*, 14.
71. "Letter to Thomas Dinesen, received 17 October, 1914 from Mbagathi Estate," in *Letters from Africa*, 17–18.
72. Ibid., 21.
73. "Letter to Ingeborg Dinesen, Ngong, 4 October, 1928" in *Letters from Africa*, 384.
74. "Letter to Ingeborg Dinesen, Mbagathi. 3 December, 1914" in *Letters from Africa*, 27.
75. "Letter to Ingeborg Dinesen, Ngong, Sunday 3 June, 1928" in *Letters from Africa*, 362.
76. MacMillan was knighted in 1918. See Chapter 3.
77. Blixen, *Out of Africa*, 77–85.
78. "Yasmina" in *Écritssur le sable*, Vol. II, 98.
79. "L'Anarchiste" in *Écrits sur le sable*, Vol. II, 131 & 133.
80. "Letter to Thomas Dinesen. April 1–3, 1926" in *Letters from Africa*, 246.
81. In her work on Olive Schreiner and Isak Dinesen, Susan R. Horton states that due to colonial policies, such as the *law* restricting the size of Kikuyu livestock, conditions worsened for the Kikuyu. She adds that Blixen "would have experienced a gradual but profound constriction of her own relations with the Kikuyu laboring on her coffee plantation." Horton, *Difficult Women, Artful Lives. Olive Shreiner and Isak Dinesen, In and Out of Africa.*, 209.
82. "Isabelle Eberhardt à Ali Abdul Wahab.Bône, 10 septembre1897" in *Écrits intimes. Lettres aux trois hommes les plus aimés*, 84.
83. Eberhardt and her mother arrived in Algeria in May 1897. Her mother died in November of the same year. For Eberhardt's sentiments regarding the death of her mother, see "Premier Journalier. Cagliari, le 1er janvier 1900" in *Écrits sur le sable*, Vol. I, 304.
84. "Troisième Journalier. Marseille, le 3 juin 1901, 9 heures du soir" in *Écrits sur le sable*, Vol. I, 391.
85. "Isabelle Eberhardt à Ali Abdul Wahab. Le 20 Rabia Al Awwal" in *Écrits intimes*, 73.
86. For Eberhardt's view on the superiority of beings driven to improve through creativity, see Genève, le 15 juin, 1900. Deuxieme journalier" in *Écrits sur le sable*, Vol. I, 316–317.
87. "Pour tuer le temps. Retour au Sud. SudOranais 2e partie" in *Écrits sur le sable*, Vol. I, 242.
88. "Genève, le 15 juin, 1900. Deuxieme journalier" in *Écrits sur le sable*, Vol. I, 317.
89. "Isabelle Eberhardt, Eloued, septembre 1900. Vers les horizons bleus" in *Écrits sur le sable*. Vol. I, 72.

90. "Isabelle Eberhardt à Ali Abdul Wahad, Bône 12 août, 1897" in Isabelle Eberhart, *Écrits Intimes*, 63.

91. "Letter to Ingeborg Dinesen, Ngong, April 13, 1924" in *Letters from Africa*, 199.

92. "Letter to Thomas Dinesen.Ngong, 24 February 1926" in *Letters from Africa*, 240–241.

93. "Un automne dans le Sahel tunisien.Vagabondages" in *Écrits sur le sable*, Vol. I, 64.

94. Quoted by Randau, *Isabelle Eberhardt,* 157.

95. Eberhardt to Randau. Algiers 12 October 1902, quoted in Randau, *Isabelle Eberhardt,* 98.

96. "Letter to Ingeborg Dinesen.Ngong, Sunday 15 October 1922" in *Letters from Africa*, 135.

97. "Wheeler, *Too Close to the Sun. The Audacious Lives and Times of Denys Finch Hatton.*, 242.

98. Randau, *Isabelle Eberhardt,* 64.

99. CAOM Serie 23X33 Letter from Bonneval to Eberhardt, March 11, 1900.

100. A certain Ms. C. d'Ambre.

101. Randau, *Isabelle Eberhardt,* 201, footnote 1.

102. "Letter to Ellen Dahl. Ngong 16 May 1926" in *Letters from Africa*, 258–265.

103. Colonial society had mostly been highly critical of Eberhardt's behavior. Her sexuality, transgender dressing, and familiarity with the Arabs came under negative scrutiny. Negative press coverage in two Algerian papers, *Les Nouvelles* and the *Union Républicaine* had been so relentless that Eberhardt had sued the latter for libel.

104. CAOM 30MIOM/28-AKHBAR, August 1922, n 13917.

105. Henriette Célarie, *Nos Soeurs Musulmanes. Scènes de la vie du Désert* (Paris: Hachette, 1925), 208.

106. CAOM 87/APOM/48-DÉJEUX, Jacques d'Espagnat, "Les Lettres françaises" in *La Revue de France*, 8 année, 1 septembre 1928, 17, 182–187 (my emphasis).

107. *La bonne nomade* (Louis Doyon, 1923), *L'amazone des sables* (Claude-Maurice Robert, 1934), *Isabelle d'Afrique* (Lucienne Favre, 1939) *Aventureuse du Sahara* (Jean Noel, 1961) and in the press *La Passionaria du desert* (Bruno Hadjih), *Notre Dame d'Afrique* and *la Séverine musulmane* (*Dépeche Algérienne*, October 29, 1904).

108. CAOM Série 23X57, Letter from the society to Barrucand, March 12, 1930.

109. CAOM 30MIOM/28-AKHBAR, "IsabelleEberhardt et Lys du Pac," October 6, 1930, no. 14,000.

110. See, for example, Claude-Maurice Robert, "Sur les traces d'Isabelle-Eberhardt" in *L'Envoûtement du Sud d'el Kantara à Djanet*," Alger, Bacconier Frères, 1934, 81–84; The first theatrical production of Eberhardt's life, by Lucienne Favre & Constance Colin, was staged at the Montparnasse theatre in 1939. This romanticized bioplay is still produced from time to time. Two films have been made of Eberhardt's life in recent years: Leslie Thornton's *There was an Unseen Cloud Moving* (1988, Women make movies) and Ian Pringle's *Isabelle Eberhardt* (1990, a French-Australian co-production).

111. Hart, *Ladies of Colonial Algeria: The Lives and Times of Aurélie Picard and Isabelle Eberhardt.*

112. "I am a storyteller. I belong to an ancient tribe of idle people who have for 2000 years sat down among the honestly hard working people of the real world and who have sometimes succeeded in creating for them another kind of reality" Karen Blixen, extract from an interview on the Karen Blixen museum website. http://www.karen-blixen.dk/index.php?option=com_content&view=article&id=73&Itemid=4&lang=en accessed March 20, 2010.

113. Dinesen, "Echoes from the Hills" in *Shadows on the Grass*, 136.

114. Kuki Gallmann, *I Dreamed of Africa* (London: Penguin Books, 1992), 205.

115. Ibid., 184.

116. Oria Douglas-Hamilton [and Dylan Thomas quoted by Douglas-Hamilton], in Gallmann, *I Dreamed of Africa*, 215. Iain and Oria Douglas-Hamilton are best known for their works on the African elephant and for their efforts to preserve African wildlife, as is Kuki Gallmann.

117. Chris Bongie, *Exotic Memories: Literature, Colonialism, and the fin de siècle* (San Francisco: Stanford University Press, 1991).

CHAPTER 3

1. Errol Trzebinski, *The Kenya Pioneers*, 1st American ed. (New York: W. W. Norton, 1986), 178. Trzebinski give the figures as 60,000 horses and mules and twice as many oxen.

2. MSS. Afr.s.2018-Miss K.A. Hill Williams, 14, See also MSS.Afr.s.1558-Margaret Elkington, chapter eleven.

3. MSS. Afr.S.504-Dobbs, 115.

4. C.S. Nicholls, *Elspeth Huxley. A Biography* 65.

5. MSS. Afr.s.2154-Box 7, Huxley papers, File 1, Letter to Vera, November 17, 1922, Kitimuru.

6. Trzebinski, *The Kenya Pioneers*, 182–183.

7. According to Trezbinski, within a few months of the outbreak of war 85 percent of the young men in the colony had joined some sort of unit, 179.

8. MSS.Afr.S. 504-Dobbs, 114–115.

9. Dane Kennedy, *Islands of White: Settler Society and Culture in Kenya and Southern Rhodesia 1890–1939* (Durham: Duke University Press, 1987), 151.

10. For details, see Robert M. Maxon, *Struggle for Kenya. The Loss and Reassertion of Imperial Initiative, 1912–1923* (London/Toronto: Associated University Presses, 1993), 85.

11. Elspeth Huxley, *White Man's Country: Lord Delamere and the Making of Kenya*, 2 vols. (New York: Praeger, 1968), 72.

12. Segregation in Kenya was administrative and not legal as it was in the United States or became in South Africa. It saved the British government from having to define by law what it overlooked in practice. See Kathryn Tidrick, *Empire and the English Character* (London: Tauris, 1992), 137.

13. Maxon, *Struggle for Kenya. The Loss and Reassertion of Imperial Initiative, 1912–1923*, 282. According to Maxon, the Colonial Office lost control of the colony during the war but regained it in 1923, as laid out in the Devonshire Declaration in July 1913. (79 and 13)

14. For a discussion of racism specific to one area in the 1920s, see C. J. D. Duder and C.P. Youé, "Paice's Place: Race and Politics in Nanyuki Districe, Kenya, in the 1920s," *African Affairs* 93, no. 371 (1994): 253–278.

15. Huxley, *White Man's Country*, 79.

16. By 1929 only 35 percent of able-bodied Kenyan men were laborers, although there were large numbers of squatters. *Colonial Report no 1510. Colony and Protectorate of Kenya. Report for 1929,* 76.

17. For a psychological analysis of master/slave concept in the colonial situation, see Octave Mannoni, *Prospero and Caliban: The Psychology of Colonization* (French ed. 1948) (Ann Arbor: University of Michigan Press, 1990). For the master servant relationship, see Douglas Hay and Paul Craven, eds., *Masters, Servants, and Magistrates in Britain and the Empire, 1562–1955* (Chapel Hill: University of North Carolina Press, 2004); Theresa M. McBride, *The Domestic Revolution: The Modernisation of Household Service in England and France, 1820–1920* (London: Croom Helm, 1976); Carolyn Steedman, *Master and Servant: Love and Labor in the English Industrial Age* (Cambridge/New York: Cambridge University Press, 2007). In the context of East Africa, see Kathryn Tidrick, "The Masai and Their Masters: A Psychological Study of District Administration," *African Studies Review* 23, no. 1 (1980); Karen T. Hansen, *Distant Companions: Servants and Employers in Zambia; 1900–1985* (Ithaca, NY: Cornell University Press, 1989).

   In colonial Algeria, according to Robert-Guaird, until the twentieth century no Algerians worked in domestic service in European households. Rather, domestic service was undertaken by Europeans. Claudine Robert-Guiard, *Des Européennes en Situation Coloniale: Algérie 1830–1939*, 158–159.

18. David Anderson, *Histories of the Hanged. Britain's Dirty War in Kenya and the End of Empire* (London: Weidenfeld & Nicolson, 2005), 15.

19. Ibid.

20. See ibid. and Charles Chenevix Trench, *Men Who Ruled Kenya* (London/ New York: The Radcliffe Press, 1993), 76; Maxon, *Struggle for Kenya The Loss and Reassertion of Imperial Initiative, 1912–1923*, 210–213; Marshall S. Clough, *Fighting Two Sides: Kenyan Chiefs and Politicians, 1918–1940*, 1st ed. (Niwot, CO: University Press of Colorado, 1990), 53–60. In 1924 the Native Authority Amendment Ordinance allowed for the establishment of local native councils (LNCs). Their members were partially elected, partially nominated and could pass by-laws and levy rates. By 1936, however, only 20 such councils remained (out of 34). No doubt their functioning was unimpeded as long as they did "what they were told." Trench, 69.

21. MSS.Afr.s.1418-Armstrong. Census figures from *Colonial Report no. 118. Colony and Protectorate of Kenya. Report for 1922,* 6. Armstrong's father followed the Second Lord Kitchner down the Nile and bought a 50 acre coffee farm, known as Thompson's Estate, 4 miles out of Nairobi. Armstrong, and her mother followed him out to Kenya.

22. The more extreme minded settlers clamored for segregation, which never became an official policy. The Colonial Office in London was fearful that an outright refusal of Indian demands would create problems in India, where Indians had many more rights than they did in East Africa. But restricting Indian immigration and economic opportunities in favor of Africans garnered sympathy among Colonial Office officials. See Maxon, *Struggle for Kenya. The Loss and Reassertion of Imperial Initiative, 1912–1923*, 162. See also

Paul Mosley, *The Settler Economies. Studies in the Economic History of Kenya and Southern Rhodesia 1900–1963* (Cambridge: Cambridge University Press, 1983), 24–25.

23. MSS. Afr.s.633, Box 3, File 3/1, folio 1-2: "Indian Question the Native outlook. Baganda and Indians. Rumours of Equal Rights for Indians with Whites" (no date), but it was the follow-up of an article which appeared in the same paper on July 1, 1921.

24. MSS. Afr.s.594 – Convention of Association. File 1/14: Statements by Ministers (past & present) and speeches in the Houses of Parliament. Extract from Winston Churchill's speech at the E.A. dinner, January 27, 1922.

25. MSS. Afr.s.594 – Convention of Association. File 1/14: Statements by Ministers (past & present) and speeches in the Houses of Parliament. Extract from Lord Delamere's speech at the E.A. dinner, January 27, 1922.

26. Nicholls, *Elspeth Huxley*, 60.

27. MSS.Afr.s.2154-Box 7-Huxley papers, file 1, Letter to Robin, March 14, 1923 from Deloraine, Njoro, Kenya Colony.

28. MSS.Afr.s.633, Box 3, File 3/1, folio 149. Letter from the East Africa Women's League, to HE Sir Robert Corydon, KCMG, Governor of Kenya, March 23, 1923.

29. Kennedy, *Islands of White: Settler Society and Culture in Kenya and Southern Rhodesia 1890–1939*, 68–69; See also Maxon, *Struggle for Kenya The Loss and Reassertion of Imperial Initiative, 1912–1923*, 52–54 & 118–120; John Lonsdale, "Kenya. Home County and African Frontier," in *Settlers and Expatriates: Britons over the Seas*, ed. Robert A. Bickers (Oxford: Oxford University Press, 2010), 74–111. 75–76.

30. Trzebinski, *The Kenya Pioneers*, 153.

31. MSS. AFr.585-Cara Buxton. Letter to Desmond, Lumbwa, March 14, 1919.

32. Dane Kennedy, "Introduction" Alyse Simpson, *The Land That Never Was* (London: Selwyn & Blount, 1937), v. For example in 1923 there were 3,450 immigrants and 3,374 emigrants; the following year there were 4,079 immigrants and 3,236 emigrants. The trend continued throughout the 1920s and 1930s. See Kennedy, *Islands of White: Settler Society and Culture in Kenya and Southern Rhodesia 1890–1939*, 195.

33. MSS. Afr.s.2154, Box 7-Huxley papers, file 3, Letter to Robin and Vera Grant from Kitimuru, March 1, 1921.

34. Simpson, *The Land That Never Was*, 104.

35. Ibid., 262.

36. Ibid., 6.

37. Florence Riddell, *I Go Wandering. A Travel Biography* (London: J. B. Lippincott 1935), 160.

38. Susan R. Horton, *Difficult Women, Artful Lives. Olive Shreiner and Isak Dinesen, in and out of Africa.* (Baltimore: The Johns Hopkins University Press, 1995), 209.

39. Kennedy, "Introduction" Simpson, *The Land That Never Was*, vi.

40. Ibid., 133.

41. Juanita Carberry and Nicola Tyrer, *Child of Happy Valley* (London: Heinemann, 1999), 31.

42. F. Duchéne, "La Femme musulmane dans l'Afrique du Nord," in *La Revue*, 1908, 470–478, Bibliothèque Marguerite Durand (henceforth BMD), DOS396AFR-Dossier-Femmes-Afrique du Nord.

43. Marius-Ary Leblond, "Préface" to Magali Boisnard, *L'alerte Au Désert: la Vie Saharienne Pendant la Guerre 1914–1916* (Paris: Perrin, 1916), vi. Marius-AryLeblond was the pseudonym for Aimé Merlo and Georges Athénas, whose joint work as critics and authors was much esteemed. According to another critic, she was "brought up to live the Arab life among the Arabs of Algeria." J. P. Dupré "*L'Alerte au Désert* by Magali Boisnard, Paris. Librairie Perrin, 1916" in *Muslim World*, Vol. 1, 1918, 94–95.

44. Magali Boisnard, *Les Endormies* (Paris: Sansot, 1909).

45. Ibid., 15.

46. Ibid., 7.

47. Ibid., 14.

48. Ibid., 15.

49. Ibid., 72.

50. Ibid., 263.

51. Ibid., 76, Also 55, 81, 111–112.

52. Charles René-Garnier, *La Conquête de L'islam Par les Femmes. Conférénce Fait à la Société Normande de Géographie le 20 Novembre 1910* (Rouen: Imprimerie Cagniard, 1911), 16, 21.

53. At the end of the nineteenth century anxieties about women's role in society found expression in unexpected places. See, for example, Mary Louise Roberts, *Disruptive Acts: The New Woman in Fin-de-Siècle France* (Chicago: University of Chicago Press, 2002).

54. Lucienne Martini, *Racines de Papier: Essai Sur L'expression Littéraire de L'identité Pieds-Noirs* (Paris: Publisud, 1997), 131.

55. In 1921 the European population in Algiers was 147,896; in Oran it was 102,210, and in Constantine it was 36,333. See Mahfoud Kaddache, *La Vie Politique à Alger de 1919 à 1939* (Algiers: SNED, 1970), 15.

56. Ibid., 11.

57. For the development of these cities along French lines, see David Prochaska, *Making Algeria French: Colonialism in Bône 1870–1920* (Cambridge/ New York: Cambridge University Press, 1990); Seth Graebner, *History's Place: Nostalgia and the City in French Algerian Literature* (New York: Lexington Books, 2007); Zeynep Çelik, *Urban Forms and Colonial Confrontations: Algiers under French Rule* (Berkeley: University of California Press, 1997); Saïd Almi, *Urbanisme et Colonisation: Présence Française en Algérie* (Sprimont, Belgique: Mardaga, 2002).

58. Martini, *Racines de Papier: Essai Sur L'expression Littéraire de L'identité Pieds-Noirs*, 131.

59. The *Code de l'indigénat* subjected the Algerians to special laws and restrictions, thus keeping them in inferior status. Algerians could be released from the indigénat through naturalization, but to be naturalized they had to renounce the Islamic personal statutes.

60. See Kaddache, *La Vie Politique à Alger de 1919 à 1939*; Jonathan K. Gosnell, *The Politics of Frenchness in Colonial Algeria, 1930–1954* (Rochester, NY: University of Rochester Press, 2002); Peter Dunwoodie, *Francophone Writing in Transition: Algeria 1900–1945* (Oxford: Peter Lang, 2005).

61. Algerian protest movements were much more developed than in Kenya. Many of Algerians who had emigrated to France for economic reasons or else had remained there after the war, joined the *Étoile Nord Africaine*, headed by Messali Hadj.

62. Annette Godin, *L'erreur de Nedjma* (Paris: Alphonse Lemerre, 1923).
    Quoted by Michel Corday, "Introduction."
63. For a discussion on Maria Bugéja's activities in Algeria, see Jeanne Bowlan,
    "Civilizing Gender Relations in Algeria: The paradoxical case of Marie Bugéja
    1919–1939" in *Domesticating the Empire,* ed. Clancy-Smith & Gouda,
    175–192. See also Sara Kimble, "Emancipation through Secularation: French
    Feminist Views of Muslim Women's Condition in Interwar Algeria" *French
    Colonial History* 7, (2006): 109–128.
64. Marie Bugéja, *EnigmeMusulmane. Lettres à uneBretonne,* Tangiers/Fez,
    Éditions internationales Pierre André, 1938, 100.
65. *Nos Soeurs musulmanes,* Algiers, Jacques Cartier, 1931 (1st published
    1921). 97
66. Ibid., 105.
67. Ibid., 115 [The work in question is: C. Mairin, *Sur l'instruction et l'éducation
    des femmes musulmanes: aux indigènes nord-africains instruits dans nos écoles,*
    Algiers, Engel, 1919]. Mixed marriages were very limited. For more on inter-
    marriage, see Robert-Guiard, *Des Européennes en Situation Coloniale: Algérie
    1830–1939,* 113–136. (For Robert-Guaird's figures see chapter 5 below,
    note 10); Jean Déjeux, *Image de L'étrangère: Unions Mixtes Franco-Maghrébines*
    (Paris: La Boîte à documents, 1989); Philippe Meylan, *Les Mariages Mixtes en
    Afrique Du Nord. Conclusion–Effets Sur la Personne et les Biens. Dissolution,* Vol.
    9, Institut des Hautes Études Marocaines. Collection des Centers D'études
    Juridiques (Paris: Librairie du Recueil Sirey, 1934); Henri Dr Marchand, *Les
    Mariages Franco-Musulmans* (Alger: Impr. Vollot-Debacq, 1954).
68. Ibid., 117.
69. *Seduction Orientale,* Algiers, Soubiron, 1931. For an analysis of the novel in
    terms of colonial ideology, see Lorcin, 2004.
70. *Visions d'Algérie,* Algiers, Baconnier frères, 1929.
71. In addition to *Seduction orientale,* she wrote *Du vice à la vertue, roman d'une
    Naïla,* Paris, Argo, 1932, *Dans la tiédeur de la tente,* Alger, La Typographie
    d'art, 1933.
72. J. Annette Godin, *Au Pays Du Myrte* (Paris: Alphone Lemerre, 1921), 59.
73. Godin's father was a military officer, hence the family's presence in Saint
    Maixint. He left the military to teach in Algeria.
74. CAOM 75APOM/16-Fonds Arnaud-Randau, manuscript of "La vie littéraire
    en Algérie." Other authors mentioned by Randau, discussed in this study, are
    Maria Bugéja, Jeanne Faure-Sardet, Mareval Bertoin, and Magali Boisnard.
75. CAOM 75APOM/16-Fonds Arnaud-Randau, "L'Association des Ecrivain-
    salgériens."
76. Martini, *Racines de Papier: Essai Sur L'expression Littéraire de L'identité
    Pieds-Noirs,* 106.
77. Godin, *L'erreur de Nedjma,* 295.
78. Ibid. Michel Corday, "Introduction."
79. See, for example, Emmanuelle Saada, *Les Enfants de la Colonie: les Métis de
    L'empire Français Entre Sujétion et Citoyenneté* (Paris: Découverte, 2007);
    Owen White, *Children of the French Empire: Miscegenation and Colonial Soci-
    ety in French West Africa, 1895–1960* (Oxford /New York: Oxford University
    Press, 1999).
80. Marie Bugéja, *Femmes Voilées, Hommes- de Même: (Récits et Impressions de
    L'extrème Sud Algérien)* (Alger: Baconnier frères, 1935), 9.

81. Ibid.

82. Marie Bugéja, *Enigme Musulmane. Lettres à Une Bretonne* (Tangiers/Fez: Éditions internationales Pierre André, 1938), 10. The book was dedicated to educators.

83. CAOM 30MIOM/28-AKHBAR Quoted in "De la femme musulmane," *Akhbar,* 31 mars, 1931.

84. The text for the Projet de Loi is as follows: "La femme indigène peut acquérir la plénitude des droits reconnus à la femme française dans les conditions et suivant la procédure prévues pour l'accession des indigènes d'Algérie à la qualité de citoyen français, soit par les articles premier, 4 et 5 du sénatus-consulte du 14 juillet 1865, sur l'état des personnes et la naturalisation en Algérie, soit par le titre premier de la loi du 4 février 1919 sur l'accession des indigènes d'Algérie aux droits politiques." BMD, DOS 396AFR. Dossier-Femmes-Afrique du Nord, Chambre des Députés, no. 1912, Session de 1925, Annexe du procès-verbal de la séance du 10 juillet 1925. Rapport fait au nom de la Commission de l'Algérie, des colonies et des protectorats chargée d'examiner le projet de loi étendant à la femme indigène d'Algérie l'application des dispositions de la loi du 4 février 1919 et du sénatus-consulte du 14 juillet 1865, sur l'accession au droit de cité. 4.

85. BMD, DOS 396AFR. Dossier-Femmes-Afrique du Nord, Chambre des Députés, no. 1912, Session de 1925, Annexe du process-verbal de la séance du 10 juillet 1925. Rapport fait au nom de la Commission de l'Algérie, des colonies et des protectorats chargée d'examiner le projet de loi *étandant à la* **femme indigène d'Algérie** *l'application des dispositions de la loi du 4 février 1919 et du sénatus-consulte du 14 juillet 1865, sur l'***accession au droit de*** cité.* 2–3.

86. See, for example, Marcelle Capy, *Le Droit et le Devoir des Femmes* (Paris: Editions de la Voix des Femmes, 1925); Maria Verone, *Pourquoi les Femmes Veulent Voter* (Epinal/Paris: Impr. Pernot, 1923).

87. Raymond Poincaré, Discours prononcé au Palais du Trocadero le 3 décembre 1921, Ligue française pour le droit de femmes, 6 BMD, DOS VER, Box 3, File 3.

Chapter 4

1. Messaouda Yahiaoui argues that the expansion of women writers in Algeria coincided with the development of the feminist movement in France: Messaouda Yahiaoui, "Regards de Romancières Françaises Sur les Sociétés Féminines d'Algérie, 1898–1960," in *Regards Sur les Littératures Coloniales Afrique Francophone*, ed. Jean-François Durand and Jean Sévry (Paris: L'Harmattan, 1999), 81.

2. For more on Rhaïs' see my: "Sex, Gender and Race in the colonial novels of Elissa Rhaïs and Lucienne Favre" in *The Color of Liberty: Histories of Race in France,* ed. Tyler Stovall and Susan Peabody (Durham, NC: Duke University Press, 2003), 108–130. See also Jean Déjeux, "Elissa Rhaïs, Conteuse Algérienne (1876–1940)," *Revue de l'Occident Musulman et de la Méditerranée* 37, no. 1 (1984): 47–79; Emily Apter, "Ethnographic Travesties: Colonial Realism, French Feminism, and the Case of Elissa Rhaïs," in *After Colonialism Imperial Histories and Postcolonial displacements,* ed. Gyan Prakash (Princeton, NJ: Princeton University Press, 1995), 299–325; Mireille

Rosello, "Elissa Rhaïs: Scandals, Impostures, Who Owns the Story?" *Research in African Literatures* 37, no. 1 (2006): 1–15.

3. Phrase quoted from *Western Mail*, appearing on the fly-page of *A Wife in Kenya*.

4. P. O. Graillet, "Rhaïs (Elissa) – Les Juifs ou la fille d'Eléazar" in *Revue Bibliographique*, no. 5 (mai 1921), 278.

5. My thanks to Julia Clancy-Smith for this information.

6. Jean Déjeux, "Élissa Rhaïs, Conteuse Algérienne (1876–1940)," *Revue de l'Occident musulman et de la Mediterranée* 37, no. 1 (1984): 61.

7. Déjeux, "Élissa Rhaïs, Conteuse Algérienne (1876–1940), 62.

8. Joseph Boumendil, *Élissa, ou, Le mystère d'une Écriture. Enquête sur la vie et l'oeuvre d'Elissa Rhaïs* (Paris, Séguier, 2008), 120.

9. Louis Bertrand was a leading figure of the Algerian literary scene. He provided Rhaïs with a letter of introduction to René Doumic. Both men were elected to the *Académie française*.

10. Luigi Pirandello, *Les Oeuvres Libres*, Recueil littéraire mensuel (Paris, Fayard, 1927); the other collected work is entitled *Blida*, and is prefaced by Louis Bertrand and included works by Gaston Ricci, Ferdinand Duchêne and Robert Migot. Duchêne was the first to receive the Grand Prix Littéraire de l'Algérie, when it was established in 1921.

11. Jules Leclerq, Rhaïs (Elissa) – La Fille des Pachas, *Revue Biblioghraphique*, no. 1 (janvier 1923), 27. For a less laudatory view of *Saâda*, see the article on Rhaïs in André Billy, *La Muse Aux Besicles* (Paris: Renaissance du Livre, 1920), 234–238.

12. Elissa Rhais, *Saada, Marockanskan* (Stockholm: Sv. førl., 1920); Elissa Rhaïs, *Eleazars Datter (Les Juifs Ou la Fille D'Éléazar)* (Kristiania, Norway: Aschehoug, 1922); Elissa Rhaïs, *Kafe-Shantan / Uniform Title: Café Chantant. Russian* (Leningrad: Izd-vo "Myslí", 1927); Elissa Rhaïs and Zukkau G. A., *Svadíba Khanify/Uniform Title: Mariage de Hanifa. Russian* (Leningrad: Izd-vo "Myslí," 1930).

13. For an analysis of her work and its significance to colony and metropole, see Lorcin "Sex, Gender and Race in the colonial novels of Elissa Rhaïs and Lucienne Favre" in *The Color of Liberty: Histories of Race in France*, ed. Stovall & Peabody Durham, NC: Duke University Press, 2003, 108–130.

14. Lucien Maury, "L'Orient des Orientaux" in *Revue Bleue*, 58, no. 1 (January 10, 1920): 25–28, 27.

15. Robert Randau, "L'exotisme de l'Houri silencieuse," CAOM, 75/APOM/16, folder 8.

16. The allure of Biskra was enhanced by the likes of André Gide and Matisse. Gide visited the town in 1893 making it the setting of his novel *L'Immoraliste*, whereas Matisse's 1907 painting "The Blue Nude" was sub-titled Souvenir de Biskra.

17. P. J. Dupré, "L'Alerte au Desert" by Magali Boisnard" in *The Moslem World*, 1916: 8/1, 94–95.

18. Robert Randau, *Le Monde coloniale illustré*, no 152, mars 1939.

19. For a discussion of Boisnard's ethnographic writings, most of which appeared in the journals of the scholarly societies of the colony, see George R. Trumbull IV, *An Empire of Facts. Colonial Power, Cultural Knowledge and Islam in Algeria, 1870–1914* (Cambridge/New York: Cambridge University Press, 2010), 78–82, 186.

20. Magali Boisnard, *Sultans de Touggourt* (Paris: Geuther, 1933); Magali Bois-
    nard, *Le Roman de Khaldoun*, 3rd ed. (Paris: H. Piazza, 1930).

21. Her collection of war poems, *Le Chant des Femmes. Poèmes de guerre et
    d'amour*. Paris, Perrin, 1917, received a prize from the *Académie française*.
    In 1934 she received the *Grand prix littéraire de l'Algérie* for her work on
    Algeria.

22. Elissa Rhaïs, *Saâda, la Marocaine* (Paris: Plon-Nourrit, 1919); *Le Café-
    Chantant. Kerkeb. Noblesse Arabe* (Paris: Plon, 1920); *Les Juifs; Ou, La
    Fille d'Éléazar* (Paris: Plon-Nourrit, 1921); *La Fille des Pachas* (Paris: Plon-
    Nourrit, 1922); *L'andalouse* (Paris: A. Fayard., 1925); *Le Mariage de Hanifa*
    (Paris: Plon-Nourrit, 1926); "Petits Pachas en Exil," *Les Oeuvres libres. Paris*
    (1927); *Par la Voix de la Musique* (Paris: Plon, 1927); *Le Sein Blanc: Roman*
    (Paris: Flammarion, 1928); *La Riffaine* (Paris: Flammarion, 1929).

23. Her novels and short stories were published or serialized in: *Revue des Deux
    Mondes, Revue de Paris. Revue Bleue, Revue Hebdomadaire*. In 1951, a poem
    by Michel Carée, based on the novella *Kerkeb* was presented at the Paris
    Opera set to the music of Samuel Rousseau. Among her most popular works
    were: *Saâda, La Marocaine* (1919, 26 editions); *Le Café chantant* (1920, 15
    editions); *Les Juifs ou la fille d'Éléazar* (1921, 19 editions); *La Fille des pachas*
    (1924, 16 editions); *La Fille du douar* (1924, 17 editions); *La Chemise qui
    porte Bonheur* (1925, later 17 editions); *Le Mariage de Hanifa* (1926, 16
    editions) and *Par la voix de la musique* (1927, 16 editions); see Jean Déjeux,
    "Élissa Rhaïs, Conteuse Algérienne (1876–1940) in *Revue de l'Occident
    musulman et de la Méditerranée* 37, no. 1 (1984): 47–79, 50.

24. According to Jules Roy (*Le Monde*, June 4, 1982, 19) Collete, Morand, and
    Mallarmé supported her, although it is not clear which Mallarmé he means,
    Stéphane Mallarmé having died in 1898.

25. Hugette Champy, "Femmes d'Aujourd'hui. Elissa Rhaïs" in *La Française*,
    samedi, 18 février, 1928.

26. Jules Leclercq, "Rhaïs, Elissa. Par la Voix de la Musique," *Revue Bibli-
    ographique*, no. 7 (July 1927): 375.

27. Champy, "Femmes d'Aujourd'hui. Elissa Rhaïs."

28. The themes of sun and sea linked to sexuality are evident in the works of
    many French-Algerian writers of the colonial period, such as Robert Randau,
    Gabriel Audisio, and Albert Camus. See, for example, Gabriel Audisio, *Jeu-
    nesse de la Méditerranée*, 2 vols., vol. II Sel de Mer (Paris: Gallimard, 1935).
    Robert Randau, *Les Colons; Roman de la Patrie Algérienne* (Paris: E. Sansot,
    1907); Randau, *Cassard le Berbère* (Algiers: Jules Carbonnel, 1926). For a
    discussion of the sexuality in these two novels, see Patricia M. E. Lorcin,
    "Women, Gender and Nation in Colonial Novels of Inter-War Algeria" *His-
    torical Reflections/Reflexions Historiques (Special issue on Algeria)* 28, no. 2
    (2002): 163–184. See also Gabriel Audisio, *Héliotrope* (Paris: Gallimard,
    1928); Audisio, *Jeunesse de la Méditerranée*. Albert Camus, *Noces, Suivi de
    L'eté* (Paris: Gallimard, 1959).

29. Rhaïs, *Saâda, la Marocaine*, 9.

30. I have discussed gender in relation to Rhaïs' work at greater length in my
    article "Sex, Gender and Race in the Colonial Novels of Elissa Rhaïs and
    Lucienne Favre."

31. Lucien Maury, "Les Lettres, Oeuvres et Idées. L'orient des Orientaux,"
    Revue Bleue 58, no. 1 (1920): 28.

32. Rhaïs, *Saâda, la Marocaine*, 109.

33. The Rif War started in 1920 between the Spaniards and the Moroccan tribes from the Rif mountains, under the leadership of Abd-el-Krim over the Moroccan territory ceded to the Spaniards by the 1912 Treaty of Fez, which transformed Morocco into a protectorate. In 1925 the French joined the Spaniards bringing the war to an end, in 1926.

34. For settler involvement in anti-Semitism, see Samuel Kalman, "'Le Combat Par Tous les Moyens': Colonial Violence and the Extreme Right in 1930s Oran," *French Historical Studies* 34, no. 1 (2011): 125–153 Samuel Kalman, "Fascism and Algérianité: The Croix de Feu, Pied-Noir Xenophobia, and the Indigenous Question in 1930s Algeria," in *The French Colonial Mind: Mental Maps of Empire and French Colonial Policy-Making*, ed. Martin Thomas (Lincoln: University of Nebraska Press, 2011); Geneviève Dermenjian, *La Crise Anti-Juive Oranaise (1895–1905), L'anti-Semétisme Dans l'Algérie Coloniale* (Paris: Harmattan, 1986).

35. Rhaïs, *La Fille des Pachas*, 96. See also 46–47.

36. Ibid., 262.

37. *Le Mariage de Hanifa* (Paris: Plon, 1926), 38; Sid Ali in *Le Mariage de Hanifa*.

38. Sid Mustapha Pacha in *La Fille des Pachas*, 4; Sid El Hadj in *La Riffaine*, 45–46.

39. Rhaïs, *La Riffaine*, 62.

40. Ibid., 119.

41. Ibid., 89.

42. Ibid., 53.

43. Jules Roy, "Le mythe d'une Algérie heureuse" *Le Monde, le 4 juin*, 1982, 19.

44. Marius-Ary Leblond, "Preface" to Magali Boisnard, *L'alerte Au Désert: la Vie Saharienne Pendant la Guerre 1914–1916* (Paris: Perrin, 1916).

45. Pierre Mille and Jean Richepin were colonial novelists. Gyp was the nom-de-plume of the Comtesse de Martel de Janville, a best-selling novelist who along with writers such as Anna de Noailles and Marie Louise de Hérédia, published romances "which largely adhered to the reassuring form of the romance while exploring the social and emotional implications of gendered identity." Diana Holmes and Carrie Tarr, *A "Belle Epoque?" Women in French Society and Culture, 1890–1914* (New York: Berghahn Books, 2006), 49; on Gyp, see also Mary Louise Roberts, *Disruptive Acts: The New Woman in Fin-de-Siècle France* (Chicago: University of Chicago Press, 2002).

46. Robert Catbeau, in *Le Dernière Heure*, Brussels, quoted by Robert Randau in "Les Écrivains de l'Outre-mer Français" in *La Nouvelle Dépêche*, jeudi (9 janvier 1936): 1–2.

47. Ibid., The Tunisian newspaper was *Ez Zohra*, 12 mars 1909.

48. CAOM, Arnaud/Randau 75APOM/51. file 36/i, clipping of an article entitled "l'Algérie dans l'Empire," no author, no date, no journal/newspaper title.

49. Ibid.

50. Magali Boisnard, *Mâadith* (Amiens: Malfère, 1921). A less elaborate analysis of Mâadith appeared in: Patricia M. E. Lorcin, "Mediating Gender, Mediating Race: Women Writers in Colonial Algeria," *Culture, Theory & Critique* 45, no. 1 (2004).

51. Boisnard, *Mâadith*, 33.

52. Ibid.,113.

53. See I. Yetiv, *Le thème de l'aliénation dans le roman maghrébin d'expression française de 1952–1956*. Sherbrooke, CELEF, 1972. In an interview with young French Muslims whose parents or grandparents were of Maghrebi origin, I asked whether they felt French or Algerian. One young woman (3rd generation French-Algerian) replied that she was culturally French—her friends were French, she liked French literature, movies, music, but that she was politically Algerian. Interview at the Paris Mosque on May 24, 2007 with a veteran of the Algerian War and a group of children and grand children of veterans, in the context of a summer course I taught in France (see http://www.hist.umn.edu/hist1910w/May24.html).

54. Magali Boisnard, *Le Roman de la Kahena, D'aprés les Anciens Textes Arabes* (Paris: H. Piazza).

55. CAOM 30MIOM/28, "Le Roman de la Kahena" in Akhbar (no. 13953), October 10, 1925 and the *Bulletin des Romaciers et Auteurs coloniaux français*, no. 3, July-August 1933.

56. CAOM, Arnaud/Randau 75APOM/51. file 36/i, clipping of an article entitled "l'Algérie dans l'Empire," no newspaper, no author, no date.

57. Boisnard, *Le Roman de Khaldoun*, 47. Andalucian in this case means the Arab Andalucia.

58. Ibid., 56.

59. Quoted by Albert Sadouillet, "Le Temoignage de Robert Randau, Écrivain et Homme d'Action" in *Algéria*, Jan-Fév, 1951, 10–13, 13.

60. Unlike Florence Riddell, whose account of her peregrinations, *I Go Wandering: A Travel Biography* (London: J. B. Lippencott, 1935) provides some information on her activities and experiences in Kenya, information about Strange's background comes from the occasional personal reference in *Kenya Today* and from the advertisements in the backmatter, or the information on the fly leaves, of her books, as well as the website, Mystery File, which contains information on mystery writers. http://mysteryfile. com/blog/index.php?paged=2&s=publishers. Accessed January 9, 2009. Strange wrote one mystery novel. Thirteen years after leaving Kenya, she returned for six months "more or less as a tourist." Nora K. Strange, *Kenya Today* (London: Stanley Paul, 1934). The one article that includes a discussion of Riddell and Strange's work does not contain anything more. C. J. D. Duder, "Love and the Lions. The Image of the White Settlements in Kenya in Popular African Fiction 1919–1939," *African* Affairs 90, no. 360 (1991): 427–438, especially 29–32.

61. Florence Riddell, *I Go Wandering. A Travel Biography*, 114.

62. Ibid., 134–135.

63. Ibid., 254.

64. Ibid., 261 and 270.

65. Florence Riddell, *Kenya Mist* (London: Thornton Butterworth, 1924), 22.

66. Ibid., 18–19.

67. Ibid., 57.

68. Ibid., 22–23.

69. Ibid., 26–27.

70. Ibid., 28.

71. Ibid., 66.

72. Ibid., 181.
73. For a discussion of the role of the Kenya novels in creating a false image of Kenya, see Duder, "Love and the Lions. The Image of the White Settlements in Kenya in Popular African Fiction 1919–1939."
74. For a recent fictionalized and much exaggerated account of Happy Valley behavior and the unsolved Errol murder, see James Fox, *White Mischief* (London: Cape, 1982). The book was made into a film in 1987.
75. Riddell, *Kenya Mist*, 66–67.
76. For Stoler on sexuality, see Ann Laura Stoler, "Carnal Knowledge and Imperial Power: Gender, Race and Morality in Colonial Asia," in *Gender at the Crossroads of Knowledge: Feminist Anthropology in the Postmodern Era,* ed. Micaela di Leonardo (Berkeley: University of California Press, 1991); Ann Laura Stoler, "Sexual Affronts and Racial Frontiers: European Identities and the Cultural Politics of Exclusion in Colonial Southeast Asia," *Comparative Studies in Society and History* 34, no. 3 (1992): 514–551; Ann Laura Stoler, "Making Empire Respectable: The Politics of Race and Sexual Morality in 20th Century Cultures," *American Ethnologist* 16, no. 4 (1985): 634–660; Ann Laura Stoler, *Race and the Education of Desire. Foucault's History of Sexuality and the Colonial Order of Things* (Durham, NC: Duke University Press, 2000).
77. Riddell, *Kenya Mist*.
78. Riddell, *I Go Wandering: A Travel Biography*, 124.
79. Riddell, *Kenya Mist*, 16 and Riddell, *I Go Wandering: A Travel Biography*, 286.
80. Florence Riddell, *Wives Win* (London: Geoffrey Bles, 1931), 75.
81. Nora K. Strange, *Imperial Mountain* (London: Hutchinson, 1941), 143.
82. Strange, *Kenya Today*, 153–154.
83. Riddell, *Wives Win*, 74–75; Florence Riddell, *Kismet in Kenya* (London: Geoffrey Bles, 1927), 33.
84. Riddell, *Kismet in Kenya*, 21 and 22.
85. Ibid., 58.
86. Florence Riddell, *Out of the Mist* (London: Thornton Butterworth, 1925), 56–57.
87. Ibid., 135 and 303.
88. Nora Kathleen Strange, *An Outpost Wooing: A Romance of East Africa*, 5th ed. (London: Stanley Paul, 1927), 12.
89. Nora Kathleen Strange, *A Wife in Kenya* (London: Stanley Paul, 1925), 199–200.
90. See, for example, Richard Griffiths, *Fellow Travellers of the Right. British Enthusiasts for Nazi Germany 1933–1939* (London: Constable, 1980); Edward VIII and Wallis Simpson, later the Duke and Duchess of Windsor, were the most prominent fascist-sympathizing aristocrats. A documentary based on recently released FBI files shedding further light on their sympathies, *Britain's Nazi Kind Revealed* directed by Clive Maltby, was aired on British television (Channel 5) on July 16, 2009.
91. Rhodes House Archive, MSS. Afr.s.2154-Box 1. Letter from Nellie Grant to Elspeth Huxley, Njoro, December 11, 1934.
92. Strange, *Imperial Mountain*, 5–6.
93. Strange, *A Wife in Kenya*, 181.
94. Strange, *Imperial Mountain*, 142.

95. Strange, *Kenya Today*, 72.

96. Ibid., 30.

97. Riddell, *I Go Wandering. A Travel Biography.*

98. Strange, *Kenya Today*, 150.

99. Ibid.

100. Riddell, *Wives Win*, 25.

101. Strange, *Kenya Today*, 14.

CHAPTER 5

1. Valentine Cunningham, *British Writers of the Thirties* (Oxford: Oxford University Press, 1988), 2.

2. More has been written about colonial urbanization in Algeria than in Kenya. For example, Zeynep Çelik, *Urban Forms and Colonial Confrontations: Algiers under French Rule* (Berkeley: University of California Press, 1997); Gwendolyn Wright, *The Politics of Design in French Colonial Urbanism* (Chicago: University of Chicago Press, 1991); Seth Graebner, *History's Place: Nostalgia and the City in French Algerian Literature* (Lanham, MD: Lexington Books, 2007). For Kenya, see Fatima Müller-Friedman, "Colonial Urbanization and Urban Management in Kenya" in *African Urban Spaces in Historical Perspective*, ed. Steven J. Salm and Toyin Falola (Rochester: University of Rochester Press, 2005); Garth Andrew Myers, "Colonial Nairobi," in *Verandahs of Power: Colonialism and Space in Urban Africa*, ed. Garth Andrew Myers (Syracuse: Syracuse University Press, 2003); John Lonsdale, "Town Life in Colonial Kenya," in *The Urban Experience in Eastern Africa, C. 1750–2000*, ed. Andrew Burton, *Azania* (Nairobi: British Institute, 2002), 207–222.

3. Charles Robert Ageron, *De L'insurrection de 1871 Au Déclenchement de la Guerre de Libération (1954), Histoire de l'Algérie Contemporaine* Vol. 2, (Paris: Presses universitaires de France, 1979), 403. For the Colonial Exhibition of 1931, see P. A. Morton, *Hybrid Modernities: Architecture and Representation at the 1931 Colonial Exposition, Paris* (Cambridge: MIT Press, 2000); Herman Lebovics, "Donner à Voir L'empire Colonial: L'exposition Coloniale Internationale de Paris en 1931," *Gradhiva*. 7, hiver (1989–1990); Charles-Robert Ageron, *De l'Algérie "Française" à l'Algérie Algérienne* (Paris: Éditions Bouchene, 2005), 369–386.

4. The centenary occasioned a prodigious literary and artistic output. The official work was the *Le Livre D'or Du Centenaire de l'Algérie Française* (Algiers: Fontana, 1930). The film commissioned for the centenary was *Le Bled*, directed by Jean Renoir. According to Ageron, *De L'insurrection De 1871 Au Déclenchement De La Guerre De Libération (1954)*, 406, the film was criticized for its inaccuracies by Louis Massignon, professor at the College de France and one of France's leading Arabists. The French public was no doubt unaware of its propaganda value.

5. Ageron, *De L'insurrection de 1871 Au Déclenchement de la Guerre de Libération (1954)*, 396.

6. George Nouelle, "A propos du centenaire de l'Algérie" in *Annales Coloniales*, April 29, 1929, CAOM holdings.

7. *La Voix indigene*, quoted by Ageron, *De L'insurrection de 1871 Au Déclenchement de la Guerre de Libération (1954)*, 410.

8. *Etats Généraux Du Féminisme 30–31 Mai 1931* (Paris: Conseil National des Femmes Françaises), 9.

9. Ibid., 16.

10. According to Robert-Guiard, there were 120 mixed marriages from 1830 to 1877; 227 from 1878–1900; 67 in 1938, and 88 in 1938. These figures do not include marriages between Europeans and indigenous Jews, which were rarer. Claudine Robert-Guiard, *Des Européennes en Situation Coloniale: Algérie 1830–1939*, 132–136. For further information on the barriers to interethnic marriages, see 115–119.

11. *Etats Généraux Du Féminisme 30–31 Mai 1931*, 18–23.

12. The *Cape Argus*, quoted in "South African Critics of Kenya Settlers. Newspaper Attacks on the Claim to Dominate" *East African Standard*, July 26, 1930: 27. Rhodes House holdings.

13. Ibid.

14. "Native Policy in Kenya, Strong Criticism of the White Paper," *East African Standard*, Saturday, August 9, 1930: 12–13, Rhodes House holdings.

15. "South African Support for Settlers Stand. "Black Dominion" in East Africa near at Hand unless Policy Changed," *East African Standard*, Saturday, August 9, 1930: 40. Rhodes House holdings.

16. "Kenya Women Confer. Closer Union and Native Policy," *East African Standard*, July 5, 1930, 19. Rhodes House holdings.

17. Ibid.

18. For a discussion of the law, see Martin S. Alexander and Keiger John F. V., *France and the Algerian War, 1954–62: Strategy, Operations and Diplomacy* (London: Frank Cass Publishers, 2002), 67–74; Charles Jonnart was governor of Algeria on three occasions: October 1900 to June 1901; May 1903 to February 1911, and January 1918 to July 1919. He believed that the colonization in Algeria remained precarious as long as France did not take concrete steps to establish a genuine reconciliation between the settlers and the indigenous population. See Charles-Robert Ageron, *Les Algériens Musulmans et la France (1871–1919)*, 2 vols, Vol. I (Paris: Presses Universitaires de France, 1968), 455.

19. L. Richardot, "Les Indigènes d'Algérie voteront-ils avant nous??" *La Française*, Saturday, May 17, 1930, Archives Brunschvicg holdings.

20. Ibid.

21. A. Fournier-Chancogne, "Le propagande sufferagiste in Algérie" *La Française*, May 17, 1930, Archives Brunschvicg holdings.

22. See Jennifer Anne Boittin, *Colonial Metropolis: The Urban Grounds of Anti-Imperialism and Feminism in Interwar Paris* (Lincoln: University of Nebraska Press, 2010); Jennifer Anne Boittin, "Exotic Mediators: French Feminists and Women Writers on Colonial North Africa, 1921–1939," *Gender & History* 22, no. 1 (2010): 131–150.

23. A letter from Jeanne Bottini-Houot to Cécile Brunschvicg on January 10, 1933 sets out the antifeminist agenda of some of the male representatives. Bottini headed the Sétif branch of the U.F.S.F. Doc. 162–163. 1AF131, Fonds Brunschvicg.

24. Marius and Ary Leblond, Ferdinand Duchêne, Musette (pseudonym for V. M. AugusteRobinet), Magali Boisnard, Maximilienne Heller, Charles Hagel, Louis Lecoq, Elissa Rhaïs, and Raymond Marival to name but a few. Their works were critiqued and published in leading metropole journals.

25. Colonial literature and colonial questions were profiled under specific headings, for example in the *Mercure de France*, where as of the 1930s, the novel rubric in "Revue de la Quinzine" was often devoted to "colonial and exotic" novels. The rubric "romans féminins" appeared in the '20s and included colonial writers such as Rhaïs'. See, for example, *Mercure de France*, no. 652 (August 15, 1925): 179–186.

26. Regionalism as a movement was essentially conservative and was a literature rooted in the "terroir." See, for example, Anne-Marie Thiesse, *Ecrire la France: le Mouvement Littéraire Régionaliste de Langue Française Entre la Belle Epoque et la Libération* (Paris: Presses universitaires de France, 1991).

27. For an elaboration of these two trends, see Marius-Ary Leblond, *Après l'exotisme de Loti, le roman colonial*, Paris, 1927. Marius-Ary Leblond is the pseudonym for the cousins Aimé Merlo and Georges Athenas who nearly always collaborated and who were considered by their peers to be authorities on colonial literature.

28. Peter Dunwoodie, *Writing French Algeria* (Oxford: Clarendon Press, 1998), 133.

29. From the manifesto of the movement, quoted by Albert Sadouillet, "Le Temoignage de Robert Randau, écrivain et hommed'action," *Algérie*, (Jan.–Feb. 1951): 10–13, 13.

30. Ibid. Among the leading novelists of the movement were: Robert Randau, Louis Le Coq, Henri Hagel, Magali Boisnard, Raymond Marival, and Ferdinand Duchêne.

    For details about the *Algerianiste* movements and the *École d'Alger*, which followed it, see Peter Dunwoodie, *Francophone Writing in Transition: Algeria 1900–1945* (New York: Oxford University Press, 2005); Dunwoodie, *Writing French Algeria*; Graebner, *History's Place: Nostalgia and the City in French Algerian Literature*.

31. For an elaboration of this reasoning, see Louis Bertrand, "Notre Afrique" in *Devant Islam* (Paris: Plon, 1926), especially, 135, 138.

32. Its most renowned adherent was Albert Camus. Other participants included Gabriel Audisio and Emmanuel Roblès.

33. See Dunwoodie, *Writing French Algeria*; Dunwoodie, *Francophone Writing in Transition: Algeria 1900–1945;* Graebner, *History's Place: Nostalgia and the City in French Algerian Literature;* Patricia M. E. Lorcin, "France and Rome in Africa: Recovering Algeria's Latin Past," *French Historical Studies* 25, no. 2 (2002).

34. From 1921 to 1952, six women were awarded the prize: Maximilienne Heller (1922), Jeanne-Faure-Sardet & Lucienne Favre (1930), Magali Boisnard (1935), Lucienne Jean-Darrouy (1945), and Mme Canavaggia (1951).

35. For Example, Nora K. Strange, *Imperial Mountain* (London: Hutchinson, 1941). The novel takes place in 1938–1939.

36. In the 1930s most European girls would have attended the Limuru Girls High School or the Nairobi Girls School before being sent (usually at the age of 11 or 12) to boarding school in Britain. European boys attended the Prince of Wales School for Boys, founded in the early 1930s, or if they were children of government officials the Nairobi Government School established in 1928. They were usually sent to boarding school in England at the early age of 7 or 8. Schooling during the colonial period was not coeducational and was racially segregated. It was only after World War II that some racial

mixing occurred in Kenya, although the schools did not become coeducational. The leading schools for Africans were the Lions High School for Boys and the Alliance Girls High School; the latter being of a lower standard than the former. Interview of Joan Considine on Monday, July 18, 2005. Although fees were relatively low during the colonial period, grants were given to poor whites as it was felt that whites had to be well educated. The exceptions were the Afrikaaners who were too poor to pay the fees [and did not qualify for grants.] They were therefore practically illiterate. Interview with Christine Nicholls on July 13, 2005. Schools were desegregated in 1962, a year before independence.

For analyses of different aspects of education in the colonies, whether of Europeans or the "indigenous" populations, see Philip G. Altbach and Gail Paradise Kelly, *Education and the Colonial Experience*, 2nd rev. ed. (New Brunswick, NJ: Transaction Books, 1984); John Anderson, *The Struggle for the School: The Interaction of Missionary, Colonial Government, and Nationalist Enterprise in the Development of Formal Education in Kenya*, Vol. 1970 (London: Longman, 1970); Elizabeth Buettner, *Empire Families: Britons and Late Imperial India* (New York: Oxford University Press, 2004); Aviston D. Downes, "From Boys to Men: Colonial Education, Cricket and Masculinity in the Caribbean, 1870–C.1920," *International Journal of the History of Sport*, 22, no. 1 (2005); Elsa M. Harik and Donald G. Schilling, *The Politics of Education in Colonial Algeria and Kenya*, Vol. 43 (Athens, OH: Ohio University Center for International Studies, 1984); Gail Paradise Kelly and David H. Kelly, *French Colonial Education: Essays on Vietnam and West Africa* (New York: AMS Press, 2000); Sarone Ole Sena, *Colonial Education among the Kenyan Maasai, 1894–1962*, no. 4 (Montreal: Department of Anthropology, McGill University, 1986); Rebecca Rogers, "Telling Stories About the Colonies: British and French Women in Algeria in the Nineteenth Century," *Gender & History* 21, no. 1 (2009); Yvonne Turin, *Affrontements Culturels Dans l'Algérie Coloniale: Écoles, Médecines, Religion, 1830–1880* (Alger: Entreprise nationale du livre, 1983).

37. Juanita Carberry and Nicola Tyrer, *Child of Happy Valley* (London: William Heinemann, 1999); Beryl Markham, *Wise Child* (USA: Pennsylvania Railroad, 1943); Beryl Markham, *West with the Night* (San Francisco, CA: North Point Press, 1983); Beryl Markham and Mary Lovell, *The Splendid Outcast: Beryl Markham's African Stories* (San Francisco, CA: North Point Press, 1987). Stephanie Zweig grew up in Kenya slightly later, in the '30s and '40s, and published an autobiographical novel in German in 1995, which was later translated into English. Stefanie Comjean Marlies Zweig, *Nowhere in Africa: An Autobiographical Novel* (Madison, WI: University of Wisconsin Press/Terrace Books, 2004).

38. Rhodes House Archives. MSS. AFR.S.2154. Box 1, File 6. Letter from Nellie Grant to Elspeth, Njoro January 1, 1938. See also C. S. Nicholls, *Elspeth Huxley. A Biography*, 286–287.

39. She wrote 48 works, which included biographies, novels, memoirs, and political commentary.

40. C. S. Nicholls, *Elspeth Huxley. A Biography*, 440.

41. *Sunday Times Magazine*, April 26, 1987, quoted by ibid., 55–56.

42. MICR.AFR. 607 (4) Helen Mayers—Autobiographical Reminiscences—1910–1931, 17

43. Nicholls, *Elspeth Huxley*, 85.

44. Phyllis Lassner, *Colonial Strangers: Women Writing the End of the British Empire* (Newark, NJ: Rutgers University Press, 2004), 119. For Lassner's take on Huxley's work, see especially chapter 3, 118–159.

45. Letter from EH to MP, May 21, 1942 in Elspeth Joscelin Grant Huxley and Margery Perham, *Race and Politics in Kenya. A Correspondence between Elspeth Huxley and Margery Perham with an Introduction by Lord Lugard* (London: Faber & Faber, 1944), 33.

46. "Prognathous jaws," for example, in Elspeth Joscelin Grant Huxley, *Murder at Government House* (New York: Viking, 1988 reprint, 1987, 1988, 1989, 1990, 1991, 1992), 21.

47. Chloe Campbell, *Race and Empire: Eugenics in Colonial Kenya* (Manchester: University of Manchester Press, 2007), 116.

48. Ibid., 118.

49. Ibid., 123.

50. Rhodes House Archives. MSS. AFR.S.2154-Box 1-file 3, Letter from Nellie Grant to Elspeth Huxley, Njoro, Wednesday, February 13, 1935.

51. Author's interview of Christine Nicholls in Oxford on July 13, 2005.

52. Eugenics in Great Britain placed the emphasis on "breeding" and never implemented eugenic practices of sterilization as did the United States and Sweden. See Gunnar Broberg and Nils Roll-Hansen, eds., *Eugenics and the Welfare State: Sterilization Policy in Denmark, Sweden, Norway, and Finland* (East Lansing, MI: Michigan State University Press, 1996); Edward J. Larson, *Sex, Race, and Science: Eugenics in the Deep South* (Baltimore, MD: The Johns Hopkins University Press, 1996); Alexandra Minna Stern, *Eugenic Nation: Faults and Frontiers of Better Breeding in Modern America* (Berkeley, CA: University of California Press, 2005); Edwin Black, *War against the Weak: Eugenics and America's Campaign to Create a Master Race* (New York: Thunder's Mouth Press, 2004).

53. "The Type of Settler Kenya Needs. Not Afraid of Manual Labor. Sir D. Hall's View," *East African Standard,* Saturday August 23, 1930: 14. Rhodes House holdings. The article concerned a talk given by Sir Daniel Hall at the Royal Society of Arts on the problems of agriculture in Kenya as practiced by white settlers.

54. Ibid.

55. Ibid.

56. Elspeth Joscelin Grant Huxley, *White Man's Country: Lord Delamere and the Making of Kenya*, New ed., 2 vols, Vol. I (London: Chatto & Windus, 1953), x.

57. Ibid., 80.

58. Ibid., 81–82.

59. Ibid., 82.

60. Ibid.

61. Ibid., 84.

62. Nicholls, *Elspeth Huxley*, 42.

63. Elspeth Huxley, *White Man's Country: Lord Delamere and the Making of Kenya*, 2 vols, Vol. II (New York: Praeger, 1968), 14.

64. Ibid.

65. Francis Scott, one of the colony's leading figures, declared that it was "perfectly supreme . . . a masterpiece. You have told the tale of Kenya from its

infancy and portrayed D very truly." Letter to EH from Francis Scott, June 10 [1935?]. Her publisher declared that he was "pleased indeed to see that the book has been so well received in the country with which it deals . . . and congratulate you on the excellent reviews which the work has received in the English press:" Letter to EH from Harold Macmillan of Macmillan & Co., London, June 20, 1925, both in MSS.AFR.s.2154-Box 10, File 1/10. Rhodes House Archives.Review in scholarly journals were mixed. The *Journal of the Royal African Society,* deemed it to be "of outstanding interest among African records" (223) whereas *International Affairs,* while praising its strong points declared it to be "tendentious and provocative" (732). H. R. T., "White Man's Country. Lord Delamere and the Making of Kenya by Elspeth Huxley," *Journal of the Royal African Society* 35, no. 139 (1936); H. A. Wyndham "White Man's Country: Lord Delamere and the Making of Kenya. By Elspeth Huxley," *International Affairs* 14, no. 5 (1925).

66. Huxley, *Murder at Government House.* Elspeth Joscelin Grant Huxley, *Murder on Safari* (New York, N. Y., U. S. A.: Viking, 1989 reprint, 1982, 1988, 2002); Elspeth Joscelin Grant Huxley, *The African Poison Murders* (New York: Viking, 1988; reprint, 1940, 1976, 1986, 1988, 1989); Elspeth Joscelin Grant Huxley, *Red Strangers* (London: New York, 1999; reprint, 1944, 1949, 1952, 954, 1959, 1965).

67. The women who formed part of the interwar golden age were Agatha Christie, Dorothy Sayers, Ngaio Marsh, Margery Allingham, and Josephine Tey. See: Jessica Mann, *Deadlier Than the Male: Why Are Respectable English Women So Good at Murder?* (New York: Macmillan, 1981).

68. Huxley, *Murder at Government House,* 7–8.

69. Ibid., 18.

70. Ibid., 58.

71. Ibid., 278.

72. Ibid., 281.

73. Ibid., 7 and 269.

74. Letter to Vera from EH, Balcome Place, Balcome, Susses, September 1, 1935. MSS.AFR.s.2154, Box 7, File 3, Letters from Elspeth Huxley to Robin and Vera Grant. Huxley papers. Rhodes House Archives.

75. Evelyn Brodhurst-Hill, *So This Is Kenya!* (London/Glasgow: Blackie & Son, 1936), 160.

76. Letter from JG to Vera, Njoro July 18, 1934. MSS.AFR.s.2154, Box 5, File 2, Letters from Josceline Grant to Vera Grant, Huxley Papers. Rhodes House Archives.

77. Letter from NG to EH, Njoro, 17.8.1938. MSS.AFR.s.2154, Box 1, File 6, Letters from Nellie Grant to Elspeth Huxley, 1938. Rhodes House Archives. A conference was convened by President Roosevelt and held in Evian, France in July 1938 to try and settle the Jewish refugee problem. Lord Winterton was the head of the British delegation and argued against the settlement of Jews in Great Britain, but envisaged the possibility of settling some in Kenya and Rhodesia.

78. Zweig, *Nowhere in Africa: An Autobiographical Novel.*

79. Letter from NG to EH, Njoro, October 31, 1941. MSS.AFR.s.2154, Box 2, File 3, Huxley papers. Rhodes House Archives.

80. The page ends in mid sentence and what follows has either disappeared or has been destroyed, for following on are two pages about the situation in

the colony. Letter from NG to Frank, October 19, 1941. MSS.AFR.s2154, Box 2, File 3, Huxley papers. Rhodes House Archives.

81. Lassner, *Colonial Strangers: Women Writing the End of the British Empire*, 140.

82. See Huxley, *The African Poison Murders*, 63. See also Brodhurst-Hill, *So This Is Kenya!*, 150–163. Brodhurst-Hill states that some sections of the Indian population took Erroll's fascism seriously (161).

83. Huxley, *The African Poison Murders*, 159.

84. Huxley, *Murder at Government House*, 167, 168.

85. Huxley, *Red Strangers*, xvi.

86. Ibid., 165.

87. Tabitha M. Kanogo, *African Womanhood in Colonial Kenya, 1900–50* (Athens, OH/Nairobi: University of Ohio Press/East African Educational Publishers, 2005), 73. Clitoridectomy was also practiced by other ethnic groups, including the Meru and the Embu.

88. Nicholls, *Elspeth Huxley*.

89. Letter from Huxley to Macmillan, quoted by ibid., 135.

90. For an analysis of the politics behind the controversy, see Susan Pedersen, "National Bodies, Unspeakable Acts: The Sexual Politics of Colonial Policy-Making," *Journal of Modern History* 63, no. 4 (1991). See also David M. Anderson, *Bodies and Souls: Female Circumcision and Christian Missions in Colonial Kenya, 1900–1939* (Cape Town: Centre for African Studies, University of Cape Town, 1994); Lynn M. Thomas, "Imperial Concerns and "Women's Affairs": State Efforts to Regulate Clitoridectomy and Eradicate Abortion in Meru, Kenya, C. 1910–1950," *Journal of African History* 39, (1998) 121–145. For a discussion of African responses to clitoridectomy, see Kanogo, *African Womanhood in Colonial Kenya, 1900–1950*, Chapter 3: 73–103; Lynn M. Thomas, "'Ngaitana (I Will Circumcise Myself)': The Gender and Generational Politics of the 1956 Ban on Clitoridectomy in Meru, Kenya," *Gender & History* 8, no. 3 (1996); reproduced in Nancy Rose Hunt, Tessie P. Liu, and Jean H. Quataert, *Gendered Colonialisms in African History* (Oxford, UK/Malden, MA, 1997), 16–41. For an account of the politics of female circumcision throughout the colonial period and beyond, see Lynn M. Thomas, *Politics of the Womb. Women, Reproduction, and the State in Kenya* (Berkeley, CA: University of California Press, 2003). For a discussion of the practice and British response in colonial Sudan, see Janice Boddy, *Civilizing Women. British Crusades in Colonial Sudan* (Princeton, NJ: Princeton University Press, 2007).

91. Bodil Folke Frederiksen, "Jomo Kenyatta, Marie Bonaparte and Bronislaw Malinowski on Clitoridectomy and Female Sexuality," *History Workshop Journal* 65, no. 1 (2008): 23–48. See also Jomo Kenyatta, *Facing Mount Kenya: The Tribal Life of the Gikuyu* (New York: Vintage Books, 1965), originally published in 1938.

92. Huxley, *Red Strangers*, 347. Kanogo also quotes Watuwa Mungu as declaring in 1934 that "Europeans [were] trying to depopulate the land by preventing circumcision of women so that the land may be taken over by Europeans," Kanogo, *African Womanhood in Colonial Kenya, 1900–1950*, 73.

93. Huxley, *Red Strangers*, 388.

94. Ibid., 168.

95. Ibid., 227–228.

96. MP to EH, March 15, 1942, Huxley and Perham, *Race and Politics in Kenya*, 17.
97. Nicholls, *Elspeth Huxley*, 136.
98. On the rivalry between Kenyatta and Leaky, see Frederiksen, "Jomo Kenyatta, Marie Bonaparte and Bronislaw Malinowski on Clitoridectomy and Female Sexuality," 36–37.
99. Nicholls, *Elspeth Huxley*, 135.
100. Renato Rosaldo, *Culture & Truth: The Remaking of Social Analysis* (Boston: Beacon Press, 1989), 69.
101. Joyce Cary's *Mister Johnson,* about an African who tried too hard to emulate his British employer, was published in the same year as *Red Strangers* but hardly sold at all. It was later considered to be among his best novels and had a postcolonial revival and a Bruce Beresford film adaptation in 1990.
102. Letter to EH from the Hon. Mr. Justice C. B. Madan, Q. C., Court of Appeal, Nairobi, December 1, 1983. MSS.AFR.s.2154, Box 15, Huxley Papers. Rhodes House Archive. See also Norman Leys, *The Colour Bar in East Africa* (London: The Hogarth Press, 1941).
103. Huxley and Perham, *Race and Politics in Kenya*, 28.
104. Evelyn Brodhurst-Hill, *The Youngest Lion: Early Farming Days in Kenya* (London: Hutchinson, 1934).
105. Ibid., 37.
106. Brodhurst-Hill, *The Youngest Lion: Early Farming Days in Kenya*, 57–58 and 64–65.
107. Most members of the Fabian society were pro-imperialist; their criticisms were about the degree of exploitation and the obtuseness of settlers with regard to Africans.
108. Marion Cran, *The Garden Beyond* (London: Herbert Jenkins Ltd., 1937), 11.
109. Ibid; Joy Adamson, *Joy Adamson's Africa* (New York: Harcourt, Brace, Jovanovich, 1972).
110. See David Anderson and Richard Grove, *Conservation in Africa: People, Policies, and Practice* (New York: Cambridge University Press, 1987); Jonathan Kingdon, *Island Africa: The Evolution of Africa's Rare Animals and Plants* (Princeton, NJ: Princeton University Press, 1989); John M. MacKenzie, *The Empire of Nature: Hunting, Conservation, and British Imperialism,* (Manchester, New York: University of Manchester Press, 1988); Edward I. Steinhart, *Black Poachers, White Hunters: A Social History of Hunting in Colonial Kenya* (Oxford/Nairobi: James Currey, 2006). It is relevant that women are among the leading conservationists in East Africa, viz. Jane Goodall, the late Dian Fossey, Kuki Gallman, Oria Douglas-Hamilton.
111. In addition to the women mentioned in previous chapters, who continued to write in the '30s, the most notable were Maximillienne Heller, Lucienne Favre, Lucienne Jean-Darrouy, Jeanne Faure-Sardet, Angèle Maraval-Bethoin. Sixty-six works of literature were published by women in the interwar period. 87. CAOM. APOM/48-Fonds Déjeux, Dossier 222.
112. See Dunwoodie, *Francophone Writing in Transition: Algeria 1900–1945.* Jonathan K. Gosnell, *The Politics of Frenchness in Colonial Algeria, 1930–1954* (Rochester: University of Rochester Press, 2002). Joshua Cole is working on Arabophone playwrights in the interwar period. Joshua

Cole, "*A Chacun son Public*: Performing Politics and Culture in Interwar French-Algeria," Paper presented at a workshop on Marginal Voices in the Colonial/Postcolonial Context at the University of Minnesota in May 2008.

113. See Mahfoud Kaddache, *La Vie Politique à Alger de 1919 à 1939* (Algiers: SNED, 1970); Ageron, *De L'insurrection de 1871 Au Déclenchement de la Guerre de Libération (1954)*, especially 313–466. Martin Thomas, *The French Empire between the Wars: Imperialism, Politics and Society*, (Manchester: University of Manchester Press, 2005).

114. 26 Jews and 20 Algerians were also wounded. Robert Attal, *Les Émeutes de Constantine: 5 Août 1934* (Paris: Romillat, 2002), 131–132.

115. Letter to Cécile Brunschvicg from Jeanne Alquier, February 27, 1935, Doc 281, 1AF 131, Fonds Brunschvicg.

116. "Un complot contre la sûreté de l'État en Algérie" in *La Dépêche algérienne*, mercredi 26 juillet, 1935. Samuel Kalman is at present working on a monograph on Fascism in Algeria. See his "Fascism and Algérianité: The Croix de Feu, Pied-Noir Xenophobia, and the Indigenous Question in 1930s Algeria," in *The French Colonial Mind*: *Mental Maps of Empire and French Colonial Policy-Making* (Lincoln, NE: University of Nebraska Press, 2011); Samuel Kalman, "'Le Combat Par Tous les Moyens': Colonial Violence and the Extreme Right in 1930s Oran," *French Historical Studies* 34, no. 1 (2011).

117. "L'Algérie va-t-elle connaître à son tour les horreurs de la guerre civile?"*La Dépêche algérienne*, jeudi 17 septembre, 1936.

118. Cecile Brunschvicg, "Le propagande suffragiste en Algérie," *La Française, samedi, 17 mai 1930.*

119. Ibid.

120. Among the U.F.S.F. delegates and pro-suffrage women to visit Algeria were the activist and Cécile Brunschvicg (1877–1946), who was the director of *La Française* from 1924, and lawyer and pacifist feminist Maria Vérone (1874–1938).

121. Violette Marchal, "Les femmesal gérienne françaises et le droit de vote," *La Française,* 17 juin, 1933.

122. Ibid.

123. See Patricia M. E. Lorcin, *Imperial Identities: Stereotyping, Prejudice and Race in Colonial Algeria*, Society and Culture in the Modern Middle East (London/New York: I.B. Tauris/St. Martin's, 1995); Patricia M. E. Lorcin, "Women, Gender and Nation in Colonial Novels of Inter-War Algeria," *Historical Reflections/Reflexions Historiques* 28, no. 2 (2002); Patricia M. E. Lorcin, "Sex, Gender and Race in the Colonial Novels of Elissa Rhaïs and Lucienne Favre," in *The Color of Liberty: Histories of Race in France*, ed. Tyler Stovall and Susan Peabody (Durham, NC: Duke University Press, 2003).

124. "Les Algériennes veulent voter," *La Dépêche algérienne*, mercredi, 10 avril, 1935. DOS 396AFR. Archives Bibliothèque Marguerite Durand. See also G. Vallé-Genairon, "Le vote des indigenes et les femmes française," *La Française,* January 30, 1937. For a sympathetic response to Viollette-Blum bill, see Claire Charles-Géniaux, "A propos du projet de loiViollette," *La Française,* February 27, 1937 both in DOS 396 ALG.

125. Blanche Icard, "Appel d'un femme algériennepaysanne et travailleuse," *La Française,* 5 octobre, 1935. DOS 396AFR. Archives Bibliothèque Marguerite Durand.

126. "Congrès des Femmes méditerranéenes," *La Française*, April 24, 1932.

127. Jeanne Bottini-Houot, "Le Féminisme en Algérie" *La Francaise*, July 16, 1933.

128. Lucienne Favre and Jeanne Faure-Sardet were jointly awarded the prize in 1931, Favre for her work to date and Faure-Sardet for her novel *Deux femmes*, which does not feature in the holdings of the Bibliothèque nationale or World Cat. According to a 1932 article in *Minèrve* on the awarding of the prize to the two women, it was a novel about "native" mores (*de moeurs indigènes*). Lucienne Jean-Darrouy received her prize in 1943 for *Au pay de la mort jaune*. For information on the prize, see Jean Déjeux, "Le Grand Prix Littéraire de l'Algérie (1921–1961)," *Revue d'Histoire Littéraire de la France* 85 (1985) 60–71; Jeanne Adam, "Polémiqueautour du premier Grand Prix Littéraire de l'Algérie. La situation des letters algériennes en 1921" in *Le Maghreb Dans L'imaginaire Français: la Colonie, le Désert, L'exil*, ed. Jean-Robert Henry (Aix-en-Provence: Edisud, 1985).

129. "Lucienne Favre, laureate du grand prix d'Algérie" in *Minèrve* published 24?.1.1932, DOS FAV, Archives of the Bibliothèque Marguerite Durand.

130. Maurice Martin du Garde, (Review of} "Prosper" in *Nouvelles Littéraires*, December 1, 1934 and an interview of Favre by Régis Leroi, "Une Femme dans la Casbahd'Alger," *Minerve*, November 14, 1937, both in DOS FAV, Archives of the Bibliothèque Marguerite Durand.

131. Prior to taking up writing she tried, unsuccessfully, to establish herself as an actress.

132. Lucienne Favre, *The Temptations of Mourad, a Novel* (New York: W. Morrow, 1948). It is the translation of Lucienne Favre, *Mille et Un Jours: Mourad* (Brussels: Editions de la Toison d'Or, 1943). As is *Lucienne Favre, Tausend Und Ein Tag: Roman, trans. Else Bredthauer (Düsseldorf: Droste-Verl., 1949)*. Her play *Prosper* was translated into English and was performed in New York, Kurt Robitschek, Gaston Baty, and Lucienne Favre, *Simoon over Algiers; A Play in Thirteen Scenes after a Novel* (New York: French American Productions, 1938).

133. Pierre Mac-Orlan, Preface to Lucienne Favre, *L'homme Derrière le Mur* (Paris: Crès, 1927), iii.

134. Jean Charpentier, "Revue de la Quinzaine," *Mercure de France*, May 17, 1927, 142.

135. Clipping of a newspaper review: Lucien Decaves "Théâtre Montparnasse, Prosper" there is no newspaper title or date, although the performance of the play in 1934 suggests that it dates from then. Sheet 3, DOS FAV in Archives of the Bibliothèque Marguerite Durand.

136. She received the *Grand Prix Littéraire de l'Algérie* in 1943. Her novels include: *Le Mariage de Mademoiselle Centhectares: Figures de Colons Algériens* (1930); *Mariette Et Le Péché* (1936); *Au Pays de la Mort Jaune* (1940); *Au Jardin de Mon Père: Contes de la Terre d'Algérie* (1942); *Les Française Dans La Guerre: Vie et Mort de Denise Ferrier: Aspirant Conductrice Au 25e Bataillon Médical 9ème D.I.C* (1946).

137. A. Fournier-Chancogne, "Une femme de letters féministe. Mme.Lucienne Jean-Darrouy" in *La Française* Saturday, June 21, 1930. Messaouda Yahiaoui claims Jean-Darrouy was a lawyer, but her article contains some errors and in my research I have not been able to confirm the fact. Messaouda Yahiaoui, "Regards de Romancières Françaises Sur les Sociétés

Féminines d'Algérie, 1898–1960," in *Regards Sur les Littératures Coloniales Afrique Francophone*, ed. Jean-François Durand and Jean Sévry (Paris: L'Harmattan, 1999), 82.

138. Extract from an article by Lucienne Jean-Darrouy, which appeared in *l'Echo d'Alger*, quoted in "Les Femmes et les Tribunaux de Commerce," *La Française*, January 14, 1934. For her appearances in other towns, see "La Propagande Suffragiste dans l'Afrique du Nord," *La Française*, January 7, 1933.

139. "'*Hélia*' de Jeanne Faure-Sardet" in *Minerve*, March 26, 1933. DOS t, Archives Bibliothèque Marguerite Durand.

140. Jeanne Faure-Sardet, *Enamorada* (Alger: P. et G. Soubiron, 1933); Jeanne Faure-Sardet, *Fille D'arabe* (Paris: E. Figuière, 1935); Jeanne Faure-Sardet, *Un Réve à Tipasa* (Alger: Aux Editions de la "Typographie d'Art," 1938); Jeanne Faure-Sardet, *Mosaïques: Impressions, Contes, Nouvelles et Souvenirs* (Algiers: Fontana, n.d.). She also wrote *Deux femmes, Hélia, Deux hommes, un fantôme …et l'Amour,* and *La Chatte Salaambô,* none of which appear in the BN or World Cat catalogues. For the importance of Roman ruins to settler identity, see Lorcin, "France and Rome in Africa: Recovering Algeria's Latin Past."

141. The praise appeared in the review of another book by Faure-Sardet: Marie Louise Armand, "Une oeuvre de femme: La Chatte Salammbô," *Minerve,* August 23, 1936.

142. Lucienne Favre, *Orientale 1930,* (Paris: B. Grasset, 1930); Lucienne Jean-Darrouy, *Le Mariage de Mademoiselle Centhectares: Figures de Colons Algériens* (Alger: P. et G. Soubiron, 1930).

143. Lucienne Favre, *Dimitri et la Mort, Roman* (Paris: J. Ferenczi et fils, 1925); Lucienne Favre, *Bab-El-Oued* (Paris: G. Crès, 1926); Lucienne Favre, *La Noce, Roman* (Paris: B. Grasset, 1929); Favre, *L'homme Derrière le Mur.* Two earlier works published in 1923, *Indulgencès plénières* and *Une Voix dans le desert,* do not feature in the holdings of the collective catalogues of France or World Cat. In 1928 she received the *Prix Corrard* for *L'homme le mur* and *Bab-el-Oued* was runner up for the *Prix Feminina.* DOS FAV, Sheet 6, Archives of the Bibliothèque Marguerite Durand.

144. For a detailed analysis of the issues of race, gender, and race in the novel, see Lorcin, "Women, Gender and Nation in Colonial Novels of Inter-War Algeria.".

145. Favre, *Orientale 1930,* 9, 12. A marbout is a holy man (living saint in Islam); a marabouta is a holy woman.
   Fatima was the prophet Muhammed's daughter. The connotations of religious subordination and marginalization are obvious.

146. Ibid., 10.

147. Robert-Guiard devotes a chapter to the demography of spousal choice in colonial Algeria. She states that until World War II, marriages between the French and the néo-French were tolerated but not encouraged. Furthermore, French women more than French men were inclined to form endogamous relationships. Robert-Guiard, *Des Européennes en Situation Coloniale: Algérie 1830–1939,* 113–136.

148. *Les Nouvelles Littéraires,* May 17, 1930, 7.

149. John Charpentier, "Revue de la Quinzine" in *Mercure de France,* February 15, 1930, 137–138.

150. Ibid.

151. She singled out Favre's portrait of Bab-el-Oued, in the novel of that name. Lucienne Jean-Darrouy, "Union Française. Apports de la littérature Algérienne.'L'Écrivain-nomade' Isabelle Eberhardt" in *L'Algérienne*, 21. 1947. CAOM. 87APOM/48-Fonds Déjeux.Dossier 229. Document 21.

152. Jean-Darrouy, *Le Mariage de Mademoiselle Centhectares: Figures de Colons Algériens*, 6.

153. Ibid., 13.

154. Ibid., 29.

155. Ibid., 23.

156. For more about spas and colonization, see Eric Thomas Jennings, *Curing the Colonizers: Hydrotherapy, Climatology, and French Colonial Spas* (Durham, NC: Duke University Press, 2006).

157. Jean-Darrouy, *Le Mariage de Mademoiselle Centhectares: Figures de Colons Algériens*, 30.

158. Ibid., 21.

159. Ibid., 19.

160. Lorcin, "Women, Gender and Nation in Colonial Novels of Inter-War Algeria"; Lorcin, "Sex, Gender and Race in the Colonial Novels of Elissa Rhaïs and Lucienne Favre"; Patricia M. E. Lorcin, "Mediating Gender, Mediating Race: Women Writers in Colonial Algeria," *Culture, Theory & Critique* 45, no. 1 (2004).

161. For an in-depth analysis of these themes see Lorcin, "Women, Gender and Nation in Colonial Novels of Inter-War Algeria."

162. Favre, *Mille et Un Jours: Mourad*, 9.

163. Ibid., 127–128, 34; Favre, *Orientale 1930*, 10.

164. Lucienne Favre, *Le Bain Juif* (Paris: Éditions B. Grasset, 1939), 19.

165. Ibid., 57–58.

166. Ibid., 59.

167. Ibid., 43. The novel was completed in 1937.

168. Ibid., 231–233.

169. Faure-Sardet, *Fille D'arabe*, 11.

170. Ibid., 13.

171. Ibid., 52.

172. Ibid., 110.

173. The trope of the virile settler man was particularly evident in the colonial novels of Louis Bertrand and Robert Randau. See in particular: Louis Bertrand, *Le Sang des Races* (Paris: P. Ollendorff, 1899); Louis Bertrand, *Pépéte, le Bien-Aimé* (Paris: A. Fayard et cie, 1909); Robert Randau, *Les Colons; Roman de la Patrie Algérienne* (Paris: E. Sansot, 1907); Robert Randau, *Cassard le Berbère* (Algiers: Jules Carbonnel, 1926).

174. Faure-Sardet, *Fille D'arabe*, 149.

175. Ibid., 175.

176. *Vient de Paraître*, publicity clipping in the novel. No date.

177. Favre also develops this theme in her novels, see in particular: Favre, *Bab-El-Oued*, 111–112; Favre, *Orientale 1930*, 242.

178. Favre, *Orientale 1930*, 70.

179. For an analysis of the legal implications of miscegenation in the colonies, see Emmanuelle Saada, *Les Enfants de la Colonie: les Métis de L'empire Français Entre Sujétion et Citoyenneté* (Paris: Découverte, 2007); Peabody and

Stovall, *The Color of Liberty: Histories of Race in France;* Owen White, *Children of the French Empire: Miscegenation and Colonial Society in French West Africa, 1895–1960* (Oxford/New York: Oxford University Press, 1999); F. Henriques, *Children of Caliban: Miscegenation* (London: Secker & Warburg, 1974); Jennifer L. Palmer, "What's in a Name? Mixed-Race Families and Resistance to Racial Codification in Eighteenth-Cenury France," *French Historical Studies* 33, no. 2 (2010); P. A. Taguieff, "Doctrines de la Race et Hantise Du Métissage. Fragments D'une Histoire de la Mixophobie Savante," *Nouvelle revue d'ethnopsychiatrie* 17 (1992).

180. See, for example the case of working class Marie from France who marries an Algerian, Ahmed, after World War I and returns to Algeria in *Orientale 1930,* although they eventually return to France to escape the "archaic" pressures of Ahmed's Muslim family. See Lorcin, "Women, Gender and Nation in Colonial Novels of Inter-War Algeria"; Lorcin, "Sex, Gender and Race in the Colonial Novels of Elissa Rhaïs and Lucienne Favre."

CHAPTER 6

1. In theory, in both colonies urban property could be purchased by anybody; in practice most Algerians or Kenyans were priced out of the market. See: Paul Mosley, *The Settler Economies. Studies in the Economic History of Kenya and Southern Rhodesia 1900–1963* (Cambridge: Cambridge University Press, 1983), 29; Mahfoud Bennoune, *The Making of Contemporary Algeria 1830–1987* (Cambridge: Cambridge University Press, 2002), 74–85. For details of the economic situation of the Africans and Algerians, see: Priscilla M. Shilaro, *A Failed Eldorado. Colonial Capitalism, Rural Industrialization, African Land Rights in Kenya, and the Kakamega Gold Rush 1930–1952* (Lanham: University Press of America, 2008); Joanna Lewis, *Empire State-Building: War and Welfare in Kenya, 1925–1952* (Athens, OH: James Currey, 2000); John Ruedy, *Modern Algeria. The Origins and Development of a Nation* (Bloomington, IN: Indiana University Press, 1992); Charles-Robert Ageron, *Les Algériens Musulmans et la France (1871–1919),* 2 vols. (Paris: Presses Universitaires de France, 1968).

2. David Anderson, *Histories of the Hanged. Britain's Dirty War in Kenya and the End of Empire* (London: Weidenfeld & Nicolson, 2005), 25–27. See also Shilaro *A Failed Eldorado. Colonial Capitalism, Rural Industrialization, African Land Rights in Kenya, and the Kakamega Gold Rush 1930–1952,* 98–132; Mosley, *The Settler Economies. Studies in the Economic History of Kenya and Southern Rhodesia 1900–1963,* 71–113 and 70–94.

3. According to Anderson, oath-taking actually started in 1944.

4. Mss.Afr.s.424. "Mau Mau ceremonies as described by participants." C. J. A. Barnett was Kenya Police Reserves Officer. He states that the copy of the papers on the Mau Mau ceremonies came into his possession c. August 1954, although he was uncertain of who compiled them. The papers itemize the commitments made by participants in taking the oath and declare that these became increasingly violent as time went by. Like all official documents drawn up in times of severe conflict, their contents cannot be taken at face value. Although I provide this information I am mindful of by whom, when, and why it was produced.

5. For details of the development of Mau Mau and the British response, see: Anderson, *Histories of the Hanged.* For a more sensationalized account,

see: Caroline Elkins, *Imperial Reckoning. The Untold Story of Britain's Gulag in Kenya* (New York: Henry Holt & Co. Ltd., 2005); Elkins was awarded the Pulitzer prize for the work in 2006, at the height of the Abu Ghraib scandal, which suggests that politics played a certain role in the awarding of the prize. Her work has been severely criticized by historians of both African and imperial history. For a discussion of these reactions, see: Daniel Branch, *Defeating Mau Mau, Creating Kenya: Counterinsurgency, Civil War, and Decolonization* (Cambridge/New York: Cambridge University Press, 2009), xiv–xv. Other works on the Mau Mau include: Bruce J. Berman, "Bureaucracy and Incumbent Violence: Colonial Administration and the Origins of the 'Mau Mau' Emergency in Kenya," *British Journal of Political Science* 6, no. 2 (1976); David Throup, *Economic & Social Origins of Mau Mau 1945–1953* (Athens, OH: J. Currey, 1988); Tabitha M. Kanogo, *Squatters and the Roots of Mau Mau 1905–1963* (Athens, OH: James Currey, 1987); Robert B. Edgerton, *Mau Mau: An African Crucible* (New York: Ballantine Books, 1991); Joanna Lewis, "Mau-Mau's War of Words: The Battle of the Pamphlets," in *Free Print and Non-Commercial Publishing since 1700*, ed. James Raven (London: Ashgate, 2000); Bruce Berman and John Lonsdale, *Unhappy Valley: Conflict in Kenya and Africa* (London J. Currey, 1992), especially, 315–504; Atieno Odhiambo, Stephen Elisha, and John Lonsdale, *Mau Mau & Nationhood Arms, Authority & Narration* (Oxford/Nairobi: James Currey, 2003); David Percox, *Britain, Kenya and the Cold War – Imperial Defence, Colonial Security and Decolonisation* (London: I. B. Tauris, 2004); Martin Shipway, *Decolonization and Its Impact: A Comparative Approach to the End of the Colonial Empires* (Oxford: Blackwell, 2008); Georgina Sinclair, *At the End of the Line: Colonial Policing and the Imperial Endgame, 1945–1980* (Manchester: Manchester University Press, 2006); Kathryn Tidrick, *Empire and the English Character* (London: Tauris, 1992), 151–71; Tidrick states that verbal violence increased greatly during the Emergency, 159.

6. Anderson, *Histories of the Hanged*, 43. Branch argues that resistance to oath-taking led to a virtual Civil War among the Kenyans. Branch, *Defeating Mau Mau, Creating Kenya: Counterinsurgency, Civil War, and Decolonization.*

7. Anderson gives the figures of Kikuyu detained at 70,000 with about 150,000 spending some time during the Emergency in the detention camps. The Special Emergency Assize Courts tried 2,609 Kikuyu on capital charges, of whom 40 percent were acquitted, 1,574 were convicted and sentenced to death, and 1090 were actually hanged. Anderson, *Histories of the Hanged*, 4–6.

8. Ibid.

9. The literature on the war is vast and impossible to enumerate. See in particular: Matthew James Connelly, *A Diplomatic Revolution: Algeria's Fight for Independence and the Origins of the Post-Cold War Era* (New York: Oxford University Press, 2002); Alistair Horne, *A Savage War of Peace: Algeria, 1954–1962* (New York: New York Review Books, 2006); James D. Le Sueur, *Uncivil War: Intellectuals and Identity Politics During the Decolonization of Algeria* (Philadelphia, PA: University of Pennsylvania Press, 2001); Irwin M. Wall, *France, the United States, and the Algerian War* (Los Angeles, CA: University of California Press, 2001); Jean-Pierre Rioux and Jean-François Sirinelli, *La Guerre d'Algérie et les Intellectuels Français* (Bruxelles: Editions Complexe, 1991).

10. For details of the landings and the ensuing political machinations in Algiers, see: Arthur Layton Funk, *The Politics of Torch; the Allied Landings and the Algiers Putsch, 1942* (Lawrence, KA: University Press of Kansas, 1974); William B. Breuer, *Operation Torch: The Allied Gamble to Invade North Africa*, 1st ed. (New York: St. Martin's Press, 1985); Anthony Verrier, *Assassination in Algiers: Churchill, Roosevelt, de Gaulle, and the Murder of Admiral Darlan* (London: Macmillan, 1991); See also relevant chapters in Connelly, *A Diplomatic Revolution: Algeria's Fight for Independence and the Origins of the Post-Cold War Era*; Martin Thomas, *The French Empire at War, 1940–1945* (Manchester: University of Manchester Press, 1998).

11. For the accounts of the events from the settlers' point of view, including a number of women's testimonies, see: Maurice Villard, *La Vérité Sur L'insurrection Du 8 Mai 1945 Dans le Constantinois: Menaces Sur l'Algérie Française* (Montpellier: Amicale des Hauts Plateaux de Sétif, 1997). This work, which in spite of its obvious pro-settler bias contains some useful material, was written as a riposte to a television program on the Sétif massacres shown on the ARTE channel of French television on May 10, 1995, which emphasized the repression and Algerian casualties to the detriment of those of the settlers. The pied-noir community originating from Sétif (L'Amicale des Hauts Plateaux de Sétif) residing in France compiled this collection of written testimonies, statistics, and photographs to manifest their "victimization" both by the Algerians in 1945 and by the French media in 1995, who, they claim, occluded their tribulations at Sétif. Needless to say there is no mention of Algerian casualties.

12. The reprisal figures vary from approximately 1,500 (official French figures) to nearly 45,000 (militant figures); Ruedy, *Modern Algeria. The Origins and Development of a Nation*, 149. See also Jean-Louis Planche, *Sétif 1945: Histoire D'un Massacre Annoncé* (Paris: Perrin, 2006); Roger Vétillard, *Sétif, Mai 1945: Massacres en Algérie* (Versailles: Editions de Paris, 2008). For an Algerian perspective on the massacres, see: Boucif Mekhaled, *Chroniques D'un Massacre: 8 Mai 1945, Sétif, Guelma, Kherrata* (Paris: Syros/Au Nom de la Mémoire, 1995); See also Martin S. Alexander, Martin Evans, and John F. V. Keiger, *The Algerian War and the French Army: Experiences, Images, Testimonies* (London: Palgrave Macmillan, 2002); Martin S. Alexander and Keiger John F. V., *France and the Algerian War, 1954–1962: Strategy, Operations and Diplomacy* (London: Frank Cass, 2002).

13. Planche argues that at the height of the repression 500 Arabs were killed daily and that the degree of the violence was linked to rumors, which had circulated for over a year in the settler community, that trouble was eminent. Planche, *Sétif 1945: Histoire d'un Massacre Annoncé*, 1 and 10. See also chapters 6 and 11.

14. Anderson, *Histories of the Hanged*, 5. For the legacy of the Algerian war of independence, see Benjamin Stora, *La Guerre des Mémoires. La France Face à Son Passé Colonial* (Paris: Éditions de l'Aube, 2007); Patricia M. E. Lorcin, ed. *Algeria & France, 1800–2000: Identity, Memory, Nostalgia* (Syracuse, UK Syracuse University Press, 2006); Martin Evans, *The Memory of Resistance: French Opposition to the Algerian War (1954–1962)* (Oxford/New York: Berg, 1997); Benjamin Stora, *La Gangrène et L'oubli: la Mémoire de la Guerre d'Algérie* (Paris: La Découverte, 1991); Jo McCormack, *The Algerian War in the French Education System: A Case Study of the Transmission of Memory*

(Loughborough: Loughborough University of Technology, 2000); Jo McCormack, *Collective Memory: France and the Algerian War (1954–1962)* (Lanham, MD: Lexington Books, 2007).

15. Anderson gives the total number of African victims of the Mau Mau as 1,819 killed and 916 wounded. Anderson, *Histories of the Hanged*, 84. The National Liberation Front (F.L.N.) divided Algeria into six Wilayas, each under an F. L. N. leader. Most of the purges occurred in Wilaya III, with the figure for that area alone varying from 2,000–3,000. See Mohammed Harbi, *Le F.L.N.: Mirage et Réalité* (Paris: Editions J.A., 1980), 235. Horne, *A Savage War of Peace: Algeria, 1954–1962*, 323; M. Hugh P. Roberts, *Algerian Socialism and the Kabyle Question* (Norwich: School of Development Studies, University of East Anglia, 1981), 261–262; Yves Courrière, *L'heure des Colonels*, His La Guerre d'Algérie, 3 (Paris: Fayard, 1970), 132–133.

16. Anderson, *Histories of the Hanged*, 178; Jacques Simon, *Le Massacre de Melouza: Algérie, Juin 1957* (Paris: Harmattan, 2006), 32–36. Branch gives figures of 74 to 100 and states that the massacre set off spiralling violence. Branch, *Defeating Mau Mau, Creating Kenya: Counterinsurgency, Civil War, and Decolonization*, 55–59. For a French reaction to the internecine struggles among the Algerians, see Charles-Robert Ageron, "Les Francais devant la guerre civile algérienne" in Charles-Robert Ageron, *De l'Algérie "Française" à l'Algérie Algérienne* (Paris: Éditions Bouchene, 2005), 495–511. Nellie Grant described the Lari massacre as "indescribably appalling, for once worse than anything the press can say." Nellie Grant, *Nellie's Story* (first published 1973) (New York: William Morrow, 1980), 189.

17. Official casualty figures for the Emergency to the end of 1956 are 11,503 "terrorists" killed, 95 Europeans of which 35 were civilians, 29 Asians of which 26 were civilians, and 1,920 "loyal" Africans. F. D. Corfield, *The Origins and Growth of Mau Mau: An Historical Survey* (Nairobi: Colony and Protectorate of Kenya, 1960), 316. Branch states that "the anti-colonial rebellion and civil war claimed the lives of approximately 25,000 Kenya Africans" (Branch, *Defeating Mau Mau, Creating Kenya: Counterinsurgency, Civil War, and Decolonization*, 5). Alastair Horne provides the following casualty figures for the Algerian War of Independence: French military losses 17,456 (including 5,966 killed "accidentally"), 64,985 wounded and injured, and 1,000 missing (including deserters). European civilian casualties of 10,000, caused by over 42,000 acts of terrorism, of which 2,788 were dead and 500 disappeared. French figures give 141,000 Algerian male combatants killed, 12,000 members of the F.L.N. killed in internecine purges, 16,000 Muslims civilians killed by the F.L.N. and a further 50,000 Muslims abducted, presumed killed, by the F.L.N., and a further 4,300 killed by the F.L.N. and M.N.A. in France. In the immediate aftermath of the war the figure given by the Algerians was 300,000 killed. Today the Algerian government gives the figure for their total war dead as 1 million. Alistair Horne, *A Savage War of Peace: Algeria, 1954–1962* (2006), 538.

18. Rhodes House Archive, MSS. Brit. Emp.s.365. Fabian Colonial Bureau-Box 46, File 119/4-Item 6. From *Fighting Talk. A Monthly Journal for Democrats*, registered at the G. P. O. as a newspaper. vol. 12, no. 6, June 1956. Issue on Eileen Fletcher, 5.

19. For Kenya, see: Anderson, *Histories of the Hanged*, 155–157 and for Algeria, see Giséle Halimi, *Le Lait de L'oranger* (Paris: Gallimard, 1988).

20. The French journalist Henri Alleg, himself a victim, exposed the use of torture in his best-selling work, *La Question*. First published in 1958 (and immediately banned) it has recently been translated into English: Henri Alleg, *The Question* (Lincoln, NE: University of Nebraska Press, 2006). Although Alleg's work created the most stir, preceding works include: Pierre Henri Simon, *Contre la Torture* (Paris: Éditions du Seuil, 1957); Georges Arnaud and Jacques Vergès, *Pour Djamila Bouhired*, Documents (Paris: Ed. de Minuit, 1957). See also Simone de Beauvoir and Gisèle Halimi, *Djamila Boupacha, the Story of the Torture of a Young Algerian Girl Which Shocked Liberal French Opinion* (New York: Macmillan, 1962). A more recent memoir on torture during the war is Louisette Ighilahriz, *L'algérienne* (Paris: Fayard, 2001). The question of the war atrocities was the subject of renewed media attention in the period 2000–2002. See the "Introduction" in *Algeria & France, 1800–2000: Identity, Memory, Nostalgia*, Lorcin ed. xix–xxx. For scholarly works, see Pierre Vidal-Naquet, *Torture: Cancer of Democracy, France and Algeria, 1954–1962* (Baltimore, MD: Penguin Books, 1963); Raphälle Branche, *La Torture et L'armée Pendant la Guerre d'Algérie: 1954–1962* (Paris: Gallimard, 2001); Marnia Lazreg, *Torture and the Twilight of Empire: From Algiers to Baghdad* (Princeton, NJ: Princeton University Press, 2008). The title is misleading as there is little about Baghdad and the account is one-sided as there is nothing about the atrocities committed by the Algerians during the war, particularly on their own people.

21. Quoted by Djamila Amrane, *Des Femmes Dans la Guerre d'Algérie: Entretiens* (Paris: Karthala, 1994), 194.

22. Quoted in ibid., 190.

23. For a journalist's account of the Yveton affair, see Jean-Luc Einaudi, *Pour L'exemple, L'affaire Fernand Yveton: Enquête* (Paris: L'Harmattan, 1986).

24. Quoted by Amrane, *Des Femmes Dans la Guerre d'Algérie: Entretiens*, 187.

25. Cited by Stora, *La Guerre des Mémoires. La France Face à Son Passé Colonial*, 94–95; Amrane, *Des Femmes*.

26. For further details, see: Hélène Bracco, *Pour Avoir Dit Non: Actes de Refus Dans la Guerre d'Algérie, 1954–1962* (Paris: Paris-Méditerranée, 2003); Marie-Pierre Ulloa, *Francis Jeanson: A Dissident Intellectual from the French Resistance to the Algerian War* (Stanford, CA: Stanford University Press, 2007); Hervé Hamon and Rotman Patrick, *Les Porteurs de Valises: la Résistance Française à la Guerre d'Algérie* (Paris: A. Michel, 1979).

27. Algerian women were very active during the war, both in France and in Algeria. See Natalya Vince, "Transgressing Boundaries: Gender, Race, Religion, and 'Françaises Musulmanes' During the Algerian War of Independence," *French Historical Studies* 33, no. 3 (2010): 446–474; Amrane, *Des Femmes Dans la Guerre d'Algérie: Entretiens*. Parminder Vir, *Algerian Women at War* (New York: Women Make Movies, 2008); Frantz Fanon, *L'an V de la Révolution Algérienne* (Paris: Découverte, 2001); Diane Sambron, *Femmes Musulmanes: Guerre d'Algérie, 1954–1962*, Collection Mémoires. Histoire (Paris: Éditions Autrement, 2007); Caroline Brac de La Perrière, *Derrière les Héros: les Employées de Maison Musulmanes en Service Chez les Européens à Alger Pendant la Guerre d'Algérie, 1954–1962* (Paris: L'Harmattan, 1987).

28. Quoted by Ranjana Khanna, *Algeria Cuts: Women and Representation, 1830 to the Present* (Stanford, CA: Stanford University Press, 2008), 83. See also

Beauvoir and Halimi, *Djamila Boupacha, the Story of the Torture of a Young Algerian Girl Which Shocked Liberal French Opinion.*

29. See Connelly, *A Diplomatic Revolution: Algeria's Fight for Independence and the Origins of the Post-Cold War Era*; Wall, *France, the United States, and the Algerian War.* On Kenya, see Percox, *Britain, Kenya and the Cold War.*

30. Anne Durand, *Idir et Thérèse* (Paris: Editions Thibaud, 1981), 71.

31. Lucienne Favre, *Mille et Un Jours: Mourad* (Brussels: Editions de la Toison d'Or, 1943); *Aventures de la Belle Doudjda* (Paris: Denoël, 1946); *Dans la Casbah, 1937–1948* (Paris: C. d'Halluin, 1949). For an analysis of Favre's novel *Mille en Un Jours: Mourad*, see Patricia M. E. Lorcin, "Sex, Gender and Race in the Colonial Novels of Elissa Rhaïs and Lucienne Favre," in *The Color of Liberty: Histories of Race in France*, ed. Peabody and Stovall.

32. Favre, *Mille et Un Jours: Mourad*; Lucienne Favre, *The Temptations of Mourad, a Novel* (New York: W. Morrow, 1948). It was also translated into German: Lucienne Favre, *Tausend Und Ein Tag: Roman*, trans. Else Bredthauer (Düsseldorf: Droste-Verl., 1949). The other novel in the series was: Lucienne Favre, *Mille et Un Jours: les Aventures de la Belle Doudjda*, 6th ed. (Paris: Gallimard, 1941).

33. Françoise Gicquel, Commissaire Divisionnaire de la Service de la Memoire et des Affaires Culturelles de la section "archives", Archives de la Prefecture de Police, recounted an anecdote told to her by a researcher of *pied-noir* origin. On being told that drilling in the Sahara had been successful the researcher's mother cried "Nous sommes foutus" (we're finished), implying that international oil interests would start meddling with the colonies internal politics to the detriment of the settlers.

34. For details of the concessions made to the Algerians in the 1944 Ordinance of the Provisional Government in Algiers and 1946 Law, see Todd Shepard, *The Invention of Decolonization: The Algerian War and the Remaking of France* (Ithaca, NY: Cornell University Press, 2006), 39–41.

35. Jeanne Montupet, *Simon: Roman*, La Fontaine Rouge (Paris: R. Laffont, 1953); *Francisca: Roman*, La Fontaine Rouge (Paris: R. Laffont, 1954); *Olivier: Roman*, La Fontaine Rouge (Paris: R. Laffont, 1955). Their bestseller status was affirmed in a review in the "Books-Authors" section of the *New York Times*, July 7, 1961, 23. Her last book was published in 1990: Jeanne (Jeannine) Montupet, *Couleurs de Paradis* (Paris: R. Laffont, 1990).

36. Jeanne Montupet, *Das Haus Vermorel: Ein Algerischer Familienroman* (Stuttgart: Deutsche Verlags-Anstalt, 1957); Jeanne Montupet, *De Rode Bron: Aïn El Hamra: Een Algerijnse Familieroman* (Baarn: Hollandia, 1958); Jeanne Montupet, *The Red Fountain*, trans. John Barlow (New York: St. Martin's Press, 1961).

37. Montupet, *The Red Fountain*, 10.

38. Ibid., 305.

39. By 1956 conscripts were openly rebelling. For an account of these events, see: Hamon and Patrick, *Les Porteurs de Valises: la Résistance Française à la Guerre d'Algérie*, 47–51.

40. Brunschvig Archives 1651 90772- "Edition d'un tract."

41. Catherine Lerouvre, *Un Feu D'enfer* (Paris: Seuil, 1958), 9.

42. Ibid., 98.

43. Ibid., 142.

44. Ibid., 118.

45. Michael O'Brien, *John F. Kennedy: A Biography*, 1st U.S. ed. (New York: Thomas Dunne Books/St. Martin's Press, 2005), 357–358. For a detailed analysis of the shifts in American policy, see Connelly, *A Diplomatic Revolution: Algeria's Fight for Independence and the Origins of the Post-Cold War Era.*, and Wall, *France, the United States, and the Algerian War.*

46. Geneviève Baïlac, "Les Grands Jours D'alger," *Revue de Paris* 67, no. 6 (1960): 57.

47. See Horne, *A Savage War of Peace: Algeria, 1954–1962*, 185–187.

48. On Tillion, see Nancy Wood, *Germaine Tillion, Une Femme-Mémoire: D'une Algérie à L'autre* (Paris: Autrement, 2003), 196–239. Tillion was criticized by pro-independence personalities, such as Jean Amrouche, for her refusal to place the blame on the French for the Algerian "shipwreck," 229. On Vincent, see Jean-Luc Einaudi, *Un Reve Algérien: Histoire de Lisette Vincent, Une Femme d'Algérie: Récit* (Paris: Editions d'Agorno, 1994).

49. In March 1931 the newspaper *Akhbar* stated that "L'oeuvre bien faisante qu'entreprend ici la France ne portera ses fruits que si la femme reçoit sa part dans cette grande éducation, car, jusqu'ici on peut dire que seuls les hommes profitent de cette œuvre de progrès . . . " CAOM, 30-MIOM/37, "De la femme musulmane" in *Akhbar,* March 31, 1931, no. 14004. For details of the 1958–1959 "emancipation" campaign, see Neil MacMaster, "The Colonial 'Emancipation' of Algerian Women: The Marriage Law of 1959 and the Failure of Legislation on Women's Rights in the Post-Independence Era," Stichproben. Wiener Zeitschrift für kritische Afrikastudien 12, no. 7 (2007). And Neil MacMaster, *Burning the Veil: Military Propaganda and the Emancipation of Women During the Algeria War 1954–1962* (Manchester: Manchester University Press, 2009).

50. MacMaster, "The Colonial 'Emancipation' of Algerian Women: The Marriage Law of 1959 and the Failure of Legislation on Women's Rights in the Post-Independence Era," 96–97.

51. French issues regarding the veil have a long history stretching from the colonial to the postcolonial period. In addition to works cited, see Frantz Fanon, "Algeria Unveiled," in *Veil: Veiling, Representation, and Contemporary Art,* ed. David A. Bailey (Cambridge, MA: MIT Press, 2003); Trica Danielle Keaton, *Muslim Girls and the Other France: Race, Identity Politics, & Social Exclusion* (Bloomington, IN: Indiana University Press, 2006); Joan Wallach Scott, *The Politics of the Veil* (Princeton, NJ: Princeton University Press, 2007). For recent literature on the veil in other contexts, see Jennifer Heath, *The Veil: Women Writers on Its History, Lore, and Politics* (Los Angles, CA: University of California Press, 2008); Ajume H. Wingo, *Veil Politics in Liberal Democratic States* (New York: Cambridge Universiy Press, 2003). In July 2010 the French parliament banned the burka from public spaces.

52. Macmaster sees it as entirely orchestrated; Horne sees it as spontaneous and, hence inexplicable. MacMaster, "The Colonial 'Emancipation' of Algerian Women: The Marriage Law of 1959 and the Failure of Legislation on Women's Rights in the Post-Independence Era," 98. Horne, *A Savage War of Peace: Algeria, 1954–1962*, 290–291.

53. Fonds Brunschvig, Union Feminine Civiqueet Sociale. 1AF463, "La Femme Algérienne in *Messages d'Algérie,* June 30, 1958.

54. Geneviève Baïlac, *Les Absinthes Sauvages; Témoignage Pour le Peuple Pieds-Noirs* (Paris: Fayard, 1972), 185.

55. Preface to: Geneviève Baïlac, *La Famille Hernandez. Théâtre Complet* (Paris: Club du Souvenir, 1966), 11.

56. Ibid., 10.

57. Patouete, the "dialect" of the *pieds-noirs,* was a hybrid of the many Southern European languages of the neo-French. For an analysis of its importance to *pied-noir* identity, see David Prochaska, "History as Literature, Literature as History: Cagayous of Algiers," *American Historical Review* 101, no. 3 (1996): 671–711.

58. In 1958 only 5 major urban areas received television and 6 percent of households had television; by 1962 the household figure had risen to 25 percent. (cited in Johnny Trutor, "Please Stand By": Reconstruction, Decolonization, and Security in British and French Public Information Films in the Postwar Era, 1945–1965 unpublished PhD thesis, UMN 2011, 72, statistics from J. Bourdon, *Histoire de la télévision sous de Gaulle* (Paris: Antropos/INA, 1990) 303, reprinted in Raymond Kuhn, The Media in France (New York: Routledge, 1995), 111.

59. Baïlac, *La Famille Hernandez. Théâtre Complet,* 12.

60. Baïlac's claim that there was no political message is disingenuous given her description of its political ramifications, when it was performed in Paris in her memoir of the war. See Baïlac, *Les Absinthes Sauvages; Témoignage Pour le Peuple Pieds-Noirs,* 211–219.

61. Anne Durand, *Idir et Thérèse: <Le Vert et le Noir.>* (Montreux: Impr. Corbaz, 1958).

62. Durand, *Idir et Thérèse,* 123.

63. In this it is reminiscent of Deepa Mehta's 1998 film, *Earth* about the post-independence partition of India.

64. Baïlac, for example, continued to believe that only a minority of Algerians sought independence ("...la plupart des Musulmans ne sont nullement coin-vancus que leur destin doive les conduire inéluctablement à l'independence d'Algérie.") Baïlac, "Les Grands Jours D'alger," 52.

65. Ibid., 49.

66. Marie Sils, Ces Forêts D'orangers (Paris: Gallimard, 1962), 13. (Marie Sils was the pseudonym of Antoinette Marchal. She was from Epinal in the Vosges, had a law degree and was married to the magistrate Jacques Scheurer. This book is significant as an illustration of the literary empathy between women writers in France and the "lost" territory)

67. Ibid., 17 and 25.

68. Ibid., 38.

69. Ibid., 364.

70. Baïlac, "Les Grands Jours d'Alger," 50.

71. A few women wrote about the impact of the war on workers in France. See Jeanine Oriano, *Driss* (Paris: Julliard, 1959); Claire Etcherelli, *Élise, Ou, La Vraie Vie* (Paris: Denoël, 1967). Of the published novels during the period 1954–1966, 77 novels were by French men, 22 by Algerian men, 17 by French women, and 2 by Algerian women. Of the 77 novels by French men most were either about military aspects of the war or were by military personnel. Statistics from Benjamin Stora, *Le Dictionnaire des Livres de la Guerre d'Algérie: Romans, Nouvelles, Poésie, Photos, Histoire, Essais, Récits Historiques, Témoignages, Biographies, Mémoires, Autobiographies: 1955–1995* (Paris: Harmattan, 1996).

72. She also goes by the name Loesch-Gagliardi.

73. Anne Loesch, *La Valise et le Cercueil* (Paris: Plon, 1963), 11.

74. Ibid., 11–12.

75. Ibid., 10.

76. Ibid., 257 and 60; ibid.

77. The French countryside at this time was depopulated and many departments had abandoned or semi-abandoned villages.

78. Loesch, *La Valise et le Cercueil*, 265.

79. For an elaboration of this ideology, see: Patricia M. E. Lorcin, "Decadence and Renascence: Louis Bertrand and the Concept of Rebarbarisation in Fin de Siècle Algeria," in *New Perspectives on the Fin de Siècle in Nineteenth- and Twentieth-Century France*, ed. Kay Chadwick and Timothy Unwin (London: Edwin Mellen, 2000), 181–197, and *Imperial Identities: Stereotyping, Prejudice and Race in Colonial Algeria*, Chapter 9.

80. Marie Elbe, *Et à L'heure de Notre Mort* (Paris: Presses de la Cité, 1963); Stora, *Le Dictionnaire des Livres de la Guerre d'Algérie: Romans, Nouvelles, Poésie, Photos, Histoire, Essais, Récits Historiques, Témoignages, Biographies, Mémoires, Autobiographies: 1955–1995*, 220. Loesch went on to have a successful literary career, publishing over a dozen works of fiction and nonfiction.

81. Francine Dessaigne, *Journal D'une Mère de Famille Pied-Noir* (Lagny-sur-Marne: L'Esprit nouveau, 1962); Francine Dessaigne, *Déracinés!* (Meaux: Éditions du Fuseau, 1964).

82. Dessaigne, *Déracinés!*

83. Ibid., 78.

84. Mohammed Dib, *Un Été Africain* (Paris: Éditions du Seuil, 1959); Mohammed Dib, *Cours Sur la Rive Sauvage* (Paris: Éditions du Seuil, 1964); Yacine Kateb, *Nedjma, Roman* (Paris: Éditions du Seuil, 1956); Yacine Kateb, *Le Cercle des Représailles, Thèâtre* (Paris: Éditions du Seuil, 1959); Mouloud Mammeri, *La Colline Oubliée* (Paris: Plon, 1952); Mouloud Mammeri, *Le Sommeil Du Juste* (Paris: Plon, 1955).

85. Rhodes House Archives.MSS.Afr.2154-Box 2-Huxley papers. Letter from NG to Frank, October 19, 1941.

86. From the cover notice of Elspeth Joscelin Grant Huxley and Margery Perham, *Race and Politics in Kenya. A Correspondence between Elspeth Huxley and Margery Perham with an Introduction by Lord Lugard* (London: Faber & Faber, 1944).

87. Michael Howard, "Soldier of fortune," *The Times Literary Supplement*, no. 5546, July 17, 2009; 5.

88. Letter from Elspeth Huxley to Margern Perham, March 10, 1942 Huxley and Perham, *Race and Politics in Kenya*, 15.

89. Ibid., 16.

90. Ibid.

91. Letter from Margery Perham to Elspeth Huxley, March 15, 1942, ibid., 18. Apartheid was introduced as a legal and political system in 1948.

92. Letter from Margery Perham to Elspeth Huxley, March 15, 1942, ibid.

93. Huxley to Perham, April 26, 1943, ibid., 144.

94. Perham to Huxley, August 20, 1943, ibid., 223.

95. Mss.Afr.s.2154-Box 10. Letter to EH from Francis Scott, Deloraine, Rongai, August 1944.

96. Elspeth Joscelin Grant Huxley, *A Thing to Love; a Novel* (London: Chatto & Windus, 1954).

97. Elspeth Joscelin Grant Huxley, *The Sorcerer's Apprentice: A Journey through East Africa* (London: Chatto and Windus, 1948).

98. C. S. Nicholls, *Elspeth Huxley: A Biography*, 195.

99. Ibid., 194.

100. Huxley, *The Sorcerer's Apprentice: A Journey through East Africa*, 36.

101. Ibid.

102. Ibid., xviii.

103. Ibid., 50.

104. Rhodes House Archive, MSS.Afr.s.2154—Box 2—Huxley Papers, File 5. Letter from Nellie Grant to Elspeth Huxley, Njoro October 7, 1945.

105. Rhodes House Archive. MSS.Afr.s.2154-Box 3: File 3/1. Letter from NG to EH, Njoro, January 20, 1946.

106. Ibid.

107. Rhodes House Archive. MSS.Afr.s.2154-Box 3: File 3/1. Letter from NG to EH, Njoro, March 13, 1946.

108. Rhodes House Archive, Micr.Afr.589-Papers of Hester Katherine ("Kit") Henn. 589/4 "Are you going to Kenya?" December 1949.

109. Nicholls, *Elspeth Huxley*, 170.

110. Elspeth Joscelin Grant Huxley, *Settlers of Kenya* (London/New York,: Longmans/Green 1948); Elspeth Joscelin Grant Huxley, *African Dilemmas*, British Commonwealth Affairs (London: New York, 1948).

111. Huxley, *Settlers of Kenya*, vii–viii.

112. Ibid., 62.

113. Ibid., 126.

114. Ibid.

115. Huxley, *African Dilemmas*, 5.

116. Ibid., 20.

117. Ibid.

118. Elspeth Huxley, "Tomorrow's Hope or Yesterday's Dream?" *The New York Times*, June 6, 1950; Elspeth Huxley, "What Life Is Like for a Settler in Kenya," *The New York Times*, June 6, 1954; Elspeth Huxley, "The Vast Challenge of Africa," *The New York Times*, July 18, 1954.

119. Elspeth Huxley, "Tomorrow's Hope or Yesterday's Dream?; Africa, the last undeveloped continent, can be converted into a virile partner of the West. Tomorrow's Hope or Yesterday's Dream?" in *The New York Times*, June 4, 1950, p. SM7 (5 pages). Other venues for her articles were: *Time & Tide, African Affairs, The National Review, The Listener, The Times [of London], Geographical Magazine, East African Standard, Kenya Sunday Times* and numerous others. For a complete list of her contributions to newspapers and periodicals, see Robert S. Cross and Michael Perkin, *Elspeth Huxley: A Bibliography* (New Castle, DE: Oak Knoll Press, 1996), 110–153 and 54–72 for her radio and television appearances.

120. Rhodes House Archive. Micr.Afr.589. "The Distaff Side," *Kenya Weekly News*, December 10, 1948, 41.

121. Rhodes House Archive, MSS.Afr.s.2199. Box 2, File 2/3: Diary September 1955–1956. Entry for October 13, 1955. Mary Casey was the niece of William Powys, one of the early settlers who had originally served as a manager on the farm of Galbraith Cole before he set up on his own and took up painting.

122. Casey kept her journal until shortly before her death in 1980. Extracts from the period 1963 to 1979 were edited and published posthumously by

Judith Lange and Louise de Bruin, as were collections of her poems and *The Kingfisher's Wing,* a "visionary recital " of the life of Plotinus. Mary Casey, Louise De Bruin, and Judith M. Lang, *A Net in Water: A Selection from the Journals* (Bath, U.K.: Powys Press, 1994).

123. MSS.Afr.s.2199. File 1/5: Diary V: The Beale Farm. Mary Casey, Entry for October 12, 1952.

124. Ibid.

125. MSS.Afr.s.2199. File 1/6: Diary VI. The Beale Farm. Mary Casey: Entry for January 13, 1953.

126. Ibid.

127. MSS.Afr.s.2199. File 1/7: Diary VII. Mary Casey: Entry for April 29, 1953.

128. MSS.Afr.s.2154-Box 3, File 5. Letter from NG to EH. Njoro, October 9, 1952.

129. Ibid.

130. MSS.Afr.s.2154-Box 3, File 5. Letter from NG to EG. Njoro, October 26, 1952.

131. MSS.Afr.s.2154-Box 3, File 5. Letter from NG to EG. Njoro, Tuesday, November 25, 1952.

132. MSS.Afr.s.2154-Box 3, File 5. Letter from NG to EG. Njoro, December 9, 1952.

133. MSS.Afr.s.2154-Box 3, File 6. Letter from NG to EG. Njoro, January 6, 1953.

134. MSS.Afr.2154-Box 3, File 7. Letter from NG to EH. Njoro, Sunday, December 5, 1954.

135. Huxley, *A Thing to Love; a Novel.* M. M. Kaye, *Death in Zanzibar & Death in Kenya* (London: St. Martins Press, 1983). Other novels written in the 1950s include: Robert Chester Ruark and Daniel Schwartz, *Something of Value* (Cutchogue, NY: Buccaneer Books, 1955); George Albert Glay, *Oath of Seven* (New York: Ace Books, 1955); Charles Ludwig, *Radio Pals in the Hands of the Mau Mau* (Wheaten, IL: Van Kampen Press, 1954); Henri de Monfreid, *Sous le Masque Mau-Mau* (Paris: B. Grasset, 1956); Victor Stafford Reid, *The Leopard* (New York: Viking Press, 1958); Walter Babington Thomas, *The Touch of Pitch: A Story of Mau Mau* (London: A. Wingate, 1956).

136. M. M. Kaye, *The Far Pavilions* (New York: St. Martin's Press, 1978); Mollie Kaye, *Six Bars at Seven* (London: First Novel library, 1940).

137. Kaye, *Death in Zanzibar & Death in Kenya.* Author's Note.

138. Ibid.

139. Ibid., 218–219.

140. Ibid., 240.

141. Ibid., 222.

142. Ibid., 296.

143. According to the review by H. R. Tate, the conversations of the Mau Mau leaders in the novel and all the details of the movement's "structure, ceremonial and organization are accurate and actual, based on information collected over the past few years by the police and 'screening teams'"; H. R. Tate, "A Thing to Love by Elspeth Huxley," *African Affairs* 54, no. 214 (1955): 67–69.

144. Huxley, *A Thing to Love; a Novel,* 15.

145. Ibid., 48.

146. Ibid., 64.
147. Ibid., 60.
148. Ibid., 66.
149. Ibid., 80–81.
150. Ibid., 210.
151. Ibid., 222.
152. Ibid., 119.
153. Ibid., 120.
154. Ibid., 210.
155. Ibid., 189.
156. MSS.Afr.2154-Box 1, File 4/2. Letter from NG to EH. Njoro, Friday, February 26, 1960.
157. Interview with Christine Nicholls, July 13, 2005. Ms. Nicholls mentioned the presence of a transcript of the interview by W. P. Kirkman in Rhodes House, Oxford. My thanks to her for this information.
158. At the 1960 Lancaster House Conference, he was against the maintenance of white settlement. As a result settler sentiment, according to Nellie Grant was "very very high against Macleod and also Renison [the governor]" Grant, *Nellie's Story*, 235.
159. MSS.Af.s.2179 Transcript of a tape-recorded interview with the Rt. Hon. Iain Macleod, M. P. Secretary of State for the Colonies, 1959–1961, interviewed by W. P. Kirkman at the White Cottage, Potters Bar, Middlesex, on December 20, 1967, 24–25. See also 49–50, where Macleod discusses what were then the Rhodesias.
160. Ibid., 88.
161. Nicholls, *Elspeth Huxley*, 309.

CHAPTER 7

1. Claude Liauzu, ed. *Dictionnaire de la colonisation française*, Larousse à présent (Paris: Larousse, 2007), 509. For press accounts, see: From our own correspondent, "Bloodshed ends Independence Parade," *The Times*, Friday, July 6, 1962, From our own correspondent, "Algeria Rebels move into Oran area," *The Times*, Saturday, July 7, 1962.
2. Liauzu, ed. *Dictionnaire de la colonisation française*, 509.
3. De Gaulle was the target of a number of assassination attempts, the best-known of which was masterminded by Lt. Col. Jean Bastien-Thiry. He was executed in March 1963 for his role in the attempt.
4. For an account of Algerian decolonization in France, see Todd Shepard, *The Invention of Decolonization: The Algerian War and the Remaking of France* (Ithaca, NY: Cornell University Press, 2006). For issues regarding *pied-noir* settlement in Europe, see Andrea L. Smith, *Colonial Memory and Postcolonial Europe: Maltese Settlers in Algeria and France*, New anthropologies of Europe (Bloomington, IN: Indiana University Press, 2006); Averell Manes, *The Pieds-Noirs 1960–2000: A Case Study in the Persistence of Subcultural Distinctiveness* (Bethesda, MD.: Academica Press, 2005); Juan David Sempere Souvannavong, *Los pieds-noirs en Alicante: las migraciones inducidas por la descolonizacion* (Alicante: Universidad de Alicante, 1997).
5. From our correspondent, "White Farmers Applaud Jomo Kenyatta 'Old Scores will be forgotten'," *The Times*, August 13, 1963.

6. "Kenya: Black & White—Harambee!" *Time*, Friday, August 23, 1963.

7. Francine Dessaigne, *Déracinés!* (Meaux: Éditions du Fuseau, 1964), 80, 126.

8. Ibid., 65.

9. Ibid., 41–42. During the final two years of the war, when the O. A. S. activity was at its height, the inhabitants of the district of Bab-el-Oued in Algiers, where many of the modest settlers lived, banged on their saucepans each night to the beat of Al-gé-rie Fran-çaise.

10. Ibid., 120.

11. Ibid., 118.

12. Marie Elbe, *Et à l'heure de notre mort* (Paris: Presses de la Cité, 1963). The novel was enlarged and reissued in 1992.

13. Elbe's other books include *Pourquoi Cologne* (Paris, Presses de la Cité, 1964), for which she received a prize from the *Société des Gens de letters*. She now lives in Majorca.

14. Marie Elbe, *A l'heure de notre mort: roman* (Paris: A. Michel, 1992), 13.

15. Ibid., 15.

16. Aron was voted into the Academy in 1974, but died a few days before his inauguration.

17. Geneviève Baïlac, *Les absinthes sauvages; témoignage pour le peuple pieds-noirs* (Paris: Fayard, 1972), 9.

18. Ibid., 14.

19. Ibid., 15.

20. For a discussion of the importance of Tipasa to the ideology of *pied-noir* identity, see Patricia M. E. Lorcin, "France and Rome in Africa: Recovering Algeria's Latin Past," *French Historical Studies* 25, no. 2 (2002): 295–329.

21. Baïlac, *Les absinthes sauvages; témoignage pour le peuple pieds-noirs*, 21. For a description of Louis Bertrand's concept of Latin Races, see chapter 9 in Lorcin, *Imperial Identities: Stereotyping, Prejudice and Race in Colonial Algeria;* and Lorcin, "Decadence and Renascence: Louis Bertrand and the Concept of Rebarbarisation in Fin de Siècle Algeria," in *New Perspectives on the Fin de Siècle in Nineteenth- and Twentieth-century France.*

22. Baïlac, *Les absinthes sauvages; témoignage pour le peuple pieds-noirs*, 24.

23. Ibid., 42–43. For an analysis of the Cagayous phenomenon, see David Prochaska, "History as Literature, Literature as History: Cagayous of Algiers," *American Historical Review* 101, no. 3 (1996): 671–711.

24. Baïlac, *Les absinthes sauvages; témoignage pour le peuple pieds-noirs*, 96.

25. Ibid., 176.

26. See, for example, Thomas F. Brady, "French Crisis: Seen from Algiers," *The New York Times*, May 18, 1958. From our own correspondent, "Warning from Algeria to President Coty," *The Times*, May 17, 1958.

27. For the text of the statement, see: Reuters, "Text of Khrushchev Statement," *The New York Times*, May 16, 1958.

28. By this time it had also become clear that an independent Algeria could mean an American share in the exploitation of its considerable oil reserves, which would not be possible if France kept Algeria.

29. Baïlac, *Les absinthes sauvages; témoignage pour le peuple pieds-noirs*, 31.

30. Ibid., 288.

31. Ibid.

32. Geneviève Baïlac, *La Famille Hernandez: L'Algérie heureuse* (Paris: R. Lafont, 1979). The plays comprising *La Famille Hernandez* were reissued a number of times, the latest being in 1992.

33. http://www.cerclealgerianiste.asso.fr/ accessed on August 8, 2009.

34. Ibid., My emphasis. The *Cercle* has branches in Lyon, Nice, Perpignan, and the Toulousain. Its main library is in Lyon.

35. http://nice.algerianiste.free.fr/pages/manifeste.html accessed on August 8, 2009.

36. The first article states: Cette Association a pour but de rechercher partout, en France et hors de France, rassembler, répertorier, conserver et faire connaître la documentation sous toutes les formes d'expression (histoire, littérature, arts plastiques, documents sonores, musique, etc.) concernant l'Algérie avant et pendant la présence française, et les suites de cette présence. Elle se donne pour règle une objectivité totale, en s'interdisant toute discrimination ou prise de position fondée sur des considérations philosophiques ou politiques. Elle se met en mesure, ainsi de fournir aux contemporains et aux générations futures un moyen fiable d'information sur la part d'histoire partagée par les Français et les Algériens pendant plus d'un siècle, et sur les conséquences proches ou lointaines qui en ont résulté pour les deux pays.

L'Association peut aussi recueillir, dans le même esprit des informations concernant la Tunisie et le Maroc. Pour favoriser la réalisation de son dessein, elle peut s'associer à d'autres institutions analogues d'intérêt spécifiquement culturel. http://www.cdha.fr/index.php?option=com_content&task=view&id=7&Itemid=6. Accessed July 12, 2010.

37. It is not possible to cover all *pied-noir* women's literature of the post-independence period. For a bibliography and discussions of such literature, see Jeanine de La Hogue and Simone Nerbonne, *Mémoire Écrite de l'Algérie depuis 1950: les auteurs et leurs oeuvres* (Paris: Editions Maisonneuve et Larose, 1992); Lucienne Martini, *Racines de papier: essai sur l'expression littéraire de l'identité pieds-noirs* (Paris: Publisud, 1997); Lucienne Martini, *Maux d'exil, mots d'exil: a l'écoute des écritures pieds-noirs* (Nice: Gandini, 2005).

38. For literary and/or feminist criticism of Cardinal's works, see Christina Angelfors, *La double conscience: la prise de conscience féminine chez Colette, Simone de Beauvoir et Marie Cardinal* (Lund, Sweden: Lund University Press, 1989); Lucille Cairns, *Marie Cardinal: Motherhood and Creativity* (Glasgow: University of Glasgow French and German Publications, 1992); Carolyn A. Durham, *The Contexture of Feminism: Marie Cardinal and Multicultural Literacy* (Urbana, IL: University of Illinois Press, 1992); Collette Trout Hall, *Marie Cardinal* (Amsterdam/Atlanta, GA: Rodopoi, 1994); Emma Webb, *Marie Cardinal: New Perspectives* (Oxford/New York: Peter Lang, 2006); Suzanne Dow, *Madness in Twentieth-century French Women's Writing: Leduc, Duras, Beauvoir, Cardinal, Hyvrard* (Oxford: Bern, 2009); Maximilian Gröne, *"Maladie ès lettres" — Krankheitsdarstellungen bei Camus, Giono, Beauvoir, Cardinal und Guibert* (Würsburg: Ergon-Verl., 2006); Alex Hughes, *Heterographies: Sexual Difference in French Autobiography* (Oxford: Berg, 1999); Françoise Lionnet-McCumber, *Autobiographical Tongues: (Self-)reading and (Self-)writing in Augustine, Nietzsche, Maya Angelou, Marie Cardinal, and Marie-Therese Humbert* (Ann Arbor: University Microfilms International, 1986). Numerous MA and PhD theses have also been written about her work. A recent example is Fiona J. Barclay,

"*Postcolonial France?: The Problematisation of Frenchness through North African Immigration: A Literary Study of Metropolitan Novels 1980–2000*" (PhD, University of Glasgow, Glasgow, 2006).

39. "Marie Cardinal" [Obituary], *The Independent*, May 12, 2001. In Salonika she held the post previously held by Michel Butor. See Marie Cardinal and Annie Leclerc, *Autrement dit* (Paris: B. Grasset, 1977), 15–16.

40. Ibid., 14.

41. Ibid., 24.

42. Marie Cardinal, *Les mots pour le dire* (Paris: Grasset, 1975), 238.

43. Ibid.

44. Ibid., 257. The novel is dedicated "to the doctor who helped me to be born."

45. Marie Cardinal, *Amour— amours—* (Paris: B. Grasset, 1998), 10.

46. Ibid., 37–38.

47. Cardinal and Leclerc, *Autrement dit*, 17.

48. Gisèle Halimi and Marie Cardinal, *La cause des femmes* (Paris: B. Grasset, 1973).

49. Cardinal and Leclerc, *Autrement dit*, 114.

50. Ibid., 146.

51. Ibid., 167–168.

52. Gabrielle Spiegel, in a recent article in the *American Historical Review*, stressed the importance of Cold War politics on Derrida's work. In fact, I would argue that his *pied-noir* roots and the traumas of World War II and the Algerian War were far more important to his theories. Gabrielle Spiegel, "The Task of the Historian," *American Historical Review* 114, no. 1 (2009): 1–15. The impact of Algeria on his work is discussed in: Lynne Huffer, "Derrida's Nostalgeria," in *Algeria & France 1800–2000, Identity, Memory, Nostalgia*, ed. Patricia M. E. Lorcin (Syracuse: Syracuse University Press, 2006), 228–246; Safaa Fathy and Jacques Derrida, *Derrida's Elsewhere* (Brooklyn, NY: First Run/Icarus, 1999), Visual Material; Michael Syrotinski, *Deconstruction and the Postcolonial: At the Limits of Theory* (Liverpool: Liverpool University Press, 2007). Works on Cixous include Anne-Emmanuelle Berger, *Algeria in Others' Languages* (Ithaca, IL: Cornell University Press, 2002), Christopher Churchill, "'L'Algérie en je' remembering colonial Algeria in the works of Hélène Cixous and Jacques Derrida" (MA thesis, Queen's University, Kingston, Canada 2001); Lynne Huffer, *Another Look, Another Woman: Retranslations of French Feminism* (New Haven, CT: Yale University Press, 1995); Mireille Rosello, "Remembering the Incomprehensible: Hélène Cixous, Leïla Sebbar, Yamina Benguigui, and the War of Algeria," in *Remembering Africa*, ed. M Elisabeth Mudimbe-boyi (Portsmouth, NH: Heinemann, 2002); and Leïla Sebbar and Alloula Malek, *Une enfance algérienne* (Paris: Gallimard, 1997).

53. In addition to the fiction and nonfiction, a large number of pictorial representations of colonial Algeria were also published. See, for example, Marie Cardinal, *Les Pieds-Noirs* (Paris: Place Furstemberg, 1994); Gérard Guicheteau and Marc Combier, *L'Algérie oubliée: images d'Algérie, 1910–1954* (Paris: Acropole, 2004); Teddy Alzieu, Oran, *Mémoire en images*, (Joué-les-Tours: A. Sutton, 2001); Elisabeth Fechner, *Oran et l'Oranie*, Souvenirs de là-bas (Paris: Calmann-Lévy, 2002); Guy Tudury, *Alger de 1830 à 1962: souvenirs et images d'une ville*, Rediviva (Nîmes: Lacour, 1994).

54. It was claimed that "un roman" had been an editorial error. Jean Déjeux, "Élissa Rhaïs, Conteuse Algérienne (1876–1940)," *Revue de l'Occiddent musulman et de la Mediterranée* 37, no. 1 (1984): 65.

55. Paul Tabet, *Elissa Rhaïs: roman* (Paris: B. Grasset, 1982), 176. Tabet refused my request to interview him.

56. Ibid., 181–182.

57. For an account of the controversy, see Déjeux, "Élissa Rhaïs, Conteuse Algérienne (1876–1940)," 67–74; Mireille Rosello, "Elissa Rhaïs: Scandals, Impostures, Who Owns the Story?," *Research in African Literatures* 37, no. 1 (2006); Emily Apter, "Ethnographic Travesties: Colonial Realism, French Feminism, and the Case of of Elissa Rhaïs," in *After Colonialism, Imperial Histories and Postcolonial displacements*, ed. Gyan Prakash (Princeton, NJ: University of Princeton Press, 1995), 302–306.

58. Apter, "Ethnographic Travesties: Colonial Realism, French Feminism, and the case of of Elissa Rhaïs," 304.

59. Jules Roy, "Le mythe d'une Algérie heureuse," *Le Monde*, June 4, 1982.

60. Jean Déjeux, *Femmes d'Algérie: légendes, traditions, histoire, littérature* (Paris: Boîte à Documents, 1987), 260.

61. Elissa Rhaïs, *Le sein blanc* (Paris: L'Archipel, 1996).

62. Déjeux, "Élissa Rhaïs, Conteuse Algérienne (1876–1940)," 68. Déjeux, who died in 1993 carried out extensive research on the Tabet "affair."

63. Rhaïs, *Le sein blanc;* Elissa Rhaïs, *La fille d'Éléazar* (Paris: L'Archipel, 1997); Elissa Rhaïs, *Le café chantant* (Saint-Denis: Bouchene, 2003); Elissa Rhaïs, *La fille des pachas*, Collection Escales (Saint-Denis, France: Editions Bouchene, 2003); Elissa Rhaïs, *Djelloul de Fés* (Saint-Denis, France: Bouchene, 2004). Otmezguine's film was produced in 1993.

64. Lucienne Jean-Darrouy, "L'Écrivain nomade. Isabelle Eberhardt" under the heading "Union Française. Apports de la Littérature Algérienne" in *L'Algérienne* (1947): 21. Newspaper clipping in CAOM 87APOM/48-Déjeux papers, dossier 229.

65. Mahmoud Bouali, "Une Musulmane anti-conformiste: Isabelle Eberhart" in *L'Action*, vendredi 18 octobre, 1974 Abdel majid Chorfi, "Isabelle Eberhardt s'est devouée à la terre de L'Islam," in *L'Action*, Dimanche 25 janvier 1976. Newspaper clippings in CAOM 87/APOM/48. Déjeux papers, dossier 226.

66. Chorfi, "Isabelle Eberhardt s'est devouée à la terre de l'Islam."

67. Mohamed Hamouda Bensaï, "Honorons la mémoire d'Isabelle Eberhardt "la belle aventureuse des sables," *La Semaine*, no. 78, March 21, 1984. CAOM 87APOM/48-Déjeux papers, dossier 228.

68. Dossier 230 of the Déjeux papers contains dozens of articles and other material written by Algerians in the 1980s and 1990s. Among this material is a poem by Chami Ahmed entitled "A Isabelle Eberhard [sic]."

69. Keltoun Staali, "Entretien avec Farouk Beloufa, "Le Cinéma, c'est la féminité..." *Revolution Africaine*, March 9–15, 1990: 1358. Beloufa was interviewed a week later by Arezki Metref on the same subject. "Farouk Beloufa. Sur les traces d'Eberhardt" in *Algérie-Actualité* March 15–21, 1990: 1274. Both in CAOM 87APOM/48-Déjeux papers, dossier 231.

70. Leslie Thornton, *There Was an Unseen Cloud Moving* (New York: Women Make Movies, 1988), Visual Material; Ian Pringle, *Isabelle Eberhardt le destin scandaleux d'un écrivain qui fut d'abord une aventurière, peut-ére*

une espionne, avant tout une femme libre (Paris: Les Films Aramis [u.a.], 1995), VHS tape. The English version of Pringle's film was first released in 1990. Djafar Damardji, *Errances (ou Terre en Cendres),* Maghreb-Fil, Alger, 1993.

71. Recent works include: Khelifa Benamara, *Isabelle Eberhardt et l'Algérie* (Alger: Editions barzakh, 2005); Marie-Odile Delacour and Jean-René Huleu, *Le voyage soufi d'Isabelle Eberhardt: essai,* Littérature française (Paris: J. Losfeld, 2008); Katherine Sheppard Irvin, "Cross-cultural dressing in Arab lands: Isabelle Eberhardt and T. E. Lawrence" (MS thesis, University of Rhode Island, Kingston, RI, 2004); Jean-Luc Manaud and Catherine Sauvat, *Isabelle Eberhardt et le désert* (Paris: Ed. du Chêne, 2003); Catherine Stoll-Simon, *Si Mahmoud ou la renaissance d'Isabelle Eberhardt* (Alger: Éditions Alpha, 2006).

72. *Yasmina ou "l'oriental Incognito"* by Serge Hureau was performed at the Theatre Musical in March–April 1987. Her reissued writings include Isabelle Eberhardt, *Oeuvres complètes: Écrits sur le sable,* ed. Marie-Odile Delacour and Jean-René Huleu, 2 vols. (Paris: Grasset, 1988).

73. Marie-Odile Delacour and Jean-René Huleu "Rebelle". "Métamorphone sahrienne ver la quête d'absolu" in *Baraka,* March 23, 1986, 3. And Elisabeth Nicolini, "Isabelle Eberhardt. La fascination de l'Islam" in *Jeune Afrique,* 1985, 14, 7–9 both in CAOM 87APOM/48-Déjeux papers, dossier 229.

74. The strip of "Mektoub" was drawn by the Australian illustrator Maria Pena and first published in Fox comics in 1989. It was later published together with three others stories about women travelers in Philip Bentley, *Passionate Nomads: A Collection of Arabian Adventures* (Sandringham, VC: Second Shore, in association with Paper Tableaux, 2006).

75. My thanks to Professor Abderrahmane Moussaoui for drawing my attention to these events. Moussaoui is currently working on the pilgrimage of St. Raphaël. The choice of these sites, both religious establishments dedicated to the Virgin Mary, is due to the fact the cathedral in Algiers, Notre Dame d'Afrique, was similarly dedicated.

76. The 2009 film by Jean-Pierre Carlon, *Paroles de pieds noirs,* encapsulates the themes of colonial nostalgia and is accompanied by the book *Parole des Pieds-Noirs: L'histoire déchirée des français d'Algérie,* Paris, Éditions Montparnasse, 2009.

77. Michael Kimmelman, "Footprints of pieds-noirs reach deep into France," *The New York Times,* March 5, 2009, C1. For an analysis of contemporary pied-noir politics, see Emmanuelle Comtat, *Le comportement politique des pieds-noirs d'Algérie: Étude de cas dans l'Isère,* Documents du C.I.D.S.P.; Série Analyses et commentaires, no. 9 (Grenoble: Institut d'Études politiques de Grenoble, Université Pierre Mendès-France, 2000); Emmanuelle Comtat, *Les pieds-noirs et la politique: quarante ans après le retour,* Sciences Po. Fait politique; Histoire (Paris: Sciences Po, 2009).

78. Denise Morel de Marnand, *Sétif de ma jeunesse* (Nice: Editions J. Gandini, 2001), 13.

79. The official material of governance of the colonies in both France and Britain was of course housed in the National Archives of each country.

80. John J. Tawney, "Personal Thoughts on a Rescue Operation: The Oxford Colonial Records Project," *African Affairs* 67, no. 269 (1968): 345–350.

As early as 1952 two prominent members of the Kenya settler community, Lady McMillan and Lord Cranworth had founded the East African European Pioneers' Society to ensure the preservation of the white history of Kenya. See: C. S. Nicholls, *Red Strangers: The White Tribe of Kenya* (London: Timewell Press, 2005), 253.

81. According to Tawney, some 15,000 known names were targeted with the hoped for result of about 10 percent, a figure which was achieved. Tawney, "Personal Thoughts on a Rescue Operation," 346.

82. Elspeth Joscelin Grant Huxley, *The Flame Trees of Thika: Memories of an African Childhood* (London: Chatto & Windus, 1959). It was published simultaneously in the United States by W. Morrow.

83. In January 1959 the colonial governors of Kenya, Uganda, and Tanganyika met at Chequers to discuss the constitutional future of the three colonies. Alan Lennox-Boyd was then Colonial Secretary and the idea was a slow move to independence over the next 20 years. After the general election of 1959, Iain Macleod replaced Lennox-Boyd and the process was speeded up. My thanks to Roger W. Horrell, O. B. E., C. M. G. for providing me with his insights on the period.

84. Robert S. Cross and Michael Perkin, *Elspeth Huxley: A Bibliography* (New Castle, DE: Oak Knoll Press, 1996), 55.

85. C. S. Nicholls, *Elspeth Huxley: A Biography*, 287.

86. McKenna, later starred in *Born Free,* the biopic of Adamson and her lions.

87. Cross and Perkin, *Elspeth Huxley: A Bibliography*, 55.

88. Laurens van der Post, "White Child's Country," *The Times*, March 5, 1959, 13.

89. Elpeth Huxley, *The Flame Trees of Thika*, 128.

90. Ibid., 83.

91. Ibid., 120.

92. Ibid.

93. Elspeth Joscelin Grant Huxley, *The Mottled Lizard* (London: Chatto & Windus, 1962). It was published in the United States as Elspeth Joscelin Grant Huxley, *On the Edge of the Rift: Memories of Kenya* (New York: Morrow, 1962). My citations come from the U.S. edition.

94. Huxley, *On the Edge of the Rift: Memories of Kenya*, 102–103.

95. Ibid., 299.

96. Elspeth Joscelin Grant Huxley and Hugo van Lawick, *Last Days in Eden* (New York: Amaryllis Press, 1984). Van Lawick had been married to Jane Goodall with whom he published a number of books connected to her research on chimpanzees.

97. Although game parks were established during the colonial period, attitudes toward game were ambiguous. Not only was hunting an important dimension of both settler existence, but during the two wars the settlers indulged in mass slaughter of animals for food both for themselves and, especially during World War II, to feed the prisoners of war (mainly Italians). On hunting and game parks, see Brian Herne, *White Hunters. The Golden Age of African Safaris* (New York: Henry Holt & Co., 1999). For a Marxist take on hunting in East Africa, see Edward I. Steinhart, *Black Poachers, White Hunters: A Social History of Hunting in Colonial Kenya* (Oxford/Nairobi: James Currey, 2006).

98. Huxley and Lawick, *Last Days in Eden*, 169.

99. Ibid., 168.

100. Joy Adamson, *Born Free, a Lioness of Two Worlds* (New York: Pantheon Books, 1960); Joy Adamson, *Living Free: The Story of Elsa and Her Cubs* (New York: Harcourt, Brace & World, 1961); Joy Adamson, *Forever Free* (New York: Harcourt, Brace & World, 1962); Joy Adamson, *The Spotted Sphinx* (New York: Harcourt, Brace & World, 1969); Joy Adamson, *Pippa, the Cheetah, and Her Cubs*, (New York: Harcourt & World, 1970).

101. Adamson illustrated several of the many editions of *Gardening in East Africa*. Arthur John Jex-Blake, *Gardening in East Africa: A Practical Handbook*, 4th ed. (London: New York, 1957); Joy Adamson, Henk Beentje, and Dhan Bhanderi, *Kenya Trees, Shrubs, and Lianas* (Nairobi, Kenya: National Museums of Kenya, 1994). It was published posthumously and contains Adamson's paintings.

102. Joy Adamson, *The Searching Spirit: An Autobiography* (London: Collins and Harvill Press, 1978), 43.

103. It starred Virginia McKenna and Bill Travers and was directed by James H. Hill and distributed by Columbia Pictures. McKenna won a Golden Globe for her portrayal of Adamson.

104. Rhodes House, Micro.Afr.580. Reel 1.Papers of Joy Adamson. 1941, 1948–1979.

105. Adamson, *The Searching Spirit: An Autobiography*, 226.

106. Ibid., Adamson, *The Spotted Sphinx*; Adamson, *Pippa, the Cheetah, and Her Cubs*.

107. Researchers from the United Kingdom and the United States, some of whom were encouraged like Adamson by Louis Leakey, joined the ranks of former settlers interested in conservation: Jane Goodall, the Douglas-Hamiltons, Diane Fossey, to name but a few.

108. Kuki Gallmann, *African Nights* (London: Perennial/Harper Collins, 2000).

109. Ibid., 35.

110. Ibid., 144. In fact Cole sold off his estate in smallish plots to Africans.

111. Ibid., 41.

112. Joan Root (1937–2006) was a renowned wildlife film-maker and ardent conservationist. Her 1978 documentary *Mysterious Castles of Clay* about termites was nominated for an Academy Award for Best Documentary Feature. She introduced Dian Fossey to the gorillas and, like Fossey, was murdered. Both Oria Douglas-Hamilton and Mirella Ricciardi are writers whose works on Kenya have had considerable success. See Lorenzo Ricciardi & Mirella Ricciardi, *African Rainbow: Across Africa by Boat* (London: Ebury Press, 1989); Mirella Ricciardi, *Vanishing Africa* (New York: Reynal, with Morrow, 1971); Mirella Ricciardi, *African Saga* (London: Collins, 1981); Mirella Ricciardi, *African Visions: The Diary of an African Photographer* (London: Cassell, 2000); Iain Douglas-Hamilton, Oria Douglas-Hamilton, and Brian Jackman, *Battle for the Elephants* (New York: Viking, 1992); Iain Douglas-Hamilton and Oria Douglas-Hamilton, *Among the Elephants* (New York: Viking Press, 1975); Oria Douglas-Hamilton, *The Elephant Family Book* (Saxonville, MA: Picture Book Studio, 1990). Ricciardi is discussed below.

113. Gallmann, *African Nights*, 70.

114. Ibid., 224.

115. http://www.Gallmannnkenya.org/ Accessed August 28, 2009.
116. Gallmann, *African Nights*, 154; ibid.
117. Ibid., 229.
118. For example, "Mwtua, The Story of Osman, The Story of Rehema, etc. Gallmann, *African Nights*.
119. Ibid., 282.
120. The term is Rítívoí's from Andreea Decíu Rítívoí, *Yesterday's Self: Nostalgia and the Immigrant Identity* (Lanham, MD: Rowman & Littlefield, 2002).
121. Ricciardi's base is in London, where, according to her website, "Her nondescript terraced house has been turned into an African haven filled with light, African artefacts and rambling plants." http://www.mirellaricciardi.com/bio.html accessed September 2, 2009.
122. Ricciardi, *African Visions: The Diary of an African Photographer*, 14.
123. Ibid., 7.
124. Ibid., 15.
125. Ibid., 38–39. For a memoir of a child of one of the members of the Happy Valley set, see Juanita Carberry and Nicola Tyrer, *Child of Happy Valley* (London: William Heinemann, 1999).
126. Ricciardi, *African Visions: The Diary of an African Photographer*, 10.
127. Ibid., 64.
128. Ibid., 9.
129. Ibid., 258.
130. Nicholls, *Red strangers: the white tribe of Kenya*.
131. Ibid., xiii.
132. Ibid., 244–255.
133. Ibid., 254.
134. Ibid., 278.
135. See, for example, Rítívoí, *Yesterday's Self: Nostalgia and the Immigrant Identity*. Christopher Shaw and Malcolm Chase, *The Imagined Past: History and Nostalgia* (New York: Manchester University Press, 1989); Svetlana Boym, *The Future of Nostalgia* (New York: Basic Books, 2001).
136. Such as Elspeth Joscelin Grant Huxley, *White Man's Country: Lord Delamere and the Making of Kenya* (London: Macmillan and Co., 1935); Elspeth Joscelin Grant Huxley, *Settlers of Kenya* (London: New York, Longmans, Green, 1948); Elspeth Joscelin Grant Huxley and Arnold Curtis, *Pioneers' Scrapbook: Reminiscences of Kenya, 1890 to 1968* (London: Evans Bros., 1980).
137. Rítívoí, *Yesterday's Self: Nostalgia and the Immigrant Identity*, 4–5.
138. Ricciardi, *African Visions: The Diary of an African Photographer*, 7.
139. Monique Ayoun, *Mon Algérie: [62 personnalités témoignent]* (Paris: Acropole, 1989); Geneviève Fournier-Giusti, *Pardon, mon Algérie: tranche de vie* (Angicourt: Editions 1900–2050, 2004); Jean-Claude Brialy, *Mon Algérie* (Boulogne-Billancourt Timée Editions, 2006); Enrico Assouline Florence Macias, *Mon Algérie* (Paris: Plon, 2001); François Molines, *C'était mon Algérie* (Marseille: F. Molines, 1973); Jean-Pierre Pellerin, *Mon Algérie* (Paris: Thélès, 2004). Most recently, there is even a community facebook page: TOUS LES PIEDS NOIRS D'ALGERIE. (http://www.facebook.com/group.php?gid=55067334781) accessed March 25, 2011.

CONCLUSION

1. Robert Randau, "L'exoticisme et l'Hourisilencieuse" CAOM 75APOM/16-Fonds Arnaud-Randau.
2. Henry Rousso, *The Vichy Syndrome: History and Memory in France since 1944/(Syndrome de Vichy)* (Cambridge: Harvard University Press, 1991), 114.

BIBLIOGRAPHY

ARCHIVAL SOURCES

Centre des Archives d'Outre-Mer, Aix-en Provence

30MIOM—PRESS
30MIOM/28, 36 & 37—Akhbar
30MIOM/31-Annales Africaines
30MIOM/320-Echo Alger
75APOM—Fonds Arnaud-Randau
75APOM/16, 18, 19, 39, 43, 45, 49–51
87APOM—Papiers Jean Déjeux
87APOM/48-Eberhardt
87APOM/54-Rhais
87APOM/56-Théâtre
87APOM/75-Femmes
87APOM/76-Femmes Ecrivains
75 APOM 39—SERIE X-31-Eberhardt
SERIE X-31/MIOM/31
SERIE X-31/MIOM/32
SERIE X-31/MIOM/17—Lyautey

Centre des Archives du Féminisme, Angers

Cécile Brunschvicg Papers:
Fonds CB/1AF 131–134, 159–160, 184, 189, 317–323, 473, 501–517, 544, 641, & 661
Union Féminine Civique et Sociale
16AF459–463

Archives de la Préfecture de Paris

Boxes: GA-U2; BA/1651–90.772.1 & 90.772.4; BA/2005; DA768

Archives de la Bibliothèque Marguerite Durand, Paris

DOS 396 AFR: Femmes-Afrique du Nord
DOS 396 ALG: 1891–1990
DOS AUC: Hubertine Auclert
DOS BOI: Magali-Boisnard

DOS CAP: Marcelle Capy
DOS CAR: Marie Cardinal
DOS CEL: Henriette Célarie
DOS CHI: Clotilde Chivas-Baron
DOS FAV: Lucienne Favre
DOS HEL: Maximilienne Heller
DOS RHAIS: Elissa Rhaïs
DOS VER: Marie Vérone, Box 1, Files 3–4

Rhodes House Archives, Oxford

MSS. Afr. s. 595: Kenya Association
MSS. Afr.s.1424-Delamere
MSS.Afr.s.594-Convention of Associations
MSS.Afr.s.633-Indian Question & Letters
MSS.Afr.s.782-Oxford Colonial Project—Papers of Elspeth Josceline Huxley, Boxes 1 & 3
MSS.Afr.s.1456-East African European Pioneers' society
MSS.Afr.s.1607-Photos
MSS.Afr.s.1670(1)-Longleat Estate
MSS.Afr.s.1849-Colchester
MSS.Afr.s.2179-Transcript of Interview of Iain Macleod, M.P. Sec. of State for the Colonies
MSS.British Empire s.365-Fabian Colonial Bureau

Women's Manuscripts and Letters

Micr.Afr.580: Adamson
Micr.Af.585: Buxton
Micr.Afr.589: Henn
Micr.Afr.591: Klapprott
Micr.Afr.607 (4): Mayers
MF.Afr.578: Scott, Lord & Lady F.
MSS.Afr.424: Jardine
MSS.Afr.s.504: Dobbs
MSS.Afr.s.950: Brindley
MSS.Afr.s.1058: La Vie Platts
MSS.Afr.s.1217: Macnaghten
MSS.Afr.s.1418: Armstrong
MSS.Afr.s.1558: Elkington
MSS.Afr.s.2018: Hill-Williams
MSS.Afr.s. 2154-Huxley Papers—Boxes 1–4,7, 10, 12, 13, 15
MSS.Afr.s.2199: Casey
MSS.Afr.s.2318: Hammond

Interviews at Oxford of Former Settlers

Christine Nicholls, interviewed on July 13, 2005, in Oxford
Joan Considine, interviewed on July 18, 2005, in Oxford

Shereen Karmali, interviewed on August 6, 2005, in Oxford
Juanita Carberry, interviewed on August 9, 2005, in London

Journals and Periodicals Consulted in the Bibliothèque Nationale and at Rhodes House

Annales Coloniales
East African Standard
France-Afrique
Journal Officiel de l'Algérie
La Française
La Nouvelle Dépeche
Minerve
Romanciers Coloniaux

PUBLISHED WORKS

Abi-Mershed, Osama. *Apostles of Modernity: Saint-Simonians and the Civilizing Mission in Algeria.* Stanford: Stanford University Press, 2010.

Ackerman, Gerald M. *Les Orientalistes de L'école Britannique.* Paris: ACR Edition, 1991.

Adamson, George. *My Pride and Joy.* New York: Simon and Schuster, 1987.

Adamson, Joy. *Born Free, a Lioness of Two Worlds.* New York: Pantheon Books, 1960.

———. *Forever Free.* New York: Harcourt, Brace & World, 1962.

———. *Joy Adamson's Africa.* New York: Harcourt Brace Jovanovich, 1972.

———. *Living Free; the Story of Elsa and Her Cubs.* New York: Harcourt, Brace & World, 1961.

———. *Pippa, the Cheetah, and Her Cubs.* New York: Harcourt, Brace & World, 1970.

———. *The Searching Spirit: An Autobiography.* London: Collins and Harvill Press, 1978.

———. *The Spotted Sphinx.* New York: Harcourt, Brace & World, 1969.

Adamson, Joy, Henk Beentje, and Dhan Bhanderi. *Kenya Trees, Shrubs, and Lianas.* Nairobi, Kenya: National Museums of Kenya, 1994.

Adas, Michael. *Machines as the Measure of Men: Science, Technology, and Ideologies of Western Dominance,* Ithaca: Cornell University Press, 1989.

Ageron, Charles Robert. *De L'insurrection de 1871 au Déclenchement de la Guerre de Libération (1954).* Histoire de l'Algérie Contemporaine; T. 2; Paris: Presses universitaires de France, 1979.

Ageron, Charles-Robert. *De l'Algérie "Française" à l'Algérie Algérienne.* Paris: Éditions Bouchene, 2005.

———. *Les Algériens Musulmans et la France (1871–1919).* 2 vols. Paris: Presses Universitaires de France, 1968.

Ahmed, Saad Noah. "Desert Quest: French and British Writers in Arabia and North Africa, 1850–1950." Dissertation: Thesis (Ph. D.)—University of Illinois at Urbana-Champaign, 1983.

Aitken, Susan Hardy. *Isak Dinesen and the Engendering of Narrative.* Chicago: University of Chicago Press, 1990.

Alexander, Martin S., Martin Evans, and John F. V. Keiger. *The Algerian War and the French Army: Experiences, Images, Testimonies.* New York: Palgrave Macmillan, 2002.

Alexander, Martin S., and John F. V. Keiger. *France and the Algerian War, 1954–1962: Strategy, Operations and Diplomacy*. London: Frank Cass Publishers, 2002.

Alleg, Henri. *La Guerre d'Algérie*. 3 vols. Paris: Temps actuels, 1981.

———. *The Question*. Lincoln: University of Nebraska Press, 2006.

Alloula, Malek. *The Colonial Harem*. Manchester: Manchester University Press, 1987.

Almi, Saïd. *Urbanisme et Colonisation: Présence Française en Algérie*, Librairie de L'architecture et de la Ville; Sprimont, Belgique: Mardaga, 2002.

Altbach, Philip G., and Gail Paradise Kelly. *Education and the Colonial Experience*. New Brunswick, NJ: Transaction Books, 1984.

Alzieu, Teddy. *Alger et Oran: Images d'Algérie de 1900 à 1960*, Saint-Cyr-sur-Loire: Alan Sutton, 2006.

———. *Oran*, Joué-les-Tours: A. Sutton, 2001.

Ames, Glenn J., and Love, Ronald S., eds. *Distant Lands and Diverse Cultures. The French Experience in Asia 1600–1700*. Westport/London: Praeger, 2003.

Amrane, Djamila. *Des Femmes Dans la Guerre d'Algérie: Entretiens*. Paris: Karthala, 1994.

Amrouche, Fadhma A. M. *Histoire de Ma Vie*. Domaine Maghrébin;. Paris: F. Maspero, 1968.

Amrouche, Marguerite Taos. *L'amant Imaginaire: Roman*. Paris: Editions Robert Morel, 1975.

Amrouche, Marguerite Taos. *Le Grain Magique. Contes, Poèmes et Proverbes Berbéres de Kabylie*. Paris: N.P., 1966.

———. *Rue des Tambourins*. Paris: La Table Ronde, 1960.

Amrouche, Marie Louise. *Jacinthe Noire, Roman*. Paris: Charlot, 1947.

Anderson, David. *Histories of the Hanged. Britain's Dirty War in Kenya and the End of Empire*. London: Weidenfeld & Nicolson, 2005.

Anderson, John. *The Struggle for the School: The Interaction of Missionary, Colonial Government, and Nationalist Enterprise in the Development of Formal Education in Kenya*. London: Longman, 1970.

Angelfors, Christina. *La Double Conscience. La Prise de Conscience Feminine Chez Colette, Simone de Beauvoir et Marie Cardinal*. Lund: Lund University Press, 1989.

Apter, Emily. "Ethnographic Travesties: Colonial Realism, French Feminism, and the Case of of Elissa Rhaïs." in *After Colonialism, Imperial Histories and Postcolonial Displacements*, ed. Gyan Prakash. Princeton: University of Princeton Press, 1995.

Ardener, Shirley. *Women and Space: Ground Rules and Social Maps*. New York: St. Martin's Press, 1981.

Arnaud, Georges, and Jacques Vergès. *Pour Djamila Bouhired*. Documents. Paris: Ed. de Minuit, 1957.

Arnaud, Jacqueline, Déjeux Jean, and Arlette Roth. *Anthologie des Écrivains Français Du Maghreb*. Paris: Présense africaine, 1969.

Arnold, Dana. *Cultural Identities and the Aesthetics of Britishness*. Studies in Imperialism. Manchester: University of Manchester Press, 2004.

Attal, Robert. *Les Émeutes de Constantine: 5 Août 1934*. Paris: Romillat, 2002.

Auclert, Hubertine. *Les Femmes Arabes en Algérie*. Paris: Société d'Éditions littéraires, 1900.

Audisio, Gabriel. *Héliotrope*. Paris: Gallimard, 1928.

————. *Jeunesse de la Méditerranée.* 2 vols. Vol. II Sel de Mer. Paris: Gallimard, 1935.

August, Thomas G. *The Selling of the Empire: British and French Imperialist Propaganda, 1890–1940.* Westport, CT: Greenwood Press, 1985.

Austin, Linda Marilyn. *Nostalgia in Transition, 1780–1917,* Charlottesville: University of Virginia Press, 2007.

Baïlac, Geneviève. *La Famille Hernandez: L'algérie Heureuse.* Paris: R. Lafont, 1979.

————. *La Famille Hernandez. Théâtre Complet.* Paris: Club du Souvenir, 1966.

————. *La Maison des Soeurs Gomez; Roman.* Paris: R. Julliard, 1958.

————. *Les Absinthes Sauvages; Témoignage Pour le Peuple Pieds-Noirs.* Paris: Fayard, 1972.

————.*Les Grands Jours D'alger.* Alger: La Maison des Livres, 1960.

Bailey, David A., and Gilane Tawadros. *Veil: Veiling, Representation, and Contemporary Art.* Cambridge: MIT Press, 2003.

Bal, Mieke, Jonathan Crewe, and Leo Spitzer, eds. *Acts of Memory. Cultural Recall in the Present.* Hanover/London: University Press of New England, 1999.

Ballantyne, Tony, and Antoinette M. Burton. *Bodies in Contact: Rethinking Colonial Encounters in World History.* Durham: Duke University Press, 2005.

Ballhatchet, Kenneth. *Race, Sex and Class under the Raj: Imperial Attitudes and Policies and Their Critics, 1793–1905.* London: Weidenfeld and Nicolson, 1980.

Barclay, Fiona J. "Postcolonial France? The Problematisation of Frenchness through North African Immigration: A Literary Study of Metropolitan Novels 1980–2000." PhD, University of Glasgow, 2006.

Barnes, Terri. "*We Women Worked So Hard*": *Gender, Urbanization, and Social Reproduction in Colonial Harare, Zimbabwe, 1930–1956.* Portsmouth, NH: Heinemann, 1999.

Baroli, Marc. *La Vie Quotidienne des Français en Algérie 1830–1914.* Paris: Hachette, 1967.

Beard, Peter H., and Jacqueline Bouvier Onassis. Afterword. *Longing for Darkness: Kamante's Tales from out of Africa.* San Francisco: Chronicle Books, 1990.

Beaulieu, Jill, and Mary Roberts. *Orientalism's Interlocutors: Painting, Architecture, Photography.* Durham: Duke University Press, 2003.

Beauvoir, Simone de, and Gisèle Halimi. *Djamila Boupacha, the Story of the Torture of a Young Algerian Girl Which Shocked Liberal French Opinion.* New York: Macmillan, 1962.

Bedjaoui, Youcef, Abbas Aroua, and Méziane Aït-Larbi. *An Inquiry into the Algerian Massacres.* Plan-les-Ouates (Genève): Hoggar, 1999.

Behad, Ali. *Belated Travelers. Orientalism in the Age of Colonial Dissolution.* ed. Stanley Fish and Fredric Jameson. Durham & London: Duke University Press, 1994.

Behlmer, George K., and F. M. Leventhal, eds. *Singular Continuities: Tradition, Nostalgia, and Identity in Modern British Culture.* San Francisco: Stanford University Press, 2000.

Bell, Morag, R. A. Butlin, and Michael J. Heffernan. *Geography and Imperialism, 1820–1940,* Manchester: Manchester University Press, 1995.

Benamara, Khelifa. *Isabelle Eberhardt et l'Algérie.* Alger: Editions Barzakh, 2005.

Bennoune, Mahfoud. *The Making of Contemporary Algeria 1830–1987.* Cambridge: Cambridge University Press, 2002.

Benstock, Shari. *Women of the Left Bank. Paris 1900–1940.* Austin: University of Texas Press, 1986.

Bentley, Philip. *Passionate Nomads: A Collection of Arabian Adventures.* Sandringham, Vic.: Second Shore in association with Paper Tableaux, 2006.

Berenson, Edward, and Eva Giloi, eds. *Constructing Charisma. Celebrity, Fame and Power in Nineteenth-Century Europe.* New York/Oxford: Berghahn Books, 2010.

Berger, Anne-Emmanuelle. *Algeria in Others' Languages.* Ithaca: Cornell University Press, 2002.

Berman, Bruce, and John Lonsdale. *Unhappy Valley: Conflict in Kenya and Africa.* London: J. Currey, 1992.

Bertrand, Louis. *Le Sang des Races.* Paris: P. Ollendorff, 1899.

———. *Pépéte, le Bien-Aimé.* Paris: A. Fayard et cie, 1909.

Betham-Edwards, Matilda. *A Winter with the Swallows.* London: Hurst and Blackett, 1867.

Betts, Raymond F. *Assimilation and Association in French Colonial Theory, 1890–1914.* New York: Columbia University Press, 1961.

Bhavnani, Kum-Kum, ed. *Feminism and Race.* Oxford: Oxford University Press, 2001.

Bickers, Robert A. *Settlers and Expatriates: Britons over the Seas,* Oxford: Oxford University Press, 2010.

Billy, André. *La Muse Aux Besicles.* Paris: Renaissance du Livre, 1920.

"Birch for the Boys. An Evening out with a Pony and Cart." *Eastern Morning News,* September 16, 1911.

Birkett, Dea. *Spinsters Abroad: Victorian Lady Explorers.* Oxford: Blackwell, 1989.

Bissell, William Cunningham. "Engaging Colonial Nostalgia." *Cultural Anthropology* 20, no. 2 (2005): 215–248.

Bjørnvig, Thorkild. *The Pact: My Friendship with Isak Dinesen.* Baton Rouge: Louisiana State University Press, 1983.

Black, Edwin. *War against the Weak: Eugenics and America's Campaign to Create a Master Race.* New York: Thunder's Mouth Press, 2004.

Blanch, Lesley. *The Wilder Shores of Love.* New York: Simon and Schuster, 1954.

Blixen, Karen. *Letters from Africa 1914–1931.* Trans. Anne Born, ed. Frans Lasson. London: Picador, 1986.

Blunt, Alison. *Travel, Gender, and Imperialism: Mary Kingsley and West Africa,* New York: Guilford Press, 1994.

Blunt, Alison, and Gillian Rose. *Writing Women and Space: Colonial and Postcolonial Geographies,* New York: Guilford Press, 1994.

Boddy, Janice. *Civilizing Women. British Crusades in Colonial Sudan.* Princeton: Princeton University Press, 2007.

Bodichon, Barbara Leigh Smith. *Algeria; Considered as a Winter Residence for the English.* London: English Woman's Journal Office, 1858.

Bodichon, Eugène. *Considérations Sur l'Algérie.* Paris: Comptoir Central de la Librairie, 1845.

———. *Études Sur l'Algérie et L'afrique.* Algiers: Chez l'Auteur, 1847.

———. *Hygiène à Suivre en Algérie. Acclimatement des Européens.* Algiers: Delavigne, 1851.

Boisnard, Magali. *L'alerte Au Désert: la Vie Saharienne Pendant la Guerre 1914–1916.* Paris: Perrin, 1916.

———. *L'enfant Taciturne: Roman.* Amiens: Malfère, 1922.

———. *Le Roman de Khaldoun.* 3. Èd. ed. Paris: H. Piazza, 1930.

———. *Le Roman de la Kahena, D'aprés les Anciens Textes Arabes.* Paris: L'Édition d'Art, 1925.

————. *Les Endormies*. Paris: Sansot, 1909.

————. *Mâadith*. Amiens: Malfère, 1921.

————. *Sultans de Touggourt*. Paris: Geuther, 1933.

Boittin, Jennifer Anne. *Colonial Metropolis: The Urban Grounds of Anti-Imperialism and Feminism in Interwar Paris*, Lincoln: University of Nebraska Press, 2010.

————. "Exotic Mediators: French Feminists and Women Writers on Colonial North Africa, 1921–1939." *Gender & History* 22, no. 1 (2010): 131–150.

Bongie, Chris. *Exotic Memories: Literature, Colonialism, and the Fin de Siècle*. San Francisco: Stanford University Press, 1991.

Booth, Howard J., and Nigel Rigby. *Modernism and Empire*. Manchester: New York, 2000.

Boris, Eileen, and Angélique Janssens, eds. *Complicating Categories: Gender, Class, Race and Ethnicity*. Cambridge: Cambridge University Press, 1999.

Bourdieu, Pierre. *The Algerians*. Boston: Beacon Press, 1962.

Boym, Svetlana. *The Future of Nostalgia*. New York: Basic Books, 2001.

Brac de La Perrière, Caroline. *Derrière les Héros: les Employées de Maison Musulmanes en Service Chez les Européens à Alger Pendant la Guerre d'Algérie, 1954–1962*, Paris: L'Harmattan, 1987.

Bracco, Hélène. *Pour Avoir Dit Non: Actes de Refus Dans la Guerre d'Algérie, 1954–1962*, Documents et Témoignages. Paris: Paris-Méditerranée, 2003.

Brady, Thomas F. "French Crisis: Seen from Algiers." *The New York Times*, May 18, 1958.

Brahimi, Denise. *Femmes Au Pays: Effets de la Migration Sur les Femmes Dans les Cultures Méditerranéennes*. Paris: Unesco, 1985.

————. *Requiem Pour Isabelle*. Paris: Publisud, 1983.

Branch, Daniel. *Defeating Mau Mau, Creating Kenya: Counterinsurgency, Civil War, and Decolonization*, New York: Cambridge, 2009.

Branche, Raphaëlle. *La Guerre d'Algérie: Une Histoire Apaisée?* Paris: Editions du Seuil, 2005.

————. *La Torture et L'armée Pendant la Guerre d'Algérie: 1954–1962*. Paris: Gallimard, 2001.

Breuer, William B. *Operation Torch: The Allied Gamble to Invade North Africa*. New York: St. Martin's Press, 1985.

Brialy, Jean-Claude. *Mon Algérie*. Boulogne-Billancourt: Timée Editions, 2006.

Bridge, Carl, and Kent Fedorowich, eds. *The British World: Diaspora, Culture, and Identity*. Portland: F. Cass, 2003.

Broberg, Gunnar, and Nils Roll-Hansen, eds. *Eugenics and the Welfare State: Sterilization Policy in Denmark, Sweden, Norway, and Finland*. East Lansing: Michigan State University Press, 1996.

Brodhurst-Hill, Evelyn. *So This Is Kenya!* London: Blackie & Son, 1936.

————. *The Youngest Lion; Early Farming Days in Kenya*. London: Hutchinson, 1934.

Brower, Benjamin Claude. *A Desert Named Peace: The Violence of France's Empire in the Algerian Sahara, 1844–1902*. New York: Columbia University Press, 2009.

Buettner, Elizabeth. *Empire Families: Britons and Late Imperial India*. New York: Oxford University Press, 2004.

Bugéja, Marie. *Coeur de Kabyle: Roman*. Tanger: Ed. internat., 1939.

————. *Dans la Tièdeur de la Tente, Roman*. Alger: Éditions de la "Typographie d'art," 1933.

————. *Du Vice à la Vertu; Roman D'une Nailia*. Paris: Editions Argo, 1932.

———. *Enigme Musulmane. Lettres à Une Bretonne.* Tangiers/Fez: Editions internationales Pierre André, 1938.

———. *Femmes Voilées, Hommes- de Même: (Récits et Impressions de L'extrème Sud Algérien).* Alger: Baconnier frères, 1935.

———. *Le Feu Du Maroc; Récits de Guerre et Réalités Du Présent.* Tanger: Éditions internationales, 1936.

———. *Nos Soeurs Musulmanes.* Paris: La revue des Études littéraires, 1921.

———. *Séduction Orientale: Roman.* Alger: P. et G. Soubiron, 1931.

Burdett, Carolyn. *Olive Schreiner and the Progress of Feminism: Evolution, Gender, Empire.* New York: Palgrave, 2001.

Burke, Edmund, Ira M. Lapidus, and Ervand Abrahamian. *Islam, Politics, and Social Movements,* Comparative Studies on Muslim Societies. Berkeley: University of California Press, 1988.

Burke, Edmund, and David Prochaska. *Genealogies of Orientalism: History, Theory, Politics.* Lincoln: University of Nebraska Press, 2008.

Burton, Antoinette M. *After the Imperial Turn: Thinking with and through the Nation.* Durham: Duke University Press, 2003.

———. *Burdens of History: British Feminists, Indian Women, and Imperial Culture, 1865–1915.* Chapel Hill: University of North Carolina Press, 1994.

———. *Dwelling in the Archive: Women Writing House, Home, and History in Late Colonial India.* Oxford: Oxford University Press, 2003.

———. *Gender, Sexuality and Colonial Modernities.* London / New York: Routledge, 1999.

Cairns, Lucille. *Marie Cardinal: Motherhood and Creativity.* Glasgow: University of Glasgow French and German Publications, 1992.

Callaway, Helen. *Gender, Culture, and Empire: European Women in Colonial Nigeria.* Urbana: University of Illinois Press, 1987.

Campbell, Chloe. *Race and Empire: Eugenics in Colonial Kenya.* Manchester: University of Manchester Press, 2007.

Camus, Albert. *Noces, Suivi de L'eté.* Paris: Gallimard, 1959.

Cannadine, David. *Ornamentalism: How the British Saw Their Empire.* Oxford/ New York: Oxford University Press, 2002.

Cantier, Jacques, and Eric Thomas Jennings. *L'empire Colonial Sous Vichy.* Paris: Odile Jacob, 2004.

Capy, Marcelle. *Le Droit et le Devoir des Femmes.* Paris: Editions de la Voix des Femmes, 1925.

Carberry, Juanita, and Nicola Tyrer. *Child of Happy Valley.* London: William Heinemann, 1999.

Cardinal, Marie. *Amour—Amours—.* Paris: B. Grasset, 1998.

———. *Au Pays de Mes Racines.* Paris: Grasset, 1980.

———. *Écoutez la Mer.* Paris: R. Julliard, 1962.

———. *Le Passé Empiété,* Le Livre de Poche. Paris: Grasset, 1983.

———. *Les Mots Pour le Dire.* Paris: Grasset, 1975.

———. *The Words to Say It: An Autobiographical Novel/Uniform Title: Mots Pour le Dire. English.* Cambridge, Mass.: VanVactor & Goodheart, 1983.

Cardinal, Marie, and Baconnier Béatrix. *Les Pieds-Noirs.* Paris: Belfond, 1988.

Cardinal, Marie, and Annie Leclerc. *Autrement Dit.* Paris: B. Grasset, 1977.

Cardinal, Marie, with notes by Lidia Parodi & Marina Vallacco. *La Clé Sur la Porte.* Genova: Cideb, 1993.

Cardinal, Marie, and Jean Luc Godard, Preface. "Deux ou trois choses que je sais". *Cet Été-Là.* Paris: Nouvelles Éditions Oswald, 1985.

Carlon, Jean-Pierre. *Paroles de Pieds-Noirs*. Paris, Editions Montparnasse, 2009. Visual Material.

———. *Pieds-Noirs: Il y a Quarante Ans Déjà L'histoire Déchirée des Français d'Algérie*. Paris: Montparnasse Editions, 2009.

Casey, Mary, Louise De Bruin, and Judith M. Lang. *A Net in Water: A Selection from the Journals*. Bath, Somerset: Powys Press, 1994.

Célarie, Henriette. *Nos Soeurs Musulmanes. Scènes de la Vie Du Désert*. Paris: Hachette, 1925.

Çelik, Zeynep. "Colonialism, Orientalism and the Canon." *Art Bulletin* 78, no. 2 (1996): 202–206.

———. *Urban Forms and Colonial Confrontations: Algiers under French Rule*. Berkeley: University of California Press, 1997.

Çelik, Zeynep, Julia Ann Clancy-Smith, and Frances Terpak, eds. *Walls of Algiers: Narratives of the City through Text and Image*. Los Angeles: Getty Research Institute, 2009.

Certeau, Michel de. *Heterologies: Discourse on the Other*. Minneapolis: University of Minnesota Press, 1986.

———. *The Practice of Everyday Life*. Berkeley: University of California Press, 1984.

Chadwick, Whitney, and Tirza True Latimer. *The Modern Woman Revisited: Paris between the Wars*. New Brunswick: Rutgers University Press, 2003.

Chailley-Bert, Joseph. *L'émigration des Femmes Aux Colonies*. Paris: A. Colin & Cie., 1897.

Chakrabarty, Dipesh. *Provincializing Europe. Postcolonial Thought and Historical Difference*. Princeton: Princeton University Press, 2000.

Chaudhuri, Nupur, and Margaret Strobel. *Western Women and Imperialism: Complicity and Resistance*. Bloomington: Indiana University Press, 1992.

Cherry, Deborah. "Earth into World, Land into Landscape: The 'Worlding' of Algeria in Nineteenth-Century British Feminism." In *Orientalism's Interlocutors: Painting, Architecture, Photography*, ed. Jill Beaulieu and Mary Roberts, 103–130. Durham: Duke University Press, 2003.

Chevalier, H. Emile. *Les Pieds-Noirs*. Paris: Calmann Lévy, 1898.

Chrisman, Laura. *Rereading the Imperial Romance: British Imperialism and South African Resistance in Haggard, Schreiner, and Plaatje*. Oxford/New York: Oxford University Press, 2000.

Churchill, Christopher. "L'algérie en je' Remembering Colonial Algeria in the Works of Hélène Cixous and Jacques Derrida." MA; Queen's University, 2001.

Clancy-Smith, Julia Ann. "Changing Perspectives on the Historiography of Imperialism: Women, Gender and Empire." in *Middle East Historiographies: Narrating the Twentieth Century*, eds. Israel Gershoni, Amy Singer, and Y. Hakan Erdem. Seattle: University of Washington Press, 2006.

———. *Exemplary Women and Sacred Journeys: Women and Gender in Judaism, Christianity, and Islam from Late Antiquity to the Eve of Modernity*. Washington, D. C.: American Historical Association, 2006.

———. "Exoticism, Erasures, and Absence. The Peopling of Algiers, 1830–1900." In *Walls of Algiers. Narratives of the City through Text and Image*, ed. Zeynep Çelick, Julia Clancy-Smith, and Frances Terpak. Seattle: University of Washington Press, 2009.

———. "Islam, Gender, and Identities in the Making of French Algeria, 1830–1962." In *Domesticating the Empire: Race, Gender, and Family Life in*

French and Dutch Colonialism, ed. Julia Clancy-Smith and Frances Gouda. Charlottesville: University Press of Virginia, 1998.

———. "L'école Rue Du Pacha, Tunis: L'ensignement de la Femme Arabe et 'la Plus Grande France (1900–1914)'." *Clio, Histoire, Femmes et Sociétés* 12, (2000): 33–55.

———. "La Femme Arabe: Women and Sexuality in France's North African Empire." In *Women, the Family and Divorce Laws in Islamic History*, ed. Amira El Azhary Sonbol, 357. Syracuse: Syracuse University Press, 1996.

———. "Le Regard Colonial: Islam, Genre et Identités Dans la Fabrication de l'Algérie Française, 1830–1962." *Nouvelles Questions Féministes* 25, no. 1 (2006).

———. *Mediterraneans: North Africa and Europe in an Age of Migration 1800–1900*. Berkeley: University of California Press, 2010.

———. ed. *North Africa, Islam, and the Mediterranean World: From the Almoravids to the Algerian War*. Portland: Frank Cass, 2001.

———. "Rebel and Saint: Muslim Notables, Populist Protest, Colonial Encounters (Algeria and Tunisia, 1800–1904)." Berkeley: University of California Press, 1994.

———. "The House of Zainab: Female Authority and Saintly Succession in Colonial Algeria." In *Women in Middle Eastern History: Shifting Boundaries in Sex and Gender*, eds. Nikki R. Keddie and Beth Baron. 254–272. New Haven: Yale University Press, 1993.

Clancy-Smith, Julia Ann, and Frances Gouda, eds. *Domesticating the Empire: Race, Gender, and Family Life in French and Dutch Colonialism*. Charlottesville, VA: University Press of Virginia, 1998.

Clough, Marshall S. "Fighting Two Sides: Kenyan Chiefs and Politicians, 1918–1940." Niwot, Colorado: University of Colorado Press, 1990.

Codell, Julie F. *Imperial Co-Histories: National Identities and the British and Colonial Press*. Madison/London: Fairleigh Dickinson University Press; Associated University Presses, 2003.

Cole, Eleanor. *Random Recollections of a Pioneer Kenya Settler*, 1975.

"Colony and Protectorate of Kenya." In *Colonial Report*, London, 1922.

"Colony and Protectorate of Kenya." In *Colonial Report*, 1929.

Comtat, Emmanuelle. *Les Pieds-Noirs et la Politique: Quarante Ans Après le Retour*, Sciences Paris: Sciences Po, 2009.

Conklin, Alice L. *A Mission to Civilize: The Republican Idea of Empire in France and West Africa, 1895–1930*. Stanford: Stanford University Press, 1997.

Connelly, Matthew James. *A Diplomatic Revolution: Algeria's Fight for Independence and the Origins of the Post–Cold War Era*. Oxford: Oxford University Press, 2002.

Cooper, Frederick. *Colonialism in Question. Theory, Knowledge, History*. Berkeley: University of California Press, 2005.

Cooper, Frederick, and Ann Laura Stoler. *Tensions of Empire: Colonial Cultures in a Bourgeois World*. Berkeley: University of California Press, 1997.

Corfield, F. D. *The Origins and Growth of Mau Mau: An Historical Survey*. Nairobi: Colony and Protectorate of Kenya, 1960.

Cornu, François. *L'afrique Dans L'oeuvre d'Elspeth Huxley*, Thèse à la Carte; Lille: Atelier national de reproduction des thèses, 2004.

Correspondent, From Our. "White Farmers Applaud Jomo Kenyatta "Old Scores Will Be Forgotten." *The Times*, August 13, 1963.

Crabbe, John. "Barbara Leigh Smith Bodichon." In *Dictionary of Women Artists*, ed. Delia Gaze, 283–286. Chicago, London: Fitzroy Dearborn, 1997.

Cran, Marion. *The Garden Beyond*. London: Herbert Jenkins Ltd., 1937.

Cron, Gretchen. *The Roaring Veldt*. New York/London: Putnam, 1938.

Cross, Robert S., and Michael Perkin. *Elspeth Huxley: A Bibliography*. New Castle, Delaware: Oak Knoll Press, 1996.

Cunningham, Valentine. *British Writers of the Thirties*. Oxford: Oxford University Press, 1988.

Curtis, Sarah. "Emilie de Vialar and the Religious Reconquest of Algeria." *French Historical Studies* 29, no. 2 (2006): 261–292.

Dames, Nicholas. *Amnesiac Selves: Nostalgia, Forgetting, and British Fiction, 1810–1870*. New York: Oxford University Press, 2001.

Daniel, Norman. *Islam and the West:The Making of an Image*. Edinburgh: Edinburgh University Press, 1960.

———. *Islam, Europe and Empire*. Edinburgh: Edinburgh University Press, 1966.

Datta, Venita. *Birth of National Icon: The Literary Avant-Garde and the Origins of the Intellectual in France*. Albany: S.U.N.Y. Press, 1999.

Daughton, J. P. *An Empire Divided: Religion, Republicanism, and the Making of French Colonialism, 1880–1914*. New York: Oxford University Press, 2006.

Davis, Fred. *Yearning for Yesterday. A Sociology of Nostalgia*. New York/London: The Free Press, 1979.

Davis, Robert K. *Christian Slaves, Muslim Masters. White Slavery in the Mediterranean, the Barbary Coast, and Italy 1500–1800*. New York: Palgrave Macmillan, 2003.

Déjeux, Jean. *Bibliographie de la Littérature "Algérienne" des Français: Bibliographie des Romans, Récits et Recueils de Nouvelles Écrits Par des Français Inspirés Par l'Algérie 1896-1975, Précédée de la Bibliographie des Études Sur la Littérature "Algérienne" des Français*, Paris: Editions du Centre national de la recherche scientifique, 1978.

———. *Bibliographie Méthodique et Critique de la Littérature Algérienne de Langue Française, 1945–1977*. Alger: Société nationale d'Édition et de diffusion, 1979.

———. *Femmes d'Algérie: Légendes, Traditions, Histoire, Littérature*. Paris: Boîte à Documents, 1987.

———. *Image de L'étrangère: Unions Mixtes Franco-Maghrébines*. Paris: La Boîte à documents, 1989.

———. *La Littérature Algérienne Contemporaine*. Paris: Presses universitaires de France, 1975.

———. *La Littérature Féminine de Langue Française Au Maghreb*. Paris: Karthala, 1994.

———. *Littérature Maghrébine de Langue Française: Introduction Générale et Auteurs*, Littératures. Sherbrooke: Naaman, 1973.

———. "Élissa Rhaïs, Conteuse Algérienne (1876–1940)." *Revue de l'Occiddent musulman et de la Mediterranée* 37, no. 1 (1984): 47–79.

Delacour, Marie-Odile, and Jean-René Huleu. *Le Voyage Soufi d'Isabelle Eberhardt: Essai*, Littérature Française; Paris: J. Losfeld, 2008.

Derderian, Richard. *North Africans in Contemporary France: Becoming Visible*. New York: Palgrave Macmillan, 2004.

Dermenjian, Geneviève. *La Crise Anti-Juive Oranaise (1895–1905), L'anti-Sémitisme Dans l'Algérie Coloniale*. Paris: Harmattan, 1986.

Deschamps, Hubert. "Et Maintenant Lord Lugard?" *Africa. Journal of the International African Institute* XXXIII, no. 4 (1963): 293–306.

Dessaigne, Francine. *Déracinés!* Meaux: Éditions du Fuseau, 1964.

———. *Jean Brune, Français d'Algérie.* Ivry-sur-Seine: Confrérie Castille, 1998.

———. *Journal D'une Mère de Famille Pied-Noir.* [Lagny-sur-Marne]: L'Esprit nouveau, 1962.

———. *La Paix Pour Dix Ans: Sétif, Guelma, Mai 1945.* Calvisson [France]: J. Gandini, 1990.

Dessaigne, Francine, and Marie-Jeanne Rey. *Un Crime Sans Assassins: Alger, 26 Mars 1962.* Alfortville: Confrérie-Castille, 1994.

Di Leonardo, Micaela. *Gender at the Crossroads of Knowledge: Feminist Anthropology in the Postmodern Era.* Berkeley: University of California Press, 1991.

Dinesen, Isak. *Isak Dinesen's Africa: Images of the Wild Continent from the Writer's Life and Words.* San Francisco: Sierra Club Books, 1985.

———. *Shadows on the Grass.* New York: Vintage Books, 1974.

Dinesen, Thomas. *My Sister, Isak Dinesen.* Trans. Joan Tate. London: Michael Joseph, 1974.

Dobie, Madeleine. *Foreign Bodies. Gender, Language and Culture in French Orientalism.* Stanford: Stanford University Press, 2001.

Donelson, Linda. *Out of Isak Dinesen in Africa: The Untold Story.* Iowa City, Iowa: Coulsong List, 1995.

Dorland, Michael. *Cadavarland. Inventing a Pathology of Catastrophe for Holocaust Survival. The Limits of Medical Knowledge and Historical Memory in France.* Walthan: Brandeis University Press, 2009.

Douglas-Hamilton, Iain, and Oria Douglas-Hamilton. *Among the Elephants.* New York: Viking Press, 1975.

Douglas-Hamilton, Iain, Oria Douglas-Hamilton, and Brian Jackman. *Battle for the Elephants.* New York: Viking, 1992.

Dow, Suzanne. *Madness in Twentieth-Century French Women's Writing: Leduc, Duras, Beauvoir, Cardinal, Hyvrard.* Oxford: Bern, 2009.

Downes, Aviston, D. "From Boys to Men: Colonial Education, Cricket and Masculinity in the Caribbean, 1870-C.1920." *International journal of the history of sport Oxfordshire, U.K.:* 22, no. 1 (2005): 3–21.

Driver, Felix, and David Gilbert. *Imperial Cities: Landscape, Display and Identity.* Manchester: Manchester University Press, 1999.

Duder, C. J. D. "The Soldier Settlement Scheme of 1919 in Kenya." Thesis/dissertation (deg); Microfiche (mfc), University of Aberdeen, 1978.

Duder, C. J. D., and C.P. Youé. "Paice's Place: Race and Politics in Nanyuki District, Kenya, in the 1920s." *African Affairs* 93, (1994): 253–278.

Duder, C. J. D. "Love and the Lions. The Image of the White Settlements in Kenya in Popular African Fiction 1919–1939." *African Affairs* 90, no. 360 (1991): 427–438.

Dunwoodie, Peter. *Francophone Writing in Transition: Algeria 1900–1945.* Oxford: P. Lang, 2005.

———. "Postface: History, Memory, and Identity—Today's Crisis, Yesterday's Issue." *French History* 20, (2006): 318–332.

———. *Writing French Algeria.* Oxford: Clarendon Press, 1998.

Dunwoodie, Peter, and Edward J. Hughes. *Constructing Memories: Camus, Algeria and Le Premier Homme,* Stirling: Stirling French Publications, 1998.

Dupré. J. P., "*L'Alerte au Désert* by Magali Boisnard" in *Muslim World* 1 (1918): 94–95.

Durand, Anne. *Idir et Thérèse.* Paris: Editions Thibaud, 1981.

————. *Idir et Thérèse: <Le Vert et le Noir.>*. Montreux: Impr. Corbaz, 1958.

Durham, Carolyn A. *The Contexture of Feminism: Marie Cardinal and Multicultural Literacy*. Urbana: University of Illinois Press, 1992.

Eberhardt, Isabelle. *Oeuvres Complètes: Écrits Sur le Sable*, ed. Delacour Marie-Odile and Huleu Jean-René. 2 vols. Paris: B. Grasset, 1988.

Eberhardt, Isabelle, and Rana Kabbani. *The Passionate Nomad: The Diary of Isabelle Eberhardt* London: Virago, 1987.

Eberhardt, Isabelle, Karim Hamdy, and Laura Rice. *Departures: Selected Writings*. San Francisco: City Lights Books, 1994.

Edgerton, Robert B. *Mau Mau: An African Crucible*. New York: Ballantine Books, 1991.

————. *The Worldwide Practice of Torture: A Preliminary Report*. Lewiston, N.Y.: Edwin Mellen Press, 2007.

Einaudi, Jean-Luc. *La Bataille de Paris: 17 Octobre 1961*. Paris: Seuil, 1991.

————. *Pour L'exemple, L'affaire Fernand Yveton: Enquête*. Paris: L'Harmattan, 1986.

————. *Un Reve Algérien: Histoire de Lisette Vincent, Une Femme d'Algérie: Récit*. Paris: Editions d'Agorno, 1994.

Elbe, Marie. *Et à L'heure de Notre Mort*. Paris: Presses de la Cité, 1963.

————. *A L'heure de Notre Mort: Roman*. Paris: A. Michel, 1992.

————. *Marie Elbe. Pourquoi Cologne?* Paris: Presses de la Cité, 1964.

Elissa-Rhais, Roland. *Dans L'intérêt de Ma France*. Paris: Éd. "Civilisation," 1931.

Elkins, Caroline. *Imperial Reckoning.The Untold Story of Britain's Gulag in Kenya*. New York: Henry Holt, 2005.

Elkins, Caroline, and Susan Pedersen, eds. *Settler Colonialism in the Twentieth Century: Projects, Practices, Legacies*. London/New York: Routledge, 2005.

Etats Généraux Du Féminisme 30–31 Mai 1931. Paris: Conseil National des Femmes Françaises.

Etcherelli, Claire. *Élise, Ou, La Vraie Vie*. Paris: Denoël, 1967.

Euben, Roxanne Leslie. *Journeys to the Other Shore: Muslim and Western Travelers in Search of Knowledge*. Princeton: Princeton University Press, 2006.

Evans, Martin. *Empire and Culture: The French Experience, 1830–1940*. New York: Palgrave Macmillan, 2004.

————. *The Memory of Resistance: French Opposition to the Algerian War (1954–1962)*. Oxford/New York: Berg, 1997.

Fanon, Frantz. "Algeria Unveiled." In *Veil: Veiling, Representation, and Contemporary Art*, ed. David A. Bailey, Cambridge, MA: MIT Press, 2003.

————. *L'an V de la Révolution Algérienne*. Paris: Découverte, 2001.

Fathy, Safaa, and Jacques Derrida. *Derrida's Elsewhere*. Brooklyn, NY: First Run/Icarus, 1999. Visual Material.

Faure-Sardet, Jeanne. *Enamorada*. Alger: P. et G. Soubiron, 1933.

————. *Fille D'arabe*. Paris: E. Figuière, 1935.

————. *Mosaiques: Impressions, Contes, Nouvelles et Souvenirs*. Algiers: Fontana, N.D.

————. *Un Réve à Tipasa*. Alger: Aux Editions de la "Typographie d'Art," 1938.

Favre, Lucienne. *Bab-El-Oued*. Paris: G. Crès, 1926.

————. *Dimitri et la Mort, Roman*. Paris: J. Ferenczi et fils, 1925.

————. *L'homme Derrière le Mur*. Paris: Crès, 1927.

————. *La Noce: Roman*. Paris: B. Grasset, 1929.

————. *Le Bain Juif* Paris: Éditions B. Grasset, 1939.

————. *Mille et Un Jours: les Aventures de la Belle Doudjda*. 6 ed. Paris: Gallimard, 1941.

————. *Mille et Un Jours: Mourad*. Brussels: Editions de la Toison d'Or, 1943.

————. *Mourad: Roman, Mille et Un Jours*. Brussels: Editions de la Toison d'Or, 1935.

————. *Orientale 1930*. Paris: B. Grasset, 1930.

————. *Tausend Und Ein Tag: Roman*. Trans. Else Bredthauer. Düsseldorf: Droste-Verl., 1949.

————. *The Temptations of Mourad, a Novel*. New York: W. Morrow, 1948.

Fechner, Elisabeth. *Oran et L'oranie*, Souvenirs de Là-Bas. Paris: Calmann-Lévy, 2002.

Feraoun, Mouloud Le Sueur James D. *Journal, 1955–1962: Reflections on the French-Algerian War/Uniform Title: Journal, 1955–1962. English*. Lincoln: University of Nebraska Press, 2000.

Fisher, Michael H. *Counterflows to Colonialism: Indian Travellers and Settlers in Britain, 1600–1857*. Delhi: Permanent Black, 2004.

Forsdick, Charles. *Travel in Twentieth-Century French and Francophone Cultures*. Oxford: Oxford University Press, 2005.

Fournier-Giusti, Geneviève. *Pardon, Mon Algérie: Tranche de Vie*. Angicourt [France]: Editions 1900–2050, 2004.

Fox, James. *White Mischief*. London: Cape, 1982.

Frederiksen, Bodil Folke. "Jomo Kenyatta, Marie Bonaparte and Bronislaw Malinowski on Clitoridectomy and Female Sexuality." *History Workshop Journal* 65, (2008): 23–48.

Fritzsche, Peter. "Specters of History: On Nostalgia, Exile and Modernity." *American Historical Review* (2001): 1587–1618.

Fulford, Tim, Peter Kitson, Tim Youngs, Debbie Lee, Indira Ghose, and Nigel Leask. *Travels, Explorations and Empires: Writings from the Era of Imperial Expansion, 1770–1835. Part 2*. London: Pickering & Chatto, 2001.

Funk, Arthur Layton. *The Politics of Torch: The Allied Landings and the Algiers Putsch, 1942*. Lawrence: University Press of Kansas, 1974.

Gallmann, Kuki. *African Nights*. London: Perennial/Harper Collins, 2000.

————. *I Dreamed of Africa*. London: Penguin Books, 1992.

Geniesse, Jane Fletcher. *Passionate Nomad: The Life of Freya Stark*. New York: Modern Library, 2001.

Genova, James Eskridge. "Colonial Ambivalence, Cultural Authenticity, and the Limitations of Mimicry in French-Ruled West Africa, 1914–1956." in *Francophone cultures and literatures, v. 45*; Peter Lang, 2004.

Ghose, Indira. *Memsahibs Abroad: Writings by Women Travellers in Nineteenth Century India*. Delhi/New York: Oxford University Press, 1998.

————. *Women Travellers in Colonial India: The Power of the Female Gaze*. Delhi: Oxford University Press, 1998.

Gilmore, Leigh. *Autobiographies: A Feminist Theory of Women's Self-Representation*. Ithaca: Cornell University Press, 1994.

Glay, George Albert. *Oath of Seven*. New York: Ace Books, 1955.

Göçek, Fatma Müge, and Shiva Balaghi, eds. *Recontrucing Gender in the Middle East. Tradition, Identity and Power*. New York: Columbia University Press, 1994.

Godin, Annette. *L'erreur de Nedjma*. Paris: Alphonse Lemerre, 1923.

————. *Au Pays Du Myrte*. Paris: Alphone Lemerre, 1921.

Golan, Romy. *Modernity and Nostalgia. Art and Politics in France between the Wars.* New Haven: Yale University Press, 1995.

Goodman, Jane E., and Paul A. Silverstein. *Bourdieu in Algeria: Colonial Politics, Ethnographic Practices, Theoretical Developments,* Lincoln: University of Nebraska Press, 2009.

Gosnell, Jonathan K. *The Politics of Frenchness in Colonial Algeria, 1930–1954.* Rochester, N.Y.: University of Rochester Press, 2002.

Graebner, Seth. *History's Place: Nostalgia and the City in French Algerian Literature.* New York: Lexington Books, 2007.

Grant, Nellie. *Nellie's Story.* New York: William Morrow, 1980 (1973).

Grewal, Inderpal. *Home and Harem: Nation, Gender, Empire and the Culture of Travel.* Durham: Duke University Press, 1994.

Griffiths, Richard. *Fellow Travellers of the Right. British Enthusiasts for Nazi Germany 1933–39.* London: Constable, 1980.

Gröne, Maximilian. *"Maladie ès Lettres"—Krankheitsdarstellungen Bei Camus, Giono, Beauvoir, Cardinal Und Guibert.* Würsburg: Ergon-Verl., 2006.

Guicheteau, Gérard, and Marc Combier. *L'Algérie oubliée: Images d'Algérie, 1910–1954.* Paris: Acropole, 2004.

Guilhaume, Jean-François. *Les Mythes Fondateurs de l'Algérie Française.* Paris: L'Harmattan, 1992.

H. R. T. "White Man's Country. Lord Delamere and the Making of Kenya by Elspeth Huxley." *Journal of the Royal African Society* 35, no. 139 (1936): 223–25.

Haddour, Azzedine. "Algeria and Its History: Colonial Myths and the Forging and Deconstructing of Identity in Pied-Noir Literature." in *French and Algerian Identities from Colonial Times to the Present: A Century of Interaction,* ed. Alec G. Hargreaves and Michael J. Heffernan. Lewiston: Edwin Mellen Press, 1993.

Halbwachs, Maurice. *On Collective Memory.* Trans. Lewis A. Coser, ed. Donald N. Mevine, The Heritage of Sociology. Chicago/London: University of Chicago Press, 1992.

Halimi, Giséle. *Le Lait de L'oranger.* Paris: Gallimard, 1988.

Halimi, Gisèle, and Marie Cardinal. *La Cause des Femmes.* Paris: B. Grasset, 1973.

Hall, Collette Trout. *Marie Cardinal.* Amsterdam/Atlanta, GA: Rodopoi, 1994.

Hall, Stuart. *Modernity: An Introduction to Modern Societies.* Cambridge, UK: Polity Press, 1995.

———. *Modernity and its Futures.* Repr. ed. Cambridge: Polity Press 1996.

———. *Understanding Modern Societies: An Introduction.* Cambridge, MA: Blackwell, 1995.

Hamon, Hervé, and Rotman Patrick. *Les Porteurs de Valises: la Résistance Française à la Guerre d'Algérie.* Paris: A. Michel, 1979.

Hannoum, Abdelmajid. *Violent Modernity. France in Algeria.* Cambridge: Harvard University Press, 2010.

Hansen, Frantz Leander, and Gaye Kynoch (trans.). *The Aristocratic Universe of Karen Blixen: Destiny and the Denial of Fate.* Brighton: Portland, 2003.

Harbi, Mohammed. *Le F.L.N.: Mirage et Réalité.* Paris: Editions J. A., 1980.

Hargreaves, Alec G. *Memory, Empire, and Postcolonialism: Legacies of French Colonialism.* New York: Lexington Books, 2005.

———. *Voices from the North African Immigrant Community in France: Immigration and Identity in Beur Fiction,* New York: Berg: Distributed in the US and Canada by St. Martin's Press, 1991.

Hargreaves, Alec G., and Michael J. Heffernan, eds. *French and Algerian Identities from Colonial Times to the Present. A Century of Interaction.* Lewiston, NY; Ontario: Edward Mellen, 1993.

Hargreaves, Alec G., and Jeremy Leaman. *Racism, Ethnicity, and Politics in Contemporary Europe.* Aldershot, England: Brookfield, VT: E. Elgar, 1995.

Hargreaves, Alec G., and Mark McKinney. *Post-Colonial Cultures in France.* London: New York, 1997.

Harik, Elsa M., and Donald G. Schilling. *The Politics of Education in Colonial Algeria and Kenya.* Athens, Ohio: Ohio University Center for International Studies, 1984.

Harmand, Jules. *Domination et Colonisation.* Paris: E. Flammarion, 1910.

Harper, Marjory, and Stephen Constantine. *Migration and Empire,* Oxford/New York: Oxford University Press, 2010.

Hart, Ursula Kingsmill. *Two Ladies of Colonial Algeria: The Lives and Times of Aurélie Picard and Isabelle Eberhardt.* Athens, Ohio: Ohio University Center for International Studies, 1987.

Hause, Steven C. *Hubertine Auclert: The French Suffragette.* New Haven: Yale University Press, 1987.

Hay, Douglas, and Paul Craven, eds. *Masters, Servants, and Magistrates in Britain and the Empire, 1562–1955.* Chapel Hill: University of North Carolina Press, 2004.

Haynes, Eugene and Isak Dinesen. *To Soar with Eagles: The European Travels, Remembrances of Isak Dinesen.* United States: Xlibris, 2000.

Heath, Jennifer. *The Veil: Women Writers on its History, Lore, and Politics.* Los Angles: University of California Press, 2008.

Henderson, Mae G. *Borders, Boundaries, and Frames. Essays in Cultural Criticism and Cultural Studies,* ed. Mae G. Henderson. New York/London: Routledge, 1995.

Henriques, F. *Children of Caliban: Miscegenation.* London: Secker & Warburg, 1974.

Henry, Jean-Robert. *Le Maghreb dans l'Imaginaire français: la Colonie, le Désert, l'Exil.* Aix-en-Provence: Edisud, 1985.

Herne, Brian. *White Hunters. The Golden Age of African Safaris.* New York: Henry Holt & Co., 1999.

Hertaud-Wright, Marie-Helene. "Masculinity, Hybridity and Nostalgia in French Colonial Fiction Films of the 1930s." Dissertation: Thesis (Ph. D.)—Loughborough University of Technology, 2000.

Himmelfarb, Gertrude. *The Roads to Modernity: The British, French, and American Enlightenments.* New York: Knopf, 2004.

Hobsbawm, Eric, and Terence Ranger, eds. *The Invention of Tradition.* Cambridge: Cambridge University Press, 1983.

Hodgkin, Katherine, and Susannah Radstone, eds. *Contested Pasts. The Politics of Memory,* ed. Paul Thompson Mary Chamberlain, Timothy Ashplant, Richard Candida-Smith, and Selma Leydesdorff. London/New York: Routledge, 2003.

Holden, Philip, and Richard R. Ruppel. *Imperial Desire: Dissident Sexualities and Colonial Literature.* Minneapolis: University of Minnesota Press, 2003.

Holmes, Diana. *French Women's Writing, 1848–1994.* London/Atlantic Highlands, NJ: Athlone, 1996.

Holmes, Diana, and Carrie Tarr. *A "Belle Epoque"? Women in French Society and Culture, 1890–1914.* New York: Berghahn Books, 2006.

Holst Petersen, Kirsten, and Anna Rutherford, eds. *A Double Colonization: Colonial and Post-Colonial Women's Writing*. Mundelstrup: Dangaroo Press, 1986.

Horne, Alistair. *A Savage War of Peace: Algeria, 1954–1962*. New York: New York Review Books, 2006.

———. *A Savage War of Peace: Algeria, 1954–1962*. New York: Viking Press, 1978.

Horton, Susan R. *Difficult Women, Artful Lives. Olive Shreiner and Isak Dinesen, in and out of Africa*. Baltimore: The Johns Hopkins University Press, 1995.

Hron, Madelaine. *Translating Pain: Immigrant Suffering in Literature and Culture*. Toronto: University of Toronto Press, 2009.

Huffer, Lynne. *Another Look, Another Woman: Retranslations of French Feminism*. New Haven: Yale University Press, 1995.

———. "Derrida's Nostalgeria." In *Algeria & France 1800–2000, Identity, Memory, Nostalgia*, ed. Patricia M. E. Lorcin, 228–246. Syracuse: Syracuse University Press, 2006.

———. *Maternal Pasts, Feminist Futures: Nostalgia, Ethics, and the Question of Difference*. San Francisco: Stanford University Press, 1998.

Hughes, Alex. *Heterographies: Sexual Difference in French Autobiography*. Oxford: Berg, 1999.

Hughes, David McDermott. "The Art of Belonging: Whites Writing Landscape in Savannah Africa." In *Conference paper presented to the Program in Agrarian Studies*. Yale University, 2006.

Hulme, Peter, and Tim Youngs, eds. *The Cambridge Companion to Travel Writing*. Cambridge: Cambridge University Press, 2008.

Hunt, Nancy Rose, Tessie P. Liu, and Jean H. Quataert. *Gendered Colonialisms in African History*. Oxford, UK: Blackwell, 1997.

Hussein, Tove. *Africa's Song of Karen Blixen*. Nairobi, Kenya: T. Hussein, 1998.

Huxley, Elspeth Joscelin Grant. *The African Poison Murders*. New York: Viking, 1988. Reprint, 1940, 1976, 1986, 1988, 1989.

———. *East Africa*. London: Penns in the rocks Press by W. Collins, 1941.

Huxley, Elpeth. *The Flame Trees of Thika*. London: Cox & Wyman, 1974.

———. *The Flame Trees of Thika; Memories of an African Childhood*. New York: W. Morrow, 1959. Reprint, 1962. 1974, 1983, 2000 (1984 & 1992 = Video Cassettes).

———. *Murder at Government House*. New York, N.Y., U.S.A.: Viking, 1988 Reprint, 1987, 1988, 1989, 1990, 1991, 1992.

———. *Murder on Safari*. New York: Viking, 1989 Reprint, 1982,1988, 2002.

———. *On the Edge of the Rift: Memories of Kenya*. New York: Morrow, 1962.

———. *Out in the Noonday Sun. My Kenya*. London: Penguin Books, 1987.

———. *Red Strangers*. London: New York, 1999. Reprint, 1944, 1949, 1952, 954, 1959, 1965.

———. *Settlers of Kenya*. London: New York, Longmans, Green, 1948.

———. *The Sorcerer's Apprentice: A Journey through East Africa*. London: Chatto and Windus, 1948.

———. *A Thing to Love; a Novel*. London: Chatto & Windus, 1954.

———. "Tomorrow's Hope or Yesterday's Dream?" *The New York Times*, June 6, 1950, 5 pages.

———. "The Vast Challenge of Africa." *The New York Times*, July 18, 1954.

———. "What Life Is Like for a Settler in Kenya." *The New York Times*, June 6, 1954, 4.

————. *White Man's Country; Lord Delamere and the Making of Kenya*. [New] ed. 2 vols. London: Chatto & Windus, 1953.

Huxley, Elspeth Joscelin Grant, and Arnold Curtis. *Pioneers' Scrapbook: Reminiscences of Kenya, 1890 to 1968*. London: Evans Bros., 1980.

Huxley, Elspeth Joscelin Grant, and Hugo van Lawick. *Last Days in Eden*. New York: Amaryllis Press, 1984.

Huxley, Elspeth Joscelin Grant, and Margery Perham. *Race and Politics in Kenya. A Correspondence between Elspeth Huxley and Margery Perham with an Introduction by Lord Lugard*. London: Faber & Faber, 1944.

Ighilahriz, Louisette. *L'algérienne*. Paris: Fayard, 2001.

Irvin, Katherine Sheppard. "Cross-Cultural Dressing in Arab Lands: Isabelle Eberhardt and T. E. Lawrence." M. S., University of Rhode Island, 2004.

Jayawardena, Kumari. *The White Woman's Other Burden: Western Women and South Asia During British Colonial Rule*. New York: Routledge, 1995.

Jean-Darrouy, Lucienne. *Au Jardin de Mon Père: Contes de la Terre d'Algérie*. Alger: E. Imbert, 1942.

————. *Au Pays de la Mort Jaune*. Algiers: Baconnier, 1940.

————. *Le Mariage de Mademoiselle Centhectares: Figures de Colons Algériens*. Alger: P. et G. Soubiron, 1930.

Jennings, Eric Thomas. *Curing the Colonizers: Hydrotherapy, Climatology, and French Colonial Spas*. Durham: Duke University Press, 2006.

————. *Vichy in the Tropics: Pétain's National Revolution in Madagascar, Guadeloupe, and Indochina, 1940–1944*. Stanford: Stanford University Press, 2001.

Jex-Blake, Arthur John. *Gardening in East Africa: A Practical Handbook*. 4th ed. London: New York, 1957.

Judt, Tony. *The Burden of Responsibility: Blum, Camus, Aron, and the French Twentieth Century*. Chicago: University of Chicago Press, 1998.

————. *Past Imperfect. French Intellecctuals, 1944–1956*. Berkeley: University of California Press, 1992.

Julien, Charles André. *Histoire de l'Algérie Contemporaine. La Conquête et les Débuts de la Colonisation (1827–1871)*. 2 vols. Vol. 1. Paris: Presses universitaires de France, 1964.

Kaddache, Mahfoud. *La Vie Politique à Alger de 1919 à 1939*. Algiers: SNED, 1970.

Kalman, Samuel. "Fascism and Algérianité: The Croix de Feu, Pied-Noir Xenophobia, and the Indigenous Question in 1930s Algeria." in *The French Colonial Mind: Mental Maps of Empire and French Colonial Policy-Making*, ed. Martin Thomas. Lincoln: University of Nebraska Press, 2011.

Kalman, Samuel. "'Le Combat Par Tous les Moyens': Colonial Violence and the Extreme Right in 1930s Oran." *French Historical Studies* 34, no. 1 (2011).

Kanogo, Tabitha M. *African Womanhood in Colonial Kenya, 1900–1950*. Athens, OH/Nairobi: University of Ohio Press/East African Educational Publishers, 2005.

————. *Squatters and the Roots of Mau Mau 1905–1963*. Athens, OH: James Currey, 1987.

Katzenellenbogen, Simon. "Femmes et Racism Dans les Colonies Européennes." *Clio, Histoiore, Femmes et Sociétés* 9, (1999): 157–178.

Kaye, M. M. *Death in Zanzibar & Death in Kenya*. London: St. Martins Press, 1983.

————. *The Far Pavilions*. London / New York: St. Martin's Press, 1978.

Kaye, Mollie. *Six Bars at Seven*. London: First Novel library, 1940.

Keaton, Trica Danielle. *Muslim Girls and the Other France: Race, Identity Politics, & Social Exclusion*. Bloomington: Indiana University Press, 2006.

Kelly, Gail Paradise, and David H. Kelly. *French Colonial Education: Essays on Vietnam and West Africa*. New York: AMS Press, 2000.

Kennedy, Dane. *Islands of White: Settler Society and Culture in Kenya and Southern Rhodesia 1890–1939*. Durham: Duke University Press, 1987.

Kenny, Michael. "A Place for Memory: The Interface between Individual and Collective Memory." *Comparative Studies in Society and History* 41, no. 3 (1999): 420–437.

"Kenya: Black & White—Harambee!" *Time*, Friday, August 23 1963.

Kenyatta, Jomo. *Facing Mount Kenya: The Tribal Life of the Gikuyu*. New York: Vintage Books, 1965.

Khanna, Ranjana. *Algeria Cuts: Women and Representation, 1830 to the Present*. Stanford: Stanford University Press, 2008.

Kimble, Sara. "Emancipation through Secularation: French Feminist Views of Muslim Women's Condition in Interwar Algeria" *French Colonial History* 7 (2006): 109–128.

Kimmelman, Michael. "Footprints of Pieds-Noirs Reach Deep into France." *The New York Times*, March 5, 2009, C1.

Knibiehler, Yvonne, and Règine Goutalier. *La Femme Au Temps des Colonies*. Paris: Stock, 1985.

Kobak, Annette. *Isabelle: The Life of Isabelle Eberhardt*. London: Chatto & Windus, 1988.

Krebs, Paula M. *Gender, Race, and the Writing of Empire: Public Discourse and the Boer War*. Cambridge/New York: Cambridge University Press, 1999.

Kuhn, Raymond. *The Media in France*. New York: Routledge, 1995.

La Hogue, Jeanine de, and Simone Nerbonne. *Mémoire Écrite de l'Algérie Depuis 1950: les Auteurs et Leurs Oeuvres*. Paris: Editions Maisonneuve et Larose, 1992.

Larson, Edward J. *Sex, Race, and Science: Eugenics in the Deep South*. Baltimore: The Johns Hopkins University Press, 1996.

Lassner, Phyllis. *Colonial Strangers: Women Writing the End of the British Empire*. Newark: Rutgers University Press, 2004.

Lazreg, Marnia. *The Eloquence of Silence: Algerian Women in Question*. New York: Routledge, 1994.

———. *Torture and the Twilight of Empire: From Algiers to Baghdad*. Princeton: Princeton University Press, 2008.

Le Gall, Michel, and Kenneth J. Perkins. eds. *The Maghrib in Question: Essays in History & Historiography*, Austin: University of Texas Press, 1997.

Le Livre D'or Du Centenaire de l'Algérie Française. Algiers: Fontana, 1930.

Le Sueur, James D. *The Decolonization Reader*. New York: Routledge, 2003.

Le Sueur, James D. *Uncivil War: Intellectuals and Identity Politics During the Decolonization of Algeria*. Philadelphia: University of Pennsylvania Press, 2001.

Le Sueur, James D., and William B. Cohen. Special edition of *France and Algeria: From Colonial Conflicts to Postcolonial Memories*, Historical Reflections/Réflexions Historiques; Vol. 28 No. 2. (2002).

Lebovics, Herman. *Bringing the Empire Back Home: France in the Global Age*. Durham: Duke University Press, 2004.

———. "Donner à Voir L'empire Colonial: L'exposition Coloniale Internationale de Paris en 1931." *Gradhiva*. 7, no. hiver (1989–1990): 18–28.

Lerouvre, Catherine. *Un Feu D'enfer*. Paris: Seuil, 1958.

Levine, Philippa, ed. *Gender and Empire*. Oxford/New York: Oxford University Press, 2004.

Levy, Anita. *Other Women: The Writing of Class, Race and Gender 1832–1898*. Princeton: Princeton University Press, 1991.

Lewis, Joanna. "Mau-Mau's War of Words: The Battle of the Pamphlets." in *Free Print and Non-Commercial Publishing since 1700*, ed. James Raven. London: Ashgate, 2000.

Lewis, Reina. *Gendering Orientalism. Race, Femininity and Representation*. London/ NY: Routledge, 1996.

Lewis, Simon. *White Women Writers and Their African Invention*. Gainesville: University Press of Florida, 2003.

Leys, Norman. *The Colour Bar in East Africa*. London: The Hogarth Press, 1941.

Leys, Norman Maclean. *A Last Chance in Kenya*. London: L. and Virginia Woolf at the Hogarth Press, 1931.

Leys, Norman Maclean, Joseph Houldsworth Oldham, and John Whitson Cell. *By Kenya Possessed: The Correspondence of Norman Leys and J. H. Oldham, 1918–1926*. Chicago: University of Chicago Press, 1976.

Liauzu, Claude. *Empire Du Mal Contre Grand Satan: Treize Siècles de Cultures de Guerre Entre L'islam et L'occident*. Paris: A. Colin, 2005.

———, ed. *Dictionnaire de la Colonisation Française*. Larousse à Présent. Paris: Larousse, 2007.

Liauzu, Claude, and Leila Blili, eds. *Colonisation: Droit D'inventaire*. Paris: A. Colin, 2004.

Lionnet, Françoise. *Postcolonial Representations: Women, Literature, Identity*. Ithaca: Cornell University Press, 1995.

Lionnet-McCumber, Françoise. "Autobiographical Tongues: (Self-)Reading and (Self-)Writing in Augustine, Nietzsche, Maya Angelou, Marie Cardinal, and Marie-Therese Humbert." Ph.D., University of Michigan 1986.

Locher-Scholten, Elsbeth. *Women and the Colonial State, Essays on Gender and Modernity in the Netherlands Indies 1900–1942*. Amsterdam: Amsterdam University Press, 2000.

Loesch, Anne. *La Valise et le Cercueil*. Paris: Plon, 1963.

Loh, Lucienne. "Beyond English Fields: Refiguring Colonial Nostalgia in a Cosmopolitan World" Ph.D., Wisconsin, 2008.

Lombardi-Diop, Cristina. "Writing the Female Frontier: Italian Women in Colonial Africa, 1890–1940." PhD, New York University, 1999.

Lonsdale, John. "Kenya. Home County and African Frontier," in *Settlers and Expatriates: Britons over the Seas*, ed. Robert A. Bickers Oxford: Oxford University Press, 2010.

———. "Town Life in Colonial Kenya." in *The Urban Experience in Eastern Africa, C. 1750–2000*, ed. Andrew Burton, 207–22. Nairobi: British Institute, 2002.

———. *The Growth and Transformation of the Colonial State in Kenya, 1929–1952*, Staff Seminar. Nairobi: University of Nairobi, Dept. of History, 1980.

Lorcin, Patricia M. E. "Decadence and Renascence: Louis Bertrand and the Concept of Rebarbarisation in Fin de Siècle Algeria." in *New Perspectives on the Fin de Siècle in Nineteenth- and Twentieth-Century France*, ed. Kay Chadwick and Timothy Unwin, 181–197. London: Edwin Mellen, 2000.

———. "France and Rome in Africa: Recovering Algeria's Latin Past." *French Historical Studies* 25, no. 2 (2002): 295–329.

————. *Imperial Identities: Stereotyping, Prejudice and Race in Colonial Algeria*. London: I. B. Tauris; New York; Distributed by St. Martin's, 1995.

————. "Imperialism, Cultural Identity and Race in Colonial Algeria. The Role of the Medical Corps: 1830–1870." *ISIS* 90, no. 4 (1999): 653–679.

————. "Mediating Gender, Mediating Race: Women Writers in Colonial Algeria." *Culture, Theory & Critique* 45, no. 1 (2004): 45–61.

————. "Sex, Gender and Race in the Colonial Novels of Elissa Rhaïs and Lucienne Favre." in *The Color of Liberty: Histories of Race in France*, ed. Tyler Stovall and Susan Peabody, Durham: Duke University Press, 2003. 108–130.

————. "Women, Gender and Nation in Colonial Novels of Inter-War Algeria." *Historical Reflections / Reflexions Historiques, (Special issue on Algeria)* 28, no. 2 (2002): 163–184.

Loth, Laura Jane. "Moving Pictures: Gender, Vision and Travel from Colonial Algeria to Contemporary France." PhD, University of Minnesota, 2005.

Lugard, Frederick John Dealtry, Baron. *The Dual Mandate in British Tropical Africa*. [5th ed. Hamden: CT] Archon Books, 1965.

Macias, Enrico, and Florence Assouline. *Mon Algérie*. Paris: Plon, 2001.

Mackworth, Cecily. *The Destiny of Isabelle Eberhardt*. New York: Ecco Press, 1975.

MacMaster, Neil. *Burning the Veil: Military Propaganda and the Emancipation of Women During the Algeria War 1954–1962*. Manchester: Manchester University Press, 2009.

————. *Colonial Migrants and Racism: Algerians in France, 1900–1962*. New York: St. Martin's Press, 1997.

————. "The Colonial 'Emancipation' of Algerian Women: The Marriage Law of 1959 and the Failure of Legislation on Women's Rights in the Post-Independence Era." *Stichproben. Wiener Zeitschrift fur kritische Afrikastudien* 12, no. 7 (2007): 91–116.

Majumdar, Margaret A. *Postcoloniality: The French Dimension*. New York: Berghahn Books, 2007.

Makdisi, Saree. *Romantic Imperialism: Universal Empire and the Culture of Modernity*. Cambridge/NY: Cambridge University Press, 1998.

Manaud, Jean-Luc, and Catherine Sauvat. *Isabelle Eberhardt et le Désert*. Paris: Ed. du Chêne, 2003.

Manes, Averell. *The Pieds-Noirs 1960–2000: A Case Study in the Persistence of Subcultural Distinctiveness*. Bethesda: Academica Press, 2005.

Mann, Jessica. *Deadlier Than the Male: Why Are Respectable English Women So Good at Murder?* New York: Macmillan, 1981.

Mannoni, Octave. *Prospero and Caliban: The Psychology of Colonization*. (French edition published 1948). New York: Praeger, 1964.

Mannoni, Pierre. *Les Français d'Algérie: Vie, Moeurs, Mentalité de la Conquête des Territoires Du Sud à L'indépendance*. Paris: Editions L'Harmattan, 1993.

Marchand, Henri Dr. *Les Mariages Franco-Musulmans*. Alger: Impr. Vollot-Debacq, 1954.

Margadant, Jo Burr. *The New Biography: Performing Femininity in Nineteenth-Century France*. Berkeley: University of California Press, 2000.

Markham, Beryl. *West with the Night*. San Francisco: North Point Press, 1983.

————. *Wise Child*. U.S.A.: Pennsylvania Railroad, 1943.

————. *World without Walls Beryl Markham's African Memoir*. Van Nuys, CA: Wild Wing Productions, 1987. Visual Material.

Markham, Beryl, and Mary S. Lovell. *The Splendid Outcast: Beryl Markham's African Stories*. San Francisco: North Point Press, 1987.

Marston, Elsa, and Donald G. Schilling. *The Politics of Education in Colonial Algeria and Kenya*, Papers in International Studies. Africa Series No. 43. Athens, Ohio: Ohio University, Center for International Studies, 1984.

Martin Shaw, Carolyn. *Colonial Inscriptions: Race, Sex and Class in Kenya*. Minneapolis: University of Minnesota Press, 1995.

Martini, Lucienne. *Maux D'exil, Mots D'exil: A L'écoute des Écritures Pieds-Noirs*. Nice: Gandini, 2005.

———. *Racines de Papier: Essai Sur L'expression Littéraire de L'identité Pieds-Noirs*. Paris: Published, 1997.

Maury, Lucien. "Les Lettres, Oeuvres et Idées. L'orient des Orientaux." *Revue Bleue* 58, no. 1 (1920): 25–28.

Maxon, Robert M. *Struggle for Kenya. The Loss and Reassertion of Imperial Initiative, 1912–1923*. London/Toronto: Associated University Presses, 1993.

Maynes, Mary Jo, Jennifer L. Pierce, and Barbara Laslett. *Telling Stories: The Use of Personal Narratives in the Social Sciences and History*. Ithaca: Cornell University Press, 2008.

McBride, Theresa M. *The Domestic Revolution: The Modernisation of Household Service in England and France, 1820–1920*. London: Croom Helm, 1976.

McCaw, Heather. *Women on Two Sides of the Divide: Gender, Identity and Colonialism in Jane Eyre and Wide Sargasso Sea*. Columbus: Ohio State University, 2000.

McClintock, Anne. *Imperial Leather: Race, Gender, and Sexuality in the Colonial Contest*. New York: Routledge, 1995.

McClintock, Anne, Aamir Mufti, and Ella Shohat. *Dangerous Liaisons: Gender, Nation, and Postcolonial Perspectives*. Minneapolis: University of Minnesota Press, 1997.

McCormack, Jo. *The Algerian War in the French Education System: A Case Study of the Transmission of Memory*. Loughborough: Loughborough University of Technology, 2000.

———. *Collective Memory: France and the Algerian War (1954–1962)*. Lanham, MD: Lexington Books, 2007.

McEwan, Cheryl. *Gender, Geography, and Empire: Victorian Women Travellers in West Africa*. Aldershot, U.K./Burlington, VT: Ashgate, 2000.

McMillan, James F. *Housewife or Harlot: The Place of Women in French Society 1870–1940*. New York: St. Martin's Press, 1981.

Meena, Alexander. *The Shock of Arrival: Reflections on Postcolonial Experience*. Boston: South End Press, 1996.

Melman, Billie. *Women's Orients. English Women and the Middle East, 1718–1918: Sexuality, Religion, and Work*. Ann Arbor: University of Michigan Press, 1992.

Memmi, Albert. *The Colonizer and the Colonized*. New York: Orion Press, 1965.

Messaadi, Sakina. *Les Romancieres Coloniales et la Femme Colonisé: Contribution à Une Étude de la Littérature Coloniale en Algérie Dans la Première Moité Du Xxe Siècle*. Alger: Entreprise nationale du livre, 1990.

———. *Nos Soeurs Musulmanes, ou, Le Mythe Féministe, Civilisateur, Évangélisateur du Messianisme Colonialiste dans l'Algérie Colonisée*. Alger: Houma, 2001.

Meylan, Philippe. *Les Mariages Mixtes en Afrique du Nord. Conclusion--Effets Sur la Personne et les Biens. Dissolution*. Vol. 9, Institut des Hautes Études Marocaines. Collection des Centres D'études Juridiques. Paris: Librairie du Recueil Sirey, S.A., 1934.

Midgley, Clare, ed. *Gender and Imperialism*. Manchester: Manchester University Press, 1998.

Mills, Sara. *Discourses of Difference: An Analysis of Women's Travel Writing and Colonialism.* London: New York, 1991.

Mills, Stephen. *Muthaiga: The History of Muthaiga Country Club; Vol. 1: 1913–1963:* Nairobi: Mills Publishing, 2006.

Molines, François. *C'était Mon Algérie.* Marseille: F. Molines, 1973.

Monfreid, Henri de. *Sous le Masque Mau-Mau.* Paris: B. Grasset, 1956.

Montupet, Jeanne. *Das Haus Vermorel: Ein Algerischer Familienroman.* Stuttgart: Deutsche Verlags-Anstalt, 1957.

———. *De Rode Bron: Aïn El Hamra: Een Algerijnse Familieroman.* Baarn: Hollandia, 1958.

———. *Francisca: Roman,* La Fontaine Rouge. Paris: R. Laffont, 1954.

———. *Olivier: Roman,* La Fontaine Rouge. Paris: R. Laffont, 1955.

———. *The Red Fountain.* Trans. John Barlow. New York: St. Martin's Press, 1961.

———. *Simon: Roman.* La Fontaine Rouge. Paris: R. Laffont, 1953.

Mooers, Colin Peter. *The New Imperialists: Ideologies of Empire.* Oxford: Oneworld, 2006.

Moore-Gilbert, B. J. *Writing India, 1757–1990: The Literature of British India.* Manchester: University of Manchester Press, 1996.

Morel de Marnand, Denise. *Sétif de Ma Jeunesse.* Nice: Editions J. Gandini, 2001.

Morton, P. A. *Hybrid Modernities: Architecture and Representation at the 1931 Colonial Exposition, Paris.* Cambridge: MIT Press, 2000.

Mosley, Paul. *The Settler Economies. Studies in the Economic History of Kenya and Southern Rhodesia 1900–1963.* Cambridge: Cambridge University Press, 1983.

Murray, Alison. "Women, Nostalgia, Memory: Chocolat, Outremer, and Indochine." *Research in African Literatures* 33, no. 2 (2002): 235–244.

Murray, Jenny. *Remembering the (Post)Colonial Self: Memory and Identity in the Novels of Assia Djebar,* Oxford: P. Lang, 2008.

Myers, Garth Andrew. "Colonial Nairobi." In *Verandahs of Power: Colonialism and Space in Urban Africa,* ed. Garth Andrew Myers, 33–54. Syracuse, NY: Syracuse University Press, 2003.

Najet, Khadda. "Naissance Du Roman Algérien Dans l'Algérie Coloniale: Un Royal Bâtard." in *Regards Sur les Littératures Coloniales Afrique Francophone,* ed. Jean-François Durant, 103–124. Paris: L'Harmattan, 1999.

Neuman, Shirley, ed. *Autobiography and Questions of Gender.* London: Frank Cass, 1991.

Nicholls, C. S. *Elspeth Huxley. A Biography.* London: St. Martins, 2002.

———. *Red Strangers: The White Tribe of Kenya.* London: Timewell Press, 2005.

Noël, Jean. *Isabelle Eberhardt, L'aventureuse Du Sahara.* Alger: Éditions Baconnier, 1961.

Noirfontaine, Pauline de. *Algérie. Un Regard Écrit.* Havre: A. Lemale, 1856.

Noose, Melita, and Nora K. Strange. *Blondes Prefer Gentlemen: The Ingenious Diary of an Amateur.* Cheltenham: Start to Finish, 2006.

Norindr, Panivong. *Phantasmatic Indochina. French Colonial Ideology in Architecture, Film and Literature.* Durham: Duke University Press, 1996.

O'Brien, Michael. *John F. Kennedy: A Biography.* New York: Thomas Dunne Books / St. Martin's Press, 2005.

Ochieng, William Robert, and Bethwell A. Ogot. *A Modern History of Kenya, 1895–1980: in Honour of B. A. Ogot.* Nairobi: Evans Brothers (Kenya), 1989.

Odhiambo, Atieno, Stephen Elisha, and John Lonsdale. *Mau Mau & Nationhood Arms, Authority & Narration.* Oxford/Nairobi: James Currey, 2003.

Ogot, Bethwell A. *Zamani: A Survey of East African History.* Nairobi: East African Pub. House, 1974.

Ogot, Bethwell A., and William Robert Ochieng, eds. *Decolonization & Independence in Kenya, 1940–1993.* Athens, OH: Ohio University Press, 1995.

Ole Sena, Sarone. *Colonial Education among the Kenyan Maasai, 1894—1962.* Discussion Paper/Dept. Of Anthropology, Mcgill University. Montreal: Department of Anthropology, McGill University, 1986.

Oliver, Roland Anthony, and J. D. Fage. *A Short History of Africa.* [*with Maps and a Bibliography.*] London: Harmondsworth, 1962.

Oriano, Jeanine. *Driss.* Paris: Julliard, 1959.

Palmer, Jennifer L. "What's in a Name? Mixed-Race Families and Resistance to Racial Codification in Eighteenth-Cenury France." *French Historical Studies* 33, no. 2 (2010): 357–385.

Patterson, J. H., and Selous Frederick Courteney. *The Man-Eaters of Tsavo and Other East African Adventures.* Whitefish, MO: Kessinger Publishing, 2000.

Peabody, Sue, and Tyler Edward Stovall. *The Color of Liberty: Histories of Race in France.* Durham: Duke University Press, 2003.

Pears, Pamela A. *Remnants of Empire in Algeria and Vietnam. Women, Words, and War.* New York: Lexington Books, 2004.

Pedersen, Susan. "National Bodies, Unspeakable Acts: The Sexual Politics of Colonial Policy-Making." *Journal of Modern History* 63, no. 4 (1991): 647–680.

Pelensky, Olga Anastasia. *Isak Dinesen: Critical Views.* Athens, OH: Ohio University Press, 1993.

———. *Isak Dinesen: The Life and Imagination of a Seducer.* Athens, OH: Ohio University Press, 1991.

Pellerin, Jean-Pierre. *Mon Algérie.* Paris: Thélès, 2004.

Percox, David. *Britain, Kenya and the Cold War—Imperial Defence, Colonial Security and Decolonisation.* London: I. B. Tauris, 2004.

Pervillé, Guy. *Dossier-Document Sur La Guerre Sans Nom: (Appelés et Rappelés Pendant la Guerre d'Algérie: 1954–1962): Un Film de Bertrand Tavernier et Patrick Rotman*: Association des Professeurs d'Histoire et de Géographie, 1992.

Peterson, Derek R. *Creative Writing: Translation, Bookkeeping, and the Work of Imagination in Colonial Kenya.* Portsmouth, NH: Heinemann, 2004.

Pickering, Jean, and Suzanne Kehde, eds. *Narratives of Nostalgia, Gender, and Nationalism.* New York: New York University Press, 1996.

Pierpont, Claudia Roth. *Passionate Minds: Women Rewriting the World.* New York: Knopf, 2000.

Pierson, Ruth Roach, Nupur Chaudhuri, and Beth McAuley. eds. *Nation, Empire, Colony: Historicizing Gender and Race.* Bloomington: Indiana University Press, 1998.

Planche, Jean-Louis. *Sétif 1945: Histoire D'un Massacre Annoncé.* Paris: Perrin, 2006.

Pommerol, Jean. *Among the Women of the Sahara; Uniform Title: Une Femme Chez les Sahariennes. English.* Trans. Mrs. Arthur Bell (N D'Anvers). London: Hurst and Blackett, 1900.

———. *Le Cas Du Lieutenant Sigmarie.* Paris: Calmann-Lévy, 1907.

———. *Le Crible, Roman.* Paris: H. Simonis Empis, 1897.

———. *La Faute D'avant, Roman.* Paris: L. Chailley, 1896.

———. *Islam Saharien: Chez Ceux Qui Guettent (Journal D'un Témoin),* Paris: A. Fontemoing, 1902.

———. "A Lady in the Unexplored Sahara" in *The World Wide Magazine,* 5, 1900, 54–62.

———. *Le Péché des Autres, Roman*. Paris: L. Chailley, 1890.

———. *Scènes Viennoises: Une de Leurs Étoiles, Son Chien, Son Père, Son Secrétaire et Ses Amis*. Paris: P. Lamm, 1897.

———. *Une Femme Chez les Sahariennes: Entre Laghouat et in-Salah*. Paris: E. Flammarion, 1900.

———. *Un Fruit et Puis Un Autre Fruit*. Paris: C. Lévy, 1911.

Pontecorvo, Gillo, Antonio Musu, Franco Solinas, Brahim Haggiag, Martin' Jean, and Yacef Saadi. *The Battle of Algiers*. Mount Cisco, NY: Axon Video Co. (Distributed by Guidance Associates), 1988. Visual Material.

Pordzik, Ralph. *The Wonder of Travel: Fiction, Tourism and the Social Construction of the Nostalgic*, Heidelberg: Winter, 2005.

Portsmouth, Gerard Vernon Wallop, Earl of. *A Knot of Roots: an Autobiography*. London: G. Bles, 1965.

Pringle, Ian. *Isabelle Eberhardt le Destin Scandaleux D'un Écrivain Qui Fut D'abord Une Aventurière, Peut-Êre Une Espionne, Avant Tout Une Femme Libre*. Paris Les Films Aramis [u.a.], 1995. VHS tape (vhs).

Prochaska, David. "History as Literature, Literature as History: Cagayous of Algiers." *American Historical Review* 101, no. 3 (1996): 671–711.

———. *Making Algeria French: Colonialism in Bône 1870–1920*. Cambridge/New York: Cambridge University Press, 1990.

Procida, Mary A. *Married to the Empire: Gender, Politics and Imperialism in India, 1883–1947*. Manchester: Manchester University Press. Distributed exclusively in the USA by Palgrave, 2002.

Prost, Antoine. *Carnets d'Algérie*. Paris: Tallandier, 2005.

Radstone, Susannah. *Memory and Methodology*. New York: Berg, 2000.

Radstone, Susannah, and Katherine Hodgkin, eds. *Regimes of Memory*. London/New York: Routledge, 2003.

Randau, Robert. *Cassard le Berbère*. Algiers: Jules Carbonnel, 1926.

———. *Les Colons; Roman de la Patrie Algérienne*. Paris: E. Sansot, 1907.

Randau, Robert, and préface: Déjeux Jean. *Isabelle Eberhardt: Notes et Souvenirs*. Paris: La Boîte à documents, 1989.

Ranger, Terence. "The Invention of Tradition Revisited: The Case of Colonial Africa." In *Legitimacy and the State in Tentieth Century Africa*, eds. Terence Ranger and O. Vaughan. Oxford: Oxford University Press 1993.

Reggui, Marcel, and Jean Amrouche. *Les Massacres de Guelma: Algérie, Mai 1945, Une Enquête Inédite Sur la Furie des Milices Coloniales*. Paris: La Découverte, 2006.

Reid, Victor Stafford. *The Leopard*. New York: Viking Press, 1958.

René-Garnier, Charles. *La Conquête de L'islam Par les Femmes. Conférénce Fait à la Société Normande de Géographie le 20 Novembre 1910*. Rouen: Imprimerie Cagniard, 1911.

Reuters. "Text of Khrushchev Statement." *The New York Times*, May 16, 1958.

Rey, Marie-Jeanne. *Mémoires D'une Écorchée Vive. Alger 1954–1962*. Versailles: Editions de l'Atlanthrope, 1987.

Rey-Goldzeiguer, Annie. *Le Royaume Arabe: la Politique Algérienne de Napoléon III, 1861–1870*. Alger: Société nationale d'édition et de diffusion, 1977.

Rhaïs, Elissa. *Beduiinitytän Tarina (Noblesse Arabe)*. Helsinki: Kirja, 1923.

———. *Der Schleier Von Algier*. Goldmann. Munchen: Goldmann, 1998.

———. *Djelloul de Fés*. Saint-Denis, France: Bouchene, 2004.

———. *Eleazars Datter (Les Juifs Ou la Fille D'Eléazar)*. Kristiania, Norway: Aschehoug, 1922.

———. *Kafe-Shantan (Café Chantant)*. Leningrad: Izd-vo "Myslí," 1927.

———. *L'andalouse*. Paris: A. Fayard & cie., 1925.

———. *La Convertie*. Paris, 1931.

———. *La Fille d'Éléazar*. Paris: L'Archipel, 1997.

———. *La Fille des Pachas*. Paris: Plon-Nourrit, 1922.

———. *La Riffaine*. Paris: Flammarion, 1929.

———. *Le Café Chantant*. Saint-Denis: Bouchene, 2003.

———. *Le Café-Chantant. Kerkeb. Noblesse Arabe*. Paris: Plon, 1920.

———. *Le Mariage de Hanifa*. Paris: Plon-Nourrit et cie, 1926.

———. *Le Sein Blanc*. Paris: L'Archipel, 1996.

———. *Le Sein Blanc: Roman*. Paris: Flammarion, 1928.

———. *Les Juifs ou, La Fille d'Éléazar*. Paris: Plon-Nourrit et cie, 1921.

———. *Par la Voix de la Musique*. Paris: Plon, 1927.

———. "Petits Pachas en Exil; Grande Nouvelle Inédite." in Les Oeuvres libres (1927); 173–242.

———. *Saâda, la Marocaine*. Paris: Plon-Nourrit & cie, 1919.

———. *Saada, Marockanskan*. Stockholm: Sv. f'rl., 1920.

Rhaïs, Elissa, Gaston Ricci, Ferdinand Duchêne, Robert Migot (preface by Louis Bertrand). *Blida*. Paris: Horizons de France, 1930.

Ricciardi, Lorenzo, and Mirella Ricciardi. *African Rainbow: Across Africa by Boat*. London: Ebury Press, 1989.

Ricciardi, Mirella. *African Saga*. London: Collins, 1981.

———. *African Visions: The Diary of an African Photographer*. London: Cassell, 2000.

———. *Vanishing Africa*. New York: Reynal, in association with Morrow, 1971.

Rice, Laura. "'Nomad Thought': Isabelle Eberhardt and the Colonial Project." *Cultural Critique* 17, no. Winter (1990–1991): 151–176.

Richardson, Lee Anne M. *New Woman and Colonial Adventure Fiction in Victorian Britain: Gender, Genre, and Empire*. Gainesville: University Press of Florida, 2006.

Ricoeur, Paul. *La Mémoire, L'histoire, L'oubli*. Paris: Seuil, 2000.

Riddell, Florence. *Castles in Kenya*. London: Geoffrey Bles, 1928.

———. *I Go Wandering. A Travel Biography*. London: J. B. Lippincott 1935.

———. *Kenya Mist*. London: Thornton Butterworth, 1924.

———. *Kismet in Kenya*. London: Geoffrey Bles, 1927.

———. *Out of the Mist*. London: Thornton Butterworth, 1925.

———. *Wives Win*. London: Geoffrey Bles, 1931.

Riley, Glenda. *Taking Land, Breaking Land: Women Colonizing the American West and Kenya, 1840–1940*. Albuquerque: University of New Mexico Press, 2003.

Rioux, Jean-Pierre, and Jean-François Sirinelli. *La Guerre d'Algérie et les Intellectuels Français*. Bruxelles: Editions Complexe, 1991.

Rítívoí, Andreea Decíu. *Yesterday's Self: Nostalgia and the Immigrant Identity*. Lanham, Md.: Rowman & Littlefield, 2002.

Robert-Guiard, Claudine. *Des Européennes en Situation Coloniale: Algérie 1830–1939*. Paris: Publications de l'Université de Provence, 2009.

Roberts, Mary Louise. *Civilization without Sexes: Reconstructing Gender in Postwar France, 1917–1927*. Chicago: University of Chicago Press, 1994.

———. *Disruptive Acts: The New Woman in Fin-de-Siècle France*. Chicago: University of Chicago Press, 2002.

Roberts, Stephen Henry. *The History of French Colonial Policy, 1870–1925*. London: Cass, 1963.

Robinson, Jane. *Wayward Women. A Guide to Women Travellers.* Oxford: Oxford University Press, 1990.

Robinson, Ronald Edward, Gallagher John, and Alice Denny. *Africa and the Victorians: The Official Mind of Imperialism.* London: Macmillan, 1981.

Robitschek, Kurt, Gaston Baty, and Lucienne Favre. *Simoon over Algiers: A Play in Thirteen Scenes after a Novel.* New York: French American Productions, 1938.

Roblès, Emmanuel. *Les Pieds-Noirs.* Collection Ces Minorités Qui Font la France. Paris: P. Lebaud, 1982.

Rogers, Rebecca. "Telling Stories About the Colonies: British and French Women in Algeria in the Nineteenth Century." *Gender & History* 21, no. 1 (2009): 39–59.

Rosaldo, Renato. *Culture & Truth: The Remaking of Social Analysis.* Boston: Beacon Press, 1989.

Rosello, Mireille. *Declining the Stereotype: Ethnicity and Representation in French Cultures,* Hanover, NH: University Press of New England, 1998.

———. "Elissa Rhaïs: Scandals, Impostures, Who Owns the Story?" *Research in African Literatures* 37, no. 1 (2006): 1–15.

———. *France and the Maghreb: Performative Encounters.* Gainesville: University Press of Florida, 2005.

———. *Infiltrating Culture: Power and Identity in Contemporary Women's Writing.* Manchester, UK: New York, 1996.

———. *Postcolonial Hospitality: The Immigrant as Guest.* Stanford: Stanford University Press, 2001.

———. "Remembering the Incomprehensible: Hélène Cixous, Leïla Sebbar, Yamina Benguigui, and the War of Algeria." in *Remembering Africa,* ed. M. Elisabeth Mudimbe-boyi, 187–205. Portsmouth, NH: Heinemann, 2002.

Rousso, Henry. *The Vichy Syndrome: History and Memory in France since 1944 / (Syndrome de Vichy).* Cambridge: Harvard University Press, 1991.

Roy, Anindyo. *Civility and Empire: Literature and Culture in British India, 1822–1922.* London/New York: Routledge, 2005.

Roy, Jules. "Le Mythe D'une Algérie Heureuse." *Le Monde,* June 4, 1982.

Ruark, Robert Chester, and Daniel Schwartz. *Something of Value.* Cutchogue, NY: Buccaneer Books, 1955.

Rubenstein, Roberta. *Home Matters: Longing and Belonging, Nostalgia and Mourning in Women's Fiction.* New York: Palgrave, 2001.

Ruedy, John. *Modern Algeria. The Origins and Development of a Nation.* Bloomington: Indiana University Press, 1992.

Rushdie, Salman. *Imaginary Homelands. Essays and Criticism 1981–1991.* London: Granta Books in association with Viking, 1991.

Saada, Emmanuelle. *Les Enfants de la Colonie: les Métis de L'empire Français Entre Sujétion et Citoyenneté.* Paris: Découverte, 2007.

Said, Edward W. *Cultural Imperialism.* New York: Knopf, 1993.

———. *Orientalism.* 1st ed. New York: Pantheon Books, 1978.

Salinas, Michèle. *Voyages et Voyageurs en Algérie 1830/1930.* Toulouse: Éditions Privat, 1989.

Salm, Steven J., and Toyin Falola, eds. *African Urban Spaces in Historical Perspective.* Rochester: University of Rochester Press, 2005.

Sambron, Diane. *Femmes Musulmanes: Guerre d'Algérie, 1954–1962.* Paris: Éditions Autrement, 2007.

———. *Les Femmes Algériennes Pendant la Colonization.* Paris: Riveneuve, 2009.

Santesso, Aaron. *A Careful Longing: The Poetics and Problems of Nostalgia*. Newark: University of Delaware Press, 2006.

Scott, Joan Wallach. *The Politics of the Veil*. Princeton: Princeton University Press, 2007.

———. *Only Paradoxes to Offer. French Feminists and the Rights of Man*. Cambridge, MA: Harvard University Press, 1996.

Sebbar, Leïla, and Alloula Malek. *Une Enfance Algérienne*. Paris: Gallimard, 1997.

Seeley, Janet. "Social Welfare in a Kenyan Town: Policy and Practice, 1902–1985." *African Affairs* 86, no. 345 (1987): 541–566.

Sempere Souvannavong, Juan David. *Los Pieds-Noirs en Alicante: Las Migraciones Inducidas Por la Descolonizacion*. Alicante: Universidad de Alicante, 1997.

Sharpe, Jenny. *Allegories of Empire: The Figure of Woman in the Colonial Text*. Minneapolis: University of Minnesota Press, 1993.

Shaw, Christopher, and Malcolm Chase. *The Imagined Past: History and Nostalgia*. Manchester: Manchester University Press, 1989.

Shepard, Todd. *The Invention of Decolonization: The Algerian War and the Remaking of France*. Ithaca: Cornell University Press, 2006.

Sherman, Daniel J. "Bodies and Names: The Emergence of Commemoration in Interwar France." *The American Historical Review* 103, no. 2 (1998): 443–466.

———. "Museums and Difference." in *21st Century Studies*. Indiana University Press, 2008.

———. *The Construction of Memory in Interwar France*. Chicago: University of Chicago Press, 1999.

Shilaro, Priscilla M. *A Failed Eldorado. Colonial Capitalism, Rural Industrialization, African Land Rights in Kenya, and the Kakamega Gold Rush 1930–1952*. Lanham/NewYork: University Press of America, 2008.

Shipway, Martin. *Decolonization and Its Impact: A Comparative Approach to the End of the Colonial Empires*. Oxford: Blackwell, 2008.

Showalter, Elaine. *A Literature of Their Own: British Women Novelists from Brontë to Lessing*. Princeton: Princeton University Press, 1977.

Sils, Marie. *Ces Forêts d'Orangers*. Paris: Gallimard, 1962.

Simon, Pierre Henri. *Contre la Torture*. Paris: Éditions du Seuil, 1957.

Simpson, Alyse. *The Land That Never Was*. London: Selwyn & Blount, 1937.

Sinclair, Georgina. *At the End of the Line: Colonial Policing and the Imperial Endgame, 1945–80*. Manchester: Manchester University Press, 2006.

Sinha, Mrinalini. "Britishness, Clubbability, and the Colonial Pubic Sphere: The Genealogy of an Imperial Institution in Colonial India." *The Journal of British Studies* 40, no. 4 (2001): 489–521.

———. *Colonial Masculinity: The "Manly Englishman" and the "Effeminate Bengali" in the Late Nineteenth Century*. Manchester: University of Manchester Press, 1995.

Smith, Andrea L. *Colonial Memory and Postcolonial Europe: Maltese Settlers in Algeria and France*, Bloomington: Indiana University Press, 2006.

Smith, Bonnie G., ed. *Women's History in Global Perspective*. Chicago: University of Illinois Press, 2004.

Spiegel, Gabrielle. "The Task of the Historian." *American Historical Review* 114, no. 1 (2009): 1–15.

Spivak, Gayatri Chakravorty. "Can the Subaltern Speak?" in *Marxism and the Interpretation of Culture*, ed. Cary Nelson and Lawrence Grossberg. Urbana: University of Illinois, 1988.

Stasiulis, Daiva, and Nira Yuval-Davis, eds. *Unsettling Settler Societies. Articulations of Gender, Race, Ethnicity and Class.* London: Sage, 1995.

Steedman, Carolyn. *Master and Servant: Love and Labour in the English Industrial Age.* Cambridge/New York: Cambridge University Press, 2007.

Steinhart, Edward I. *Black Poachers, White Hunters: A Social History of Hunting in Colonial Kenya.* Oxford/Nairobi: James Currey, 2006.

Steinmetz, George. *The Devil's Handwriting. Precoloniality and the German Colonial State in Qindao, Samoa, and Southwest Africa.* Chicago: University of Chicago Press, 2007.

Stern, Alexandra Minna. *Eugenic Nation: Faults and Frontiers of Better Breeding in Modern America.* Berkeley: University of California Press, 2005.

Stocking, George W. *Victorian Anthropology.* New York: Free Press: London, 1987.

Stoler, Ann Laura. "Carnal Knowledge and Imperial Power: Gender, Race and Morality in Colonial Asia." in *Gender at the Crossroads of Knowledge: Feminist Anthropology in the Postmodern Era* ed. Micaela di Leonardo. Berkeley: University of California Press, 1991.

———. *Carnal Knowledge and Imperial Power: Race and the Intimate in Colonial Rule.* Berkeley: University of California Press, 2002.

———. "Haunted by Empire: Geographies of Intimacy in North American History." in *American encounters/global interactions.* Durham: Duke University Press, 2006.

———. "Making Empire Respectable: The Politics of Race and Sexuality Morality in 20th Century Cultures." *American Ethnologist* 16, no. 4 (1985): 634–660.

———. *Race and the Education of Desire. Foucault's History of Sexuality and the Colonial Order of Things.* Durham: Duke University Press, 2000.

———. "Sexual Affronts and Racial Frontiers: European Identities and the Cultural Politics of Exclusion in Colonial Southeast Asia." *Comparative Studies in Society and History* 34, (1992): 514–551.

Stoler, Ann Laura, Carole McGranahan, and Peter C. Perdue. *Imperial Formations.* In *School for Advanced Research advanced seminar series.* Oxford: James Currey, 2007.

Stoll-Simon, Catherine. *Si Mahmoud ou la Renaissance d'Isabelle Eberhardt.* Alger: Éditions Alpha, 2006.

Stora, Benjamin. *Histoire de la Guerre d'Algérie, 1954–1962.* Paris: La Découverte, 1993.

———. *Ils Venaient d'Algérie: L'immigration Algérienne en France (1912–1992),* Paris: Fayard, 1992.

———. *La Gangrène et L'oubli: la Mémoire de la Guerre d'Algérie.* Paris: La Découverte, 1991.

———. *La Guerre des Mémoires. La France Face à Son Passé Colonial.* Paris: Éditions de l'Aube, 2007.

———. *Le Dictionnaire des Livres de la Guerre d'Algérie: Romans, Nouvelles, Poésie, Photos, Histoire, Essais, Récits Historiques, Témoignages, Biographies, Mémoires, Autobiographies: 1955–1995.* Paris: Harmattan, 1996.

Stora, Benjamin, and Mohammed Harbi. *La Guerre d'Algérie: 1954–2004, la Fin de L'amnésie.* Paris: R. Laffont, 2004.

Strange, Nora Kathleen. *Courtship in Kenya.* London: Stanley Paul, 1900.

———. *Kenya Calling.* London: Stanley Paul, 1928.

———. *Kenya Dawn.* London: Stanley Paul, 1928.

———. *Latticed Windows.* London: Stanley Paul, 1924.

———. *An Outpost Wooing: A Romance of East Africa.* 5th ed. London: Stanley Paul, 1927.

Strobel, Margaret. *European Women and the Second British Empire.* Bloomington: Indiana University Press, 1991.

———. *A Wife in Kenya.* London: Stanley Paul, 1925.

———. *Gender, Sex and Empire.* Washington: American Historical Association, 1993.

Suleiman, Susan Rubin, ed. *Exile and Creativity. Signposts, Travelers, Outsiders, Backward Glances.* Durham: Duke University Press, 1998.

Surkis, Judith. *Sexing the Citizen: Morality and Masculinity in France, 1870–1920.* Ithaca: Cornell University Press, 2006.

Syrotinski, Michael. *Deconstruction and the Postcolonial: At the Limits of Theory.* Liverpool: Liverpool University Press, 2007.

Tabet, Paul. *Elissa Rhaïs: Roman.* Paris: B. Grasset, 1982.

Tageldin, Shaden M. "Reversing the Sentence of the Impossible Nostalgia: The Poetics of Postcolonial Migration in Sakinna Boukhedenna and Agha Shahid Ali." *Comparative Literature Studies* 40, no. 3 (2003): 232–261.

Taguieff, P. A. "Doctrines de la Race et Hantise du Métissage. Fragments D'une Histoire de la Mixophobie Savante." *Nouvelle revue d'ethnopsychiatrie* 17 (1992): 53–100.

Talbayev, Edwige Tamalet. "Between Nostalgia and Desire: L'École d'Alger's Transnational Identifications and the Case for a Mediterranean Relation." *International Journal of Francophone Studies* 10, no. 3 (2007): 359–376.

Tate, H. R. "A Thing to Love by Elspeth Huxley." *African Affairs* 54, no. 214 (1955): 67–99.

Tawney, John J. "Personal Thoughts on a Rescue Operation: The Oxford Colonial Records Project." *African Affairs* 67, no. 269 (1968): 345–350.

Thiesse, Anne-Marie. *Ecrire la France: le Mouvement Littéraire Régionaliste de Langue Française Entre la Belle Epoque et la Libération.* Paris: Presses universitaires de France, 1991.

Thomas, Lynn M. "Imperial Concerns and 'Women's Affairs': State Efforts to Regulate Clitoridectomy and Eradicate Abortion in Meru, Kenya, C. 1910–1950." *Journal of African History* (1998): 121–146.

———. "'Ngaitana (I Will Circumcise Myself)': The Gender and Generational Politics of the 1956 Ban on Clitoridectomy in Meru, Kenya." *Gender & History* 8, no. 3 (1996): 338–363.

———. *Politics of the Womb. Women, Reproduction, and the State in Kenya.* Berkely: University of California Press, 2003.

Thomas, Martin. *The French Empire at War, 1940–45.* Manchester: University of Manchester Press, 1998.

———. *The French Empire between the Wars: Imperialism, Politics and Society.* Manchester: University o Manchester Press, 2005.

———. *The French North African Crisis: Colonial Breakdown and Anglo-French Relations, 1945–62.* New York: Macmillan Press/St. Martin's Press, 2000.

Thomas, Martin, Bob Moore, and L. J. Butler, eds. *Crises of Empire: Decolonization and Europe's Imperial States, 1918–1975.* Berkeley: University of California Press, 2007.

Thomas, Walter Babington. *The Touch of Pitch: A Story of Mau Mau.* London: A. Wingate, 1956.

Thornton, Leslie. *There Was an Unseen Cloud Moving.* New York: Women Make Movies, 1988. Visual Material.

Thurman, Judith. *Isak Dinesen: The Life of a Storyteller*. 1st ed. New York, N.Y.: St Martin's Press, 1982.

Tidrick, Kathryn. *Empire and the English Character*. London: Tauris, 1992.

———. "The Masai and Their Masters: A Psychological Study of District Administration." *African Studies Review*, 23, no. 1 (1980): 15–31.

Tilburg, Patricia A. *Colette's Republic. Work, Gender and Popular Culture in France, 1870–1914*. New York/Oxford: Berghahn Books, 2009.

Tillion, Germaine. *France and Algeria: Complementary Enemies*. New York: A. A. Knopf, 1961.

———. *Le Harem et les Cousins*, Paris: Éditions du Seuil, 1966.

Tindall, Gillian. *Countries of the Mind. The Meaning of Place to Writers*. Boston: Northeastern University, 1991.

Trench, Charles Chenevix. *Men Who Ruled Kenya*. London/New York: The Radcliffe Press, 1993.

Trzebinski, Errol. *Silence Will Speak: A Study of the Life of Denys Finch Hatton and His Relationship with Karen Blixen*. Chicago: University of Chicago Press, 1977.

———. *The Kenya Pioneers*. New York: W. W. Norton, 1986.

Tudury, Guy. *Alger de 1830 à 1962: Souvenirs et Images D'une Ville*, Rediviva; Nîmes: Lacour, 1994.

Turin, Yvonne. *Affrontements Culturels Dans l'Algérie Coloniale: Écoles, Médecines, Religion, 1830–1880*. Alger: Entreprise nationale du livre, 1983.

Ulloa, Marie-Pierre. *Francis Jeanson: A Dissident Intellectual from the French Resistance to the Algerian War/Uniform Title: Francis Jeanson. English*. Stanford: Stanford University Press, 2007.

———. *Francis Jeanson: Un Intellectuel en Dissidence: de la Résistance à la Guerre d'Algérie*. Paris: Berg, 2001.

Valérian, Dominique. *Bougie, Port Maghrébin, 1067–1510*. Rome: École française de Rome, 2006.

Vallory, Louise (Louise Mesnier). *A L'aventure en Algérie*. Paris: Hetzel, 1863.

van der Post, Laurens. "White Child's Country." *The Times*, March 5, 1959, 13; col C.

van Hees, Annelies. *The Ambivalent Venus: Women in Isak Dinesen's Tales (Condensed Version of Van Hees' Doctoral Thesis: De Ambivalente Venus in Het Werk Van Karen Blixen)*. Minneapolis: University of Minnesota Press, 1991.

Vergès, Françoise. *Monsters and Revolutionaries: Colonial Family Romance and Métissage*. Durham: Duke University Press, 1999.

Verone, Maria. *Pourquoi les Femmes Veulent Voter*. Epinal/Paris: Impr. Pernot, 1923.

Verrier, Anthony. *Assassination in Algiers: Churchill, Roosevelt, de Gaulle, and the Murder of Admiral Darlan*. London: Macmillan, 1991.

Vidal-Naquet, Pierre. *Torture: Cancer of Democracy, France and Algeria, 1954–62*. Baltimore: Penguin Books, 1963.

Villard, Maurice. *La Vérité Sur L'insurrection Du 8 Mai 1945 Dans le Constantinois: Menaces Sur l'Algérie Française*. Montpellier: Amicale des Hauts Plateaux de Sétif, 1997.

Vince, Natalya. "Transgressing Boundaries: Gender, Race, Religion, and 'Françaises Musulmanes' During the Algerian War of Independence." *French Historical Studies* 33, no. 3 (2010): 445–474.

Vir, Parminder. *Algerian Women at War*. New York, NY: Women Make Movies, 2008. Visual Material.

Wagner, Tamara S. *Longing: Narratives of Nostalgia in the British Novel, 1740–1890*. Lewisburg: Bucknell University Press, 2004.

Wall, Irwin M. *France, the United States, and the Algerian War*. Berkeley, Los Angeles: University of California Press, 2001.

Ward, H. F., and J. W. Milligan. *Handbook of British East Africa*. Nairobi: Sifton Praed, 1912.

Webb, Emma. *Marie Cardinal: New Perspectives*. Oxford/New York: Peter Lang, 2006.

Webster, Wendy. *Englishness and Empire, 1939–1965*. Oxford/New York: Oxford University Press, 2005.

Wheeler, Sara. *Too Close to the Sun. The Audacious Live and Times of Denys Finch Hatton*. New York: Random House, 2006.

White, Luise. *The Comforts of Home: Prostitution in Colonial Nairobi*. Chicago: University of Chicago Press, 1990.

———. *Speaking with Vampires: Rumor and History in Colonial Africa*, Los Angeles: University of California Press, 2000.

White, Owen. *Children of the French Empire: Miscegenation and Colonial Society in French West Africa, 1895–1960*. Oxford/New York: Oxford University Press, 1999.

Whitlock, Gillian. *The Intimate Empire: Reading Women's Autobiography*. New York: Cassell, 2000.

Wildenthal, Lora. *German Women for Empire, 1884–1945*. Durham: Duke University Press, 2002.

Williams, Mrs. Branch. *Mosaics*. Nashville: Southern Methodist Publishing House, 1881.

Williams, Patrick, and Laura Chrisman. *Colonial Discourse and Post-Colonial Theory: A Reader*. New York: Columbia University Press, 1994.

Wilson, Janelle L. *Nostalgia: Sanctuary of Meaning*. Lewisburg: Bucknell University Press, 2005.

Wilson, Kathleen. *A New Imperial History: Culture, Identity, and Modernity in Britain and the Empire, 1660–1840*. Cambridge/New York: Cambridge University Press, 2004.

———. *The Island Race: Englishness, Empire and Gender in the Eighteenth Century*. London/New York: Routledge, 2003.

Wingo, Ajume H. *Veil Politics in Liberal Democratic States*, Cambridge/New York: Cambridge Universiy Press, 2003.

Wood, Nancy. *Germaine Tillion, Une Femme-Mémoire: D'une Algérie à L'autre*. Paris: Autrement, 2003.

Woollacott, Angela. *Gender and Empire*. New York: Palgrave Macmillan, 2006.

Wright, Gwendolyn. *The Politics of Design in French Colonial Urbanism*. Chicago: University of Chicago Press, 1991.

Yahiaoui, Messaouda. "Regards de Romancières Françaises Sur les Sociétés Féminines d'Algérie, 1898–1960." in *Regards Sur les Littératures Coloniales Afrique Francophone*, ed. Jean-François Durand and Jean Sévry, 79–94. Paris: L'Harmattan, 1999.

Youngs, Tim. *Travellers in Africa. British Travelogues, 1850–1900*. Manchester & New York: St. Martin Press, 1994.

Zakine, Hubert. *Il Était Une Fois . . . Bab El-Oued: 1830–1962: Étude Historique, Sociologique et Nostalgique D'un Monde Disparu*. Toulon: Presses du Midi Editions, 2010.

Zengos, Hariclea. "A World without Walls: Race, Politics and Gender in the African Works of Elspeth Huxley, Isak Dinesen, and Beryl Markham." PhD Thesis, Tufts University, 1989.

Zweig, Stefanie. *Nirgendwo in Afrika: Autobiographischer Roman*. 2. Aufl. ed. München: Langen Müller, 1995.

———. *Une Enfance Africaine: Roman Autobiographique*. Monaco: Éditions du Rocher, 2002.

Zweig, Stefanie, and Marlies Comjean. *Nowhere in Africa: An Autobiographical Novel*. Madison, WI: University of Wisconsin Press/Terrace Books, 2004.

INDEX

A Thing to Love (Huxley), 158, 166
A Thing of Value (Huxley), 164–6
Abbas, Ferhat, 152
Académie française, 174, 235n9
Achebe, Chinua, 123
Action Française, 127
Adamson, George, 187
Adamson, Joy, 39, 187, 200
African Dilemmas (Huxley), 160–1
African Nights (Gallmann), 187
African Poison Murders (Huxley), 122
African Visions (Ricciardi), 190
Afrikaner, 37, 117, 167, 170
Akhbar (news bulletin), 61, 81
Algeria
  colonial history of, 3–8, 21–3
  and defensive nostalgia, 148–56
  and demographics, 5
  and direct rule, 4
  female European presence in, 27–35
  independence (1962), 171
  and land expropriation, 22–3, 25,
    46–7
  literary developments in, 111–14
  and literary realism in, 127–38
  and literary scene, 4–5
  and modernity, 73–82
  mythologies of settlement, 25–6
  néo-French argument, 129
  in the 1920s, 67–83, 85
  in the 1930s, 108–11, 127–38
  and nostalgia and identity, 172–82
  and Orientalism, 85
  reasons for studying, 3–5
  settler population of, 46–9
  and "teaching the native," 73–82
  travel to, 8
  and women's space, 7–8
  and women's writing, 5–7

Algeria; considered as a winter residence
  for the English (1858), 29
Algerian War of Independence, 145–6,
  150, 152, 154, 201, 238n53,
  241n18, 254n14, 255n17, 266n52
Algérianiste movement, 79, 96, 112,
  175–6, 242n30
Algiers, 4a, 21–3, 28, 76, 107, 129,
  131–3, 146–51, 153–4, 173,
  175–7, 182
Algiers, battle of (1957), 147
Allied states, 145, 147, 149, 200
Alquier, Jeanne, 127–8
Alsace-Lorraine annexation (1870), 27
Amar, Rabbi Moise, 86
Anderson, David, 143–5
Annales Coloniales, 108
anti-Semitism, 23, 31, 90, 121–2,
  127–8, 136, 150, 199
Apostrophes (popular cultural program),
  179
Arabs, 17, 21–3, 28, 30–1, 52, 61,
  87, 90, 93–5, 135, 137, 150–1,
  228n103, 232n43, 254n13
Armand, Marie-Louise, 132
Armstrong, K., 70
Aron, Robert, 174
Arrow of God (1967) (Achebe), 123
assimilation theory, 4
Association of Algerian writers, 79
Association du Centre de
  Documentation Historique sur
  l'Algérie, 182
Association des Ecrivains Algériens, 112
association theory, 4
Au pays du Myrte (Godin), 79–80
Auclert, Hubertine, (1848–1914),
  29–32
Autrement Dit (Cardinal), 178

Bache, Eva, 126. *See* Evelyn
　　Brodhurst-Hill
Baïlac, Geneviève, 150–2, 156, 169,
　　171, 174–5, 202
Bally, Peter, 187
Barbaresque, 79
Beauvoir, Simone de, 147
Beloufa, Farouk, 181
Bensaï, Mohamed Hamouda, 181
Berbers, 21, 23, 30, 93, 95, 135,
　　213n1
Berenson, Edward, 45, 223n2
Bernhardt, Sarah, 46
Bertrand, Louis, 86, 133, 155, 174
Blixen, Karen, 1–2, 16, 39, 43, 45–64,
　　72, 113–15, 119, 183–4, 188–90,
　　197–8, 203, 212n55, 223n2,
　　227n81, 229n112
　　Danish ethnicity of, 46, 48
　　and female icons, 60–3
　　and fiction and reality, 57–9
　　on love of Africa, 47
　　and masculine chivalric ideal, 53–7
　　and paradox, 59–60
　　pen name, 47
　　See *Out of Africa*
Blixen-Finecke, Bror, 49, 55–6, 225n27
Blundell, Michael, 163, 169
Bodichon, Barbara Leigh Smith, 28–30,
　　217n43,45
Bodichon, Eugène, 29–30, 217n46,
　　218n49
Boisnard, Magali (1882–1945), 17,
　　61–2, 74–5, 85–8, 93–6, 99,
　　106, 112, 198, 232n43, 235n19,
　　237n50
Bolshevism, 127
Bône, 4, 23, 49, 76, 107
Bongie, Chris, 64
Bonheur, Rosa, 46
Bonneval, J., 60
Booth, Howard J., 12
Born Free (Adamson), 187
Bouali, Mahmoud, 180
Bougie, 4, 79, 107
Boumendil, Rosine, 86
Boupacha, Djamila, 147
Boym, Svetlana, 10, 95
British East Africa, 3, 24, 26, 35, 38,
　　49, 69, 96

British Fascisti, 103
British Pacifist Journal, 146
British Union of Fascists, 103
Brodhurst-Hill, Evelyn, 126–7, 200,
　　246n82
Brunschvicg, Cécile, 128, 241n23
Bugéja, Marie (1875?–1957), 78–81,
　　130, 198
Burmese independence, 160–1
Burton, Antoinette, 11–12
Buxton, Cara, 68, 72

Campbell, Chloe, 116
Camus, Albert, 79, 112, 175
Carberry, Juanita, 73, 113, 202
Cardinal, Marie (1929–2001), 176–8,
　　202, 265n38, 266n39
carrot and the stick, 124–5
Casey, Mary (1915–1980), 162–3,
　　262n121, 122
Castle, Barbara, 147
Catholicism, 22, 27, 74, 93, 137,
　　211n50
Celarié, Henriette, 61, 108
*Centre de Culture, de Recherche et
　　Documentation historique sur
　　l'Algérie*, 176
*Centre de Documentation Historique sur
　　l'Algérie*, 176
*Centre Regionale d'Art Dramatique
　　d'Alger* (CRAD), 151
Certeau, Michel de, 43
Ces forets d'orangers, 153, 259n66
Cezilly, George (1904–?), 152.
　　See Anne Durand
Chadwick, Whitney, 12
Chailley-Bert, Joseph, 48
Chakrabarty, Dipesh, 12
Champy, Hugette, 88
Chania-Totseland federation scheme,
　　120
charisma, 45
Charpentier, John, 131, 133
Chemouil, Mardochée (Maurice), 86
Child of Happy Valley (Carberry), 202
*Childhood Memories from Colonial East
　　Africa* (Considine), 202
Chorfi, Abdelmajid, 180–1
Christians, 22, 30, 32, 70, 90, 93–4,
　　123, 136–8, 149, 168, 211n50

Christie, Agatha, 119
Churchill, Winston, 71
circumcision, 124
cities, 1, 4, 8, 10–17, 23, 26–7, 41, 60, 67–9, 76–82, 85, 89, 98, 101, 107–8, 110–11, 117, 119, 127, 129, 131–3, 138, 143–4, 148–50, 153–5, 159, 166, 168–70, 171–2, 177–8, 184, 192, 195–203, 235n13, 241n24
Cixous, Hélène (b.1937), 178, 266n52
Cleland-Scott, Helen, 56–7
clitoridectomy, 124
Closer Union in East Africa, 109
Closer Union White Paper, 120
coffee, 35, 38–9, 49–50, 54, 68, 70, 97, 224n22, 227n81, 230n21
Cold War, 147, 174–5
Cole, Berkeley, 54
Cole, Eleanor (Nellie), 38
Cole, Galbraith, 36, 38
Colette, 88, 131, 179
colon (settler), 17, 80, 112, 130, 133–6, 149, 154
Colonial Exhibition in France (1931), 108
colonial nostalgia, 2, 7–16, 172, 183, 195, 198, 202–3
Colonial Office, 67, 69, 71, 102–3
Colonial Records Project (Oxford University), 42, 168–9, 183, 202
colonial realism, 112
colonialism
  and approval, 47–8
  and children, 185
  and nostalgia, 8–13
  and novels, memoirs, and letters, 13–15
  and realism, 112
  and women, 2–8, 26–7, 45–6
colonization, 1–11, 64, 76, 78, 119, 129, 135, 139–40, 143, 149, 180, 184, 197, 199
Commision des Colonies, 108
Compton, Fay, 183
Conference of the International Women's Alliance (1935) (Istanbul, Turkey), 128
Congress of Mediterranean Women (Constantine) (1932), 130

conservation, 186–7
Considine, Joan, 202, 242n36
Constantine, 4, 23, 52, 76, 79, 107, 127–8, 130, 136
Constantine pogrom (1934), 127
Constructing Charisma, 45
Cooke, Alistair, 183
Cornell Daily Sun, 115
Corydon, Robert, 71
CRAD. See *Centre Regionale d'Art Dramatique d'Alger*
Cran, Marion, 126–7, 200
Crémieux Law (1870), 23
Crespin, Lucienne, 61
Crespin, Pierre, 87
Croix de Feu, 128
Crown Land Ordinance (1902), 24
Crown Land Ordinance (1915), 69
Cuénat, Hélène, 147
Cunningham, Valentine, 107
Curtis, Sarah, 27–8

d'Houdelot, Adolphe, 28
Da Costa, M., 86
Daily Mail, 97
Danish ethnicity, 46, 48
Davis, Emily, 29
Davis, Fred, 10
De Gaulle, Charles, 147, 150, 171, 175
The Death of an Aryan (Huxley), 122
Death in Kenya (Kaye), 164–6
decolonization, 3, 15, 17, 94, 143–70, 171, 176–8, 192, 201–2
defensive nostalgia, 147–55
Déjeux, Jean, 86, 180
Delacroix, Eugène, 28
Delamere, Lord Hugh, 24, 35–6, 38, 48, 54, 71, 97, 117, 119, 139, 160, 172, 182, 188, 203, 221n99, 231n25
Dépêche Algérienne (newspaper), 81, 173
Der Zauberlehrling (Goethe), 158
Déracinés! (Dessaigne), 155, 172–3
Derrida, Jacques (1930–2004), 178
Descaves, Lucien, 131
Dessaigne, Francine, 155–6, 172–3
Devonshire Declaration, 71, 229n13
Dib, Mohammed (1920–2003), 156
Dimitriet la Mort (Favre), 131

Dinesen, Ingeborg (Blixen's mother), 50

Dinesen, Isak, 47, 53. *See* Karen Blixen

Dinesen, Thomas (Blixen's brother), 50, 54, 56, 58

"The Distaff Side" (*Kenya Weekly News*), 162

Djamardji, Djafar, 181

Dobbs, Marion, 21, 36, 38, 41–2, 68

Dorland, Michael, 11

Douglas-Hamilton, Iain, 188

Douglas-Hamilton, Oria, 63, 188, 229n116, 247n110, 270n107, 112

Doumic, René, 86

Dreyfus Affair, 90, 136

Driver, Felix, 15

The Dual Mandate in British tropical Africa (Lord Lugard), 4

Duchène, Ferdinand, 73–4

Duder, C. J. D., 55

Durand, Anne, 152

Durand, Marguerite, 60

East African Association, 70

East African Dinner (1922), 71

East African Turf Club, 40

East African Women's League, 40, 71, 109–10, 159, 221n99

Eberhardt, Isabelle (1877–1904), 16, 29, 43, 45–64, 75, 96, 133, 179–81, 197–8, 232n55
  and female icons, 60–3
  and fiction and reality, 57–9
  on love of Africa, 47
  and masculinity, 50–3
  and paradox, 59–60
  Russian ethnicity, 46, 48

eccentricity, 46

École d'Alger, 112

École polytechnique, 137

École des Religeuse de la Doctrine, 86

Ecoutez la mer (Cardinal), 176

Ehnni, Slimène, 52

Elbe, Marie, 155, 173–4

Eliot, Charles, 24–5

Elissa Rhaïs, un roman (Tabet), 179

Elkington, Margaret, 37, 39, 56–7

Elle, 176

Elsa Wild Animal Appeal Trust, 187

Emergency in Kenya, 144–7, 158, 163–8

The Englishwoman's Journal, 29

Enlightenment, 13, 30, 34

Errances (ou Terre en Cendres) (Djamardji), 181

Et à l'heure de notre mort (Elbe), 155, 173

États Généraux du Féminisme (1931), 108

Ethiopia, invasion of (1935–1936), 122

eugenics, 116–17, 122, 140, 200, 244n52

European Pioneers' Society, 37

Evian peace accords (1962), 171

Facing Mount Kenya (Kenyatta), 125

Falklands war, (1982), 9

The Far Pavilions (Kaye), 164

fascism, 17, 103, 107, 118, 120–2, 127

Faure-Sardet, Jeanne, 130–2, 136–8, 247n111, 249n128

Favre, Lucienne (1896–1958), 107, 130–3, 135–6, 138–9, 148

female icons, 60–3

"feminine" novels, 111

feminism, 5, 26, 29–32, 38, 60, 79, 93, 108, 110, 128, 130–1, 147, 176, 178, 180

Femmes de Demain, 131

Fenech, Maximilienne, 112

Fille d'Arabe, 132, 136, 138

Financial Delegation of Algeria, 129

Finch-Hatton, Dennis, 46, 54, 114, 188, 190

The Flame Trees of Thika, Memories of an African Childhood (Huxley), 183–5, 201

Fletcher, Eileen, 146

FLN. *See* National Liberation Front

freedom, 36, 47, 49–51, 53, 58–9, 61–3, 73, 80, 89, 103, 106, 147, 149–50, 161, 166–7, 180, 187, 190

French colonialism, 4, 12–13, 29, 48, 75, 78, 90, 108, 146

French identity/Frenchness, 76, 78, 80, 83, 104, 137–8, 147, 169, 174, 196, 202

French North Africa, 2, 89, 95

Fromentin, Eugène, 28

Gallmann, Kuki, 62–3, 187–90, 202–3, 229n116
Gallmann Memorial Foundation, 189
The Garden Beyond (Cran), 127
Gautier, Théophile, 28
gender, 2, 5–11, 26–7, 32, 35, 38–41, 46, 48, 50–7, 60–1, 63–4, 68, 76, 79–83, 89, 91–4, 97–9, 101–2, 105–6, 111, 123, 128, 135, 140, 145, 147–54, 178–80, 197–200
genocide, 155
German colonies, 3
Geographical Society of Normandy, 75
Geographical Society of North Africa, 75
Gilbert, David, 15
Giloi, Eva, 45
Godin, J. Annette (1875–1958), 67, 79–80, 87, 198, 233n73. See *Au pays du Myrte*; *L'Erreur de Nedjma*
Goethe, Johann Wolfgang von, 158
Golan, Romy, 11–12
Gouda, Frances, 16
Grand Concours littéraire du centenaire de l'Algérie de la Ville de Paris, 78
Grand Prix Littéraire de l'Algérie, 112, 131–2, 235n10, 236n21, 249n128
Grant, Eleanor ("Nellie") (1885–1977), 68–9, 71, 103, 112–14, 116–18, 121, 123, 156–9, 163–4, 168, 172, 184, 200–1
Grant, Josceline, 121
Grant, Vera Campbell, 121
Grogan, Ewart Stewart, 41
Guelma (1945), 200
Guerroudj, Jacqueline, 146

Halimi, Gisèle, 147, 178
Hall, Mary, 49
Hammond, Alice, 27
Haouch Aïn el Hamra-La Fontaine Rouge, 149
Hardinge, Arthur, 24
Heller, Maximilienne, 112
Henri-Levy, Bernard, 179
Hill-Williams, K. A., 39, 222n109, 112
Himmelfarb, Gertrude, 13
Hinderer, Anna Martin (1827–1870), 49
Histories of the Hanged (Anderson), 143

Hitler, Adolf, 120–1
Hobsbawm, Eric, 10
Hofer, Johannes, 9
Holmes, Diana, 13
Holocaust, 148
Howard, Michael, 156
Huxley, Aldous, 114
Huxley, Elspeth (1907–1997), 42, 69, 72, 107, 113–26, 139, 156–64, 166–9, 171, 183–91, 198–201. See *Red Strangers*; *White Man's Country*

I Dreamed of Africa (1991) (Gallmann), 62, 187–8, 203, 229n116
Icard, Blanche, 130
Idir et Thérèse, 152–4
Imperial British East Africa Company, 24
imperial nostalgia, 8–13, 195, 203
Imperial Mountain (Strange), 100, 104–5
indigènes, 17, 89, 108, 110, 136
India, 3, 5, 17, 26, 96, 101, 147–8, 160, 164, 200
Indian independence (1947), 147, 160–1
Indians, 24–5, 55, 68–72, 77, 81, 102–3, 109, 170, 199
indigène, 79, 96, 112, 218n47, 234n84,85
Indochina (French), 3, 200
Indochine, 9
Institute of Commonwealth Studies, 183
Isabelle d'Afrique (Favre), 131
Isabelle Eberhardt, 181
Islam, 21–2, 25, 28, 31, 34, 43, 49–50, 52, 57, 59, 61–2, 73–9, 81–2, 86–90, 92–4, 96, 106, 108, 110, 128, 132–3, 135–8, 150–1, 171, 175, 179–82, 196
Italy, 5, 103, 121, 129, 151, 188–90

Jean-Darrouy, Lucienne, 129–35, 180, 247n111, 249n128, 137, 250n138, 251n151
Jeanson, Colette, 143, 1477
Jewish people, 5, 21, 23, 90, 121–2, 127, 135–6, 151, 182, 241n10, 245n77, 248n11

Jex-Blake, Muriel, 187
Joan of Arc, 94–5
Jonnart Law (1919), 110
Journal d'une mere de famille pied-noir
    (Dessaigne), 155

Kahena (1925) (Boisnard), 93
Karen Coffee Company Ltd., 50
Kaye, Mary Margaret ("Mollie")
    (1908–2004), 164
Kennedy, Dane, 38, 55, 72
Kennedy, John F., 150
Kenya
    and animism, 22
    colonial history of, 3–8, 21–5
    and demographics, 5
    and female European presence,
        35–43
    independence (1963), 171
    and Indians. *See* Indians
    and indirect rule, 4
    in the 1920s, 67–8, 85
    in the 1930s, 108–11, 114–27
    and land expropriation, 25
    literary developments in, 111–14
    literary realism in, 114–27
    and mythologies of settlement, 25–6
    and nostalgia as reality, 156–69
    reasons for studying, 3–5
    and reality expressed, 68–73
    and red strangers, 182–91
    settler society in, 46–9
    travel to, 8
    and a vanishing Africa, 182–91
    White Papers (1930), 109–10
    and wild animals, 39, 43, 186–9,
        200, 203
    and wildness, 85
    and women's space, 7–8
    and women's writing, 5–7
Kenya Emergency (1952–1960), 144–7,
    158, 163–8
Kenya Mist (Riddell), 97–8
Kenya Society for the Study of Race
    Improvement (KSSRI), 116–17
Kenya-Uganda railway, 4
Kenya Weekly News, 162
Kenyan Legislative Council, 109
Kenyatta, Jomo, 124–5, 166, 172, 182,
    201

Khaldoun, Ibn, 88, 95
Khrushchev, Nikita, 175
Kikuyu (clan), 17, 22, 41, 70, 73,
    100, 119, 123–5, 139, 144–5,
    157, 161–3, 165–8, 184–5, 191,
    227n81, 253n7
Kikuyu Association, 70
Kimmelman, Michael, 182
Kingsley, Mary, 49
Kismet in Kenya (1927) (Riddell),
    100–1
KSSRI. *See* Kenya Society for the Study
    of Race Improvement

L'Action, 180
L'Algérianiste, 175–6
L'Algérie heureuse, 175
L'Athénée, 60
l'Echo d'Alger, 131, 173
L'Echo de Paris, 39
L'Erreur de Nedjma (Godin), 80
L'Express, 176
La Cause des Femmes (Halimi), 178
La Dépêche algérienne, 128, 248n116
La famille Hernandez, 151–2, 175
La Fille des Pachas (1922) (Rhaïs), 90
La Fontaine Rouge (Montupet), 148–9
La Française, 93, 110–11, 129–30
La Fronde, 60
La Kahena (1925), 93–5
La loi du 23 Avril (1887), 23
La maison des soeurs Gomez (Baïlac),
    151
La Mer Rouge, 112
La Revue de France, 61
La Riffaine (1929) (Rhaïs), 90–1
La valise et le cercueil (Loesch), 154
La Vandale (1907) (Boisnard), 93
La Vie Platts, Madeleine, 42
Labour government, 103, 124, 147
The Land that Never Was (Simpson),
    72, 127, 231n32
Lari massacre (1953), 145
Lassner, Phyllis, 12, 115–16, 122
Last Days in Eden (Huxley), 186
Later than you Think (Kaye), 164–5
Latimer, Tirza, 12
Lawick, Hugo van, 186
Lawrence, T. E., 61
Le Bain Juif (Favre), 135–6

Le Cercle algérianiste, 175–6
Le Figaro, 93
Le Gall, Noura, 75
Le Mariage de Hanifa (Rhaïs), 90–1
*Le marriage de Mademoiselle
    Centhectaires* (Jean-Darrouy), 132
Le Monde, 92–3, 133, 147, 179
Le mythe d'une Algérie heureuse (article),
    92–3
Le Roman de Khaldoun (1930)
    (Boisnard), 93, 95
Le roman de la Kahena, 95
Le Secret d'Elissa Rhaïs (Otmezguine),
    180
Le Sein Blanc (Rhaïs), 179–80
Le Temps, 93
Le tombeau de la chrétienne (Loesch), 155
Leakey, Louis, 125, 144, 187
Leblond, Marius-Ary, 74, 93, 232n43,
    242n27
Légion d'honneur, 179
Lerouvre, Catherine, 149–50
Les Endormies, 74–5, 93
Les Femmes arabes en Algérie (Auclert),
    30–2
Les Juifs, ou la fille d'Eléazar (1921)
    (Rhaïs), 90
Les mots pour le dire (Cardinal), 176,
    178
Les Nouvelles Littéraires, 133
letters, 13–15
Letters from Africa (Blixen), 1
Lévrier, Antonin, 30
Libya, 9, 21
*Ligue française pour le droit des
    femmes* (Trocadero Palace) (1921),
    82
Limuru Girls High School, 27
Loesch, Anne, 154–6, 173
Loi Warnier (1873), 22
London School of Economics (LSE),
    123
Longden, Anne, 29
Loti, Pierre, 112
Loup, Elyette, 146
"Love and the Lions" (Riddell), 97
LSE. *See* London School of Economics
Lugard, Frederick (1st Baron Lugard)
    (Lord Lugard), 4
Lyautey, Hubert, 53, 89–90, 181

Mâadith (1921) (Boisnard), 93–4
Mac-Orlan, Pierre, 131
Macleod, Iain, 168–9
Macmillan, 124
Macmillan, Harold, 245n65
Macmillan, Lucy, 68, 203
MacMillan, William Northrup, 38–9,
    57, 68
MacNaghten, Hilda, 38, 42
Madden, A. F., 182
male gaze, 35, 92
Malinowski, Bronislaw, 123, 125
Mammeri, Mouloud (1917–1989), 156
March on Rome (1922), 103
Marchal, Antoinette, 259n66
Marchal, Violette, 129
Margadant, Jo Burr, 13
Marion, Cécile, 147
Markham, Beryl, 113, 200
Marnard, Denise Morel de, 202
Martini, Lisette, 79
Master and Servant Ordinance (1906), 41
Maswali Matatu League, 159
Matu (character) (*Red Strangers*), 123,
    125
Mau Mau, 144–7, 158, 162–8, 200–1,
    252n4, 253n5, 255n15, 16,
    263n143
    Uprising. *See* Kenya Emergency
Maxon, Robert M., 69
McDonell family, 27
McKenna, Virginia, 183
Mead, Margaret, 178
memoirs, 13–15
methodology, 16–17
Mille, Pierre, 93, 237n45
Mille et un jours: Mourad, 131, 148
Minerve (Favre), 131–2
mission civilisatrice, 13, 59
Mitidja, 23, 149
Mobile Masterpiece Theatre, 183
modernity/modernism, 7–13, 15, 17,
    34, 38–40, 43, 51, 64, 69–70,
    73–83, 88–92, 106, 107, 111,
    123–5, 134–5, 139–40, 150–1,
    154, 157–8, 161–2, 179, 196–7,
    199, 201–2
*Modernity and Nostalgia, art and
    politics in France between the wars*
    (Golan), 11–12

Mombasa, 8, 22, 24, 36, 38, 40, 158
Montupet, Jeanne (Jeannine) (1920–?), 148–9
Morand, Colette, 88
Morand, Paul, 88
Morel, Denise, 182, 202
Moseley, Oswold, 103
The Mottled Lizard (Huxley), 171, 185, 269n93
Mourad (Favre), 131, 148
Mozabites, 34, 213n1
Murder at Government House (Huxley), 119–20
Mussolini, Benito, 103, 120–2
musulmans, 17
Muthaiga Club (Nairobi), 40

Nairobi, 4, 40, 68, 70, 76, 102, 107, 109, 144, 162, 167
Nasser, Gamal Abdel, 175
National Academy of Design in New York, 29
National Council of French Women, 108
National Liberation Front (FLN), 145, 147, 150–2, 154–5, 170, 177, 201, 255n15, 17
National Museum of Kenya, 187
nationalism, 124, 126, 143, 175, 199–200
the "native," 4, 17, 23–5, 31, 41, 53, 60, 71–3, 77–8, 86–97, 99, 101, 104–6, 108–12, 117–20, 122, 124, 126–7, 136, 138, 175, 197, 218n47, 226n56, 230n20, 231n23, 249n128
  and nostalgia, 86–96
Native Policy in East Africa, 109
Native Registration Ordinance (1915), 41
Nazism, 121–2
New Mayflower, 121
New York Times, 161, 175, 182
Nicholls, Christine, 37, 117, 125, 168–9, 191, 202
Njoro Settlers' Association, 159
Noirfontaine, Pauline, 21, 28–9
Northey, Sir Edward, 69, 71
Nos Soeurs musulmanes (1921), 78
Nostalgérie, 155–6, 172, 177, 180–2, 185, 203

nostalgia
  as the "call of Africa," 96–106
  and colonialism, 8–13
  defensive, 148–55
  and female icons, 60–3
  and "the native," 86–96
  as reality, 156–69
Notre Rive, 131
Nouelle, Georges, 108
novels, 13–15
Nuffield College, 156
Nyanza, Victoria, 24–5

O'Shea, T. J., 109
O. A. S. *See* Organisation armée secrete
Operation Epérvier (1986), 9
Operation Torch (1942), 145
Operation Uncomfortable (Grant), 163
Operations de maintain d'ordre (1954), 144
Oran, 4, 22–3, 38, 60, 76, 107, 109, 130–1, 149, 171, 182
Organisation armée secrete (O. A. S.), 154, 171, 173, 182, 264n9
Orientale 1930 (Favre), 107, 132, 135, 250n145, 252 n180
Orientalism, 34–5, 43, 57, 62, 75, 85–9, 91–4, 107, 132, 135
Orm, Rotha Linton, 103
Otmezguine, Jacques, 180
Out of Africa (Blixen), 47–8, 57–8, 62, 113–15, 119, 183–4
Out of Africa (film) (Pollack) (1985), 62
Out of the Mist (Riddell), 101
An Outpost Wooing (Strange), 101
Overseas Service Pensioners' Association, 202
Oxford Colonial Records Project, 42
Oxford University, 42, 156, 183, 202

Panchasi, Roxanne, 10
Parti Communiste Algérien (PCA), 146
patriarchy, 8, 13–14, 27, 82
Paulignan, Henri, 79
PCA. See *Parti Communiste Algérien*
Peace News, 146
Perham, Margery (1895–1982), 116, 125–6, 147, 156–8, 183
Petite Gironde, 59

Picard, Aurelie (1849–1933), 27, 62
pied-noirs, 79, 88, 91, 133, 151, 154–6, 171–83, 185, 192–3, 200–3
Pieds-Noirs (Cardinal), 202
"pioneer," 11, 25, 27, 37–9, 42–3, 55, 62, 101, 117–18, 127, 149, 159, 161–2, 165, 182–3, 185, 188–9, 191, 196, 201
Pirandello, Luigi, 86
Pivot, Bernard, 179
Podolinsky, Nicolas, 51
Poincaré, Raymond, 82
Pollack, Stanley, 62
polygamy, 31, 218n52
Pommerol, Jean, 32, 34–5
Popular Front (France), 128
Pringle, Ian, 181, 228n110
Problems of Racial Relation in the Settled Areas. A Possible Aid to their study, 159
progress, 12–13, 31, 34, 38, 80–1, 108, 115–17, 122–3, 133, 135, 151
Prosper (Favre), 131
Pujol, Jean-Marc, 182

racism/race, 5–8, 12, 29–30, 34, 37, 40–1, 46, 48, 63–4, 70–2, 76, 79–81, 83, 93–4, 96, 99–100, 104–5, 107, 109, 111–12, 115–17, 120, 123–4, 126–8, 135–9, 147–52, 155, 157–60, 162, 168, 172, 174, 183, 185, 191, 196–200, 202–3
Randau, Robert, 52, 79, 87, 198
Ranger, Terence, 10
Red Fountain, 201
Red Strangers (Huxley), 107, 123, 125, 139, 171–93, 200, 246n92
Red Strangers. The White Tribe of Kenya (Nicholls), 191, 202, 215n24
Renaud, Jean, 137
René-Garnier, Charles, 75, 77
Revue des Deux Mondes, 86, 88, 93
Rhaïs, Elissa, 17, 61–2, 85–93, 95–6, 98–9, 106, 179–80, 198. See *Saâda, La Marocaine*
Ricciardi, Mirella, 188, 190, 192, 202, 270n112, 271n121
Richard, Charles, 32
Richepin, Jean, 93, 237n45

Riddell, Florence, 17, 37, 73, 85–6, 96–102, 104–6, 113, 198
Rif War (1920–1926), 90
Rift Valley, 22, 144, 164, 184, 224n10
Rigby, Nigel, 12
Riley, Glenda, 11
Rítívoí, Andreea Decíu, 11, 192
Roberts, Mary Louise, 46, 71
romans de bibliothèque de gare (romantic fiction), 86
Romanticism, 62, 133, 180
Root, Joan, 188
Rosaldo, Renato, 125
Roseveare, Mary, 27, 216n33
Rousselot, 133–5
Rousso, Henry, 200–1
Roux-Freissineng, M., 82
Roy, Jules, 92, 179
Royal Academy in London, 29
Russian ethnicity, 46, 48
Rutinau, Georges, 166

Saâda, La Marocaine (1919) (Rhaïs), 86–90
Saadi, Mahmoud, 52, 75
Sainte-Croix, Avril de, 108
Sarradet, Jean, 155
Scott, Francis, 158, 245n65
Scott, Helen Cleland, 39, 203
Sekanyola (Ugandan African paper), 70
"self," 6–7, 11, 13–15, 47, 49, 50, 59, 86, 190, 192
Sénatus-Consulte (1865), 82
Serrano, Rosa, 146
Sétif clashes (1945), 145, 200
Sétif de ma jeunesse (Morel), 182, 202, 254n11
The Settlers of Kenya (Huxley), 160–1
Séverine, 60–1, 181
Sewell, Billy, 38
sex/sexuality, 5–6, 26, 32, 35, 43, 57, 60–1, 80, 87–9, 91–2, 95, 97–101, 104–5, 133–5, 137, 140, 177–8, 198–9
Shadows on the Grass (Blixen), 54, 57–8, 190
Sils, Marie (1914–1982), 153–4, 259n66
Simpson, Alyse, 42–3, 67, 72–3, 126–7
Sir Northrup MacMillan Memorial Library, 68

Slessor, Mary (1848–1915), 49
Smith, Benjamin Leigh, 29
So This is Kenya! (1936)
     (Brodhust-Hill), 126–7
Soldier Settlement Scheme, 25, 71, 83
*The Sorcerer's Apprentice: A journey
     through East Africa* (Huxley), 158,
     160–1
Southern Highlands of Tanganyika,
     160
Southern Rhodesia, 25, 69, 160, 201–2
Stalinism, 107
Spain, 5, 23, 54, 77, 128–9, 136–8,
     146, 149, 151
Spanish Civil War, 128
Stavisky affair, 128, 136
Steinmetz, George, 3
stereotype, 5, 57, 62, 87–9, 94, 122,
     126, 135, 137, 207
Stewart, Kathleen, 9
Stoler, Ann, 11, 16, 99
Strange, Nora K. (1884–1974), 17, 86,
     96, 100–6, 113, 198
Strobel, Margaret, 16
Sufi brotherhood, 27, 53
Sultans de Touggourt, 95
Sunday Times, 114

Tabet, Paul (b. 1942), 179–80
Tageldin, Shaden, 10
Tanganyika, 24, 109, 121, 160
Taouti, Mohammed, 81–2
Teitgen, Paul, 146–7
There was an Unseen Cloud Moving, 181
Things Fall Apart (1958) (Achebe),
     123
Thiong'o, Ngugi Wa, 11
Third Republic, 127
Thomas, Dylan, 63
Thornton, Leslie, 181
Thuku, Harry, 70
Thurman, Judith, 1
Tidjanniya, 27
Tillion, Germaine, 150
Tilly, Charles, 11
The Times (London), 172, 175
Times Literary Supplement, 158
torture, 91, 105, 146–7, 150, 152,
     167, 201, 256n20
travel writing, 6, 28–9

tribalism, 117, 160
Trophimowsky, Alexander, 49, 224n19
Turner, R. B., 110

U. F. S .F. See *Union française pour le
     suffrage des femmes*
Uganda, 3–4, 24, 70, 109, 269n83
Uganda railway, 3–4, 24
Un Feu d'Enfer (Lerouvre), 149–50
*Une femmes chez les Sahariennes: entre
     Laghouat et In-salah* (Pommerol),
     32
Union coloniale française, 48
Union des femmes françaises de la Seine,
     149
*Union française pour le suffrage des
     femmes* (U. F. S. F.), 110–11,
     128–31
urban living/urbanism, 1, 4, 12, 15,
     23, 26, 76–7, 89, 101, 107,
     132–3, 138, 143–4, 148–9, 154,
     168–9, 196–200, 240n2
Utopian socialists, 4, 30

Vachell, Superintendent (character)
     (*Murder at Government* House),
     119–20, 122
Vallory, Louise, 28
Vanishing Africa (Ricciardi), 190–1,
     203
Vialar, Emilie de (1797–1856), 27–8, 49
Vichy France, 134, 145, 147, 150, 200
Vidalkaha, La ferme africaine, 1
Vient de Paraître, 137
Vincent, Lisette, 150
violence, 9, 12, 72, 87, 91–2, 108,
     135–6, 144–6, 152, 154, 162,
     164, 166–8, 173, 182, 199
Viollette, Maurice, 108
Viollette-Blum bill, 128
voting, 82, 129–30

Wahab, Ali Abdul, 51, 58
Westenholz, Aage, 50
"white man's burden," 13
"white man's country," 3, 25, 116–17,
     192
*White Man's Country: Lord Delamere
     and the Making of Kenya* (Huxley),
     117–19, 123, 125, 200

White Papers (1930) (Kenya), 109–10
A Wife in Kenya (Strange), 102–4
Wilaya III, 145
Williams, Raymond, 26
Wilson, Janelle, 10
Wives Win (Riddell), 105–6
Woman's War Work League, 68
Women's Army Corps, 145
Women's Hour (BBC), 183
Women's Suffrage Committee, 29
World War I, 12, 25, 37, 67, 73, 78,
    82, 85, 96, 101–2, 106, 107, 110,
    117–18, 131, 134, 185, 198, 200,
    222n116

World War II, 37, 128, 143, 145, 149,
    151, 156, 159, 164, 170, 180,
    182, 200, 242n36
Wright, Gwendolyn, 15

Yacine, Kateb (1929–1989),
    156
Yesterday's Self (Rítívoí), 11
Yveton, Fernand, 146
The Youngest Lion (Brodhurst-Hill),
    126

Zanzibar, 9, 24
Zweig, Stephanie, 121, 243n37